THE CONCISE
CAMBRIDGE BIBLIOGRAPHY
OF
ENGLISH LITERATURE
600–1950

THE CONCISE
CAMBRIDGE BIBLIOGRAPHY
OF
ENGLISH LITERATURE
600–1950

EDITED BY

GEORGE WATSON

SECOND EDITION

CAMBRIDGE
AT THE UNIVERSITY PRESS
1965

PUBLISHED BY
THE SYNDICS OF THE CAMBRIDGE UNIVERSITY PRESS
Bentley House, 200 Euston Road, London, N.W. 1
American Branch: 32 East 57th Street, New York 22, N.Y.
West African Office: P.O. Box 33, Ibadan, Nigeria

©

CAMBRIDGE UNIVERSITY PRESS
1958

SECOND EDITION
©

CAMBRIDGE UNIVERSITY PRESS
1965

First edition   1958
Second edition 1965

Printed in Great Britain at the University Printing House, Cambridge
(Brooke Crutchley, University Printer)

CONTENTS

Ref 16
Z
2011
W3
1965

Preface   *page* vii

Abbreviations   xi

GENERAL INTRODUCTION

Bibliographies   3
Other Reference Works   4
Literary History and Criticism   5
Collections and Anthologies   7
Prosody   8
Book Production and Distribution   8
Grammars, Dictionaries etc.   10

THE OLD ENGLISH PERIOD (600–1100)

Bibliography   15
Literary History   15
Collections and Anthologies   16
Grammars and Dictionaries   17
Authors etc. (Ælfric to Wulfstan)   17

THE MIDDLE ENGLISH PERIOD (1100–1500)

Bibliographies   29
Literary History   29
Collections and Anthologies   30
Authors etc. (*Alexander Romances* to Wiclif)   31

THE RENAISSANCE TO THE RESTORATION (1500–1660)

Bibliographies   51
Literary History and Criticism   51
Collections and Anthologies   53
Authors etc. (Andrewes to Wyatt)   55

THE RESTORATION TO THE ROMANTICS (1660–1800)

Bibliographies   105
Literary History and Criticism   105
Collections and Anthologies   106
Authors (Addison to Young)   107

CONTENTS

THE NINETEENTH CENTURY (1800–1900)

Bibliographies   *page* 151
Literary History and Criticism   151
Collections and Anthologies   153
Authors (Acton to Yeats)   153

THE EARLY TWENTIETH CENTURY (1900–1950)

Bibliographies   213
Literary History and Criticism   213
Anthologies and Periodicals   214
Authors (Auden to Virginia Woolf)   215

Index   265

PREFACE

THE object of this book is to provide a concise statement of the bibliography of all periods of English literature from Caedmon to Dylan Thomas. Apart from its final section (1900–1950), it is a compression by rigorous selection of the only comprehensive work in this field, the *Cambridge Bibliography of English Literature* (Cambridge 1940) and of its *Supplement* (Cambridge 1957). Six periods are treated: the Old English period (600–1100), the Middle English (1100–1500), the Renaissance to the Restoration (1500–1660), the Restoration to the Romantics (1660–1800), the Nineteenth Century (1800–1900) and the Early Twentieth Century (1900–1950). It is obvious that strict limits must be set to so vast a scheme, and I have tried to observe the following throughout:

(i) *Scope of the work.* Only writers in English native to or mainly resident in the British Isles have been included. This means that (as in *C.B.E.L.* itself) American literature as such has been excluded—its bibliography is in course of being treated in admirable detail in Mr Jacob Blanck's *Bibliography of American Literature* (8 vols. New Haven 1955– , for the Bibliographical Society of America)—though sections on Henry James and T. S. Eliot will be found in their appropriate periods. It means too that the present work excludes Anglo-Indian, English–Canadian, English–South African and Australian and New Zealand literature, all of which were briefly treated at the end of Volume III of *C.B.E.L.* No such national limits, however, have applied to the choice of biographical and critical studies concerning the British and Irish writers considered here.

(ii) *Principles of selection.* Only some four hundred writers have been considered at all, and these have been arranged within their periods in simple alphabetical order. In practice this has meant including almost all the writers ranking as major in *C.B.E.L.*, with a few added from the sections called 'Minor' and from such special sections as the 'Literature of Science'. In the case of the period 1900–1950, of course, a selection of about eighty writers has had to be made *de nouveau*, and in such a matter the taste of a single editor is no certain guide. Balance is called for as much as discrimination, and a firm emphasis upon literary as opposed to quasi-literary values. Throughout the book, and especially in its last section, I have worked on the principle that the object of a reference book is to predict questions and then simply and lucidly to answer them; and I have tried to include such authors, space permitting, as the reader of a bibliography of English literature might ordinarily expect to find there, each author being treated in as much detail as the scale of the book seemed to allow. The book begins with lists of general bibliographies, literary histories etc., and each of the six periods begins similarly with general works concerned solely or largely with a single period.

(iii) *Arrangement.* The canon of an author's works is represented only in selection; and when, as in most cases, a list of biographical and critical works is added, only standard biographies and major and general critical studies are entered. The emphasis is heavily upon books as opposed to articles, and though critical essays of eminence have often been listed specialist articles are never included. The division establishes the most elementary distinction in enumerative bibliography, that between primary and secondary, 'works by' and 'works about'. The canon is preceded, where they exist, by standard bibliographies, concordances and other reference books concerned with a single author. The structure of each author-section is therefore as follows:

NAME (dates of birth and death)

Reference works, e.g. bibliographies and concordances

A SELECTION FROM THE CANON, in order of publication
Collected works, letters and journals

Standard biographies and critical studies

(iv) *Style of entries.* The short title of each book is entered as it appears on the title-page of the first known edition, unless otherwise noted, except that punctuation is systematically enforced, capitalization reduced to the usage of current prose, contractions expanded and the use of i, j, u and v modernized. The short title is followed by the name of the editor, if any, the place of publication (unless it is London)[1] and year of the first edition,[2] whether such information appears in the book or not, followed by the year of publication of the author's final revision, if any, and details of the most modern and scholarly editions. But in this last respect some concessions have been made to the principle of availability, and useful modern reprints as well as scholarly editions have often been entered. It will be seen that *Concise C.B.E.L.*, unlike *C.B.E.L.* itself, attempts to list only the most *significant* early editions, namely the first edition and that representing the author's final intention—the

---

[1] For this purpose all books published in England by the Oxford University Press have been entered as 'Oxford'.

[2] No attempt has been made, however, to adjust the year of publication as recorded in the book itself when a discrepancy of months between the recorded and actual dates of publication is such that the book actually appeared in the year before or after the recorded date.

viii

probable foundations of the text of a modern edition.[1] Changes other than revision are specifically noted, e.g. 'enlarged', 'abridged' etc. Editorial notes are bracketed or distinguished by italic type.

Acknowledgements. My first thanks are due to the Syndics of the Cambridge University Press, whose invitation to prepare this book single-handed came as my work as editor of the *C.B.E.L. Supplement* was nearing its end. The invitation forced me to put my ideas on the nature and purpose of bibliographical reference into strict order, and if I have solved the essential problem of achieving conciseness in this complex field without gross falsification, it is due to the sympathy with which they considered my first specimens and their advice at later stages. Professor John W. Clark, Mr J. C. Maxwell and Professor George Whalley, along with many other patient and obliging friends, have made an important contribution at the proof stage, and I have been fortunate, too, in enlisting the help of six scholars who have each read one period-section and who, without subscribing to all my methods and conclusions, have made many hundreds of suggestions and saved me from many errors: Mr R. W. Burchfield in the Old English section, Dr J. A. W. Bennett in the Middle English, Dr Ethel Seaton in the Renaissance, Mr Herbert Davis in the eighteenth century, Mr Michael Sadleir in the nineteenth and Mr H. S. Harvey in the twentieth. A seventh scholar, Mr F. W. Bateson, has a graver responsibility. It was he who first introduced me to the work of the *Cambridge Bibliography* six years ago, when it stood in urgent need of a Supplement, and who urged me to undertake a *Concise C.B.E.L.* For so much encouragement, and for his suggestive comments on reading the book in manuscript, I wish here to record my thanks.

GEORGE WATSON

---

[1] In a few cases (e.g. FitzGerald's *Rubáiyát*), intermediate editions representing successive revisions of special interest have also been recorded.

PREFACE TO THE SECOND EDITION

The demand for a second edition has enabled me to make some corrections and many additions to this bibliography, especially in publications of the last seven years.

G. W.

St John's College, Cambridge
March 1964

ABBREVIATIONS

Acad.	Academy	MS(S).	manuscript(s)
addn(s)	addition(s)	OE	Old English
AS	Anglo-Saxon	OSA	Oxford Standard
b.	born		Authors
bk(s)	book(s)	pbd	published
d.	died	pbn(s)	publication(s)
ed.	edited by	Proc.	Proceedings
edn(s)	edition(s)	pt(s)	part(s)
EETS	Early English Text Society	ptd	printed
		Q(q)	quarto(s)
EL	Everyman's Library	rev.	revised
EML	English Men of Letters	RL	Reynard Library
facs.	facsimile	rptd	reprinted
Fr.	French	ser.	series
illustr.	illustrated by	Soc.	Society
introd.	introduction	tr.	translated by
It.	Italian	trn	translation
lib.	library	univ.	university
lit.	literature	unpbd	unpublished
ME	Middle English	vol(s)	volume(s)
ML	Muses' Library	WC	World's Classics

GENERAL INTRODUCTION

GENERAL INTRODUCTION

Period bibliographies, literary histories, anthologies, grammars etc. will be found at the beginning of period-sections, below.

Bibliographies

Watt, Robert. Bibliotheca britannica: or a general index to British and foreign literature. 4 vols. Edinburgh 1824. *With subject-index.*

Lowndes, William T. The bibliographer's manual of English literature. 4 vols. 1834; 11 vols. 1857–64 (rev. H. G. Bohn).

Catalogue of the printed books in the British Museum. 393 pts. 1881–1900; Supplement [1882–99], 40 pts. 1900–5; General catalogue, *c.* 300 vols. 1931– (*complete revision*).

Halkett, Samuel and John Laing. A dictionary of the anonymous and pseudonymous literature of Great Britain. Ed. Catharine Laing, 4 vols. Edinburgh 1882–8; 7 vols. Edinburgh 1926–34 (rev. and enlarged by James Kennedy *et al.*); vols. viii–ix, 1900–50, by Dennis E. Rhodes and Anna E. C. Simoni, Edinburgh 1956.

Lee, Sidney *et al.* The year's work in English studies. Oxford 1921– (English Assoc.). *Annual collections of essays by various hands on current pbns since 1919.*

Peers, E. Allison *et al.* Bibliography of English language and literature. Cambridge 1921– (Modern Humanities Research Assoc.). *Annual lists of current pbns since 1920.*

American bibliography. PMLA, xxxvii– (1922–). *An annual record of modern language pbns (American pbns only before 1957) since 1921.*

Wise, Thomas J. The Ashley library: a catalogue of the printed books, manuscripts and autograph letters collected by Wise. 11 vols. 1922–36.

Northup, Clark S. A register of the bibliographies of the English language and literature. New Haven 1925.

Batho, Edith C. *et al.* Summary of periodical literature. Review of English studies, I–. (1925–). *Quarterly lists of current periodical articles.*

Kennedy, Arthur G. A bibliography of writings on the English language. Cambridge, Mass. 1927; 1961.

—— A concise bibliography for students of English. Palo Alto, Cal. 1940; 1960 (*enlarged by Donald B. Sands*).

Davies, Godfrey *et al.* Bibliography of British history. Oxford 1928–.

Esdaile, Arundell. The sources of English literature: a guide for students. Cambridge 1928.

Brussel, I.R. Anglo–American first editions, Pt i, East to west, 1826–1900. 1935; Pt ii, West to east, 1786–1930, 1936.

Cross, Tom P. Bibliographical guide to English studies. Chicago 1938; 1963 (*revised and enlarged by Donald F. Bond as* A reference guide to English studies).

Besterman, Theodore. A world bibliography of bibliographies. 3 vols. 1939–40; 4 vols. Geneva 1955–6 (*enlarged*).

Spargo, John W. A bibliographical manual for students of the language and literature of England and the US. Chicago 1939; 1941.

Bateson, F.W. (ed.). The Cambridge bibliography of English literature [600–1900]. 4 vols. Cambridge 1940; Supplement 600–1900, ed. George Watson, Cambridge 1957.

A catalog of books represented by Library of Congress printed cards to 1942. 167 vols. Ann Arbor 1942–6; Supplement, 42 vols. 1948. *Supplements in progress.*

Hayward, John. English poetry: a catalogue of first and early editions from Chaucer to the present day. Cambridge 1947; 1950.

Baldensperger, F. and W.P.Friederich. Bibliography of comparative literature. Chapel Hill, N.C. 1950.

Matthews, William. British diaries: an annotated bibliography of diaries written between 1442 and 1942. Berkeley, Cal. 1950.

Stewart, James D. *et al.* British union-catalogue of periodicals. 4 vols. 1955–.

Sawin, Lewis *et al.* Abstracts of English studies, 1– (1958–). *Monthly summaries of periodical literature.*

Other Reference Works

Chambers, Robert. Cyclopaedia of English literature. 2 vols. Edinburgh 1843–4, 4 vols. 1857–60; ed. David Patrick, 3 vols. 1901–3, 1938 (*enlarged*).

Brewer, E.Cobham. Dictionary of phrase and fable. 1870; 1949.

Stephen, Leslie, Sidney Lee *et al.* The dictionary of national biography. 21 vols. 1885–1909; Supplements, London (*later* Oxford) 1909–. *Complete to 1950. See p. 201, below.*

Cousin, John W. Biographical dictionary of English literature. 1910, 1938; 1958, 1962 (Dictionary of literary biography, English and American), rev. D. C. Browning (EL).

Ekwall, Eilert. The concise Oxford dictionary of English place-names. Oxford 1936; 1960.

Harvey, Paul. The Oxford companion to English literature. Oxford 1932, 1946; The concise Oxford dictionary of English literature, ed. John Mulgan, Oxford 1939.

Ghosh, J.C. and E.G.Withycombe. Annals of English literature, 1475–1925. Oxford 1935; 1961 (*continued to 1950*).

Smith, W.G. The Oxford dictionary of English proverbs. Oxford 1935; 1948 (rev. Paul Harvey).

The Oxford dictionary of quotations. Oxford 1941; 1953.

Tilley, Morris P. A dictionary of the proverbs in England in the sixteenth and seventeenth centuries. Ann Arbor 1950.

Hartnoll, Phyllis. The Oxford companion to the theatre. Oxford 1951; 1957 (*with supplement*).

Opie, Iona and Peter. The Oxford dictionary of nursery rhymes. Oxford 1951; 1952.

Steinberg, S.H. Cassell's encyclopaedia of literature. 2 vols. 1953.

Literary History and Criticism

Warton, Thomas (1728–90). The history of English poetry from the eleventh to the eighteenth century. 3 vols. 1774–81. *Completed to c. 1600.*

Johnson, Samuel. Prefaces biographical and critical to the works of the English poets. 10 vols. 1779–81. '*Lives of the poets*'.

Hazlitt, William. Lectures on the English poets. 1818.

—— Lectures on the English comic writers. 1819.

Hallam, Henry. Introduction to the literature of Europe in the fifteenth, sixteenth and seventeenth centuries. 4 vols. 1837–9.

Taine, Henri. Histoire de la littérature anglaise. 4 vols. Paris 1863–4; tr. 2 vols. Edinburgh 1871.

Jusserand, J.-J. Histoire littéraire du peuple anglais. 2 vols. Paris 1894–1904; tr. 3 vols. 1895–1909. *A history of English literature to the Civil War.*

Courthope, W.J. A history of English poetry. 6 vols. 1895–1910.

Hales, John (ed.). Handbooks of English literature. 11 vols. (10 pts). 1895–1903.

Wülker, Richard. Geschichte der englischen Literatur. Leipzig 1896; 2 vols. Leipzig 1906–7.

Saintsbury, George (ed.). Periods of European literature. 12 vols. Edinburgh 1897–1908.

—— A short history of English literature. 1898.

—— A history of criticism and literary taste in Europe. 3 vols. Edinburgh 1900–4; A history of English criticism: being the English chapters of the History revised, Edinburgh 1911.

Ward, A.W. and A.R.Waller (edd.). The Cambridge history of English literature. 14 vols. Cambridge 1907–16; 1932 (*without bibliographies*); vol. xv: Index, Cambridge 1927. *See under Sampson, below.*

Baker, Ernest A. The history of the English novel. 10 vols. 1924–39.

Legouis, Emile and Louis Cazamian. Histoire de la littérature anglaise. Paris 1924; tr. 2 vols. 1926–7; 1 vol. 1930, 1957; A short history of English literature, by Emile Legouis, Oxford 1934–5 (abridged).

Nicoll, Allardyce. British drama. 1925; 1947.

—— A history of English drama, 1660–1900. 6 vols. Cambridge 1952–9. A revision of his period histories.

Barfield, Owen. Poetic diction: a study in meaning. 1928; 1952.

Chambers, R.W. The continuity of English prose. In Nicholas Harpsfield, Sir Thomas More, ed. E.V.Hitchcock, 1932; 1950 (separately) (EETS).

Williams, Charles. The English poetic mind. Oxford 1932.

Eliot, T.S. The use of poetry and the use of criticism. 1933.

Elton, Oliver. The English muse. 1933.

Bateson, F.W. English poetry and the English language. 1934.

—— English poetry: a critical introduction. 1950.

Bodkin, Maud. Archetypal patterns in poetry. Oxford 1934.

Dobrée, Bonamy (ed.). Introductions to English literature. 5 vols. 1938–58; 1950–2 (vols. iii and i). With bibliographies.

Leavis, F.R. Revaluation: tradition and development in English poetry. 1936.

Sampson, George. The concise Cambridge history of English literature. Cambridge 1941; 1961 (with addn by R.C.Churchill).

Atkins, J.W.H. English literary criticism. 3 vols. Cambridge (later London) 1943–51. Completed to 1800.

Grierson, Herbert and J.C.Smith. A critical history of English poetry. 1944; 1947.

Wilson, F.P. and Bonamy Dobrée (edd.). The Oxford history of English literature. 14 vols. (12 pts). Oxford 1945–. With bibliographies.

Brooks, Cleanth. The well wrought urn: studies in the structure of poetry. New York 1947.

Baugh, Albert C. et al. A literary history of England. New York 1948.

Craig, Hardin et al. A history of English literature. New York 1950.

Ford, Boris (ed.). A guide to English literature. 7 vols. 1954–61 (Pelican). Studies by various hands, with anthology in vol. I.

Allen, Walter. The English novel: a short critical history. 1954.

Tillyard, E.M.W. The English epic and its background. 1954.

Kinsley, James (ed.). Scottish poetry: a critical survey. 1955.

Wellek, René. A history of modern criticism, 1750–1950. 4 vols. New Haven 1955– . Literary criticism in Europe and N. America.

Frye, Northrop. Anatomy of criticism: four essays. Princeton 1957.

Wimsatt, W.K. and Cleanth Brooks. Literary criticism: a short history. New York 1957. Classical criticism, and English since 16th century.

Daiches, David. A critical history of English literature. 2 vols. New York 1960.

Watson, George. The literary critics: a study of English descriptive criticism. 1962 (Penguin); 1964.

Davies, Hugh Sykes and George Watson (edd.). The English mind: studies in the English Moralists presented to Basil Willey. Cambridge 1964.

Collections and Anthologies

Johnson, Samuel. The works of the English poets. 68 vols. 1779–81; 75 vols. 1790 (*enlarged*). *Incorporated in Chalmers, below.*

Ellis, George. Specimens of the early English poets. 1790, 3 vols. 1801 (*enlarged*); Specimens of the later English poets, ed. Robert Southey, 3 vols. 1807.

Anderson, Robert. The works of the British poets, with prefaces. 14 vols. Edinburgh 1792–1807.

Chalmers, Alexander. The works of the English poets. 21 vols. 1810. *See Johnson, above.*

Child, Francis J. English and Scottish ballads. 8 vols. Boston 1857–8; The English and Scottish popular ballads, ed. Child, 5 vols. Boston 1882–98, ed. Helen C. Sargent and Kittredge, Cambridge, Mass. 1904 (*selection*). *See* Matthew Hodgart, The ballads, 1950.

Palgrave, Francis T. The golden treasury. 1861; 1891; Oxford 1907, 1940 (OSA) (*enlarged*).

Arber, Edward. An English garner. 8 vols. 1877–96; ed. Thomas Seccombe, 12 vols. 1903–4 (*enlarged*).

—— British anthologies. 10 vols. 1899–1901.

Saintsbury, George. Specimens of English prose style. 1885.

Quiller-Couch, Arthur. The Oxford book of English verse. Oxford 1900; 1939 (*enlarged*).

—— The Oxford book of ballads. Oxford 1910.

—— The Oxford book of English prose. Oxford 1925.

Dixon, W. Macneile and Herbert Grierson. The English Parnasaus: an anthology chiefly of longer poems. Oxford 1909.

Auden, W.H. and John Garrett. The poet's tongue. 1935.

Auden, W.H. The Oxford book of light verse. Oxford 1938; 1939.

—— and Norman H. Pearson. Poets of the English language. 5 vols. New York 1951.

Brooks, Cleanth and Robert Penn Warren. Understanding poetry: an anthology for college students. New York 1938; 1950.

Roberts, D. Kilham. The centuries' poetry. 4 vols. 1938–53 (Penguin).

Bennett, H.S., C.S.Lewis *et al.* Fifteen poets. Oxford 1941.

Davies, Hugh Sykes. The poets and their critics. 1943 (Pelican); 2 vols. 1960–2 (*enlarged*).

Sutherland, James. The Oxford book of English talk. Oxford 1953.

Allott, Kenneth *et al*. The Pelican book of English prose. 5 vols. 1956 (Pelican).

Hayward, John. The Penguin book of English verse. 1956 (Penguin).

Pinto, V. de Sola and A.E. Rodway. The common muse: an anthology of popular British ballad poetry, XVth–XXth century. 1957.

Allott, Miriam. Novelists on the novel. 1959.

Prosody

For a bibliography see Karl Shapiro, A bibliography of modern prosody, Baltimore 1948.

Schipper, Jakob. Englische Metrik. 3 vols. Bonn 1882–8; 1 vol. Vienna 1895 (Grundriss) (*abridged*), tr. Oxford 1910.

Mayor, Joseph B. Chapters on English metre. 1886.

—— A handbook of modern English metre. Cambridge 1903.

Bridges, Robert. Milton's prosody. Oxford 1893; 1921 (*enlarged*).

Sievers, Eduard. Altgermanische Metrik. Halle 1893.

Omond, Thomas S. A study of metre. 1903.

—— English metrists. Oxford 1921.

Saintsbury, George. A history of English prosody from the twelfth century. 3 vols. 1906–10.

—— Historical manual of English prosody. 1910.

—— A history of English prose rhythm. Edinburgh 1912.

Abercrombie, Lascelles. Principles of English prosody, pt i. 1923.

Smith, Egerton. The principles of English metre. Oxford 1923.

Lewis, C.S. The fifteenth-century heroic line. Essays and studies, xxiv (1938).

—— The alliterative metre. *In his* Rehabilitations, Oxford 1939.

Shapiro, Karl. English prosody and modern poetry. Baltimore 1947.

Ing, Catharine. Elizabethan lyrics. 1951.

Book Production and Distribution

Ames, Joseph. Typographical antiquities: being an historical account of printing in England. 1749; 3 vols. 1785–90 (rev. William Herbert); 4 vols. 1810–19 (rev. Thomas F. Dibdin); Index, 1899.

Reed, Talbot B. A history of the old English letter foundries. 1887; 1952 (rev. and enlarged by A.F. Johnson).

Plomer, Henry R. A short history of English printing, 1476–1898. 1900; 1915 (*popular edn*).

Plomer, Henry R. A dictionary of booksellers and printers, 1641 to 1667. 1907.

—— et al. A dictionary of printers and booksellers, 1668 to 1725. 1922.

—— et al. A dictionary of printers and booksellers, 1726 to 1775. 1932.

Duff, E. Gordon. A century of the English book-trade [1457–1557]. 1905.

—— The printers, stationers and booksellers of London from 1476 to 1535. Cambridge 1906.

McKerrow, Ronald B. (ed.). A dictionary of printers and booksellers in England, Scotland and Ireland, 1557–1640. 1910.

—— Printers' and publishers' devices in England and Scotland, 1485–1640. 1913.

—— and F. S. Ferguson. Title-page borders used in England and Scotland, 1485–1640. 1932.

—— An introduction to bibliography for literary students. Oxford 1927; 1928.

Mumby, Frank A. The romance of bookselling: a history. 1910; 1930.

—— Publishing and bookselling. 1930; 1947.

Aldis, Harry G. The printed book. Cambridge 1916; 1941, 1951 (rev. John Carter and Brooke Crutchley).

Updike, Daniel B. Printing types: their history, form and use. 2 vols. Cambridge, Mass. 1922; 1962.

Morison, Stanley. Four centuries of fine printing. 1924; 1960.

—— Type designs of the past and present. 1926; 1962 (re-entitled On type designs, past and present).

de Ricci, Seymour. English collectors of books and manuscripts (1530–1930). Cambridge 1930.

Sadleir, Michael. The evolution of publishers' binding styles, 1770–1900. 1930.

Carter, John. Binding variants in English publishing, 1820–1900. 1932.

—— Taste and technique in book-collecting. Cambridge 1947.

—— ABC for book-collectors. 1952; 1961.

—— Books and book-collectors. 1956.

Johnson, A. F. Type designs: their history and development. 1934.

Davies, Hugh W. Devices of the early printers, 1457–1560. 1935.

Simpson, Percy. Proof-reading in the sixteenth, seventeenth and eighteenth centuries. Oxford 1935.

Berry, W. Turner and A. F. Johnson. Catalogue of specimens of printing type by English and Scottish printers and founders, 1665–1830. 1935.

—— Encyclopaedia of type faces. 1953.

Labarre, E. J. A dictionary of paper and paper-making terms. Amsterdam 1937.

Plant, Marjorie. The English book trade: an economic history. 1939.

Bowers, Fredson. Principles of bibliographical description. Princeton 1949.
—— Textual and literary criticism. Cambridge 1959.
Steinberg, S. H. Five hundred years of printing. 1955; 1961 (Penguin).
Greg, W. W. Some aspects and problems of London publishing between 1550 and 1650. Oxford 1956.
Glaister, Geoffrey A. Glossary of the book. 1960.

Grammars, Dictionaries, Histories of the Language

For a bibliography see Arthur G. Kennedy, A bibliography of writings on the English language to 1922, Cambridge, Mass. 1927; *and for an account of the dictionary before Johnson,* DeWitt T. Starnes and Gertrude E. Noyes, The English dictionary from Cawdrey to Johnson, 1604–1755, Chapel Hill, N. C. 1946.

Johnson, Samuel. A dictionary of the English language. 2 vols. 1755; 1773.

Roget, Peter M. Thesaurus of English words and phrases. 1852; 1936, 1949 (enlarged by Samuel R. Roget); ed. D. C. Browning, 1952 (EL).

Ellis, Alexander J. On early English pronunciation, with especial reference to Shakspere and Chaucer. 5 pts. 1869–89.

Morris, Richard. Historical outlines of English accidence. 1872; 1895 (rev. L. Kellner and Henry Bradley).

Sweet, Henry. Handbook of phonetics. Oxford 1877.
—— History of English sounds. Oxford 1888.
—— A new English grammar, logical and historical. 2 pts. Oxford 1891–8.
—— Short history of English grammar. Oxford 1892.

Skeat, Walter W. An etymological dictionary of the English language. 4 pts. 1879–82, 1 vol. 1909 (*enlarged*); A concise etymological dictionary, Oxford 1882, 1956.
—— Principles of English etymology. 2 ser. Oxford 1887–91; 1892 (ser. 1).
—— A glossary of Tudor and Stuart words. Ed. A. L. Mayhew, Oxford 1914.

Murray, James, Henry Bradley, W. A. Craigie and C. T. Onions. A new English dictionary on historical principles. 20 vols. (10 pts). Oxford 1888–1928; Introduction, supplement and bibliography, Oxford 1933; The Oxford English dictionary, being a corrected reissue, 13 vols. (*with supplement*), Oxford 1933; The shorter Oxford English dictionary, ed. William Little *et al.*, 2 vols. Oxford 1933; 1957. *See also Fowler, below.*

Emerson, Oliver F. The history of the English language. New York 1894; An outline history, New York 1906.

Wright, Joseph. The English dialect dictionary. 6 vols. Oxford 1898–1905.

Kaluza, Max. Historische Grammatik der englischen Sprache. 2 vols. Berlin 1900–1; 1906–7.

Bradley, Henry. The making of English. 1904.

Jespersen, Otto. Growth and structure of the English language. Leipzig 1905; Oxford 1954.

—— A modern English grammar. 7 vols. Heidelberg (*later* Copenhagen) 1909–49 (completed by Niels Haislund); 1949 (vols. i–iv).

—— Essentials of English grammar. 1933.

Ripman, Walter. The sounds of spoken English. 1905; 1931 (*re-entitled* English phonetics, *with supplement*).

Fowler, H.W. and F.G. The King's English. Oxford 1906; 1930.

—— The concise Oxford dictionary of current English, adapted from the Oxford dictionary. Oxford 1911; 1964 (rev. E.McIntosh).

—— The pocket Oxford dictionary. Oxford 1924; 1942 (rev. H.G.Le Mesurier and E.McIntosh).

Wyld, Henry C. The historical study of the mother tongue. 1906.

—— The growth of English. 1907.

—— A short history of English. 1914; 1927 (*enlarged*).

—— A history of modern colloquial English. 1920; 1936.

—— The universal dictionary of the English language. 1932.

Jones, Daniel. The pronunciation of English. Cambridge 1909; 1956.

—— An English pronouncing dictionary on strictly phonetic principles. 1917; 1956, 1963 (EL).

—— An outline of English phonetics. Leipzig 1918; Cambridge 1932, 1962.

—— The phoneme: its nature and use. Cambridge 1950.

Smith, Logan Pearsall. The English language. 1912; Oxford 1952 (with epilogue by R.W.Chapman) (Home univ. lib.).

Classen, E. Outlines of the history of the English language. 1919.

Weekley, Ernest. A concise etymological dictionary of modern English. 1921; 1952.

Fowler, H.W. A dictionary of modern English usage. Oxford 1926; 1937.

Ward, Ida C. The phonetics of English. Cambridge 1929; 1945.

Davies, Constance. English pronunciation from the fifteenth to the eighteenth century. 1934.

Baugh, Albert C. History of the English language. New York 1935; 1957.

Serjeantson, Mary S. A history of foreign words in English. 1935.

Partridge, Eric. A dictionary of slang and unconventional English. 1937; 1949 (*enlarged*).

Wrenn, C.L. The English language. 1949; 1952.

Brunner, Karl. Die englische Sprache: die geschichtliche Entwicklung. 2 vols. Halle 1950–1.

Horn, Wilhelm. Laut und Leben: englische Lautgeschichte der neueren Zeit (1400–1950). Ed. Martin Lehnert, 2 vols. Berlin 1954.

Clark, John W. Early English: a study of Old and Middle English. 1957.

Dobson, E. J. English pronunciation, 1500–1700. 2 vols. Oxford 1957.

THE OLD ENGLISH PERIOD
(600–1100)

THE OLD ENGLISH PERIOD
(600–1100)

Bibliography

Bonser, Wilfrid. An AS and Celtic bibliography (450–1087). 2 vols. Oxford 1957. *A bibliography of history; for literature see Renwick and Orton, below.*

Ker, N.R. Catalogue of manuscripts containing AS. Oxford 1957.

Literary History

Earle, John. AS literature. 1884.

Ker, W.P. Epic and romance. 1896; 1908. *On the Germanic and French epic before Chaucer.*

—— The dark ages. Edinburgh 1904. *A history of European literature, Latin and vernacular, A.D. 500–1100.*

Brooke, Stopford A. English literature from the beginning to the Norman Conquest. 1898.

Brandl, Alois. Geschichte der altenglischen Literatur. *In* Grundriss der germanischen Philologie, ed. Hermann Paul, Strasbourg 1908.

Chadwick, H.Munro. The heroic age. Cambridge 1912.

Thomas, P.G. English literature before Chaucer. 1924.

Chambers, R.W. England before the Norman Conquest. 1926.

Laistner, Max L.W. Thought and letters in western Europe, A.D. 500 to 900. 1931; Ithaca, N.Y. 1957.

Crawford, Samuel J. AS influence on western Christendom, 600–800. Oxford 1933.

Hodgkin, R.H. History of the Anglo-Saxons [to 900]. 2 vols. Oxford 1935; 1952.

Wardale, E.E. Chapters on OE literature. 1935.

Douglas, D.C. English scholars, 1660–1730. 1939; 1951.

Renwick, W.L. and Harold Orton. The beginnings of English literature to Skelton, 1509. 1939; 1952. *With bibliography.*

Kennedy, Charles W. The earliest English poetry. New York 1943.

Stenton, F.M. AS England. Oxford 1943; 1947 (Oxford history of England, vol. ii).

Levison, Wilhelm. England and the Continent in the eighth century: Ford lectures. Oxford 1946.

Anderson, George K. The literature of the Anglo-Saxons. Princeton 1949.

Whitelock, Dorothy. The beginnings of English society. 1952 (Pelican history of England, vol. ii).

Wilson, R.M. The lost literature of medieval England. 1952.

Sisam, Kenneth. Studies in the history of OE literature. Oxford 1953.

Blair, Peter Hunter. An introduction to AS England. Cambridge 1956.

Collections and Anthologies

Hickes, George. Linguarum veterum septentrionalium thesaurus. 3 vols. Oxford 1703–7.

Thorpe, Benjamin. Analecta anglo-saxonica. Oxford 1834; 1846.

Grein, C.W.M. Bibliothek der angelsächsischen Poesie. 4 vols. Göttingen (*later* Cassel *and* Göttingen) 1857–64; Cassel (*later* Leipzig) 1881–98 (rev. Richard Wülker). *Vols. iii–iv are rptd as* Sprachschatz, 2 vols. Cassel 1861.

——, Richard Wülker *et al.* Bibliothek der angelsächsischen Prosa. 13 vols. Cassel (*later* Leipzig *and* Hamburg) 1872–1933.

Sweet, Henry. An AS reader. Oxford 1876; 1922, 1954 (rev. C.T. Onions).

Bright, J.W. An AS reader. New York 1891; 1935 (rev. James R. Hulbert).

Wyatt, A.J. An elementary OE reader (early West Saxon). Cambridge 1901.

—— An AS reader. Cambridge 1919.

Cook, Albert S. and C.B. Tinker. Select translations from OE poetry. Boston 1902; Select translations from OE prose, Boston 1908.

Dickins, Bruce. Runic and heroic poems of the old Teutonic peoples. Cambridge 1915 (*with trns*).

Sedgefield, W.J. An AS verse book. Manchester 1922; An AS prose book, Manchester 1928.

Sampson, George. Prose and verse, to the cycles of romance. Cambridge 1924. *An anthology of trns.*

Gordon, R.K. AS poetry translated. 1926, 1954 (EL).

Krapp, George P. and Elliott van K. Dobbie. The AS poetic records. 6 vols. New York 1931–53.

Kennedy, Charles W. OE elegies translated into alliterative verse. Princeton 1936.

—— Early English Christian poetry translated into alliterative verse. New York 1952.

Bone, Gavin. AS poetry: an essay with specimen translations in verse. Oxford 1943.

Whitelock, Dorothy. English historical documents, *c.* 500–1042. 1955.

*The bulk of OE poetry, collected in Grein and Krapp-Dobbie (above), is
contained in four MSS:*

Beowulf MS (Brit. Museum, Cotton Vitellius A xv). Ed. Julius
Zupitza, 1882 (EETS) (*facs.*); ed. Dobbie, New York 1953
(vol. iv). *See under* Beowulf *and* Judith, *below.*

Cædmon MS (Bodley, Junius 11). Ed. Israel Gollancz, Oxford
1927 (*facs.*); ed. Krapp, New York 1931 (vol. i). *See under
Cædmon, below.*

Exeter book (Exeter Cathedral). Ed. R.W.Chambers, Max
Förster and Robin Flower, Bradford 1933 (*with facs.*); ed.
Krapp and Dobbie, New York 1936 (vol. iii); tr. Israel Gollancz
and W.S.Mackie, 2 vols. 1895–1934 (EETS). *See under
Cynewulf* (Crist; Guðlac; Harrowing of hell; Juliana; Phoenix;
Physiologus), Riddles, Ruin, Widsið, *below.*

Vercelli book (Vercelli Cathedral). Ed. Max Förster, Rome 1913
(*facs.*); ed. Krapp, New York 1932 (vol. ii). *See under Cynewulf*
(Address of soul to body; Andreas; Dream of rood; Elene; Fates
of apostles), *below.*

Grammars and Dictionaries

Bosworth, Joseph. An AS dictionary. Ed. T.Northcote Toller,
4 pts. Oxford 1882–8; Supplements, Oxford 1908, 1921.

Sievers, Eduard. Angelsächsische Grammatik. Halle 1882; 1942,
1951 (rev. Karl Brunner); tr. Albert S.Cook, Boston 1885.

Sweet, Henry. AS primer. 1882; 1953 (rev. Norman Davis).

―― A student's dictionary of AS. Oxford 1897.

Clark Hall, John R. A concise AS dictionary. Cambridge 1894; 1961.

Wyatt, A.J. An elementary OE grammar (early West Saxon).
Cambridge 1897.

Wright, Joseph and Elizabeth M. OE grammar. Oxford 1908; 1925.

Wardale, E.E. An OE grammar. 1922; 1926.

Holthausen, F. Altenglisches etymologisches Wörterbuch. Heidelberg 1934.

Brook, G.L. An introduction to OE. Manchester 1955.

Quirk, Randolph and C.L.Wrenn. An OE grammar. 1955; 1957.

Campbell, Alistair. OE grammar. Oxford 1959.

Bessinger, J.B. A short dictionary of AS poetry. Toronto 1960.

ÆLFRIC (*c.* 955–*c.* 1020)

A SAXON TREATISE concerning the Old and New Testament. Ed.
William L'Isle, 1623 (*with trn*); ed. C.W.M.Grein, Cassel 1872 (Prosa,
vol. i); ed. Samuel J. Crawford, 1922 (EETS) (*with* Heptateuch, *below*).

DICTIONARIUM SAXONICO-LATINO-ANGLICUM, cum glossario. Ed. William Somner, Oxford 1659; ed. Julius Zupitza, Berlin 1880.

HEPTATEUCHUS, liber Job, evangelium Nicodemi et Judith. Ed. Edward Thwaites, Oxford 1698; ed. C.W.M.Grein, Cassel 1872 (Prosa, vol. i); Heptateuch, treatise on the Old and New Testament and preface to Genesis, ed. Samuel J.Crawford, 1922 (EETS).

COLLOQUIUM. Ed. Heinrich Leo, Halle 1835; 1838 (in Sprachproben); ed. G.N.Garmonsway, 1939, 1947 (Methuen's OE lib.).

DE TEMPORIBUS ANNI. Ed. Thomas Wright, 1841 (in Popular treatises on science); ed. Heinrich Henel, 1942 (EETS).

PASTORAL LETTERS. Ed. Benjamin Thorpe, 1840 (in Ancient laws and institutes of England); ed. Bernard Fehr, Hamburg 1914 (Prosa, vol. ix).

HOMILIES. Ed. Benjamin Thorpe, 2 vols. 1844–6 (in Homilies of the AS Church): Selected homilies, ed. Henry Sweet, Oxford 1885, 1896.

METRICAL LIVES OF SAINTS. Ed. Walter W.Skeat, 4 vols. 1881–1900 (EETS) (with trn); ed. Bruno Assmann, Cassel 1889 (Prosa, vol. iii).

LATIN LIFE OF ÆTHELWOLD. Ed. Joseph Stevenson, 1858 (Rolls ser.); tr. Dorothy Whitelock, 1955 (in English historical documents, c. 500–1042).

White, Caroline L. Ælfric: his life and writings. New Haven 1898.

Dubois, Marguérite-Marie. Ælfric: sermonnaire, docteur et grammairien. Paris 1942.

Sisam, Kenneth. Ælfric's Catholic homilies; The order of Ælfric's early books. Both in his Studies in the history of OE literature, Oxford 1953.

KING ALFRED (849 – 899)

BEDAE HISTORIA ECCLESIASTICA. Ed. Abraham Wheloc(k), 2 vols. Cambridge 1643–4 (Alfred's OE version with Latin original); ed. Thomas Miller, 4 vols. 1890–8 (EETS) (with trn); ed. Jakob Schipper, Leipzig, 2 vols. 1897–9 (Prosa, vol. iv).

BOETHI CONSOLATIO philosophiae libri v redditi ab Alfredo. Ed. Christopher Rawlinson, Oxford 1698; ed. J.S.Cardale, 1829 (with trn); ed. W.J.Sedgefield, Oxford 1899; tr. Sedgefield, Oxford 1900.

OROSIUS. Ed. Daines Barrington, 1773 (OE version with trn); tr. Joseph Bosworth, 1855; ed. Bosworth, 1859; OE text and Latin original, ed. Henry Sweet, 1883 (EETS); Extracts, ed. Sweet, Oxford 1885; The Tollemache Orosius, ed. Alistair Campbell. Copenhagen 1953 (facs.).

GREGORY'S PASTORAL CARE. Ed. Henry Sweet, 2 vols. 1871–2 (EETS); ed. N.R.Ker, Copenhagen 1956 (facs.); Prefaces, tr. Dorothy Whitelock, 1955 (in English historical documents, c. 500–1042).

For the AS Chronicle, *begun in Alfred's reign and perhaps under his inspiration, see* Chronicle, *below.*

Whole works. Ed. J.A.Giles, 3 vols, Oxford 1852-8.

Asser, Bishop (d. 909)? De rebus gestis Ælfredi magni. Ed. Matthew Parker, 1574; ed. W.H.Stevenson, Oxford 1904, 1959; tr. L.C.Jane, 1908; [extracts], tr. Dorothy Whitelock, 1955 (*in* English historical documents, *c.* 500-1042).

Plummer, Charles. The life and times of Alfred the Great. Oxford 1902.

Lees, B.A. Alfred the Great, the truth-teller. New York 1919.

Oman, Carola. Alfred, king of the English. 1939.

Duckett, Eleanor S. Alfred the Great. Chicago 1956.

BEDE (BAEDA VENERABILIS) (*c.* 672 – 735)

Jones, Putnam F. A concordance to the Historia ecclesiastica. Cambridge, Mass. 1929.

Laistner, Max L.W. and H.H.King. A handlist of Bede manuscripts. Ithaca, N.Y. 1943.

HISTORIA ECCLESIASTICA gentis Anglorum. Strasbourg *c.* 1475; tr. Thomas Stapleton, Antwerp 1565; ed. Abraham Wheloc(k), 2 vols. Cambridge 1643-4 (*with OE version*); ed. John Smith, Cambridge 1722 (*with OE version*); ed. Charles Plummer, 2 vols. Oxford 1896; ed. J.E.King, 1930 (Loeb) (*with trn*); tr. Leo Sherley-Price, 1955 (Penguin); The Leningrad Bede, ed. Olof Arngart, Copenhagen 1952 (*facs.*). *For the OE version see under Alfred, above.*

BEDAS METRISCHE VITA sancti Cuthberti. Ed. W.Jaager, Leipzig 1935.

TWO LIVES OF ST CUTHBERT: a life by an anonymous monk of Lindisfarne and Bede's prose life. Ed. Bertram Colgrave, Cambridge 1940 (*with trns*).

OPERA DE TEMPORIBUS. Ed. Charles W.Jones, Cambridge, Mass. 1943.

Opera. Paris 1544; 8 vols. Basle 1563; ed. J.A.Giles, 12 vols. 1843-4; ed. J.P.Migne, Paris 1850-62 (Patrologia, vols xc-xcv).

For the apocryphal works see Bedae pseudepigrapha: scientific writings falsely attributed to Bede, ed. Charles W.Jones, Ithaca, N.Y. 1939.

Thompson, A.Hamilton *et al.* Bede: his life, times and writings. Oxford 1935.

Chambers, R.W. Bede. Proc. Brit. Acad. xxii (1936). *Rptd in his* Man's unconquerable mind, 1939.

Duckett, Eleanor S. *In her* AS saints and scholars, New York 1947. *On Aldhelm, Bede, Boniface, Wilfrid.*

BEOWULF AND FINNSBURG

BEOWULF. Ed. G.J.Thorkelin, Copenhagen 1815; ed. Julius Zupitza, 1882, 1959 (EETS) (*MS. facs.*); ed. A.J.Wyatt, Cambridge 1894, 1914 (rev. R.W.Chambers); ed. Fr.Klaeber, Boston 1922, 1950; ed. C.L.Wrenn, 1953.

Prose trn by John R.Clark Hall, 1901; 1940, 1950 (rev. C.L.Wrenn). *Verse trns by* Gavin Bone, Oxford 1945 (*incomplete*) *and by* E.Morgan, Aldington, Kent 1952.

FINNSBURG. Ed. George Hickes, Oxford 1705 (*in* Thesaurus, vol. ii). *Also in modern edns of* Beowulf, *above.*

Chambers, R.W. Beowulf: an introduction. Cambridge 1921; 1959 (rev. C.L.Wrenn).
—— Beowulf and the 'heroic age'. *In his* Man's unconquerable mind, 1939.
Lawrence, W.W. Beowulf and epic tradition. Cambridge, Mass. 1928.
Hoops, Johannes. Kommentar zum Beowulf. Heidelberg 1932.
Girvan, Ritchie. Beowulf and the seventh century. 1935.
Tolkien, J.R.R. Beowulf: the monsters and the critics. Proc. Brit. Acad. xxii (1936).
Bonjour, Adrien. The digressions in Beowulf. Oxford 1950.
Whitelock, Dorothy. The audience of Beowulf. Oxford 1951.

BLICKLING HOMILIES (971?)

THE BLICKLING HOMILIES. Ed. Richard Morris, 3 vols. 1874–80 (EETS); ed. Rudolph Willard, Copenhagen 1960 (*facs.*). *Written or transcribed in 971.*

BYRTHFERTH (11th cent.)

BYRTHFERTH'S MANUAL (A.D. 1011). Vol. 1. Ed. Samuel J.Crawford, 1929 (EETS) (*with trn*).

CÆDMON (late 7th cent.)

HYMN. *Bede's* Historia ecclesiastica *contains his Latin paraphrase of the hymn and an account of Cædmon's inspiration. The OE original was inserted in some MSS of the* Historia. Ed. A.H.Smith, 1933 (*in* Three Northumbrian poems) (Methuen's OE lib.).
PARAPHRASIS POETICA GENESIOS. Ed. Franciscus Junius, 1655; ed. C.W.M.Grein and Richard Wülker, Leipzig 1894 (Poesie, vol. ii); The Cædmon MS., ed. Israel Gollancz, Oxford 1927 (*facs.*); The Junius MS., ed. G.P.Krapp, New York 1931; tr. Charles W. Kennedy, 1916. *Paraphrases of Genesis, Exodus, Daniel etc.*

The Genesis. Ed. Fr. Klaeber, Heidelberg 1913, 1931; ed. B. J. Timmer, Oxford 1948, 1954.

Exodus. Ed. F. A. Blackburn, Boston 1907; ed. E. B. Irving, New Haven 1953.

Sievers, Eduard. Der Heliand und die angelsächsische Genesis. Halle 1875.

Dustoor, P. E. Legends of Lucifer in early English and in Milton. Anglia, liv (1930).

Dobbie, Elliott van K. The manuscripts of Cædmon's Hymn and Bede's Death song. New York 1937.

Wrenn, C. L. The poetry of Cædmon. Proc. Brit. Acad. xxxii (1946).

CHARMS

LEECHDOMS, wortcunning and starcraft in early English. Ed. Oswald Cockayne, 3 vols. 1864–6 (Rolls ser.); AS charms, ed. Felix Grendon, Journal of Amer. folklore, xxii (1909), New York 1930.

Storms, G. AS magic. The Hague 1948. *A study, with texts and trns.*

Grattan, J. H. G. and C. Singer. AS magic and medicine. 1952.

CHARTERS AND LAWS

'Αρχαιονομία: sive de priscis Anglorum legibus libri. Ed. William Lambarde, 1568; ed. Abraham Wheloc(k), Cambridge 1644 (*in* Bedae Historia ecclesiastica, vol. ii); Leges anglo-saxonicae, ed. David Wilkins, 1721; Ancient laws and institutes of England, ed. Benjamin Thorpe, 2 vols. 1840; ed. F. Liebermann, 3 vols. Halle 1903–16; The laws of the earliest English kings, ed. F. L. Attenborough, Cambridge 1922 (*with trns*); ed. Agnes J. Robertson, Cambridge 1925 (*with trns*).

CODEX DIPLOMATICUS aevi saxonici. Ed. J. M. Kemble, 6 vols. 1839–48; Diplomatarium anglicum, ed. Benjamin Thorpe, 1865; Select charters, ed. William Stubbs, Oxford 1866; Cartularium saxonicum, ed. W. de G. Birch, 3 vols. 1885–93; A handbook to the land charters, ed. John Earle, Oxford 1888; AS charters, ed. Agnes J. Robertson, Cambridge 1939 (*with trns*); AS wills, ed. Dorothy Whitelock, Cambridge 1930; AS writs, ed. F. E. Harmer, Manchester 1952.

For trns of many charters, laws and wills see English historical documents c. 500–1042, ed. Dorothy Whitelock, 1955.

CHRONICLE (891? – 1154?)

CHRONICON. Ed. Abraham Wheloc(k), Cambridge 1644 (*in* Bedae Historia ecclesiastica, vol. ii); ed. Edmund Gibson, Oxford 1692 (*with Latin trn*); [six texts, A–F], ed. Benjamin Thorpe, 2 vols. 1861

(Rolls ser.) (*with trn*); Two of the chronicles parallel [A and E], ed. John Earle, Oxford 1865; 2 vols. 1892-9 (rev. Charles Plummer), 1952; tr. G.N. Garmonsway, 1953, 1955 (EL) and Dorothy Whitelock, 1955 (*in* English historical documents, *c*. 500-1042), 1961 (*separately*). *Seven MS. compilations have survived (A–G), most beginning with annals of English history from 55 B.C. written in OE in Alfred's reign:*

A. Parker chronicle (–1070). Ed. Earle and Plummer (*above*); ed. Robin Flower and Hugh Smith, 1941 (EETS) (*facs.*); 832–900, ed. A.H. Smith, 1935, 1951 (Methuen's OE lib.).

B. (–977). Ed. Thorpe (*above*).

C. (–1066). Ed. Harry A. Rositzke, Bochum 1940; [Æthelred, 978–1016], ed. Margaret Ashdown, Cambridge 1930 (*in* English and Norse documents relating to Ethelred).

D. (–1130). Ed. E. Classen and F.E. Harmer, Manchester 1926.

E. Peterborough chronicle (–1154). Ed. Earle and Plummer (*above*); ed. Dorothy Whitelock, Copenhagen 1954 (*facs.*); 1070–1154, ed. Cecily Clark, Oxford 1958; tr. Harry A. Rositzke, New York 1951.

F. (–1058). Ed. F.P. Magoun, Medieval studies, ix (1947). *Latin–English.*

G. (–1070). Ed. Wheloc(k) (*above*). *Otherwise called Aⁱ—a transcript of A made* c. *1025.*

See the histories of AS England by Chambers, Hodgkin, Stenton and Whitelock, pp. 15–6 above.

CYNEWULF (9th cent.?)

CODEX EXONIENSIS. Ed. Benjamin Thorpe, 1842 (*with trns*); The Exeter book, ed. Israel Gollancz and W.S. Mackie, 2 vols. 1895–1934 (EETS) (*with trns*); ed. R.W. Chambers, Max Förster and Robin Flower, Bradford 1933 (*with facs.*); ed. G.P. Krapp and Elliott van K. Dobbie, New York 1936. *Includes six poems attributed to Cynewulf:* Crist, Guðlac, Harrowing of hell, Juliana, Phoenix, Physiologus.

CODEX VERCELLENSIS. Ed. J.M. Kemble, 1843 (*with trns*); ed. Max Förster, Rome 1913 (*facs.*); ed. G.P. Krapp, New York 1932. *Includes* Andreas, Dream of the rood, Elene, Fates of the apostles.

Andreas and The fates of the apostles. Ed. G.P. Krapp, Boston 1906; ed. Kenneth R. Brooks, Oxford 1961.

Crist. Ed. Israel Gollancz, 1892 (*with trn*); ed. Albert S. Cook, Boston 1900.

The dream of the rood. Ed. Bruce Dickins and A.S.C. Ross, 1934, 1954 (Methuen's OE lib.).

Elene. Ed. Julius Zupitza, Berlin 1877, 1899; ed. Albert S. Cook, New Haven 1919 (*with* Phoenix *and* Physiologus); ed. P. O. E. Gradon, 1958 (Methuen's OE lib.).

The fates of the apostles. Ed. Krapp (*with* Andreas, *above*).

Juliana. Ed. William Strunk, Boston 1904; ed. Rosemary Woolf, 1955 (Methuen's OE lib.).

Phoenix. Ed. Cook (*with* Elene, *above*).

Physiologus. Ed. Cook (*with* Elene, *above*).

For prose trns see Charles W. Kennedy, Poems of Cynewulf translated, New York 1910, *and for verse trns his* Early English Christian poetry, New York 1952.

Sisam, Kenneth. Cynewulf and his poetry. Proc. Brit. Acad. xviii (1932). *Rptd in his* Studies in the history of OE literature, Oxford 1953.

Dubois, Marguérite-Marie. Les éléments latins dans la poésie religieuse de Cynewulf. Paris 1942.

DEOR'S LAMENT

See under Exeter book, *p. 17 above*

DEOR. Ed. Kemp Malone, 1933, 1949 (Methuen's OE lib.).

GNOMIC VERSES

See under Exeter book, *p. 17 above*

GNOMIC POETRY IN AS. Ed. Blanche C. Williams, New York 1914.

GOSPELS

THE GOSPELS translated in the olde Saxons tyme out of Latin. Ed. John Foxe, 1571; The Gothic and AS Gospels, with the versions of Wycliffe and Tyndale, ed. Joseph Bosworth and George Waring, 1865; ed. J. W. Bright, 4 vols. 1904–6; Glossary, ed. M. A. Harris, Boston 1899.

St Matthew. Ed. J. M. Kemble and C. Hardwick, Cambridge 1858; St Mark, ed. Walter W. Skeat, Cambridge 1871; St Luke, ed. Skeat, Cambridge 1874; St John, ed. Skeat, Cambridge 1878.

THE LINDISFARNE AND RUSHWORTH GOSPELS. Ed. John Stevenson and George Waring, 4 vols. 1854–65; Lindisfarne Gospels, ed. Eric G. Millar, 1923 (*facs. of 39 leaves*); Glossary, ed. Albert S. Cook, Halle 1894.

EVANGELIUM NICODEMI. Ed. Edward Thwaites, Oxford 1698 (*with* Heptateuch); The Gospel of Nicodemus, ed. Samuel J. Crawford, Edinburgh 1927.

JUDITH (late 9th or early 10th cent.)

HISTORIAE JUDITH FRAGMENTUM. Ed. Edward Thwaites, Oxford 1698 (*with* Heptateuch); ed. Albert S. Cook, Boston 1888 (*with trn*); ed. B. J. Timmer, 1952 (Methuen's OE lib.).

MALDON (991) AND *BRUNANBURH* (937)

MALDON. Ed. Thomas Hearne, Oxford 1726 (*in* Johannis Glastoniensis chronica); ed. Margaret Ashdown, Cambridge 1930 (*in* English and Norse documents) (*with trn*); ed. E. D. Laborde, 1936 (*with* Byrhtnoth); ed. E. V. Gordon, 1937, 1949 (Methuen's OE lib.); tr. W. P. Ker (1887), 1926 (*in* R. W. Chambers, England before the Norman Conquest).

BRUNANBURH. Ed. Abraham Wheloc(k), Cambridge 1644 (*in* Bedae Historia ecclesiastica, vol. ii: Chronicon); ed. Alistair Campbell, 1938; tr. Alfred Tennyson, 1880 (*in his* Ballads). *In MSS A, B, C and D of* Chronicle (*see under* Chronicle, *above*). *For this and other poems preserved in the* Chronicle, *see* AS minor poems, ed. Elliott van K. Dobbie, New York 1942.

RIDDLES

See under Exeter book, *p. 17 above*

THE RIDDLES OF THE EXETER BOOK. Ed. Frederick Tupper, Boston 1910; ed. A. J. Wyatt, Boston 1912; ed. Moritz Trautmann, Heidelberg 1915; tr. Paull F. Baum, Durham, N.C. 1963.

RUIN

See under Exeter book, *p. 17 above*

RUINAE. Ed. Heinrich Leo, Halle 1865; Poem of a city in ruins, supposed to be Bath, ed. John Earle, Bath 1872 (*with trn*); tr. Charles W. Kennedy, Princeton 1936 (*in his* OE elegies).

SEAFARER

For early edns see under Exeter book, *p. 17 above*

THE SEAFARER. Ed. Ida L. Gordon, 1960 (Methuen's OE lib.); tr. Ezra Pound, 1912 (*in his* Ripostes); tr. Gavin Bone, Oxford 1943 (*in his* AS poetry); tr. Dorothy Whitelock, 1955 (*in* English historical documents, *c.* 500–1042).

Anderson [-Arngart], O.S. The seafarer: an interpretation. Lund 1937.

Whitelock, Dorothy. The interpretation of the Seafarer. *In* The early cultures of north-west Europe, ed. Cyril Fox and Bruce Dickins, Cambridge 1950.

See also under Wanderer, *below*

WALDERE

TWO LEAVES OF KING WALDERE'S LAY. Ed. George Stephens, Copenhagen 1860 (*with facs. and trn*); ed. F. Holthausen, Gothenburg 1899 (*with facs.*); ed. Bruce Dickins, Cambridge 1915 (*in* Runic and heroic poems); ed. F. Norman, 1933 (Methuen's OE lib.); ed. Fr. Klaeber, Boston 1922, 1950 (*with* Beowulf).

WANDERER

For edns see under Exeter book, *p. 17 above*

THE WANDERER. Tr. Gavin Bone, Oxford 1943 (*in his* AS poetry); tr. Dorothy Whitelock, 1955 (*in* English historical documents, *c*. 500–1042).

Huppé, Bernard F. The Wanderer: theme and structure. Journal of English and Germanic philology, xlii (1943).
Gordon, Ida L. Traditional themes in the Wanderer and the Seafarer. Review of English studies, new ser. v (1954).
Stanley, E. G. OE poetic diction and the interpretation of the Wanderer, the Seafarer and the Penitent's prayer. Anglia, lxxiii (1956).

WIDSIÐ

See under Exeter book, *p. 17 above*

TRAVELLER'S SONG. Ed. J. M. Kemble, 1833 (*in* The AS poems of Beowulf); Widsið, ed. R. W. Chambers, Cambridge 1912 (*with trn*); ed. Kemp Malone, 1936 (Methuen's OE lib.), Copenhagen 1962.

Chambers, R. W. Widsith: a study in OE. heroic legend. Cambridge 1912.

WULFSTAN (d. 1023)

SERMO LUPI AD ANGLOS. Ed. William Elstob, Oxford 1705 (*in* Hickes's Thesaurus, vol. ii, *from a letter to Hickes with a text based on MS. Cotton Nero A 2 and with Latin trn*); ed. Dorothy Whitelock, 1939, 1952 (Methuen's OE lib.) (*Nero A 1*); tr. Whitelock, 1955 (*in* English historical documents, *c*. 500–1042).
HOMILIES. Ed. A. S. Napier, Berlin 1883; ed. Dorothy Bethurum, Oxford 1957.

Napier, A. S. Über die Werke des altenglischen Erzbischofs Wulfstan. Weimar 1882.
Becher, C. F. R. Wulfstans Homilien. Leipzig 1910.
McIntosh, Angus. Wulfstan's prose. Proc. Brit. Acad. xxxiv (1948).
Jost, Karl. Wulfstanstudien. Berne 1950.

THE MIDDLE ENGLISH PERIOD
(1100–1500)

THE MIDDLE ENGLISH PERIOD
(1100–1500)
INCLUDING THE SCOTTISH CHAUCERIANS

Bibliographies

Geddie, William. A bibliography of Middle Scots poets. Edinburgh 1912 (Scottish Text Soc.).

Brown, Carleton. A register of ME religious and didactic verse. 2 vols. Oxford 1916–20.

—— and R.H.Robbins. The index of ME verse. New York 1943. *An expansion of the* Register, *adding secular poems.*

Wells, J.E. A manual of the writings in ME, 1050–1400. New Haven 1916; Nine supplements, 1919–52. *Complete to 1945.*

Tucker, Lena L. and Allen R.Benham. A bibliography of fifteenth-century literature. Seattle 1928.

de Ricci, Seymour. Census of medieval and Renaissance MSS in the US and Canada. 3 vols. New York 1935–40; Supplement, New York 1961.

Loomis, R.S. Introduction to medieval literature chiefly in England. New York 1939; 1948.

Literary History

Warton, Thomas (1728–90). History of English poetry [to *c.* 1600]. 3 vols. 1774–81. *Unfinished.*

Saintsbury, George. The flourishing of romance and the rise of allegory. Edinburgh 1897.

Ker, W.P. English literature, medieval. 1912 (Home univ. lib.).

Owst, G.R. Preaching in medieval English: an introduction to sermon MSS of *c.* 1350–1450. Cambridge 1926.

—— Literature and pulpit in medieval England. Cambridge 1933; Oxford 1961 (*with addns*).

Lewis, C.S. The allegory of love. Oxford 1936.

—— The discarded image: an introduction to medieval and Renaissance literature. Cambridge 1964.

Renwick, W.L. and H.Orton. The beginnings of English literature to Skelton, 1509. 1939; 1952. *With bibliography.*

Wilson, R.M. Early ME literature. 1939.

—— The lost literature of medieval England. 1952.

Atkins, J.W.H. English literary criticism: the medieval phase. Cambridge 1943.

Chambers, E.K. English literature at the close of the Middle Ages. Oxford 1945 (Oxford history of English lit., vol. II, ii).

Bennett, H.S. Chaucer and the fifteenth century. Oxford 1947 (Oxford history of English lit., vol. II, i).

Kane, George. ME literature: a critical study of the romances, the religious lyrics, Piers Plowman. 1951 (Methuen's OE lib.).

Everett, Dorothy. Essays on ME literature. Ed. Patricia Kean, Oxford 1955.

Speirs, John. Medieval English poetry: the non-Chaucerian tradition. 1957.

Spearing, A.C. Criticism and medieval poetry. 1964.

Collections and Anthologies

Ritson, Joseph. Ancient Engleish metrical romanceës. 3 vols. 1802.

Morris, Richard. Specimens of early English, 1250–1400. Oxford 1867; 2 vols. Oxford 1872–82, 1894–8 (with Walter W. Skeat); Specimens, 1394–1579, ed. Skeat, Oxford 1871, 1880.

Emerson, Oliver F. ME reader. New York 1905; 1915.

Chambers, E.K. and Frank Sidgwick. Early English lyrics, amorous, divine, moral and trivial. 1907.

Weston, Jessie L. Romance, vision and satire. Boston 1912. *Translations*.

—— Chief ME poets. Boston 1914. *Translations*.

Brandl, Alois and Otto Zippel. Mittelenglische Sprach- und Literaturproben. Berlin 1915; 1927.

Cook, Albert S. A literary ME reader. Boston 1915.

Neilson, W.A. and K.G.T. Webster. Chief British poets of the fourteenth and fifteenth centuries. Boston 1916.

Hall, Joseph. Selections from early ME. 2 vols. Oxford 1920.

Sisam, Kenneth. Fourteenth-century verse and prose. Oxford 1921; 1937.

Brown, Carleton. Religious lyrics of the fourteenth century. Oxford 1924; 1952 (rev. G.V. Smithers).

—— English lyrics of the thirteenth century. Oxford 1932.

—— Religious lyrics of the fifteenth century. Oxford 1939.

Sampson, George. Prose and verse, to the cycles of romance. Cambridge 1924. *An anthology of trns.*

Hammond, Eleanor P. English verse between Chaucer and Surrey. Durham, N.C. 1927.

French, W.H. and C.B. Hale. ME metrical romances. New York 1930.

Chambers, R.W. and Marjorie Daunt. A book of London English, 1384–1425. Oxford 1931.

Greene, Richard L. The early English carols. Oxford 1935.

—— A selection of English carols. Oxford 1962.

Brook, G.L. The Harley lyrics: MS. Harley 2253. Manchester 1948; 1956.
Mossé, Fernand. Manuel de l'anglais du moyen âge. Pt ii, Moyen-anglais. Paris 1949; tr. and rev. Baltimore 1952.
Dickins, Bruce and R.M.Wilson. Early ME texts. Cambridge 1951; 1952.
Robbins, R.H. Secular lyrics of the xivth and xvth centuries. Oxford 1952.
—— Historical poems of the xivth and xvth centuries. New York 1959.
Davies, R.T. Medieval English lyrics. 1963.

Grammars and Dictionaries

Stratmann, F.H. and Henry Bradley. ME dictionary. Oxford 1891.
Wright, Joseph and Elizabeth M. An elementary ME grammar. Oxford 1923; 1928.
Craigie, W.A. A dictionary of the older Scottish tongue, from the twelfth century to the end of the sixteenth. Chicago 1930–.
Brunner, Karl. Abriss der mittelenglischen Grammatik. Halle 1938.
Mossé, Fernand. Manuel de l'anglais du moyen âge. Pt ii, Moyen-anglais. Paris 1949; tr. and rev. Baltimore 1952.
Kurath, H. and S.H.Kuhn. ME dictionary. Ann Arbor 1953–.

ALEXANDER ROMANCES (14th and 15th cent.)

LYFE OF ALISAUNDER. Ed. Henry Weber, Edinburgh 1810 (*in* Metrical romances, vol. i); ed. G.V.Smithers, 2 vols., 1952–7 (EETS). *A selection was pbd in Thomas Warton's* History of English poetry, 1774–81.
THE BUIK OF ALEXANDER, by John Barbour. Ed. David Laing, 1831; ed. R.L.Graeme Ritchie, 4 vols. Edinburgh 1921–9 (Scottish Text Soc.) (*with Fr. original*). *A trn of two Fr. poems, completed in 1438, probably by a disciple of Barbour.*
ALISAUNDER: fragment A. Ed. Walter W.Skeat, 1867 (EETS) (*with* Palerne), ed. F.P.Magoun, Cambridge, Mass. 1929 (*in* Gests of Alexander); Fragment B, ed. Joseph Stevenson, 1849, ed. Skeat, 1878 (EETS) (*in* Alexander and Dindimus); Fragment C, ed. Stevenson (with B), ed. Skeat, 1886 (EETS) (The wars of Alexander) *Early fourteenth-century alliterative trns of a Latin romance,* Historia Alexandri de preliis, *A and B being probably by the same translator.*
PROSE ALEXANDER. Ed. J.S.Westlake, vol. i, 1911 (EETS).

ANCRENE RIWLE (late 12th cent.)

ANCREN RIWLE: a treatise on the rules and duties of monastic life. Ed. James Morton, 1853 (*with trn*) (*MS. Cotton Nero A. xiv*), 1905 (*trn only*), ed. Mabel Day, 1952 (EETS); ed. R. M. Wilson, 1954 (EETS) (*MS. Caius College 234*); ed. Albert C. Baugh, 1956 (EETS) (*British Museum MS. Royal 8 C. 1*); ed. F. M. Mack, 1963 (EETS) (Titus D, xviii).

ANCRENE WISSE. Ed. J. R. R. Tolkien, 1962 (EETS) (*MS. Corpus Christi College Cambridge 402*); Parts six and seven, ed. Geoffrey Shepherd, Edinburgh 1959.

The Rule, an anonymous manual in eight parts written for three noble anchoresses, was revised for wider use as Ancrene wisse *and tr. into French* (EETS, 1944 *and* 1958) *and Latin* (EETS, 1944).

Macaulay, G. C. The Ancren riwle. Modern language rev. ix (1914).

Dymes, D. M. E. Original language of the Ancren riwle. Essays and studies, ix (1923).

Tolkien, J. R. R. Ancrene wisse and Hali meiðhad. Essays and studies, xiv (1928).

ARTHURIAN LITERATURE

Ackerman, Robert W. An index of the Arthurian names in ME. Palo Alto, Cal. 1952. *For a bibliography see* Bruce, *below, supplemented by* John J. Parry, A bibliography of critical Arthurian literature 1922–9, New York 1931; 1930–5, New York 1936; *continued annually in* Modern language quarterly, 1–, 1940–.

GILDAS (516?–570). De calamitate, excidio et conquestu Britanniae. Ed. Polydore Vergil, 1525; ed. Thomas Gale, Oxford 1691; ed. Theodor Mommsen, Berlin 1894 (*in* Monumenta Germaniae historica, vol. xiii); tr. J. A. Giles, 1841.

NENNIUS (*fl.* 796). Historia britonum. Ed. Gale, Mommsen, tr. Giles (*with* Gildas, *above*).

GEOFFREY OF MONMOUTH (d. 1154). Historia regum Britanniae. Paris 1508; ed. A. Schulz, Halle 1853; ed. Edmond Faral, Paris 1929 (*in* La légende Arthurienne, vol. iii); tr. Sebastian Evans, 1904.

WACE (*d. after* 1171). Roman de Brut or Geste des Bretons. Ed. Le Roux de Lincy, 2 vols. Rouen 1836–8; ed. Ivor Arnold, 2 vols. Paris 1938–40. *An Anglo-Norman verse trn of Geoffrey, above.*

LAȝAMON (*fl. c.* 1200). Brut: or Chronicle of Britain. Ed. Frederic Madden, 3 vols. 1847 (*two texts*); ed. G. L. Brook and R. F. Leslie, 3 vols. 1963– (EETS); ed. Brook, Oxford 1963 (*selection*). *An alliterative verse chronicle, partly a trn of Wace, above, written c. 1205.*

SIR GAWAYNE AND THE GRENE KNIGHT. *See under* Pearl Group, *p. 46 below.*

LE MORTE ARTHUR. 1819; ed. F.J.Furnivall, 1864; ed. James D.Bruce, 1903 (EETS). *A stanzaic romance of the late fourteenth century.*

MORTE ARTHURE. Ed. J.O.Halliwell, 1847; ed. George G.Parry, 1865, 1871 (rev. Edmund Brock) (EETS); ed. M.M.Banks, 1900; ed. E. Björkman, Heidelberg 1915. *An alliterative verse romance, written c. 1400.*

Malory, Sir Thomas. *See p. 42 below.*

Ritson, Joseph. The life of King Arthur. 1825.

Weston, Jessie L. From ritual to romance. Cambridge 1920.

Bruce, James D. The evolution of Arthurian romance to 1300. 2 vols. Göttingen 1923.

Chambers, E.K. Arthur of Britain. 1927.

Faral, Edmond. La légende Arthurienne: études et documents. Pt i: les plus anciens textes. 3 vols. Paris 1929.

Reid, Margaret J.C. The Arthurian legend: comparison of treatment in modern and medieval literature. Edinburgh 1938.

Williams, Charles. The figure of Arthur. *In* Arthurian torso, ed. C.S. Lewis, Oxford 1948. *Unfinished.*

Loomis, R.S. Arthurian tradition and Chrétien de Troyes. New York 1949.

—— Wales and the Arthurian legend. Cardiff 1956.

—— (ed.). Arthurian literature in the Middle Ages: a collaborative history. Oxford 1959.

Tatlock, John S.P. The legendary history of Britain. Berkeley 1950.

For the historical background see R.G.Collingwood *and* J.N.L.Myres, Roman Britain and the English settlements, Oxford 1936.

AYENBITE OF INWYT (1340)

Ed. Joseph Stevenson, 1855; ed. Richard Morris, 1866 (EETS). *A trn of the French treatise by Friar Lorens, Somme des vices et des vertus, by the Kentish monk Michael of Northgate.*

For BALLADS *see p. 7 above.*

JOHN BARBOUR (c. 1320 – 1395)

THE BRUCE. Edinburgh 1571?; ed. Andrew Hart, Edinburgh 1616; ed. John Pinkerton, 1790; ed. Cosmo Innes, Aberdeen 1856; ed. Walter W.Skeat, 4 pts. 1870–9 (EETS), 4 pts. 1893–5 (Scottish Text Soc.); ed. W.Mackay Mackenzie, 1909; tr. G.Eyre-Todd, Glasgow 1907. *An epic of traditional Scottish history, 1304–33. For the* Buik of Alexander, *which has been doubtfully attributed to Barbour, see under* Alexander romances, *above.*

Neilson, George. Barbour: poet and translator. 1900.

2   33   WCB

BESTIARY (early 13th cent.)

Ed. Thomas Wright, Leipzig 1837 (*in* Altdeutsche Blätter, vol. ii); ed. Richard Morris, 1872 (*in* An old English miscellany) (EETS). *A verse paraphrase, mainly of the Latin* Physiologus *by Thetbaldus, an eleventh-century Italian monk. A twelfth-century Latin version is tr.* T.H. White, The book of beasts, 1954.

WILLIAM CAXTON (*c.* 1422 – 1491)

de Ricci, Seymour. A census of Caxtons. 1909.

The fifteenth-century first edns of the following were all ptd by Caxton:

THE RECUYELL of the historyes of Troye. Bruges 1475?; ed. H.Oskar Sommer, 2 vols. 1894. *A trn of the French collection of Raoul Le Fevre, with prologue, interpolation and epilogue.*

THE GAME AND PLAYE OF THE CHESSE. 1476; ed. V. Figgins, 1855 (*facs.*); ed. W.E.A.Axon, 1883. *A trn of two Fr. versions of* Jacques de Cessolis, Liber de ludo scaccorum, *with dedication, interpolation and epilogue.*

THE HISTORIES OF JASON. 1477; ed. John Munro, 1912 (EETS). *A trn from the Fr. romance of Raoul Le Fevre, with prologue and epilogue.*

REYNART THE FOXE. 1481; 1489; ed. Edward Arber, 1878; ed. Donald B.Sands, Cambridge, Mass. 1960. *A prose trn of the beast-epic from the Flemish, with prologue and epilogues.*

GODEFFROY OF BOLOYNE. 1481; ed. Mary N.Colvin, 1893 (EETS). *A trn from the Fr. narrative of William Archbp of Tyre, with prologue and epilogue.*

POLYCHRONICON. 1482. *Trevisa's trn of Higden's history, with a continuation (bk viii), prologue and epilogue. See under Trevisa, below.*

LEGENDA AUREA. 1483? *See under English Bible, p. 58 below.*

FABLES. 1484; ed. Joseph Jacobs, 2 vols. 1889. *A trn of Aesop from the Fr. version of Machault, with epilogue.*

ENEYDOS. 1490?; ed. M.T.Culley and F.J.Furnivall, 1890 (EETS). *A prose Virgil from the Fr. adaptation of 1483, with prologue and epilogue.*

SIX BOOKES OF METAMORPHOSEOS. Ed. George Hibbert, 1819; ed. Stephen Gaselee and H.F.B.Brett-Smith, Oxford 1924. *A prose trn of Ovid made from a Fr. version in c. 1480 but apparently never ptd by Caxton.*

Also edns of trns by Antony Wydeville, Earl Rivers, of Dicts or sayings of the philosophers (1477) *and of* Christine de Pisan (1478); *and edns of Chaucer's* Canterbury tales (1478?), *Gower's* Confessio amantis (1483) *and Malory's* Morte Darthur (1485). *For his trns of the Charlemagne romances see under* Charlemagne romances, *below.*

Prologues and epilogues. Ed. W.J.B.Crotch, 1928 (EETS). *See also Aurner, below.*

Blades, William. The life and typography of Caxton. 2 vols. 1861–3; 1 vol. 1882 *(rev. and abridged).*
Duff, E. Gordon. William Caxton. Chicago 1905.
Aurner, Nellie S. Caxton: a study of the literature of the first English press. 1926. *With an edn of the prologues, interpolations and epilogues.*
Bennett, H.S. English books and readers, 1475–1557. Cambridge 1952.

CHARLEMAGNE ROMANCES

CHARLES THE GRETE. 1485 (Caxton); ed. Sidney J.H.Herrtage, 2 pts. 1880–1 (EETS).
FOURE SONNES OF AYMON. *c.* 1489 (Caxton); ed. Octavia Richardson, 2 pts. 1884–5 (EETS).
HUON DE BORDEUXE. *c.* 1534. *See under Lord Berners, p. 58 below.*
TAILL OF RAUF COILȜEAR. Ed. Robert Lekpreuik, St Andrews 1572; ed. Herrtage, 1882 (EETS); ed. W.H.Browne, Baltimore 1903.
OTUEL. Ed. H.W.B.Nicholson, 1836; ed. Herrtage, 1882 (EETS).
ROLAND AND VERNAGU. Ed. Nicholson, Herrtage *(with* Otuel, *above).*
THE SOWDONE OF BABYLONE. 1854; ed. Emil Hausknecht, 1881 (EETS).
SIR FIRUMBRAS. Ed. Herrtage, 1879 (EETS).
SONG OF ROLAND. Ed. Herrtage, 1880 (EETS).
SEGE OF MELAYNE. Ed. Herrtage *(with* Song of Roland, *above).*
DUKE ROWLANDE AND SIR OTTUELL. Ed. Herrtage, 1880 (EETS).
FILLINGHAM OTUEL AND FIRUMBRAS. Ed. M.J.O'Sullivan, 1935 (EETS).

GEOFFREY CHAUCER (*c.* 1340 – 1400)

Hammond, Eleanor P. Chaucer: a bibliographical manual. New York 1908.
Spurgeon, Caroline F.E. Five hundred years of Chaucer criticism and allusion, 1357–1900. 7 pts. 1914–24; 3 vols. Cambridge 1925.
Both supplemented by Dudley D.Griffith, Bibliography of Chaucer, 1908–53, Seattle 1955.
Tatlock, John S.P. and Arthur G.Kennedy. A concordance to the complete works. Washington 1927.

In conjectural order of composition:
ROMAUNT OF THE ROSE. 1532 (*in* Workes, ed. Thynne, *below*), ed. F.J. Furnivall, 1911; ed. Max Kaluza, 1891 *(with Fr. original).*
BOOK OF THE DUCHESS. 1532 (Thynne).

HOUS OF FAME. 1486? (Caxton).

BOETHIUS, DE CONSOLATIONE PHILOSOPHIAE. 1478? (Caxton); 1532 (Thynne); ed. Richard Morris, 1868 (EETS); ed. F.J.Furnivall, 1886.

PARLIAMENT OF FOULES. 1478? (*entitled* The temple of bras) (Caxton); ed. D.S.Brewer, Edinburgh 1960.

TROILUS AND CRISEYDE. 1482? (Caxton); ed. R.K.Root, Princeton 1926, 1945. *See also under* Robert Henryson, *below*.

LEGEND OF GOOD WOMEN. 1532 (Thynne); ed. Walter W.Skeat, Oxford 1889.

CANTERBURY TALES. 1478? (Caxton); ed. Thomas Tyrwhitt, 5 vols. 1775–8; ed. J.M.Manly, New York 1928 (*selected*); ed. Manly and Edith Rickert, 8 vols. Chicago 1940 (The text studied on the basis of all known manuscripts); ed. A.C.Cawley, 1958 (EL). *A facs. of the Ellesmere MS. was pbd 2 vols. Manchester 1911.*

[Works]. Ed. Richard Pynson, 3 pts. 1526; ed. William Thynne, 1532, ed. Walter W.Skeat, 1905 (*facs*.); ed. John Stow, 1561; ed. Thomas Speght, 1598, 1598; ed. John Urry, 1721; Complete works, ed. Skeat, 7 vols. Oxford 1894–7, 1 vol. Oxford 1895 (Student's Chaucer); Poetical works, ed. F.N.Robinson, Boston 1933, 1957 (*re-entitled* Works).

Dryden, John. *In his preface to* Fables, 1700.

Tyrwhitt, Thomas. An essay upon his language and versification. 1775 (*in his edn of* Canterbury tales, *above*).

Root, R.K. The poetry of Chaucer. Boston 1906; 1922.

Tatlock, John S.P. The development and chronology of Chaucer's works. 1907.

Coulton, G.G. Chaucer and his England. 1908; 1963.

Kittredge, G.L. Chaucer and his poetry. Cambridge, Mass. 1915.

Brusendorff, Aage. The Chaucer tradition. Copenhagen 1925.

Manly, J.M. Some new light on Chaucer. New York 1926.

French, Robert D. A Chaucer handbook. New York 1927; 1947.

Lowes, John Livingston. Chaucer and the development of his genius. Boston 1934.

Lewis, C.S. *In his* The allegory of love, Oxford 1936.

Bennett, H.S. *In his* Chaucer and the fifteenth century, Oxford 1947.

Coghill, Nevill. The poet Chaucer. Oxford 1949 (Home univ. lib.).

Lawrence, W.W. Chaucer and the Canterbury tales. New York 1950.

Clemen, Wolfgang H. Der junge Chaucer. Cologne 1953; tr. and enlarged, 1963 (Chaucer's early poetry).

Bennett, J.A.W. The parlement of foules: an interpretation. Oxford 1957.

Muscatine, Charles. Chaucer and the French tradition. Berkeley, Cal. 1957.

Robertson, D.W. A preface to Chaucer. Princeton 1963.

For an edn of sources see Sources and analogues of Chaucer's Canterbury tales, ed. W.F.Bryan and Germaine Dempster, Chicago 1941.

GAVIN DOUGLAS (*c.* 1474 – 1522)

THE PALYCE OF HONOUR. Edinburgh? 1530? (*fragment*); London 1553?; Edinburgh 1579, ed. J.G.Kinnear, 1827 (*facs.*).

KING HART. Ed. John Pinkerton, 1786 (*in* Ancient Scotish poems). *Attributed to Douglas.*

THE XIII BUKES OF ENEADOS translatet into Scottish meter. 1553 (*corrupt text*); ed. Thomas Ruddiman, Edinburgh 1710 (*corrected from Ruthven MS.*); ed. George Dundas, 2 vols. Edinburgh 1839 (*vol. ii unpbd*) (*Cambridge MS.*); ed. David F.C.Coldwell, 4 vols. Edinburgh 1957– (Scottish Text Soc.). *A trn of Virgil in heroic couplets, with prologues to each book, an epilogue and commentary to part of bk i.*

Select works. Perth 1787; Selections, ed. David F.C.Coldwell, Oxford 1964.

Poetical works. Ed. John Small, 4 vols. Edinburgh 1874. *With a memoir.*

Watt, Lauchlan M. Douglas's Aeneid. Cambridge 1920.

MEDIEVAL DRAMA

Stratman, Carl J. Bibliography of medieval drama. Berkeley, Cal. 1954.

THE SUMMONING OF EVERYMAN. 1510–19?, ?(Pynson) (*two fragmentary edns*), ed. W.W.Greg, Louvain 1910 (Bang); *c.* 1530 (John Skot), ed. Greg, 2 vols. 1904–9 (Bang); ed. A.C.Cawley, Manchester 1961.

CHESTER MYSTERIES. Ed. J.H.Markland, 1818; ed. Thomas Wright, 2 vols. 1843–7; ed. Hermann Deimling and Matthews, 2 vols. 1893– 1916 (EETS). *One or more plays ed. Collier, Pollard, Manly, Hemingway, Adams, below; also* Antichrist, ed. W.W.Greg, Oxford 1935.

COVENTRY PLAYS: The pageant of the shearmen and tailors, ed. Thomas Sharp, Coventry 1825 (*in* A dissertation on the Coventry mysteries; ed. Manly, Adams, *below*); The presentation in the temple: a pageant [The weavers' play], ed. John B.Gracie, Edinburgh 1836.

Two Coventry Corpus Christi plays. Ed. Hardin Craig, 1902 (EETS).

DIGBY PLAYS. Ed. Thomas Sharp, Edinburgh 1835; ed. F.J.Furnivall, 1882, 1896 (EETS). *One or more plays ed. Manly, Adams, below.*

TOWNELEY PLAYS. Ed. J.Raine and James Gordon, 1836; ed. George England and A.W.Pollard, 1897 (EETS). *One or more plays ed. Manly, Hemingway, Adams, below.*

LUDUS COVENTRIAE [N-town cycle]: a collection of mysteries. Ed. J.O. Halliwell, 1841; ed. K.S.Block, 1922 (EETS). *One or more plays ed. Pollard, Manly, Hemingway, Adams, below.*

ABRAHAM AND ISAAC [Brome]: a mystery play. Ed. Lucy Toulmin Smith, Anglia, vii (1884), Norwich 1886 (*in* A common-place book of the fifteenth century); ed. Manly, Adams, *below*; [Chester Abraham and Isaac], ed. Rudolf Brotanek, Halle 1898.

YORK PLAYS. Ed. Lucy Toulmin Smith, Oxford 1885; tr. Margaret S. Mooney, New York 1915. *One or more plays ed. Pollard, Manly, Hemingway, Adams, below.*

MACRO PLAYS. Ed. F.J.Furnivall and A.W.Pollard, 1904 (EETS). *First complete text of three morality plays written 1425–75.*

The origin of the English drama. Ed. Thomas Hawkins, 3 vols. Oxford 1773.

Five miracle plays. Ed. John Payne Collier, 1836.

English miracle plays, moralities and interludes. Ed. A.W.Pollard, Oxford 1890; 1927.

Specimens of the pre-Shakespearean drama. Ed. J.M.Manly, 2 vols. Boston 1897.

Early English dramatists. Ed. John S.Farmer, 12 vols. 1905–8.

English nativity plays. Ed. S.B.Hemingway, New York 1909.

The non-cycle mystery plays. Ed. Osborn Waterhouse, 1909 (EETS).

Chief pre-Shakespearean dramas. Ed. J.Q.Adams, Boston 1924.

Everyman, and medieval miracle plays. Ed. A.C.Cawley, 1956 (EL).

Chambers, E.K. The medieval stage. 2 vols. Oxford 1903.
—— The English folk-play. Oxford 1933.
—— *In his* English literature at the close of the Middle Ages. Oxford 1945.

Young, Karl. The drama of the medieval Church. Oxford 1933.

Gardiner, Harold C. Mysteries' end; the last days of the medieval religious stage. New Haven 1946.

Craig, Hardin. English religious drama of the Middle Ages. Oxford 1955.

WILLIAM DUNBAR (*c.* 1456 – *c.* 1513)

[THE CHEPMAN AND MYLLAR PRINTS]. 9 tracts. Edinburgh 1508; ed. George Stevenson, Edinburgh 1918 (Scottish Text Soc.); ed. William Beattie, Edinburgh 1950 (*facs.*). *Six Dunbar poems, including* The golden targe *and* The flyting of Dunbar and Kennedy.

THE EVER GREEN. Ed. Allan Ramsay, 2 vols. Edinburgh 1728. *Includes free versions of 24 Dunbar poems.*

ANCIENT SCOTTISH POEMS. Ed. David Dalrymple, Lord Hailes, Edinburgh 1770. *32 poems from Bannatyne MS.*

ANCIENT SCOTISH POEMS. Ed. John Pinkerton, 2 vols. 1786. *23 poems.*

Poems. Ed. David Laing, 2 vols. Edinburgh 1834; ed. John Small *et al.*, 3 vols. Edinburgh 1884–93 (Scottish Text Soc.); ed. Jakob Schipper, 5 pts. Vienna 1892–4; ed. W. Mackay Mackenzie, 1932, 1960 (rev. Bruce Dickins); ed. James Kinsley, Oxford 1958 (*selection*).

Mackay, Æ. J. G. William Dunbar. 1889.

Taylor, Rachel A. Dunbar: the poet and his period. 1931.

Baxter, J. W. William Dunbar. Edinburgh 1952.

THE FLOURE AND THE LEAFE (c. 1450–75)

THE FLOURE AND THE LEAFE. 1598 (*in Speght's edn of Chaucer's works*); ed. Walter W. Skeat, 1897 (*in* Chaucer, Complete works, vol. vii); ed. D. A. Pearsall, Edinburgh 1962.

THE ASSEMBLY OF LADIES. 1532 (*in Thynne's edn of Chaucer's works*); ed Skeat, Pearsall, *above.*

Two allegorical poems in rhyme royal, of unknown and probably separate authorship, formerly attributed to Chaucer.

SIR JOHN FORTESCUE (c. 1394 – c. 1476)

DE POLITICA ADMINISTRATIONE et legibus civilibus commentarius. 1546; 1567 (*with trn by Richard Mulcaster*); 1616 (*with trn by John Selden, re-entitled* De laudibus legum Angliae); ed. S. B. Chrimes, Cambridge 1942.

THE DIFFERENCE between an absolute and a limited monarchy. Ed. John Fortescue-Aland, 1714; ed. Charles Plummer, Oxford 1885 (*entitled* The governance of England: a revised text).

Works. Ed. Thomas Fortescue, Lord Clermont, 2 vols. 1869.

JOHN GOWER (1330? – 1408)

MIROUR DE L'OMME. Oxford 1899 (*in* Complete works, *below*). Speculum hominis *or* Speculum meditantis, *a verse manual in French on the vices and virtues, first attributed to Gower by G. C. Macaulay.*

VOX CLAMANTIS. Ed. H. O. Coxe, 1850. *A description of English society, in Latin elegiac verse.*

CONFESSIO AMANTIS. 1483 (Caxton); ed. Reinhold Pauli, 3 vols. 1857; The English works, ed. G. C. Macaulay, 2 vols. 1900–1 (EETS); Selections, ed. Macaulay, Oxford 1903.

Complete works. Ed. G.C.Macaulay, 4 vols. Oxford 1899–1902.

Ker, W.P. *In his* Essays on medieval literature, 1905.
Lewis, C.S. *In his* The allegory of love, Oxford 1936.

LAY OF HAVELOK (late 13th cent.)

HAVELOK THE DANE. Ed. Frederic Madden, 1828 (*with Fr. text*); ed.
Walter W.Skeat, 1868, 1889 (EETS), Oxford 1902, 1915 (rev.
Kenneth Sisam); tr. A.J.Wyatt, 1913.

STEPHEN HAWES (*c.* 1475 – 1523?)

THE EXAMPLE OF VERTU. 1504?
THE PASSETYME OF PLEASURE. 1509 (*fragment*); 1517 (*complete*); ed.
William E.Mead, 1928 (EETS).
THE CONVERCYON OF SWERERS. 1509; ed. David Laing, 1865.
COMFORT OF LOVERS. 1512?

ROBERT HENRYSON (*c.* 1430 – *c.* 1505)

THE MORALL FABILLIS OF ESOPE, compylit in eloquent and ornate Scottis
meter. Edinburgh 1570; 1571; tr. Richard Smith, 1577 (The
fabulous tales, Englished); Edinburgh 1621; ed. A.R.Diebler,
Anglia, ix (1886) (*from Harleian MS.*).
ORPHEUS AND EURYDICE. *In the Chepman and Myller prints, Edinburgh
1508 (incomplete). See under Dunbar, above, for edns of the prints.*
TESTAMENT OF CRESSEID. Ed. William Thynne, 1532 (*in* The workes of
Chaucer); Edinburgh 1593; ed. Walter W.Skeat, Oxford 1897 (*in*
Chaucerian and other pieces); ed. Bruce Dickins, Edinburgh 1925,
London 1943; ed. R.K.Gordon, 1934 (*in* The story of Troilus, as told
by Benoît de Sainte-Maure, Boccaccio, Chaucer, Henryson). *Included
as Chaucer's own continuation (bk vi) of his* Troilus and Criseyde *in
edns of his works till Urry (1721).*

Poems and fables. Ed. David Laing, Edinburgh 1865; Poems, ed. G.
Gregory Smith, 3 vols. Edinburgh 1906–14 (Scottish Text Soc.);
Poems and fables, ed. H.Harvey Wood, Edinburgh 1933, 1958;
Poems, ed. Charles Elliott, Oxford 1963 (*selected*).

Kynaston, Sir Francis. *His unique narrative of Henryson's life accom-
panied a Latin version of Chaucer's* Troilus and Criseyde *and of the*
Testament *made c. 1640 and pbd in* Poems, ed. G. Gregory Smith,
above.
Tillyard, E.M.W. Testament of Cresseid. *In his* Five poems, 1948.
Stearns, Marshall W. Robert Henryson. New York 1949.

WALTER HILTON (d. 1396)

THE SCALE OF PERFECTION. *c.* 1494 (de Worde); ed. Evelyn Underhill, 1923 (*modernized*); tr. Leo Sherley-Price, 1957 (Penguin).

EPISTLE ON MIXED LIFE. *c.* 1494 (*as bk iii of* The scale of perfection, *above*); ed. George G.Perry, 1866, 1921 (*in* English prose treatises of Richard Rolle) (EETS); ed. Dorothy Jones (*in* Minor works, *below*). *Also attributed to Rolle.*

Minor works. Ed. Dorothy Jones, 1929.

THOMAS HOCCLEVE OR OCCLEVE
(*c.* 1368 – *c.* 1450)

THE LETTER OF CUPID. 1532 (*in* Workes of Chaucer, ed. Thynne); ed. Walter W. Skeat, Oxford 1897 (*in* Chaucerian and other pieces) (*with two ballades,* To the King *and* To the Knightes of the Garter).

THE REGEMENT OF PRINCES. Ed. Thomas Wright, 1860. *A verse trn made 1411–12, mainly of* Aegidius Romanus, De regimine principum.

THE TALE OF JONATHAS. 1614 (*modernized and abridged by William Browne of Tavistock in his* Shepheards pipe).

OF THE VIRGIN and her sleeveless garment. Ed. Arthur Beatty, 1902 (*entitled* A new ploughman's tale).

Poems, selected. Ed. George Mason, 1796.

Works. Ed. F.J.Furnivall and Israel Gollancz, 3 vols. 1892–1925 (EETS).

JAMES I, KING OF SCOTLAND (1394 – 1437)

THE KINGIS QUAIR. Ed. William Tytler, Edinburgh 1783 (*in* Poetical remains); ed. Walter W. Skeat, 1884, 1911 (Scottish Text Soc.); ed. W.Mackay Mackenzie, 1939.

Craigie, W.A. The language of The Kingis quair. Essays and studies, xxv (1939).

JULIANA LAMPIT (JULIAN OF NORWICH)
(*c.* 1343 – *c.* 1415)

XVI REVELATIONS OF DIVINE LOVE. Ed. R. F. S. Cressy, 1670 (*modernized*); ed. Grace Warrack, 1901 (*modernized*); The shewings of the Lady Julian, 1373, ed. Dundas Harford, 1925; ed. Roger Hudleston, 1927, 1952.

KATHERINE GROUP (early 13th cent.)

*Four alliterative prose tracts in praise of virginity, perhaps by the same
author.*

HALI MEIDENHAD. Ed. Oswald Cockayne, 1866; 1920 (EETS).

SAWLES WARDE. Ed. Richard Morris, 1868 (*in* Old English homilies,
ser. 1) (EETS); ed. R. M. Wilson, Leeds 1936.

KATHARINE. Ed. James Morton, 1841; ed. E. Einenkel, 1884 (EETS).

JULIANA. Ed. Oswald Cockayne and Edmund Brock, 1872 (EETS).

MARGERY KEMPE (*c.* 1373 – *c.* 1440)

THE BOOK OF MARGERY KEMPE. Vol. I. Ed. Sanford B. Meech and Hope
Emily Allen, 1940 (EETS); tr. W. Butler-Bowdon, 1936, Oxford
1954 (WC). *Short extracts pbd by Wynkyn de Worde, 1501?*

WILLIAM LANGLAND (*c.* 1332 – *c.* 1400)

VISION OF PIERCE PLOWMAN. Ed. Robert Crowley, 1550, 1561 (*with*
Crede of Pierce Plowman); ed. Thomas Wright, 2 vols. 1842, 1895
(*B text*); ed. Walter W. Skeat, 6 vols. 1867–84 (EETS) (*A, B and C
texts*); Three parallel texts, together with Richard the Redeless, ed.
Skeat, 2 vols. Oxford 1886, 1954 (*with bibliography*); Prologue, passus
i–vii, ed. J. F. Davis, 1896, 1928 (rev. E. S. Olsewska); The Hunting-
ton Library manuscript, ed. R. W. Chambers, San Marino, Cal. 1936;
A critical edition of the A-version, ed. Thomas A. Knott and David
C. Fowler, Baltimore 1952; ed. George Kane, 1959. *Since Skeat's
EETS tract of 1866 the MSS of the poem have been classed as three
texts: A (written c. 1362), the first and shortest version; B (c. 1377), an
expanded version of A; and C (1390–), a second and final revision.
There are modern versions by H. W. Wells (1935) and Nevill Coghill
(1949) (selection).*

*Two anonymous alliterative poems of the fourteenth century are associated
with Piers Plowman:* The parlement of the thre ages *and* Wynnere
and Wastoure, *both* ed. Israel Gollancz, 1897; Parlement, ed. M. Y.
Offord, 1959 (EETS). Mum and the sothsegger, *formerly known as*
Richard the Redeless, ed. Mabel Day and R. Steele, 1936 (EETS),
is not now thought to be by Langland.

Jusserand, J.-J. L'épopée mystique de Langland. Paris 1893; tr. and
rev. 1894.

Bright, Allan H. New light on Piers Plowman. Oxford 1928.

Dunning, T. P. Piers Plowman: an interpretation of the A-text.
Dublin 1937.

Chambers, R. W. Piers Plowman: a comparative study. *In his* Man's
unconquerable mind, 1939.

Donaldson, E. Talbot. Piers Plowman: the C-text and its poet. New Haven 1949.

Robertson, D.W. and Bernard F. Huppé. Piers Plowman and scriptural tradition. Princeton 1951.

Lawlor, John J. Piers Plowman: an essay in criticism. 1962.

Salter, Elizabeth. Piers Plowman: an introduction. Oxford 1962.

JOHN LYDGATE (c. 1370 – c. 1450)

In conjectural order of composition:

THE CHORLE AND THE BIRD. 1477? (Caxton), Cambridge 1906 (*facs.*); ed. H.N.MacCracken (*in* Minor poems, vol. ii, *below*). *A beast-fable, written* c. *1400*.

THE TEMPLE OF GLASS. 1478? (Caxton), Cambridge 1905 (*facs.*); ed. J.Schick, 1891 (EETS). *Written* c. *1403*.

RESON AND SENSUALLYTE. Ed. Ernst Sieper, 2 vols. 1901–3 (EETS). *Written* c. *1408*.

THE HYSTORYE, sege and dystruccyon of Troye. 1513 (Pynson); tr. Thomas Heywood, 1614 (*as* The life and death of Hector); ed. Henry Bergen, 4 vols. 1906–35 (EETS). *A verse paraphrase of* Guido delle Colonne, Historia troiana, *written 1412–21*.

THE SIEGE OF THEBES. 1500? (de Worde); ed. Axel Erdmann and Eilert Ekwall, 2 vols. 1911–30 (EETS). *A verse adaptation made in 1421–2 of an unknown Fr. prose romance.*

[THE ASSEMBLY OF THE GODS]. 1498 (de Worde), Cambridge 1906 (*facs.*); ed. Oscar L.Triggs, Chicago 1895 (EETS, 1896). *Written after 1422*.

THE PILGRIMAGE OF THE LIFE OF MAN. Ed. F.J.Furnivall and K.B. Locock, 3 vols. 1899–1904 (EETS). *A verse trn of* Guillaume de Deguileville, Le pèlerinage de la vie humaine, *begun in 1426*.

THE FALLE OF PRINCIS. 1494 (Pynson); ed. Henry Bergen, 4 vols. 1924–7 (EETS). *A verse trn of an enlarged Fr. version of* Boccaccio, De casibus virorum illustrium, *made 1431–8*.

THE TESTAMENT OF LYDGATE. 1515? (Pynson); ed. H.N.MacCracken (*in* Minor poems, vol. i, *below*).

Minor poems. Ed. J.O.Halliwell, 1840 (*selection*); ed. H.N.Mac-Cracken and Merriam Sherwood, 2 vols. 1911–34 (EETS).

Schirmer, Walter F. John Lydgate. Tübingen 1952; tr. 1961.

SIR THOMAS MALORY (d. 1471?)

LE MORTE DARTHUR reduced in to Englysshe. Ed. William Caxton, 1485; ed. William Stansby, 1634; ed. Edward Strachey, 1884 (*Caxton's text*); ed. H.Oskar Sommer, 2 vols. 1900; ed. Eugène Vinaver, 3 vols. Oxford 1947, 1963 (*from Winchester MS.*), 1 vol. 1954

(OSA). *The Winchester College MS., discovered in 1934, showed the work to be not one narrative but eight. The last has been pbd separately,* The tale of the death of King Arthur, ed. Vinaver, Oxford 1955.

Ker, W.P. *In his* Essays on medieval literature, 1905.

Kittredge, G.L. Sir Thomas Malory. Barnstable 1925.

Vinaver, Eugène. Sir Thomas Malory. Oxford 1929.

Chambers, E.K. *In his* English literature at the close of the Middle Ages, Oxford 1945.

Bradbrook, M.C. Sir Thomas Malory. 1958 (Br. Council pamphlet).

Essays on Malory. Ed. J.A.W.Bennett, Oxford 1963.

'SIR JOHN MANDEVILLE'

For a bibliography of versions of the Travels *in eight languages see Bennett, below.*

[TRAVELS]. 1496? (Pynson); 1499 (de Worde); 1568 (East); ed. David Caskey? 1725 (*first full text*); ed. P.Hamelius, 2 vols. 1919–23 (EETS) (*from MS.*); The Bodley version, ed. M.C.Seymour, 1963 (EETS) (*an abridged version in MS.*). *Modernized texts by A.W. Pollard (1901) and Malcolm Letts (2 vols. 1953).*
A trn of a Fr. travel-book of c. 1356. The English translator, claiming to be both author and traveller, calls himself in the preface Sir John Mandeville.

Letts, Malcolm. Sir John Mandeville: the man and his book. 1949.

Bennett, Josephine W. The rediscovery of Mandeville. New York 1954.

ROBERT MANNYNG of BRUNNE (*c.* 1280 – *c.* 1340)

HANDLYNG SYNNE. Ed. F.J.Furnivall, 1862; 2 vols. 1901–3 (EETS). *A verse treatise on sin based on* William of Wadington, Manuel de pechiez, *and begun in 1303.*

MEDITATIONS ON THE SUPPER OF OUR LORD. Ed. F.J.Furnivall, 1875 (EETS). *A verse trn of* Bonaventure, Vita Christi, *perhaps by Mannyng.*

CHRONICLE OF ENGLAND. Part i, ed. F.J.Furnivall, 2 vols. 1887 (Rolls ser.) (*based on Wace's* Brut); Part ii [A.D. 689–1327], ed. Thomas Hearne, 2 vols. Oxford 1725 (*based on the Fr. chronicle of Pierre de Langtoft*). *Completed in 1338.*

Crosby, Ruth. Mannyng: a new biography. PMLA, lvii (1942).

LAURENCE MINOT (14th cent.)

POEMS on events in the reign of Edward III. Ed. Joseph Ritson, 1795; Political poems and songs, vol. i, ed. Thomas Wright, 1859 (Rolls ser.); Poems of Minot, ed. Joseph Hall, Oxford 1887, 1914.

SIR ORFEO (early 14th cent.)

Ed. Joseph Ritson, 1802 (*in* Ancient Engleish metrical romanceës, vol. ii); ed. David Laing, 1822 (*in* Selected remains of ancient popular poetry of Scotland); ed. O. Zielke, Breslau 1880 (*critical text*); ed. Kenneth Sisam, Oxford 1921, 1937 (*in* Fourteenth-century verse and prose); ed. A. J. Bliss, Oxford 1954. *A lay tr. from a Fr. source.*

ORRMULUM (early 13th cent.)

Ed. R. M. White, Oxford 1852; 2 vols. 1878 (rev. R. Holt). *539 lines added in* N. R. Ker, Unpublished parts of the Ormulum, Medium aevum, ix (1940). *An unfinished homily in syllabic verse by Orrm, being an English version of the Latin Gospels in the Mass book with interpolations.*

THE OWL AND THE NIGHTINGALE (c. 1200)

Ed. Joseph Stevenson, 1838; ed. J. E. Wells, Boston 1907; ed. J. W. H. Atkins, Cambridge 1922 (*with trn*); ed. J. H. G. Grattan and G. F. H. Sykes, 1935 (EETS) (*parallel texts from the two MS.*); ed. E. G. Stanley, Edinburgh 1960; Facsimile from the surviving manuscripts, ed. N. R. Ker, 1963 (EETS). *A verse altercation between two birds, perhaps by Nicholas of Guildford.*

THE PASTONS (15th cent.)

PASTON LETTERS [1422–1509]. Ed. John Fenn, 5 vols. 1787–1823; ed. Mrs Archer Hind, 2 vols. 1924, 1956 (*with appendix*) (EL); 3 vols. 1872–5, 6 vols. 1904 (rev. and enlarged by James Gairdner).

Selections by Alice D. Greenwood (1920), A. H. R. Ball (1949) and Norman Davis (1958); and in modern spelling, ed. Davis (1963) (WC).

Bennett, H. S. The Pastons and their England. Cambridge 1922.

PEARL GROUP

Four alliterative poems preserved in the same unique MS. and probably by the same author.

Early English alliterative poems. Ed. Richard Morris, 1864; 1901 (EETS). *Pearl, Purity, Patience.*

Pearl, Cleanness, Patience and Sir Gawain, reproduced in facsimile from MS. Cotton Nero A x. Ed. Israel Gollancz, 1923 (EETS).

PEARL. Ed. Israel Gollancz, 1891, 1921 (*with trn*); ed. E. V. and Ida L. Gordon, Oxford 1953; ed. A. C. Cawley, 1962 (EL); tr. Mary V. Hillmann, New York 1961.

PATIENCE. Ed. H. Bateson, Manchester 1912, 1918; ed. Israel Gollancz, 1913, 1924.

PURITY [*or* Cleanness]. Ed. Robert J. Menner, New Haven 1920; ed. Israel Gollancz and Mabel Day, 2 vols. 1921–33.

SIR GAWAYNE and the grene knight. Ed. Frederic Madden, 1839; ed. Richard Morris, 1864, 1912 (rev. Israel Gollancz) (EETS); ed. J. R. R. Tolkien and E. V. Gordon, Oxford 1925, 1936; ed. Gollancz and Mabel Day, 1940 (EETS); ed. A. C. Cawley, 1962 (EL) (*with* Pearl, *above*).

Kittredge, G. L. A study of Gawain and the green knight. Cambridge, Mass. 1916.

Oakden, J. P. Alliterative poetry in ME. 2 vols. Manchester 1930–5.

Everett, Dorothy. The alliterative revival. *In her* Essays on ME literature, Oxford 1955.

Savage, Henry L. The Gawain-poet. Chapel Hill, N. C. 1957.

Borroff, Marie. Sir Gawain and the green knight: a stylistic and metrical study. New Haven 1962.

REGINALD PECOCK (*c.* 1395 – *c.* 1460)

A TREATISE proving Scripture to be the rule of faith. Ed. Henry Wharton, 1688 (*pt ii, with summary of pt i*); ed. J. L. Morison, Glasgow 1902 (pts i–ii) (*re-entitled* Book of faith).

THE REPRESSOR of overmuch blaming of the clergy. Ed. Churchill Babington, 2 vols. 1860 (Rolls ser.). *With biography and bibliography*.

THE DONET. Ed. E. V. Hitchcock, 1921 (EETS); The folewer to the Donet, ed. Hitchcock, 1924 (EETS).

THE REULE OF CRYSTEN RELIGIOUN. Ed. W. C. Greet, 1927 (EETS).

PROVERBS OF ALFRED (12th cent.)

Ed. Thomas Wright and J. O. Halliwell, 1841 (*in* Reliquiae antiquae, vol. i); ed. Richard Morris, 1872 (EETS); ed. Walter W. Skeat, Oxford 1907; ed. O. S. Anderson-Arngart, 2 vols. Lund 1942–55. *A collection of alliterative and riming verse homilies of unknown authorship.*

RICHARD ROLLE (*c.* 1300 – 1349)

For a bibliography see H. E. Allen, below.

PRICKE OF CONSCIENCE. Ed. Richard Morris, Berlin 1862–4. *A didactic poem formerly attributed to Rolle.*

ENGLISH PROSE TREATISES. Ed. George G. Perry, 1866, 1921 (EETS).

THE PSALTER AND CERTAIN CANTICLES. Ed. H. R. Bramley, Oxford 1884. *The* Psalter *is based on the Latin commentary on the psalms by Peter Lombard.*

THE FIRE OF LOVE and the mending of life, tr. Richard Misyn, 1434–45. Ed. R. Harvey, 1896 (EETS); tr. G. C. Heseltine, 1935.
MEDITATIO DE PASSIONE. Ed. Harold Lindkvist, Upsala 1917.

Yorkshire writers: Rolle. Ed. C. Horstman, 2 vols. 1895–6. *All the English works except the* Psalter.
Minor works. Tr. and ed. Geraldine E. Hodgson, 1923.
Selected works. Ed. G. C. Heseltine, 1930.
English writings. Ed. Hope Emily Allen, Oxford 1931. *For an edn of the lyrics see Comper, below.*

Middendorff, H. H. B. Studien über Rolle. Magdeburg 1886.
Allen, Hope Emily. Writings ascribed to Rolle and materials for his biography. New York 1927.
Comper, Frances M. M. The life of Rolle, with an edition of his English lyrics. 1928.

JOHN OF TREVISA (*c.* 1330 – 1402)

POLYCHRONICON. 1482 (Caxton) (*with Caxton's bk viii, A.D. 1357–1460*); ed. Churchill Babington and J. R. Lumby, 9 vols. 1865–86 (Rolls ser.) (*with Latin original*). *A trn, completed in 1387, of the Latin history in seven books by Ranulf Higden (d. 1364), written c. 1350.*
A DIALOGUE betwene a knyght and a clerke. *c.* 1540 (*with Latin original*); ed. Aaron J. Perry, 1925 (EETS) (*from Harleian MS., with English text of 1540*). *A trn from William of Occam (d. 1349?).*
DE PROPRIETATIBUS RERUM. 1494 (de Worde). *A trn, completed in 1398, of the encyclopaedia of natural science by Bartholomew Anglicus (fl. 1230–50).*

THOMAS USK (d. 1388)

TESTAMENT OF LOVE. Ed. William Thynne, 1532 (*in* The workes of Chaucer); ed. Walter W. Skeat, Oxford 1897 (*in* Chaucerian and other pieces). *A prose allegory.*

JOHN WICLIF (*c.* 1325 – 1384)

Shirley, Walter W. A catalogue of the original works of Wyclif. Oxford 1865; London 1924 (*re-entitled* A catalogue of the extant Latin works) (rev. Johann Loserth).

DIALOGORUM LIBRI QUATTUOR. Basle 1525; ed. Victor Lechler, Oxford 1869 (*entitled* Trialogus).
WYCKLYFFES WYCKET. London? 1546; ed. T. P. Pantin, Oxford 1828. *A popular treatise on the Sacrament.*

ARTICULI: sive aphorismi. Ed. John Foxe, Amsterdam 1554.

LAST AGE OF THE CHURCH. Ed. J.H.Todd, Dublin 1840.

TREATISE OF MIRACLIS PLEYINGE. Ed. Thomas Wright and J.O.Halliwell, 1841 (*in* Reliquiae antiquae, vol. i).

DE OFFICIS PASTORALI. Ed. Victor Lechler, Leipzig 1863.

APOLOGY FOR LOLLARD DOCTRINES. Ed. J.H.Todd, 1842.

THE HOLY BIBLE in the earliest English versions. Ed. Josiah Forshall and Frederic Madden, 4 vols. Oxford 1850. *The first complete edn of the Wicliffite Bible, the earlier and later versions in parallel texts with the General Prologue. The trn was inspired by Wiclif and was partly made by him. The later version of the New Testament was first ptd in 1731, ed. John Lewis, and again in 1841 (in* The English hexapla): *and the earlier in 1848, ed. Lea Wilson. The Prologue was first pbd in 1550.*

REMONSTRANCE AGAINST ROMISH CORRUPTIONS in the Church. Ed. Josiah Forshall, 1851. *A trn of the Latin Conclusions, first ptd in Lewis, below, and ed. Walter W. Shirley as* Fasciculi zizaniorum, 1858 (Rolls ser.). *The Thirty-seven conclusions are an expansion of the Twelve written by Wiclif's followers to present to Parliament in 1395. The Latin version of the* Twelve conclusions *was tr. John Foxe in his* Actes and monuments (1563) *and their probable English original ed.* H.S.Cronin, English historical review, xx (1907).

DE MANDATIS DIVINIS. Ed. Johann Loserth and F.D.Matthew, 1922.

SUMMA DE ENTE. Ed. S.H.Thomson, Oxford 1930.

Tracts and treatises. Ed. Robert Vaughan, 1845; Three treatises, ed. J.H.Todd, Dublin 1851; Select English works, ed. Thomas Arnold, 3 vols. Oxford 1869–71; Select English writings, ed. H.E.Winn, Oxford 1929.

The English works hitherto unprinted. Ed. F.D.Matthew, 1880 (EETS).

Lewis, John. The history of the life and sufferings of Wicliffe. 1720; Oxford 1820.

Lechler, Victor. Wiclif und die Vorgeschichte der Reformation. Leipzig 1873; tr. and rev. 1878, 1884.

Trevelyan, G.M. England in the age of Wycliffe. 1899, 1909; The Peasants' Rising and the Lollards: unpublished documents, 1899.

Deanesly, Margaret. The Lollard Bible and other medieval Biblical versions. Cambridge 1920.

Workman, H.B. John Wyclif. 2 vols. Oxford 1926.

Craigie, W.A. The English versions (to Wyclif). *In* The Bible in its ancient and English versions, ed. H.Wheeler Robinson, Oxford 1940; 1954.

McFarlane, K.B. Wycliffe and the beginnings of English non-conformity. 1952.

THE RENAISSANCE TO THE RESTORATION
(1500–1660)

THE RENAISSANCE TO THE RESTORATION
(1500–1660)

Bibliographies

Arber, Edward. A transcript of the register of the Company of Stationers, 1554–1640. 5 vols. 1875–94; 1650–1708, 3 vols. 1913–14. *The Court records of the Company have been ed. W.W. Greg and E.Boswell (vol. i) and William A.Jackson (vol. ii), 2 vols. 1930–57.*

Sayle, Charles E. Early English printed books in the University Library, Cambridge, 1475–1640. 4 vols. Cambridge 1900–7.

Hoe, Robert. Catalogue of books by English authors before 1700. 5 vols. New York 1903–5.

Greenlaw, Edwin, Hardin Craig et al. Recent literature of the English renaissance. Studies in philology, xiv– (1917–). *Annual lists of modern studies since 1916.*

Pollard, A.W. and G.R.Redgrave. A short-title catalogue of books, 1475–1640. 1926; W.W.Bishop, A checklist of American copies, Ann Arbor, 1944, 1950; David Ramage, A finding-list of English books to 1640 in libraries in the British Isles, Durham 1958. *For continuation see Wing, p. 105 below.*

Davies, Godfrey. Stuart period, 1603–1714. Oxford 1928; Conyers Read, Tudor period, 1485–1603, Oxford 1933, 1959 (Bibliography of British history).

Case, Arthur E. A bibliography of English poetical miscellanies, 1521–1750. 1935.

Tannenbaum, Samuel A. Elizabethan bibliographies. New York 1937–.

Greg, W.W. A bibliography of the English printed drama to the Restoration. 4 vols. 1939–59.

Harbage, Alfred. Annals of English drama, 975–1700: an analytical record. Philadelphia 1940; London 1964 (rev. Samuel Schoenbaum).

Williams, Franklin B. Index of dedications and commendatory verses in English books before 1641. 1962.

See also under John Bale, below.

Literary History and Criticism

Hazlitt, William. Lectures chiefly on the dramatic literature of the age of Elizabeth. 1820.

Gosse, Edmund. From Shakespeare to Pope. Cambridge 1885.

Saintsbury, George. A history of Elizabethan literature. 1887.

Creizenach, Wilhelm. Geschichte des neueren Dramas. 5 vols. Halle 1895–1916; vol. iv (bks i–viii), tr. 1916 (*entitled* The English drama in the age of Shakespeare).

Boas, F. S. Shakspere and his predecessors. 1896.

—— University drama in the Tudor age. Oxford 1914.

—— An introduction to Tudor drama. Oxford 1933; An introduction to Stuart drama, Oxford 1946.

Spingarn, J. E. A history of literary criticism in the Renaissance. New York 1899; 1925.

Greg, W. W. Pastoral poetry and pastoral drama. 1906. *William Browne, John Fletcher, Jonson, Milton, Spenser etc.*

Schelling, F. E. Elizabethan drama, 1558–1642. 2 vols. Boston 1908.

Swinburne, A. C. The age of Shakespeare. 1908.

—— Contemporaries of Shakespeare. 1919.

Shakespeare's England. 2 vols. Oxford 1916.

Berdan, J. M. Early Tudor poetry, 1485–1547. New York 1920.

Chambers, E. K. The Elizabethan stage. 4 vols. Oxford 1923. *Continued from 1616 by Bentley, below.*

Williamson, George. The Donne tradition. Cambridge, Mass. 1930.

—— The Senecan amble: a study in prose form from Bacon to Collier. 1951.

Willey, Basil. The seventeenth-century background. 1934. *Bacon, Hobbes, Henry More etc.*

Bradbrook, M. C. Themes and conventions of Elizabethan tragedy. Cambridge 1935.

—— The rise of the common player. 1962.

Craig, Hardin. The enchanted glass: the Elizabethan mind in literature. New York 1936.

Ellis-Fermor, Una. The Jacobean drama. 1936; 1953.

Eliot, T. S. Elizabethan essays. 1936.

White, Helen. The metaphysical poets: a study in religious experience. New York 1936; 1956.

Knights, L. C. Drama and society in the age of Jonson. 1937. *Dekker, Thomas Heywood, Jonson, Massinger, Middleton etc.*

—— Explorations: essays in criticism mainly on the seventeenth century. 1946. *Bacon, George Herbert, Henry James, Shakespeare, Yeats, Restoration comedy etc.*

Baldwin, C. S. and D. L. Clark. Renaissance literary theory and practice. New York 1939.

Bentley, Gerald E. The Jacobean and Caroline stage [1616–42]. 7 vols. Oxford 1941–.

Rubel, Veré L. Poetic diction in the English Renaissance. New York 1941.

Tillyard, E.M.W. The Elizabethan world picture. 1943.

Bush, Douglas. English literature in the earlier seventeenth century. Oxford 1945; 1962 (Oxford history of English lit., vol. v).

Wilson, F.P. Elizabethan and Jacobean. Oxford 1946.

Tuve, Rosemond. Elizabethan and metaphysical imagery. Chicago 1947.

Ing, Catherine. Elizabethan lyrics. 1951.

Smith, Hallett. Elizabethan poetry. Cambridge, Mass. 1952.

Jones, Richard F. The triumph of the English language: a survey of opinions concerning the vernacular. Palo Alto, Cal. 1953.

Lewis, C.S. English literature in the sixteenth century, excluding drama. Oxford 1954 (Oxford history of English lit., vol. iii).

Martz, Louis L. The poetry of meditation. New Haven 1954; 1962. *On religious poetry of Crashaw, Donne, Herbert, Milton, Southwell.*

Clemen, Wolfgang H. Die Tragödie vor Shakespeare. Heidelberg 1955; tr. 1961.

Lever, J.W. The Elizabethan love sonnet. 1956.

Wickham, Glynne. Early English stages, 1300–1660. 3 vols. 1959–.

Jacobean theatre; Elizabethan poetry, ed. John R. Brown and Bernard Harris, 1960 (Stratford studies, nos 1–2).

Alvarez, A. The school of Donne. 1961.

Elizabethan drama: modern essays in criticism. Ed. R.J. Kaufmann, New York 1961.

Seventeenth-century English poetry: modern essays in criticism. Ed. William R. Keast, New York 1962.

See also under Fuller, Leland and Walton, below, and Aubrey, p. 108 below.

Collections and Anthologies

Tottel, Richard. Songes and sonettes written by Surrey and other. 1557; 1557; ed. Hyder E. Rollins. 2 vols. Cambridge, Mass. 1928–9. '*Tottel's miscellany.*' *See under Surrey and Wyatt, below.*

Fraunce, Abraham. The Arcadian rhetorike. 1588; ed. Ethel Seaton, Oxford 1950. *A rhetoric book, with examples from Sidney et al.*

The passionate pilgrime. 1599. *Includes poems by Barnfield, Marlowe, Ralegh, Shakespeare.*

Ling, Nicholas? Englands Helicon. 1600, 1614 (*enlarged*); ed. Hugh Macdonald, 1925, 1950 (ML); ed. Hyder E. Rollins, 2 vols. Cambridge, Mass. 1935.

Allott, Robert. Englands Parnassus. 1600.

Dodsley, Robert. A select collection of old plays. 12 vols. 1744; ed. W. Carew Hazlitt, 15 vols. 1874–6 (*enlarged from 60 to 83 plays*).

Lamb, Charles. Specimens of English dramatic poets. 1808.

Pollard, A.W. English miracle plays, moralities and interludes. Oxford 1890; 1927.

Henley, W.E. Tudor translations. 44 vols. 1892–1909; Charles Whibley, ser. 2, 12 vols. 1924–7.

Manly, J.M. Specimens of pre-Shakespearean drama. 2 vols. Boston 1897–8.

Bang, W. *et al.* Materialien zur Kunde des älteren englischen Dramas. Louvain 1902–.

Gayley, Charles M. *et al.* Representative English comedies. 3 vols. New York 1903–14.

Gregory Smith, G. Elizabethan critical essays. 2 vols. Oxford 1904.

Lee, Sidney. Elizabethan sonnets. 2 vols. 1904.

Farmer, John S. Early English dramatists. 12 vols. 1905–8. *A collection of 'lost' and anon. plays.*

—— *et al.* Tudor facsimile texts. 143 vols. 1907–14.

Saintsbury, George. Minor poets of the Caroline period. 3 vols. Oxford 1905–21.

—— Shorter novels, Elizabethan and Jacobean. 1929 (EL).

Greg, W.W., F.P.Wilson *et al.* Malone Society reprints. 1907–.

Spingarn, J.E. Seventeenth-century critical essays. 3 vols. Oxford 1908–9.

Thorndike, A.H. Minor Elizabethan drama. 2 vols. 1910 (EL).

Dover Wilson, J. Shakespeare's England: a book of Elizabethan prose. Cambridge 1911.

Cunliffe, J.W. Early English classical tragedy. Oxford 1912.

Nichol Smith, D. Characters from the histories and memoirs of the seventeenth century. Oxford 1918.

Grierson, Herbert. Metaphysical lyrics and poems. Oxford 1921.

—— and Geoffrey Bullough. The Oxford book of seventeenth-century verse. Oxford 1934.

Adams, J.Q. Chief pre-Shakespearean dramas. Boston 1924.

Ault, Norman. Elizabethan lyrics from the original texts. 1925; 1949.

—— Seventeenth-century lyrics from the original texts. 1928; 1950.

Murphy, Gwendolen. A cabinet of characters. Oxford 1925.

Hebel, J.William and Hoyt H.Hudson. Poetry of the English Renaissance, 1509–1660. New York 1929; Prose, New York 1952.

Rollins, Hyder E. The Pepys ballads. 8 vols. Cambridge, Mass. 1929–32.

Howarth, R.G. Minor poets of the seventeenth century. 1931; 1953 (EL). *Carew, Herbert of Cherbury, Lovelace, Suckling.*

Chambers, E.K. The Oxford book of sixteenth-century verse. Oxford 1932.

Gebert, Clara. An anthology of Elizabethan dedications and prefaces. Philadelphia 1933.

Tucker Brooke, C.F. and N.Burton Paradise. English drama, 1580–1642. New York 1933.

Boas, F.S. Five pre-Shakespearean comedies. Oxford 1934 (WC).

McIlwraith, A.K. Five Elizabethan comedies. Oxford 1934 (WC); Five Elizabethan tragedies, Oxford 1938 (WC).

Gilbert, Allan H. Literary criticism, Plato to Dryden. New York 1940.

Bullett, Gerald. Silver poets of the sixteenth century: Wyatt, Surrey, Sidney, Raleigh, Sir John Davies. 1947 (EL).

Gardner, Helen L. The metaphysical poets. 1957 (Penguin); Oxford 1961.

Nicoll, Allardyce. The Elizabethans. Cambridge 1957.

Donno, Elizabeth S. Minor Elizabethan epics. 1963.

For Anderson and Chalmers see under 1660–1800, p. 106 below.

LANCELOT ANDREWES (1555 – 1626)

THE WONDERFULL COMBATE betweene Christ and Satan, opened in seven sermons. 1592. *11 further sermon-books pbd 1604–20.*

XCVI sermons. Ed. William Laud and John Buckeridge, 1629.

TORTURA TORTI: ad Matt. Torti liberum responsio. 1609; Oxford 1851 (Lib. of Anglo-Catholic theology).

A MANUAL FOR THE SICK. Tr. Richard Drake, 1648 (*from Greek MS.*); ed. F.E.Brightman, 1909.

A MANUAL OF PRIVATE DEVOTIONS. Tr. Richard Drake, 1648 (*pt 1 only, from Greek MS.*); Preces privatae, graece et latine, ed. John Lamphire, 1675 (*original Greek and Latin*); tr. J.H.Newman and J.M. Neale, 2pts Oxford 1842–4; ed. Henry Veale, 1895, Cambridge 1899 (*enlarged*); ed. F.E.Brightman, 1903.

[Works]. 11 vols. Oxford 1841–54 (Lib. of Anglo-Catholic theology).

Eliot, T.S. *In his* For Lancelot Andrewes, 1928.

Higham, Florence. Lancelot Andrewes. 1952.

Reidy, Maurice F. Andrewes: Jacobean court preacher. Chicago 1955.

Welsby, Paul A. Lancelot Andrewes. 1958.

ROGER ASCHAM (1515 – 1568)

TOXOPHILUS: the schole of shootinge. 1545; 1571; ed. Edward Arber, 1868.

THE SCHOLEMASTER: or plain and perfite way of teachyng children the Latin tong. 1570; ed. Edward Arber, 1870.

Whole works. Ed. J.A.Giles, 4 vols. 1864–5; English works, ed. W. Aldis Wright, Cambridge 1904.

Ryan, Lawrence V. Roger Ascham. Palo Alto, Cal. 1963.

FRANCIS BACON, 1ST BARON VERULAM, later VISCOUNT ST ALBANS (1561 – 1626)

Gibson, R.W. Bacon: a bibliography to 1750. Oxford 1950.

ESSAYES. 1597 (*10 essays*); 1612 (*38*); 1625 (*58*), ed. W.Aldis Wright, 1862, 1865; ed. Geoffrey Grigson, Oxford 1937 (WC); A harmony of the Essays, ed. Edward Arber, 1895.

THE PROFICIENCE and advancement of learning. 1605; ed. W.Aldis Wright, 1868, 1873. *See* De augmentis *below*.

DE SAPIENTIA VETERUM liber. 1609; tr. Arthur Gorges, 1619.

INSTAURATIO MAGNA, pars secunda: novum organum, sive indicia vera de interpretatione naturae. 1620; tr. Peter Shaw, 1725 (*in his English edn of Bacon's works*); ed. Thomas Fowler, Oxford 1878, 1889.

THE HISTORIE of the raigne of King Henry the seventh. 1622; ed. J.R. Lumby, Cambridge 1876.

DE AUGMENTIS SCIENTIARUM. 1623; tr. Gilbert Wats, 1640. *A Latin version of* The advancement of learning, *above, recast and greatly enlarged*.

SYLVA SYLVARUM: or a naturall historie. Ed. William Rawley, 1627. *Includes the unfinished* New Atlantis.

Certaine miscellany works. Ed. William Rawley, 1629; Remaines, being essayes and letters, 1648; Resuscitatio, ed. Rawley, 2 pts. 1657–70.

Works. Ed. James Spedding, R.L.Ellis and D.D.Heath, 14 vols. 1857–74; Philosophical works, ed. J.M.Robertson, 1905.

Rawley, William. [Life of Bacon.] *In* Resuscitatio, 1657, *above*.

Macaulay, Thomas. *In his* Critical and historical essays, 1843.

Levi, Adolfo. Il pensiero di Bacon. Turin 1925.

Williams, Charles. Bacon. 1933.

Wallace, Karl R. Bacon on communication and rhetoric. Chapel Hill N.C. 1943.

Knights, L.C. Bacon and the seventeenth-century dissociation of sensibility. *In his* Explorations, 1946.

Anderson, F.H. The philosophy of Bacon. Chicago 1948.

JOHN BALE (1495 – 1563)

Davies, W.T. A bibliography of Bale. Proc. Oxford Bibliog. Soc. v (1940).

A TRAGEDYE or enterlude manyfestyng the chefe promyses of God, compyled 1538. Wesel 1547?

JOHAN BAPTYSTES PREACHYNGE, compyled 1538. Wesel 1547?; London 1744 (*in* Harleian miscellany, vol. i). *No copy extant of* 1547.

THE TEMPTACYON OF OUR LORDE, compyled 1538. Wesel 1547?

THRE LAWES, of nature, Moses and Christ, compyled 1538. Antwerp 1548?

KYNGE JOHAN. Ed. John Payne Collier, 1837; ed. J.H.P.Pafford, 1931. *Written 1534–47.*

ILLUSTRIUM MAIORIS BRITANNIAE scriptorum summarium. Wesel 1548; Catalogus, 2 pts. Basle 1557–9 (*enlarged*); Index, ed. R.L.Poole and Mary Bateson, Oxford 1902. *1902 is the first pbn of a notebook used 1549–57 as material for the* Catalogus.

Select works. Ed. Henry Christmas, Cambridge 1849.

Dramatic writings. Ed. John S.Farmer, 1907.

Harris, Jesse W. John Bale. Urbana, Ill. 1940.

McCusker, Helen. Bale: dramatist and antiquary. Bryn Mawr, Pa. 1942.

ALEXANDER BARCLAY (1475? – 1552)

THE SHYP OF FOLYS of the worlde, translated out of Laten, Frenche and Doche. 1509; 1570; ed. T.H.Jamieson, 2 vols. Edinburgh 1874. *Tr. mainly from Latin and French versions of Sebastian Brant's* Narrenschyff (1494).

EGLOGUES. 1515? (i–iii); The boke of Codrus and Mynalcus, 1521 (iv); The fyfte eglog, 1521.

Certayne eglogues. 1570 (*in* The shyp of folys, *above*); ed. Beatrice White, 1928 (EETS).

Herford, C.H. *In his* Studies in the literary relations of England and Germany in the sixteenth century, Cambridge 1886.

Pompen, Aurelius. The English versions of The ship of fools. 1925.

RICHARD BARNFIELD (1574 – 1627)

THE AFFECTIONATE SHEPHEARD. 1594; ed. J.O.Halliwell, 1842.

GREENES FUNERALLS. 1594; ed. Ronald B.McKerrow, 1911.

CYNTHIA, WITH CERTAIN SONNETS and the Legend of Cassandra. 1595.

THE ENCOMION OF LADY PECUNIA. 1598.

Poems in divers humors. 1598.

Poems. Ed. A.B.Grosart, 1876; ed. A.H.Bullen, 1903 (*in* Some longer Elizabethan poems).

FRANCIS BEAUMONT (1585? – 1616) and
JOHN FLETCHER (1579 – 1625)

THE FAITHFUL SHEPHEARDESSE. 1609?; ed. F.W.Moorman, 1896. *By Fletcher.*

THE KNIGHT OF THE BURNING PESTLE. 1613; 1635; ed. M. Joan Sargeaunt, 1928. *By Beaumont.*

A KING AND NO KING. 1619.

THE MAIDES TRAGEDY. 1619; ed. A.H.Thorndike, Boston 1906.

PHYLASTER. 1620; ed. F.S.Boas, 1898.

THE LIFE OF KING HENRY THE EIGHT. *In* Shakespeares comedies, histories and tragedies, 1623. *By Shakespeare and Fletcher?*

THE TWO NOBLE KINSMEN, written by Mr John Fletcher and Mr William Shakespeare. 1634.

THE BLOODY BROTHER. 1639; Oxford 1640 (*re-entitled* Rollo Duke of Normandy); ed. J.D.Jump, Liverpool 1948. *Attributed to Chapman, Fletcher, Ben Jonson and Massinger.*

THE WILD-GOOSE CHASE: a comedy. 1652. *By Fletcher.*

Poems by Beaumont. 1640; 1653 (*enlarged*); ed. A.B.Grosart, 1869.

Comedies and tragedies. 1647 (*34 unpbd plays*); Fifty[-two] comedies and tragedies, 1679.

Works. Ed. A.H.Bullen *et al.*, 4 vols. 1904–12 (*unfinished*); ed. Arnold Glover and A.R.Waller, 10 vols. Cambridge 1905–12; [Six] plays, ed. G.P.Baker, 1911, 1953 (EL).

Macaulay, G.C. Beaumont: a critical study. 1883.

Appleton, William W. Beaumont and Fletcher: a critical study. 1956·

Leech, Clifford. The John Fletcher plays. 1962.

JOHN BOURCHIER, 2ND BARON BERNERS (1467–1533)

FROYSSART: the cronycles of England, Fraunce, Spayne. 2 vols. 1523–5; ed. W.P.Ker, 6 vols. 1901–3.

HUON DE BORDEUXE. 1534?; ed. Sidney Lee, 4 pts. 1884–7 (EETS).

THE GOLDEN BOKE OF MARCUS AURELIUS. 1535; ed. J.M.Galvez, Berlin 1916 (*in his* Guevara in England, Palaestra cix). *Tr. from the Spanish of Guevara's* Marco Aurelio (1529) *through Bertant's French version.*

THE CASTELL OF LOVE. 1540? (*fragment*); 1549? *Tr. from Diego de San Pedro.*

ARTHUR OF LYTELL BRYTAYNE. 1555; ed. E.V.Utterson, 1814.

THE ENGLISH BIBLE

Darlow, T.H. and H.F.Moule. Historical catalogue of the printed editions of Holy Scripture. 2 vols. 1903–11.

Titles are merely descriptive or conventional:

The golden legend. 1483?; 1487?; ed. F.S.Ellis, 3 vols. 1892. *Trn by Caxton of the* Legenda aurea *of Jacobus de Voragine, containing most of the Pentateuch and Gospels.*

Tindale, William (1494?–1536). New testament: the Cologne fragment. Cologne 1525 (c. *40 leaves, suppressed*); Worms 1525 (1526?) (*complete*).

—— Pentateuch. Marburg 1530; 1534 (Genesis *rev.*).

—— Jonas. Antwerp? 1531? *For modern edns, see pp. 96–7, below.*

Tindale tr. the O.T. as far as Chronicles; the material was used in Matthew's Bible, below.

Coverdale, Miles (1488–1568). Bible. Marburg, *or* Antwerp, *or* Cologne 1535, pbd Samuel Bagster, 1838, 1847; Southwark 1537. *First complete English Bible. See also under Great Bible, below.*

'Matthew, Thomas' (*probably* John Rogers, c. *1500–1555*). Bible. London (ptd Antwerp) 1537. *A combination of Tindale and Coverdale.*

Taverner, Richard (1505?–1575). Bible. 1539. *A revision of Matthew's Bible.*

The Great Bible. 1539 ('*Cromwell's Bible*'); 1540 (*with Cranmer's prologue*), 1540 ('*Cranmer's Bible*'). *Coverdale's revision of Matthew's Bible. Includes the Prayer Book version of the Psalter.*

Cheke, Sir John (1514–1557). St Matthew. 1543.

Whittingham, William (1524?–1579). New Testament. Geneva 1557; 1842 (*facs.*). *A Protestant exile version by Calvin's brother-in-law.*

—— *et al.* Geneva Bible. Geneva 1560; London 1575. *The 'Breeches Bible'.*

The Bishops' Bible. 1568; 1572. *An official revision of the Great Bible under Archbp Parker's direction.*

Martin, Gregory *et al.* Douai-Rheims Bible: New testament, Rheims 1582; Old testament, 2 vols. Douai 1609–10. *A new version from the Vulgate by Catholic refugees in France.*

King James' Bible: or the authorized version. 1611; 1611; ed. W. Aldis Wright, 5 vols. Cambridge 1909 (*literatim*); ed. A. W. Pollard, Oxford 1911 (*facs.*).

The English Hexapla of the New testament. Pbd Samuel Bagster, 1841; 1872. *The Wiclif, Tindale, Cranmer, Geneva, Rheims and Authorized versions with the Greek text.*

Westcott, Brooke Foss. A general view of the history of the English Bible. 1868; 1905 (rev. W. Aldis Wright).

Pollard, A. W. Records of the English Bible, 1525–1611. Oxford 1911.

Isaacs, J. *In* The Bible in its ancient and English versions, ed. H. Wheeler Robinson, Oxford 1940; 1954.

Butterworth, Charles C. The literary lineage of King James Bible, 1340–1611. Philadelphia 1941.

Daiches, David. The King James version, with special reference to the Hebrew tradition. Chicago 1941.

Lewis, C. S. The literary impact of the Authorised Version. 1950; *rptd in his* They asked for a paper, 1962.

Mozley, J. F. Coverdale and his Bibles. 1953.

See also under AS. Gospels, p. 23, Wiclif, pp. 47–8 above, and Sandys and Tindale, below.

NICHOLAS BRETON (1555? – 1626?)

A FLOORISH UPON FANCIE. 1577; 1582 *(enlarged)*.

THE WORKES OF A YOUNG WYT. 1577.

BRITTONS BOWRE OF DELIGHTS. 1591; ed. Hyder E. Rollins, Cambridge, Mass. 1933 *(facs.)*. *Partly by Breton.*

THE PILGRIMAGE TO PARADISE, with the Countesse of Pembrookes love. Oxford 1592.

THE WIL OF WIT. 1597; 1599; ed. J. O. Halliwell, 1860. *Many prose pamphlets follow, 1597–1626.*

PASQUILS MAD-CAP. 2 pts. 1600; Pasquils mistresse, 1600; Pasquils passe and passeth not, 1600.

MELANCHOLIKE HUMOURS. 1600; ed. G. B. Harrison, 1929.

THE PASSIONATE SHEPHEARD. 1604.

CHARACTERS. 1615.

STRANGE NEWS out of divers countries. 1622.

Other poems in Englands Helicon (1600).

Works in verse and prose. Ed. A. B. Grosart, 2 vols. 1879.

A mad world my masters and other prose works. Ed. Ursula Kentish-Wright, 2 vols. 1929. *15 pieces.*

Poems not hitherto reprinted. Ed. Jean Robertson, Liverpool 1952. *With biography and bibliography.*

SIR THOMAS BROWNE (1605 – 1682)

Keynes, Geoffrey. A bibliography of Browne. Cambridge 1924; 1957.

RELIGIO MEDICI. 1642 *(two unauthorized edns)*; 1643 *(authorized)*; 1682; ed. W. A. Greenhill, 1881; ed. Jean-Jacques Denonain, Cambridge 1953, 1955 *(collated with MS.)*.

PSEUDODOXIA EPIDEMICA: or enquiries into received tenets and commonly presumed truths. 1646; 1672 *(enlarged)*. *Re-entitled* Vulgar errors *in* Works (1686), *below.*

HYDRIOTAPHIA: URNE-BURIALL; with The garden of Cyrus. 1658; ed. W. A. Greenhill, 1896; 1927 *(facs.)*; ed. John Carter, 1932, 1958.

CERTAIN MISCELLANY TRACTS. 1683.

A LETTER TO A FRIEND. 1690.

CHRISTIAN MORALS. Ed. John Jeffery, Cambridge 1716 (*from MS.*); ed. Samuel Johnson, 1756.

Works. 1686; Posthumous works, 1712; Works, including his life and correspondence, ed. Simon Wilkin, 4 vols. 1835–6; Works, ed. Geoffrey Keynes, 6 vols. 1928–31, 1964; Religio medici and other works, ed. L. C. Martin, Oxford 1964.

Digby, Kenelm. Observations upon Religio medici. 1643; Oxford 1909 (*with* Religio medici).

Johnson, Samuel. Life. *In* Christian morals, 1756, *above.*

Coleridge, S. T. *In his* Literary remains, 1836–9.

Stephen, Leslie. *In his* Hours in a library, ser. 2, 1876.

Gosse, Edmund. Sir Thomas Browne. 1905 (EML).

Dunn, William P. Browne: a study in religious philosophy. Menasha, Wis. 1926; Minneapolis 1950.

Bennett, Joan. Browne: 'a man of achievement in literature'. Cambridge 1962.

WILLIAM BROWNE of Tavistock (1590? – 1645?)

AN ELEGY [on Henry, Prince of Wales]. 1613. *Recast for* Pastorals, *I. v, below.*

BRITTANNIA'S PASTORALS, bk i. 1613; 1616 (*with ii*); i–ii, 1625; bk iii (*incomplete*), ed. T. Crofton Croker, 1852.

THE SHEPHEARDS PIPE. 1614. *With eclogues by George Wither et al.*

INNER TEMPLE MASQUE. 1772 (*in* Works, *below*); ed. Gwyn Jones, 1954 (*re-entitled* Circe and Ulysses). *Acted Jan. 1614.*

ORIGINAL POEMS never before published. Ed. S. Egerton Brydges, 1815.

Works. Ed. Thomas Davies, 3 vols. 1772; Whole works, ed. W. Carew Hazlitt, 2 vols. 1868–9; Poems, ed. Gordon Goodwin, 2 vols. 1894 (ML).

ROBERT BURTON (1577 – 1640)

Jordan-Smith, Paul. Bibliographia Burtoniana. Palo Alto, Cal. 1931.

THE ANATOMY OF MELANCHOLY. Oxford 1621; 1624; 1628; 1632; 1638; 1651 (*variously rev. and enlarged*); ed. A. R. Shilleto, 3 vols. 1893; ed. Floyd Dell and Paul Jordan-Smith, 2 vols. New York 1927; ed. Holbrook Jackson, 3 vols. 1932 (EL).

PHILOSOPHASTER; POEMATA COLLECTA. Ed. W. E. Buckley, 1862; ed. Paul Jordan-Smith, Palo Alto, Cal. 1931 (*with trn*).

Wood, Anthony. *In his* Athenae oxonienses, 1691–2.

Whibley, Charles. *In his* Literary portraits, 1904.

Osler, William *et al*. Burton and the Anatomy. Proc. Oxford Bibliog. Soc. i (1927).

Mueller, William R. The anatomy of Burton's England. Berkeley, Cal. 1952.

WILLIAM CAMDEN (1551 – 1623)

BRITANNIA: chorographica descriptio. 1586; 1607 (*enlarged*); tr. Philemon Holland, 1610; tr. Edmund Gibson, 1695.

REMAINES OF A GREATER WORKE concerning Britaine. 2 pts. 1605; 1 vol. 1870.

ANNALES RERUM anglicarum et hibernicarum, pt i (–1588). 1615; pt ii (1589–1603), Leyden 1625 (*with i*); ed. Thomas Hearne, 3 vols. Oxford 1717; tr. 2 pts. 1625–9.

EPISTOLAE. Ed. Thomas Smith, 1691. *Includes* Memorabilia de seipso·

THOMAS CAMPION (1567 – 1620)

POEMATA; Liber elegiarum; Liber epigrammatum. 1596.

A BOOKE OF AYRES. 1601. *Music and some lyrics by Philip Rosseter.*

OBSERVATIONS IN THE ART OF ENGLISH POESIE. 1602; ed. G. Gregory Smith, Oxford 1904 (*in* Elizabethan critical essays). *Reply by Samuel Daniel*, A defence of ryme, 1603.

THE DESCRIPTION OF A MASKE presented at White-Hall. 1607. *Two further masques, 1613 and 1614.*

TWO BOOKES OF AYRES. 1610; The thirde and fourth booke of ayres, 1617? *Words and music by Campion.*

SONGS OF MOURNING, bewailing the untimely death of Prince Henry. 1613.

EPIGRAMMATUM LIBRI II; Umbra; Elegiarum liber unus. 1619.

Poetical works in English. Ed. Percival Vivian, 1907 (ML); Works, ed. Vivian, Oxford 1909.

Fellowes, E. H. The English school of lutenist song writers, ser. 2, 1926. *Includes an edn of Campion's music.*

Kastendieck, Miles M. England's musical poet: Campion. New York 1938.

THOMAS CAREW (1594/5 – 1640)

COELUM BRITANNICUM: a masque at Whitehall. 1634; 1634.

Poems. 1640; 1642; 1651 (*both enlarged*); ed. Rhodes Dunlap, Oxford 1949.

GEORGE CHAPMAN (1559? – 1634)

HERO AND LEANDER. 1598; ed. C. F. Tucker Brooke, Oxford 1910 (*in* Works of Marlowe); ed. L. C. Martin, 1931 (*in* Marlowe's Poems). *Pt i by Marlowe, ii by Chapman.*

SEAVEN BOOKES of the Iliades of Homere. 1598 (*bks i, ii, vii–xi*); Achilles shield: his eighteenth booke, 1598; Homer, prince of poets, in twelve bookes, 161C? (Seaven bookes *rptd with iii–vi and xii*); The Iliades, 1611 (*i–ii rev., with xiii–xxiv*).

TWENTY-FOUR BOOKES of Homers Odisses. 1615?

The whole works of Homer. 1616; 5 vols. Oxford 1930–1; ed. Allardyce Nicoll, 2 vols. New York 1956.

EASTWARD HOE, made by Chapman, Ben Jonson, Joh. Marston. 1605.

MONSIEUR D'OLIVE: a comedie. 1606.

BUSSY D'AMBOIS: a tragedie. 1607, ed. Nicholas Brooke, 1964; 1641, ed. F.S.Boas, Boston 1905.

THE REVENGE OF BUSSY D'AMBOIS. 1613; ed. F.S.Boas, Boston 1905.

THE MEMORABLE MASQUE of the Innes of Court. 1613?

THE GEORGICKS OF HESIOD. 1618.

HOMERS BATTAILE OF FROGS AND MISE; his hymns and epigrams. 1624?

Works. Ed. R.H.Shepherd, 3 vols. 1874–5; Plays and poems, ed. T.M.Parrott, 2 vols. 1910–14 (*plays only*).

Poems. Ed. Phyllis B.Bartlett, New York 1941.

Swinburne, Algernon. Chapman: a critical essay. 1875; 1908 (*in his* The age of Shakespeare).

Spens, Janet. Chapman's ethical thought. Essays and studies, xi (1925).

Ellis, Havelock. Chapman, with illustrative passages. 1934.

Jacquot, Jean. Chapman: sa vie, sa poésie, son théâtre, sa pensée. Paris 1951.

Lewis, C.S. Hero and Leander. Proc. Brit. Acad. xxxviii (1952).

ABRAHAM COWLEY (1618 – 1667)

POETICALL BLOSSOMES. 1633; 1636 (*with* Sylva).

THE MISTRESS: love-verses. 1647.

Poems. 1656. *Includes* The mistress, Pindarique odes *and the epic* Davideis.

A VISION concerning Cromwell the wicked. 1661.

VERSES WRITTEN ON SEVERAL OCCASIONS. 1663.

Works. Ed. Thomas Sprat, 1668; 3 vols. 1707–8 (*enlarged*). 1668 *includes first pbn of* Discourses by way of essays.

English writings. Ed. A.R.Waller, 2 vols. Cambridge 1905–6.

Prose works. Ed. J.R.Lumby, Cambridge 1887, 1923 (*re-entitled* Essays) (rev. Arthur Tilley); ed. A.B.Gough, Oxford 1915.

The mistress, with other select poems. Ed. John Sparrow, 1929 (Nonesuch Press); Poetry and prose, with Sprat's Life, ed. L.C. Martin, Oxford 1949.

Sprat, Thomas. The life and writings of Cowley. *In* Works, 1668, *above*.

Johnson, Samuel. *In his* Lives, 1779–81.

Loiseau, Jean. Cowley: sa vie, son œuvre. Paris 1931.

Nethercot, Arthur H. Cowley: the Muse's Hannibal. Oxford 1931.

Eliot, T.S. A note on two odes of Cowley. *In* Seventeenth-century studies presented to Sir Herbert Grierson, Oxford 1938.

Walton, Geoffrey. *In his* Metaphysical to Augustan, 1955.

Hinman, Robert B. Cowley's world of order. Cambridge, Mass. 1960.

RICHARD CRASHAW (1612/13 – 1649)

EPIGRAMMATUM SACRORUM LIBER. Cambridge 1634; 1670; tr. Clement Barksdale, 1682.

STEPS TO THE TEMPLE: sacred poems; with the delights of the Muses. 1646; 1648 (*enlarged*); Carmen Deo nostro: sacred poems collected, corrected, augmented, ed. Thomas Car, Paris 1652; Steps to the temple, 1670.

[Poems]. Ed. A.R. Waller, Cambridge 1904; Poems, English, Latin, and Greek, ed. L.C. Martin, Oxford 1927, 1957 (*with addns*).

Eliot, T.S. *In his* For Lancelot Andrewes, 1928.

Wallerstein, Ruth C. Richard Crashaw. Madison, Wis. 1935.

Warren, Austin. Crashaw: a study in baroque sensibility. Baton Rouge, La. 1939.

SAMUEL DANIEL (1563? – 1619)

Sellers, H. A bibliography of Daniel, 1585–1623. Proc. Oxford Bibliog. Soc. ii (1930).

DELIA, with The complaint of Rosamond. 1592; 1594 (*with* Cleopatra); ed. Arundel Esdaile, 1908 (*with Drayton's* Idea). *24 of the 50 Delia sonnets were first pbd in a pirated edn of Sidney's* Astrophel and Stella, 1591.

THE CIVILE WARS. 1595 (bks i–iv); i–v, 1599 (*in* Poeticall essayes, *below*); i–vi, 1601 (*in* Works, *below*); 1609 (i–viii) (*unfinished verse chronicle*); ed. Laurence Michel, New Haven 1958.

Poeticall essayes. 1599. *Includes* Musophilus *and* A letter from Octavia.

Works newly augmented. 1601.

PANEGYRIKE TO THE KING; Certain epistles; with A defence of ryme. 1603.

Defence. Ed. G. Gregory Smith, Oxford 1904 (*in* Elizabethan critical essays). *A reply to Campion's* Observations, 1602.

THE VISION OF THE 12. GODDESSES. 1604. *A royal masque first pbd in a pirated edn, 1604.*

CERTAINE SMALL POEMS, with the tragedie of Philotas. 1605; 1611 (*enlarged*). *Includes* Ulisses and the syren.

Philotas. Ed. Laurence Michel, New Haven 1949.

THE HISTORIE OF ENGLAND. 1612 (pt i); 1618? (*complete*).

HYMENS TRIUMPH. 1615.

Whole workes in poetrie. 1623; Complete works, ed. A.B.Grosart, 5 vols. 1885; Poems and A defence of ryme, ed. A.C.Sprague, Cambridge, Mass. 1930.

SIR WILLIAM DAVENANT (1606 – 1668)

MADAGASCAR, WITH OTHER POEMS. 1638.

A DISCOURSE UPON GONDIBERT. Paris 1650; London 1651 (*as preface to* Gondibert); ed. J.E. Spingarn, Oxford 1908 (*in* Seventeenth-century critical essays). *Reply by* Hobbes, The answer to D'Avenant's Preface, Paris 1650 (*in* Spingarn).

GONDIBERT: an heroick poem. 1651. *Unfinished.*

THE SIEGE OF RHODES. 1656 (*libretto*); 1663 (*enlarged as heroic play in two pts*).

Works. 1673. *Includes 26 plays, 20 pbd separately 1629–74.*

Firth, C.H. Davenant and the revival of drama during the Protectorate. Eng. historical review, xviii (1903).

Harbage, Alfred. Sir William Davenant. Philadelphia 1935.

Nethercot, Arthur H. D'avenant: poet laureate and playwright-manager. Chicago 1938.

SIR JOHN DAVIES (1569 – 1626)

EPIGRAMMES AND ELEGIES. 2 pts. Middelburg (Holland) 1590? *A verse trn of Ovid's epigrams, with Marlowe's trn of the elegies.*

ORCHESTRA: or a poeme of dauncing. 1596; ed. E.M.W. Tillyard, 1945.

NOSCE TEIPSUM: this oracle expounded in two elegies. 1599; 1602; 1622 (*with* Hymnes of Astraea *and* Orchestra).

Poetical works, 1773; Works, ed. A.B.Grosart, 3 vols. 1869–76; Poems in facsimile from the first editions in the Huntington Library, ed. Clare Howard, New York 1941.

THOMAS DEKKER (1572? – 1632)

OLD FORTUNATUS. 1600.

THE SHOMAKERS HOLIDAY. 1600; ed. James Sutherland, Oxford 1928.

SATIRO-MASTIX. 1602. *A reply to Jonson's* Poetaster, *perhaps with Marston.*

THE HONEST WHORE. 1604, 1605 (*with Middleton*); The second part, 1630.

For collaborations see under Ford, Massinger, Middleton and Webster, below.

Dramatic works. Ed. R.H.Shepherd, 4 vols. 1873; ed. Fredson Bowers and Cyrus Hoy, 5 vols. Cambridge 1953–.

NEWES FROM HELL. 1606; 1607 (*re-entitled* A knights conjuring); ed. E.F.Rimbault, 1842.

THE SEVEN DEADLY SINNES of London. 1606; ed. H.F.B.Brett-Smith, Oxford 1922.

THE GULS HORNE-BOOKE. 1609; ed. Ronald B.McKerrow, 1904. *A satire on the Jacobean gallant.*

Non-dramatic works. Ed. A.B.Grosart, 5 vols. 1884–6.

The plague pamphlets. Ed. F.P.Wilson, Oxford 1925. *Six pamphlets, 1603–30.*

THOMAS DELONEY (1543? – 1600)

THE PLEASANT HISTORIE of Jack of Newberie. 1597?; 1619; ed. George Saintsbury, 1929 (*in* Shorter novels) (EL).

THOMAS OF READING. ?; 1612; ed. Saintsbury (*with above*).

THE GENTLE CRAFT. 2 pts. 1597–8?; 1637–9; ed. W.J.Halliday, 1928.

STRANGE HISTORIES. 1602; 1607; ed. John Payne Collier, 1842.

Works. Ed. Francis O.Mann, Oxford 1912; Novels, ed. Merritt E. Lawlis, Bloomington, Ind. 1961.

SIR JOHN DENHAM (1615 – 1669)

COOPERS HILL. 1642; 1655 (*first authorized edn, enlarged*); 1668 (*iu* Poems, *below*).

Poems and translations, 1668; Poetical works, ed. Theodore H.Banks, New Haven 1928.

Johnson, Samuel. *In his* Lives, 1779–81.

Aubrey, John. *In his* Lives, 1813.

JOHN DONNE (1571? – 1631)

Keynes, Geoffrey. A bibliography of Donne. 1914; Cambridge 1932, 1958 (*enlarged*).

Combs, H.C. and Z.R.Sullens. A concordance to the English poems. Chicago 1940.

PSEUDO-MARTYR. 1610. *A Protestant prose tract for English Catholics.*

CONCLAVE IGNATI. 1611; Ignatius his conclave, 1611, ed. Charles M. Coffin, New York 1941 (*facs.*). *The Latin and English versions of an anti-Jesuit tract.*

AN ANATOMY OF THE WORLD. 1611; ed. Geoffrey Keynes, Cambridge 1951 (*facs.*); The second anniversary: of the progres of the soule, 1612 (*with* The first anniversary); New York 1932 (*facs.*); 1633 (*in* Poems, *below*); The anniversaries, ed. Frank Manley, Baltimore 1963. *An elegy on Elizabeth Drury.*

SERMON. 1622. *Eight further volumes of sermons pbd 1622–38.*

DEVOTIONS UPON EMERGENT OCCASIONS. 1624; ed. John Sparrow, Cambridge 1923.

POEMS. 1633; 1635; 1650; 1669 (*all enlarged*). 1633 *prints for the first time 51 of the 55* Songs and sonets, *16 of the 19* Epigrams, *11 of the 20* Elegies, *the 5* Satyres *and 28 of the 39* Divine poems, *including the 19* Holy sonnets.

JUVENILIA: or certaine paradoxes and problemes. 1633; ed. Geoffrey Keynes, 1923 (Nonesuch Press); ed. Roger E. Bennett, New York 1936 (*facs.*).

BIATHANATOS. 1646; ed. J. William Hebel, New York 1930 (*facs.*).

ESSAYES IN DIVINITY. 1651; ed. Evelyn M. Simpson, Oxford 1952.

LXXX SERMONS. 1640 (*with Walton's* Life); Fifty sermons, 1649; XXVI sermons, 1660; Selected passages, ed. Logan Pearsall Smith, Oxford 1919; Ten sermons, ed. Geoffrey Keynes, 1923 (Nonesuch Press); Sermons, ed. George R. Potter and Evelyn M. Simpson, 10 vols. Berkeley, Cal. 1953– (*first complete edn*).

Works. Ed. Henry Alford, 6 vols. 1839; Complete poetry and selected prose, ed. John Hayward, 1929, 1930 (Nonesuch Lib.); ed. Charles M. Coffin, New York 1952 (Modern Lib.).

Poems. Ed. Herbert Grierson, 2 vols. Oxford 1912, 1 vol. Oxford 1929 (OSA) (*without notes*); ed. Roger E. Bennett, Chicago 1942 (*modernized*).

Divine poems. Ed. Helen L. Gardner, Oxford 1952.

Songs and sonets. Ed. Theodore Redpath, 1956.

Walton, Izaak. The life of Donne. 1640 (*in* Sermons, *above*); 1658 (*enlarged*).

Gosse, Edmund. The life and letters of Donne. 2 vols. 1899.

Simpson, Evelyn M. A study of the prose works of Donne. Oxford 1924; 1948.

Legouis, Pierre. Donne the craftsman. Paris 1928.

Spencer, Theodore, T. S. Eliot *et al.* A garland for Donne. Cambridge, Mass. 1931.

Coffin, Charles M. Donne and the new philosophy. New York 1937.

3-2

Lewis, C.S. Donne and love poetry. *In* Seventeenth-century studies presented to Herbert Grierson, Oxford 1938. *Reply by Joan Bennett, ibid.*

Leishman, J.B. The monarch of wit. 1951; 1961.

MICHAEL DRAYTON (1563 – 1631)

THE SHEPHEARDS GARLAND fashioned in nine eglogues. 1593; ed. John Payne Collier, 1870 *(facs.).*

IDEAS MIRROUR: amours in quaterzains. 1594; 1619 *(re-entitled* Idea); ed. Arundell Esdaile, 1908 *(with Daniel's* Delia).

ENDIMION AND PHOEBE. 1595; 1606 *(re-entitled* The man in the moone) *(in* Poems, *below);* ed. J.William Hebel, Oxford 1925.

ENGLANDS HEROICALL EPISTLES. 1597; 1598 *(enlarged);* 1600 *(with* Idea *above).*

THE LIFE of Sir John Oldcastle. 1600; 1908 *(facs.). Partly by Drayton.*

THE OWLE. 1604.

THE BARRONS WARS. 1605 *(in* Poems, *below).*

POLYOLBION. 1612; 1622 *(re-entitled* A chorographical description of Great Britain) *(enlarged).*

THE BATTAILE OF AGINCOURT. 1627. *For the* Ballad of Agincourt, *see under* Poems, *below.*

THE MUSES ELIZIUM, being ten nymphalls. 1630.

Poems. 1605; 1606; 1619 *(both enlarged);* ed. John Buxton, 2 vols. 1953 (ML). To the Cambro-Britans: the ballad of Agincourt *first pbd in* 1606, *rev. in* 1619.

Minor poems. Ed. Cyril Brett, Oxford 1907.

Complete works. Ed. J.William Hebel, Kathleen Tillotson and Bernard H.Newdigate, 5 vols. Oxford 1931–41; 1961.

Elton, Oliver. Drayton: a critical study. 1905.

Newdigate, Bernard H. Drayton and his circle. Oxford 1941.

WILLIAM DRUMMOND of Hawthornden (1585 – 1649)

TEARES ON THE DEATH of Meliades. Edinburgh 1613.

POEMS. Edinburgh? 1614?; 1616 *(enlarged).*

FLOWRES OF SION; Cypresse grove. Edinburgh 1623; 1630 *(enlarged). The* Grove, *a prose meditation on death, is ed. Kastner, below.*

The history of Scotland, 1423–1542. 1655. *A collection of the prose works.*

Poems. Ed. Edward Phillips, 1656. *Incomplete, but adds 33 unpbd poems.*

Works. Ed. John Sage and Thomas Ruddiman, Edinburgh 1711.

The poetical works with A cypresse grove. Ed. L.E.Kastner, 2 vols. Manchester 1913.
Ben Jonson's conversations with Drummond. Ed. David Laing, 1833; ed. R.F.Patterson, 1923; ed. C.H.Herford and Percy Simpson, Oxford 1925 (*in their edn of* Jonson, vol. i). *Record of a visit by Jonson to Hawthornden in 1619.*

Laing, David. Account of the Hawthornden manuscripts in the possession of the Society, with extracts. Trans. Soc. of Antiquaries of Scotland, iv (1831).
Masson, David. Drummond of Hawthornden. 1873.
Joly, Augustin. Drummond de Hawthornden. Lille 1934.

JOHN EARLE (1601? – 1665)

Murphy, Gwendolen. *In her* Bibliography of English character-books, 1608–1700, Oxford 1925.

MICRO-COSMOGRAPHIE: essayes and characters. 1628 (*54 characters*); 1629 (*77*); 1633 (*78*); ed. Philip Bliss, 1811 (*with verse*), Bristol 1897 (rev. S.T.Irwin); ed. Gwendolen Murphy, 1928 (Nonesuch Press).

Clarendon, Earl of. *In his* Life, Oxford 1719; *rptd in* Characters, ed. D.Nichol Smith, Oxford 1918.

SIR THOMAS ELYOT (*c.* 1490 – 1546)

THE BOKE NAMED THE GOVERNOUR. 1531; ed. H.H.S.Croft, 2 vols. 1883.
OF THE KNOWLEDGE whiche maketh a wise man. 1533; ed. E.J.Howard, Oxford, Ohio 1946.
THE EDUCATION OF CHILDREN, translated out of Plutarche. 1535?
DICTIONARY. 1538; 1545 (*re-entitled* Bibliotheca Elyotae). *The first Latin-English dictionary.*
THE CASTEL OF HELTH. 1539; 1541; New York 1937 (*facs.*).
THE DEFENCE OF GOOD WOMEN. 1540; ed. E.J.Howard, Oxford, Ohio 1940.

EDWARD FAIRFAX (1580? – 1635)

GODFREY OF BULLOIGNE: or the recoverie of Jerusalem. 1600; ed. Henry Morley, 1890. *An ottava rima trn of Tasso's* Gerusalemme liberata (1581).

GILES FLETCHER the younger (1585/6 – 1623)

CHRISTS VICTORIE and triumph over and after death. 2 pts. Cambridge 1610.

Poems. Ed. A.B.Grosart, 1868; 1876; Poetical works of Giles and Phineas Fletcher, ed. F.S.Boas, 2 vols. Cambridge 1908–9.

For John Fletcher see under Beaumont and Fletcher, *above.*

PHINEAS FLETCHER (1582 – 1650)

BRITTAIN'S IDA. 1628; ed. Ethel Seaton, Oxford 1926 (*entitled* Venus and Anchises) (*from MS.*). *Formerly attributed to Spenser.*
SYLVA POETICA. Cambridge 1633.
THE PURPLE ISLAND, with piscatorie eclogs. 2 pts. Cambridge 1633.

Poems. Ed. A. B. Grosart, 4 vols. 1869; Poetical works of Giles and Phineas Fletcher, ed. F. S. Boas, 2 vols. Cambridge 1908–9.

Langdale, Abram B. Phineas Fletcher: man of letters, science and divinity. New York 1937.

JOHN FLORIO (1553? – 1626)

FIRST FRUTES. 1578, ed. A. de Re, Formosa 1936; Second frutes, 1591. *An It. phrase-book and grammar.*
THE ESSAYES OF MONTAIGNE. 1603; 1632 (*with index*); ed. George Saintsbury, 6 vols. 1892–3; ed. J. I. M. Stewart, 2 vols. 1931 (Nonesuch Press).

Matthiessen, F. O. *In his* Translation: an Elizabethan art, Cambridge, Mass. 1931.
Yates, Frances A. John Florio. Cambridge 1934.

JOHN FORD (1586 – 1639)

THE LOVERS MELANCHOLY. 1629.
THE BROKEN HEART: a tragedy. 1633.
LOVES SACRIFICE: a tragedie. 1633.
TIS PITTY SHEES A WHORE. 1633.
THE CHRONICLE HISTORIE of Perkin Warbeck. 1634.
THE WITCH OF EDMONTON: a tragi-comedy by W. Rowley, Dekker, Ford etc. 1658.

Dramatic works. Ed. William Gifford, 2 vols. 1827; 3 vols. 1869, 1895 (rev. Alexander Dyce); ed. W. Bang and H. de Vocht, 2 vols. Louvain 1908–27 (Bang).
[Five plays]. Ed. Havelock Ellis, 1888 (Mermaid).

Eliot, T. S. *In his* Selected essays, 1932.
Sargeaunt, M. Joan. John Ford. Oxford 1935.
Davril, Robert. Le drame de Ford. Paris 1955.
Oliver, H. J. The problem of Ford. Melbourne 1955.
Leech, Clifford. Ford and the drama of his time. 1957.

JOHN FOXE (1517 – 1587)

ACTES AND MONUMENTS. 1563; 1583; 3 vols. 1641; ed. S.R.Cattley, 8 vols. 1837–41; 1853–70 (rev. Josiah Pratt). *First entitled* The book of martyrs *in Madan's edn (1776)*.

Foxe, Simeon? Life of Foxe. *In* Actes, 1641, *above*. *Attributed to one of Foxe's sons*.

Mozley, J.F. Foxe and his book. 1940.

Haller, William. Foxe's Book of martyrs and the Elect Nation. 1963.

THOMAS FULLER (1608 – 1661)

Gibson, Strickland. A bibliography of Fuller. Proc. Oxford Bibliog. Soc. iv (1936).

THE HISTORIE OF THE HOLY WARRE. Cambridge 1639.

THE HOLY STATE; The profane state. Cambridge 1642; ed. M.G. Walten, 2 vols. New York 1938 (*facs*.).

THE CHURCH-HISTORY OF BRITAIN, of the University of Cambridge and of Waltham Abbey. 1655.

THE HISTORY of the worthies of England. 1662; ed. P.Austin Nuttall, 3 vols. 1840; ed. J.Freeman, 1952 (*abridged*).

Poems. Ed. A.B.Grosart, Edinburgh 1868.

Specimens. Ed. Charles Lamb, Reflector, iv (1811); Selections, ed. E.K.Broadus, Oxford 1929.

Collected sermons. Ed. J.E.Bailey and W.E.A.Axon, 2 vols. 1891.

Coleridge, S.T. *In his* Literary remains, 1836–9.

Bailey, J.E. The life of Fuller. 1874.

Houghton, Walter E. The formation of Fuller's Holy and profane states. Cambridge, Mass. 1938.

GEORGE GASCOIGNE (1539? – 1577)

A HUNDRETH SUNDRIE FLOWRES. 1573, ed. C.T.Prouty, Columbia, Missouri 1942; 1575 (*re-entitled* Posies).

1573 *includes the comedy* Supposes, *the tragedy* Jocasta *and the novel* Master F.J. 1575 *adds* Certayne notes of instruction concerning the making of verse.

Supposes: a comedie by Ariosto englished. 1573 (*above*); ed. R. Warwick Bond, Oxford 1911 (*in* Early plays from Italian).

Jocasta: a tragedie by Euripides translated and digested. 1573 (*above*); ed. J.W.Cunliffe, Boston 1906.

THE GLASSE OF GOVERNMENT: a tragicall comedie. 1575; ed. John S. Farmer, 1914 (*facs.*).

THE STELE GLAS: a satyre. 1576.

Pleasauntest works. 1587; Complete works, ed. J.W.Cunliffe, 2 vols. Cambridge 1907–10.

Whetstone, George. A remembraunce of Gaskoigne. 1577; ed. Edward Arber, 1868 (*with* The stele glas).

Schelling, F.E. The life and writings of Gascoigne. Boston 1893.

Prouty, C.T. Gascoigne: Elizabethan courtier, soldier and poet. New York 1942.

ROBERT GREENE (1558 – 1592)

PANDOSTO. 1588; ed. James Winny, Cambridge 1957 (*in* The descent of Euphues: three Elizabethan romance stories). *A prose romance, the source of Shakespeare's* Winter's tale.

REPENTANCE. 1592; Groats-worth of witte, 1592; ed. G.B.Harrison, 1923 (*together*).

FRIER BACON AND FRIER BONGAY. 1594; ed. A.W.Ward, Oxford 1878, 1901 (*with Marlowe's* Faustus); ed. W.W.Greg, 1926.

JAMES THE FOURTH. 1598; ed. A.E.H.Swaen and W.W.Greg, 1921.

Life and complete works. Ed. A.B.Grosart, 15 vols. 1881–6.

Plays and poems, ed. J.Churton Collins, 2 vols. Oxford 1905.

FULKE GREVILLE, 1ST BARON BROOKE (1554–1628)

THE TRAGEDY OF MUSTAPHA. 1609.

THE LIFE OF SIR PHILIP SIDNEY. 1652; ed. Nowell C. Smith, Oxford 1907.

Workes written in his youth. 1633; Remains, 1670. 1633 *includes* Caelica, *a sequence of 110 poems.*

Works. Ed. A.B.Grosart, 4 vols. 1870; Poems and dramas, ed. Geoffrey Bullough, 2 vols. 1939.

WILLIAM HABINGTON (1605 – 1654)

CASTARA. 2 pts. 1634; 1635; 3 pts. 1639–40 (*both enlarged*).

Poems. Ed. Kenneth Allott, 1948.

RICHARD HAKLUYT (1552? – 1616)

DIVERS VOYAGES touching the discoverie of America. 1582; ed. J.Winter Jones, 1850.

THE PRINCIPALL NAVIGATIONS, voiages and discoveries of the English nation. 1589; 3 vols. 1600 (*much enlarged*); ed. Walter Raleigh, 12 vols. 1903–5; ed. John Masefield, 10 vols. 1927–8.

WESTERN DISCOVERIES. 1877. *Written in Paris in 1584.*

Original writings and correspondence of the two Richard Hakluyts. Ed. E.G.R.Taylor, 2 vols. 1935.

Froude, J.A. *In his* Short studies, 1867–83.
Raleigh, Walter. The English voyages of the sixteenth century. Glasgow 1906. *The introd. to his edn, above, revised.*
Parks, George B. Hakluyt and the English voyages. New York 1928.

JOSEPH HALL (1574 – 1656)

VIRGIDEMIARUM: first three bookes, of toothless satyrs. 1597, 1598; The three last bookes, of byting satyres, 1598.

Works. 3 vols. 1625–62; ed. Philip Wynter, 10 vols. Oxford 1863. *Includes the theological works.*
Collected poems. Ed. Arnold Davenport, Liverpool 1949.

SIR JOHN HARINGTON (1561 – 1612)

ORLANDO FURIOSO in English heroical verse. 1591. *An ottava rima trn of Ariosto's epic (1516–32).*

A briefe apologie of poetrie. 1591 (Preface *to above*); ed. G.Gregory Smith, Oxford 1904 (*in* Elizabethan critical essays).

EPIGRAMS. 1618; ed. McClure (*below*).

Nugae antiquae: original papers. Ed. Henry Harington, 2 vols. 1769–75; ed. Thomas Park, 2 vols. 1804.
Letters and epigrams. Ed. Norman E.McClure, Philadelphia 1930.

JAMES HARRINGTON (1611 – 1677)

THE COMMON-WEALTH OF OCEANA. 1656; ed. S.B.Liljegren, Lund 1924.
POLITICAL DISCOURSES. 1660.

Oceana and other works. Ed. John Toland, 1700; 1737 (*enlarged*).
Blitzer, Charles. An immortal commonwealth: the political thought of Harrington. New Haven 1960.

EDWARD, BARON HERBERT OF CHERBURY (1583 – 1648)

DE VERITATE. Paris 1624. *First London edn, 1645. A Latin treatise on metaphysics, tr. Bristol 1937.*
OCCASIONAL VERSES. 1665; Poems, ed. G.C.Moore Smith, Oxford 1923; ed. R.G.Howarth, 1931 (EL) (*in* Minor poets of the seventeenth century).
THE LIFE OF LORD HERBERT written by himself. Ed. Horace Walpole, Strawberry Hill 1765 (*from MS.*); ed. Sidney Lee, 1886, 1906.

GEORGE HERBERT (1593 – 1633)

Palmer, George H. A Herbert bibliography. Cambridge, Mass. 1911.
Mann, Cameron. A concordance to the English poems. Boston 1927.

THE TEMPLE: sacred poems and private ejaculations. Ed. Nicholas
   Ferrar, Cambridge 1633; 1638; 1641 (*with Christopher Harvey's*
   Synagogue); 1674 (*with Walton's* Life); ed. Francis Meynell, 1927
   (Nonesuch Press) (*from MS.*); Poems, ed. Helen L. Gardner, Oxford
   1961 (WC).
REMAINS. Ed. Barnabas Oley, 1652. *Includes the prose* A priest to the
   temple, *pbd separately 1671.*

Works. Ed. William Pickering, 2 vols. 1835–6 (*with Coleridge's notes*);
   ed. F.E. Hutchinson, Oxford 1941, 1945.

Walton, Izaak. The life of Herbert. 1670; 1674 (*with* Temple, *above*).
Coleridge, S.T. *In his* Biographia literaria, 1817.
Knights, L.C. *In his* Explorations, 1946.
Tuve, Rosemond. A reading of Herbert. Chicago 1952.
Bottrall, Margaret. George Herbert. 1954.
Summers, J.H. George Herbert. Cambridge, Mass. 1954.

ROBERT HERRICK (1591 – 1674)

MacLeod, Malcolm. A concordance to the poems. New York 1936.

HESPERIDES: or works both humane and divine. 1648. *Includes* Noble
   numbers: or his pious pieces.

Poetical works. Ed. F.W. Moorman, Oxford 1915; ed. L.C. Martin,
   Oxford 1956; Poems, ed. John Hayward, 1961 (Penguin) (*selected*).

Moorman, F.W. Herrick: a biographical and critical study. 1910;
   1924.
Delattre, Floris. Robert Herrick. Paris 1912.

JOHN HEYWOOD (1497? – 1580?)

THE FOURE P.P. *c.* 1545; ed. J.Q. Adams, Boston 1924 (*in* Chief pre-
   Shakespearean dramas). *Four earlier interludes separately pbd in
   1533, a sixth below.*
WYTTY AND WYTLESS. Ed. F.W. Fairholt, 1846 (*abridged*); 1909 (*facs.*).
Dramatic writings. Ed. John S. Farmer, 1905.
Woorkes. 1562; ed. John S. Farmer, 1906; ed. B.A. Milligan, Urbana,
   Ill. 1956. *Epigrams and a collection of proverbs.*

Bolwell, Robert G.W. The life and works of John Heywood. New York 1921.

Maxwell, Ian. French farce and John Heywood. Melbourne 1946.

THOMAS HEYWOOD (1574? – 1641)

Clark, Arthur M. A bibliography of Thomas Heywood. Proc. Oxford Bibliog. Soc. i (1925).

EDWARD THE FOURTH. 2 pts. 1599; ed. Seymour de Ricci, 1922 (*facs.*).

A WOMAN KILDE WITH KINDNESSE. 1607; 1617; ed. R.W. Van Fossen, 1961.

A YORKSHIRE TRAGEDY. 1608; 1619. *Attributed by Clark, above.*

THE FAIR MAID OF THE WEST. 2 pts. 1631.

THE ENGLISH TRAVELLER. 1633.

DICK OF DEVONSHIRE. Ed. A.H.Bullen, 1883 (*in* Collection of old English plays); 1955 (Malone Soc.).

Thomas Heywood claimed a hand in 220 plays, most now lost. See also under Webster, below.

Dramatic works. Ed. R.H.Shepherd, 6 vols. 1874; [Five plays], ed. A.Wilson Verity, 1888 (Mermaid).

Clark, Arthur M. Thomas Heywood: playwright and miscellanist. Oxford 1931.

Eliot, T.S. *In his* Selected essays, 1932. *A review of Clark, above.*

Boas, F.S. Thomas Heywood. 1950.

THOMAS HOBBES (1588 – 1679)

Macdonald, Hugh and Mary Hargreaves. Hobbes: a bibliography. 1952.

DE CIVE. Paris 1642; Amsterdam 1647, 1647; tr. 1651. *Third section of philosophic treatise, followed by first and second sections, 1655–8, below.*

HUMANE NATURE: or the fundamental elements of policie. 1650.

DE CORPORE POLITICO: or the elements of law. 1650.

The elements of law, natural and politic. Ed. Ferdinand Tönnies, 1889. *Circulated in MS. in 1640, first pbd as two separate works in 1650, above.*

THE ANSWER to D'Avenant's Preface before Gondibert. Paris 1650 (*in* Davenant, A discourse upon Gondibert); ed. G.Gregory Smith, Oxford 1904 (*in* Elizabethan critical essays). *An essay on heroic poetry.*

DE CIVE. Amsterdam 1651.

LEVIATHAN. 1651; ed. A.R. Waller, Cambridge 1904; ed. Michael Oakeshott, Oxford 1946.

DE CORPORE. 1655, tr. 1656; De homine, 1658. *First and second sections; see De cive, above.*

TRACTS. 2 vols. 1681–2. *Includes* Behemoth.

The English works. Ed. William Molesworth, 11 vols. 1839–45.

Aubrey, John. *In his* Lives, 1813.

Robertson, George Croom. Hobbes. Edinburgh 1886.

Strauss, Leo. The political philosophy of Hobbes. Oxford 1936; Chicago 1952.

Warrender, Howard. The political philosophy of Hobbes. Oxford 1957.

Mintz, Samuel I. The hunting of Leviathan: seventeenth-century reactions to the materialism and moral philosophy of Hobbes Cambridge 1962.

RICHARD HOOKER (1554 – 1600)

OF THE LAWES of ecclesiastical politie: eight bookes. 1593 (*bks i–iv only*); The fift booke, 1597, ed. R.Bayne, 1902; i–v, ed. John Spenser, 1604, 1611; The sixth and eighth books, 1648, 1651; vii, 1662 (*in* Works, *below*); i–v, ed. Bayne, 2 vols. 1907, 1954 (rev. Christopher Morris) (EL).

Works. Ed. John Gauden, 1662; 1666 (*with Walton's* Life); ed. John Keble, 3 vols. Oxford 1836, 1888 (rev. R.W.Church and F.Paget).

Walton, Izaak. The life of Hooker. 1665; 1666 (*in* Works, *above*); 1670, 1675 (*in his* Lives). *Written under Archbp Sheldon's direction, its facts demolished by Sisson, below.*

Sisson, C.J. The judicious marriage of Mr Hooker and the birth of the Laws. Cambridge 1940.

BEN JONSON (1572 – 1637)

Ford, H.L. Collation of the Jonson folios, 1616–31–40. Oxford 1932.

EVERY MAN OUT OF HIS HUMOR. 1600 (*3 quartos*); Q1, ed. W.W.Greg and F.P.Wilson, 1920 (Malone Soc.); Qq. 2 & 3, ed. W.Bang and W.W.Greg, Louvain 1907 (Bang).

EVERY MAN IN HIS HUMOR. 1601; ed. W.Bang and W.W.Greg, Louvain 1905 (Bang).

THE FOUNTAINS OF SELFE-LOVE: or Cynthias revels. 1601; ed. W.Bang and L.Krebs, Louvain 1908 (Bang).

POETASTER: or the arraignment. 1602; ed. H.de Vocht, Louvain 1934. (Bang).

SEJANUS HIS FALL. 1605; ed. H.de Vocht, Louvain 1935 (Bang).

VOLPONE: OR THE FOXE. 1607; ed. H.de Vocht, Louvain 1935 (Bang).

CATILINE HIS CONSPIRACY. 1611.

THE ALCHEMIST. 1612; ed. H.de Vocht, Louvain 1950 (Bang).

EPICOENE: or the silent woman. 1612? (*lost*); 1616 (*in* Workes, *below*).

EPIGRAMMES; THE FORREST. *In* Workes, 1616, *below. Two verse collections.*

BARTHOLOMEW FAYRE. *In* Workes, 1631, *below*; ed. E. A. Horsman, 1960.

THE SAD SHEPHERD. 1640 (*in* Workes); ed. W. W. Greg, Louvain 1905 (Bang).

UNDER-WOODS: consisting of divers poems. *In* Workes, 1640.

THE ENGLISH GRAMMAR. 1640 (*in* Workes); ed. Strickland Gibson, 1928.

TIMBER: or discoveries. 1640 (*in* Workes); ed. F. E. Schelling, Boston 1892; ed. Maurice Castelain, Paris 1906.

Workes. 1616 (*corrected text*); vol. II, 1631; ed. Kenelm Digby, 1640. *1616 folio includes 17 masques, 1640 adds another 17.*

[Works]. Ed. C. H. Herford, Percy and Evelyn M. Simpson, 11 vols. Oxford 1925–52.

Complete plays. Ed. F. E. Schelling, 2 vols. 1910 (EL); Five plays, Oxford 1953 (WC).

Poems. Ed. Bernard H. Newdigate, Oxford 1936; ed. George B. Johnston, 1954 (ML) (*selected*); Complete poetry, ed. William B. Hunter, New York 1963.

Conversations with William Drummond of Hawthornden. Ed. David Laing, 1833; ed. R. F. Patterson, 1923; ed. Herford and Simpson, Oxford 1925 (*in* Works, vol. i, *above*). *Record by Drummond of a visit by Jonson to Hawthornden in 1618–19.*

Dryden, John. *In his* Of dramatick poesie, 1668. *An examen of* Epicoene.

Aubrey, John. *In his* Lives, 1813.

Gregory Smith, G. Ben Jonson. 1919 (EML).

Eliot, T. S. *In his* The sacred wood, 1920.

Bradley, Jesse F. and J. Q. Adams. The Jonson allusion-book, 1597–1700. New Haven 1922.

Herford, C. H. and Percy Simpson. Life of Jonson. *In* Works, vols. i–ii, Oxford 1925, *above*.

Gilbert, Allan H. The symbolic persons in the masques of Jonson. Durham, N.C. 1948.

Walton, Geoffrey. The tone of Jonson's poetry. *In his* Metaphysical to Augustan, 1955.

Partridge, Edward B. The broken compass: a study of the major comedies of Jonson. 1958.

Barish, Jonas A. Jonson and the language of prose comedy. Cambridge, Mass. 1960.

Trimpi, Wesley. Jonson's poems: a study of the plain style. Palo Alto, Cal. 1962.

THOMAS KYD (1558 – 1594)

Crawford, Charles. A concordance to the works. 3 pts. Louvain 1906–10 (Bang).

THE SPANISH TRAGEDIE. ?; 1594?; 1602 (*with addns*); ed. W.W.Greg, 1902 (Malone Soc.); ed. Philip Edwards, 1959.
ARDEN OF FEVERSHAM. 1592; ed. Hugh Macdonald, 1947 (Malone Soc.).
A number of anonymous plays, including Arden of Feversham, *as well as the lost* Hamlet, *have been attributed to Kyd.*

Works. Ed. F.S.Boas, Oxford 1901; 1955.

Carrère, Félix. Le théâtre de Kyd. Toulouse 1951.

JOHN LELAND (1506? – 1552)

ASSERTIO ARTURII. 1544; tr. Richard Robinson, 1582; *both* ed. W.E. Mead, 1925 (EETS) (*in* Christopher Middleton, Chinon of England). *A defence of Arthurian legends in reply to Polydore Vergil.*
LABORIOUSE JOURNEY and serche for Englandes antiquitees: a Newe Yeares gyfte to Henry VIII. Ed. John Bale, 1549; 1710 (*with* Itinerary, *below*).
COMMENTARII de scriptoribus britannicis. Ed. Anthony Hall, 1709. *MS. used by Bale for his* Summarium *and* Catalogus.
ITINERARY [*c.* 1535–43]. Ed. Thomas Hearne, 9 vols. Oxford 1710–2; 1745; ed. Lucy Toulmin Smith, 5 vols. 1906–10.
DE REBUS BRITANNICIS COLLECTANEA. Ed. Thomas Hearne, 6 vols. 1715; 1774 (*enlarged*).

SIR DAVID LINDSAY (1485 – 1555)

THE DREME. Edinburgh? 1530?; Rouen 1558.
THE COMPLAYNTE OF A POPINJAY. Edinburgh 1530; tr. London 1538.
    The first Scottish edns (1530) are both lost.
ANE DIALOG betuix experience and ane courteour. St Andrews? 1554?; tr. London 1566.
A HISTORIE of squyer Mildrum. Edinburgh 1594; ed. James Kinsley, Edinburgh 1959.
ANE SATYRE of the thrie estaits. Edinburgh 1602; ed. James Kinsley, 1954. *A morality played before James V in 1540.*

Warkis. Edinburgh 1568; Poetical works, ed. Douglas Hamer, 4 vols. 1931–6 (Scottish Text Soc.).

THOMAS LODGE (1558? – 1625)

[HONEST EXCUSES: a defence of poetry, music and stage plays.] 1579?; ed. David Laing, 1853; ed. G. Gregory Smith, Oxford 1904 (*in* Elizabethan critical essays) (*extracts*). *An unnamed reply to* Stephen Gosson, Schoole of abuse, 1579.

ROSALYNDE: Euphues golden legacie. 1590; ed. W.W. Greg, 1907, 1931. *A novel which served Shakespeare as the source of* As you like it.

A LOOKING GLASSE for London and England by Lodge and Greene. 1594; ed. W.W. Greg, 1932 (Malone Soc.).

PHILLIS: pastorall sonnets. 1593; ed. Sidney Lee, 1904 (*in* Elizabethan sonnets).

A FIG FOR MOMUS: satyres, eclogues and epistles. 1598.

Complete works. Ed. Edmund Gosse, 4 vols. Glasgow 1883.

Paradise, N. Burton. Thomas Lodge. New Haven 1931.

Sisson, C. J. Lodge and his family. *In* Lodge and other Elizabethans, ed. Sisson, Cambridge, Mass. 1933.

RICHARD LOVELACE (1618 – 1657?)

LUCASTA: epodes, odes, sonnets, songs. 1649.

LUCASTA: posthume poems. 1659.

Poems. Ed. C. H. Wilkinson, 2 vols. Oxford 1925, 1 vol. Oxford 1930; ed. R. G. Howarth, 1931 (*in* Minor poets of the seventeenth century) (EL).

JOHN LYLY (1554? – 1606)

EUPHUES: the anatomy of wit. 1578, 1579 (*enlarged*); Euphues and his England, 1580, 2 pts, 2 vols. 1581; ed. Edward Arber, 1868; ed. Morris W. Croll and Harry Clemons, 1916; ed. James Winny, Cambridge 1957 (*in* The descent of Euphues: three Elizabethan romance stories).

ALEXANDER, CAMPASPE AND DIOGENES. 1584; ed. W.W. Greg, 1934 (Malone Soc.). *First of eight comedies.*

SAPHO AND PHAO. 1584.

ENDIMION: the man in the moone. 1591.

GALLATHEA. 1592.

MIDAS. 1592.

MOTHER BOMBIE. 1594; ed. K. M. Lea, 1948 (Malone Soc.).

THE WOMAN IN THE MOONE. 1597.

LOVES METAMORPHOSIS. 1601.

Complete works. Ed. R. Warwick Bond, 3 vols. Oxford 1902.

Dover Wilson, J. John Lyly. Cambridge 1905.

Feuillerat, Albert. John Lyly. Cambridge 1910.

Tilley, Morris P. Elizabethan proverb lore in Euphues and in Pettie's Petite pallace. New York 1926.

Hunter, G. K. Lyly: the humanist as courtier. 1962.

CHRISTOPHER MARLOWE (1564 – 1593)

Crawford, Charles. The Marlowe concordance. 5 pts. Louvain 1911–32 (Bang).

EPIGRAMMES AND ELEGIES. 2 pts. Middelburg (Holland) 1590? *A verse trn of some of Ovid's elegies, with ten of the epigrams tr. Sir John Davies.*

TAMBURLAINE THE GREAT: two tragicall discourses. 1590.

EDWARD THE SECOND. 1594; ed. W. W. Greg, 1926 (Malone Soc.).

THE TRAGEDIE OF DIDO, queene of Carthage, by Marlowe and Nash. 1594; ed. Ronald B. McKerrow, 1904 (*in* Works of Nashe).

HERO AND LEANDER. 1598; 1598 (*with Chapman's continuation*).

THE MASSACRE AT PARIS. 1600?; ed. W. W. Greg, 1929 (Malone Soc.).

THE TRAGICALL HISTORY OF D. FAUSTUS. 1604 (*bad quarto*), ed. A. W. Ward, Oxford 1878, 1901 (*with Greene's* Bacon and Bungay); 1616 (*good quarto*); Parallel texts, ed. W. W. Greg, Oxford 1950; Conjectural reconstruction, ed. Greg, Oxford 1950.

THE RICH JEW OF MALTA. 1633.

Works. Ed. C. F. Tucker Brooke, Oxford 1910; ed. R. H. Case *et al.*, 6 vols. 1930–3, 1955–.

Plays. Oxford 1939 (WC).

Eliot, T. S. Notes on the blank verse of Marlowe. *In his* The sacred wood, 1920.

Ellis-Fermor, Una. Christopher Marlowe. 1927.

Boas, F. S. Marlowe: a biographical and critical study. Oxford 1940; 1953.

Bakeless, John E. The tragicall history of Marlowe. 2 vols. Cambridge, Mass. 1942.

Poirier, Michel. Christopher Marlowe. 1950.

Levin, Harry. The overreacher: a study of Marlowe. Cambridge, Mass. 1952.

Wilson, F. P. Marlowe and the early Shakespeare. Oxford 1953.

Steane, J. B. Marlowe: a critical study. Cambridge 1964.

JOHN MARSTON (1576 – 1634)

THE METAMORPHOSIS of Pigmalions image and certaine satyres. 1598; The scourge of villanie, 1598 (*10 satires*), 1599 (*with addn*), 1599. *Attacks on Joseph Hall.*

ANTONIO AND MELLIDA: the first part. 1602; Antonios revenge: the second part, 1602; 2 pts, ed. W.W.Greg, 1922 (Malone Soc.).

THE MALCONTENT. 1604; 1604 (*with Webster's addns*).

THE DUTCH COURTEZAN. 1605.

PARASITASTER: or the fawne. 1606; 1606.

THE WONDER OF WOMEN: or Sophonisba. 1606.

Marston collaborated with Chapman and Jonson in Eastward hoe! *and perhaps with Dekker in* Satiro-mastix.

Works. Ed. A.H.Bullen, 3 vols. 1887; Plays, ed. H.Harvey Wood, 3 vols. Edinburgh 1934–9; Poems, ed. Arnold Davenport, Liverpool 1961.

Eliot, T.S. *In his* Elizabethan essays, 1934.

Axelrad, A.José. Un malcontent élizabéthain: Marston. Paris 1955.

Peter, John. *In his* Complaint and satire, Oxford 1956.

Caputi, Anthony. John Marston, satirist. Ithaca, N.Y. 1961.

ANDREW MARVELL (1621 – 1678)

THE FIRST ANNIVERSARY of the government under the Lord Protector. 1655.

THE REHEARSAL TRANSPROS'D. 1672, 1672; The second part, 1673. *A reply to* Samuel Parker, Ecclesiastical politie, 1670.

MISCELLANEOUS POEMS. Ed. Mary Palmer ('Mary Marvell'), 1681; Poems, ed. Hugh Macdonald, 1952 (ML).

THE LAST INSTRUCTIONS to a painter. *In* Poems on affairs of state, 1689. *The other satires were also posthumously pbd in collections.*

Works. Ed. A.B.Grosart, 4 vols. 1872–5.

Poems and letters. Ed. H.M.Margoliouth, 2 vols. Oxford 1927; 1952.

Selected poetry and prose. Ed. Dennis Davison, 1952.

Marvell: tercentenary tributes by Birrell, T.S.Eliot, Gosse *et al.* Ed. W.H.Bagguley, Oxford 1922.

Legouis, Pierre. Marvell: poète, puritain, patriote. Paris 1928.

Bradbrook, M.C. and M.G.Lloyd Thomas. Andrew Marvell. Cambridge 1940; 1961.

PHILIP MASSINGER (1583 – 1640)

THE VIRGIN MARTIR: a tragedie. 1622. *With Thomas Dekker.*

THE DUKE OF MILLAINE: a tragedie. 1623.

THE BOND-MAN. 1624; ed. B.T.Spencer, Princeton 1932.

THE ROMAN ACTOR: a tragaedie. 1629; ed. W.L.Sandidge, Princeton 1929.

THE PICTURE: a tragecomedie. 1630.

THE RENEGADO: a tragaecomedie. 1630.

THE EMPEROUR OF THE EAST: a tragaecomoedie. 1632.

THE FATALL DOWRY: a tragedy. 1632. *With Nathaniel Field.*

THE MAID OF HONOUR. 1632.

A NEW WAY TO PAY OLD DEBTS: a comoedie. 1633; ed. A.H.Cruickshank, Oxford 1926.

THE UNNATURALL COMBAT: a tragedie. 1639.

THREE NEW PLAYES. 1655.

BELIEVE AS YOU LIST. Ed. T.Crofton Croker, 1849; ed. C.J.Sisson, 1928 (Malone Soc.).

THE PARLIAMENT OF LOVE. Ed. K.M.Lea, 1929 (Malone Soc.).

Massinger probably collaborated with John Fletcher and may have had a share in Two noble kinsmen *(under Shakespeare, below).*

Plays. Ed. William Gifford, 4 vols. 1805; [Ten plays], ed. Arthur Symons, 2 vols. 1887–9 (Mermaid); [Four plays], ed. L.A. Sherman, New York 1912.

Stephen, Leslie. *In his* Hours in a library, ser. 2, 1876.

Cruickshank, A.H. Philip Massinger. Oxford 1920.

Eliot, T.S. *In his* The sacred wood, 1920. *A review of Cruickshank.*

Chelli, Maurice. Le drame de Massinger. Lyons 1923.

Dunn, T.A. Massinger: the man and the playwright. Edinburgh 1957.

THOMAS MIDDLETON (1580 – 1627)

MICRO-CYNICON: sixe snarling satyres. 1599.

THE GHOST OF LUCRECE. 1600; ed. J.Q.Adams, New York 1937 (*with facs.*). *A continuation of Shakespeare's* Lucrece (1594).

THE HONEST WHORE [pt i]. 1604; 1605. *With Thomas Dekker.*

THE REVENGERS TRAGAEDIE. 1607. *Formerly attributed to Tourneur.*

A TRICKE TO CATCH THE OLD-ONE. 1608.

A MAD WORLD, MY MASTERS. 1608.

THE ROARING GIRLE: or Moll Cut-purse. 1611. *With Dekker.*

A GAME AT CHESSE. 1625; ed. R.C.Bald, Cambridge 1929.

A CHAST MAYD IN CHEAPE-SIDE: a comedy. 1630.

THE CHANGELING. 1653; ed. N.W.Bawcutt, 1958, 1961 (*with addns*). *With William Rowley.*

TWO NEW PLAYES, viz. More dissemblers besides women: a comedy; Women beware women: a tragedy. 1657.

THE MAYOR OF QUINBOROUGH: a comedy. 1661; ed. R.C.Bald, New York 1938 (*entitled* Hengist, King of Kent) (*from MS.*). *A tragedy.*

THE WITCH. 1778; ed. L.Drees and H.de Vocht, Louvain 1945 (Bang); ed. W.W.Greg, 1950 (Malone Soc.).

Middleton also wrote a number of masques.

Works. Ed. Alexander Dyce, 5 vols. 1840; ed. A.H.Bullen, 8 vols. 1885–6; [Ten plays], ed. A.C.Swinburne and Havelock Ellis, 2 vols. 1887–90 (Mermaid).

Eliot, T.S. *In his* For Lancelot Andrewes, 1928.

Schoenbaum, Samuel. Middleton's tragedies: a critical study. New York 1955.

Barker, Richard H. Thomas Middleton. New York 1958.

JOHN MILTON (1608 – 1674)

Bradshaw, John. A concordance to the poetical works. 1894.

Stevens, David H. Reference guide to Milton from 1800. Chicago 1930.

A MASKE presented at Ludlow Castle, 1634. 1637; Cambridge 1906 (*facs.*). '*Comus*'.

LYCIDAS. Cambridge 1638 (*in* Justa Edouardo King); London 1645, 1673 (*in his* Poems, *below*).

EPITAPHIUM DAMONIS. *c.* 1639–40. *Latin elegy on his friend Charles Diodati,* d. *1638.*

OF REFORMATION touching Church discipline. 1641.

THE DOCTRINE and discipline of divorce. 1643; 1643 (*enlarged*).

OF EDUCATION. 1644.

AREOPAGITICA: a speech for the liberty of unlicenc'd printing. 1644; ed. Richard C.Jebb, Cambridge 1918.

Poems, both English and Latin. 1645, Oxford 1924 (*facs.*), ed. Cleanth Brooks and John E.Hardy, New York 1951; 1673. *Includes* On the morning of Christ's nativity, L'allegro, Il penseroso *and reprints* Comus, Lycidas, *above. The MS. at Trinity College, Cambridge, of* Arcades, Comus, Lycidas, *several sonnets etc. has been ed. in facs. by* W.Aldis Wright, Cambridge 1899 *and* Frank A.Patterson, New York 1933.

THE TENURE of kings and magistrates. 1649.

PRO POPULO anglicano defensio. 1650; Defensio secunda, 1654. *Latin pamphlets in reply to Claude de Saumaise (Salmasius), a Fr. controversialist.*

PARADISE LOST: a poem written in ten books. 1667; in twelve books, revised and augmented, 1674; ed. Richard Bentley, 1732; MS. of book i, ed. Helen Darbishire, Oxford 1931 (*with facs.*).

PARADISE REGAIN'D; Samson Agonistes. 1671; Samson Agonistes, ed. F.T.Prince, Oxford 1957.

EPISTOLARUM FAMILIARUM liber unus; Prolusiones oratoriae. 1674; Private correspondence and academic exercises, tr. Phyllis B.Tillyard, ed. E.M.W.Tillyard, Cambridge 1932.

DE DOCTRINA CHRISTIANA. Ed. and tr. C.R.Sumner, 1825 (*from MS.*).

Works: Columbia edition. Ed. Frank A. Patterson *et al.*, 20 vols. New York 1931–40; The student's Milton, ed. Patterson, New York 1930, 1933; Complete poems and major prose, ed. Merritt Y. Hughes, New York, 1957.

Poetical works. Ed. H. C. Beeching, Oxford 1904, 1958 (rev. Helen Darbishire) (OSA); Poems in chronological order, ed. Herbert Grierson, 2 vols. 1925; English poetical works, ed. Charles Williams, Oxford 1940 (WC); Complete poetical works in facsimile, ed. Harris F. Fletcher, 4 vols. Urbana, Ill. 1943–8; Poetical works, ed. Helen Darbishire, 2 vols. Oxford 1952–5.

Latin and Italian poems. Tr. William Cowper, ed. William Hayley, 1808.

Complete prose works. Ed. Don M. Wolfe *et al.*, 8 vols. New Haven 1953–; Prose selected, ed. Malcolm W. Wallace, Oxford 1925 (WC).

Phillips, Edward. The life of Milton. *In* Milton's Letters of state, 1694; ed. Helen Darbishire *in* The early lives of Milton, 1932, *with lives by John Aubrey, John Phillips (?), Anthony Wood, John Toland, Jonathan Richardson.*

Addison, Joseph. [On Paradise lost]. Spectator (Jan.–May 1712); ed. Albert S. Cook, Boston 1892.

Johnson, Samuel. *In his* Lives, 1779–81.

Masson, David. The life of Milton. 7 vols. 1859–94; 1881 (vol. i).

Pattison, Mark. Milton. 1879 (EML).

Raleigh, Walter. Milton. 1900.

Saurat, Denis. Milton: man and thinker. 1925; 1944 (*with addns*).

Hanford, James H. A Milton handbook. New York 1926; 1946.

—— John Milton, Englishman. New York 1949.

Tillyard, E. M. W. Milton. 1930; 1956.

—— The Miltonic setting. 1947.

—— Studies in Milton. 1951.

Eliot, T. S. A note on the verse of Milton. Essays and studies, xxi (1936).

—— Milton. Proc. Brit. Acad. xxxiii (1947). *Both rptd in his* On poetry and poets, 1957.

Lewis, C. S. A preface to Paradise lost. Oxford 1942. *Reply by* Arthur J. A. Waldock, Paradise lost and its critics, Cambridge 1947.

The life records of Milton. Ed. J. Milton French, 5 vols. New Brunswick N. J. 1949–.

Prince, F. T. The Italian element in Milton's verse. Oxford 1954.

Adams, Robert M. Ikon: Milton and the modern critics. Ithaca, N.Y. 1955.

Tuve, Rosemond. Images and themes in five poems by Milton. Cambridge, Mass. 1957.

Broadbent, J.B. Some graver subject: an essay on Paradise lost. 1960.
Empson, William. Milton's God. 1961.
Ricks, Christopher. Milton's grand style. Oxford 1963.

HENRY MORE (1614 – 1687)

ΨΥΧШΔΙΑ PLATONICA, or a Platonicall song of the soul: foure poems. Cambridge 1642; Philosophicall poems, Cambridge 1647 (*enlarged*); ed. Geoffrey Bullough, Manchester 1931 (Psychozoia and minor poems).
AN ANTIDOTE AGAINST ATHEISM. 1652; 1655 (*enlarged*).
ENTHUSIASMUS TRIUMPHATUS: or a discourse of enthusiasme. 1656.
ENCHIRIDION ETHICUM. 1667. *Partly tr. by More in Joseph Glanvill's* Saducismus triumphatus, 1681.
DIVINE DIALOGUES. 1668.

Philosophical writings. 1662; Opera, 3 vols. 1675–9 (*More's Latin trn*); Philosophical writings, ed. F.I. MacKinnon, New York 1925 (*selection*).
Complete poems. Ed. A.B. Grosart, Edinburgh 1878.

Ward, Richard. Life of Henry More. 1710; ed. M.H. Howard, 1911 (*with selection of poems*).
Campagnac, E.T. *In his* The Cambridge Platonists, Oxford 1901.
Powicke, F.J. *In his* The Cambridge Platonists, 1926.

SIR THOMAS MORE (1478 – 1535)

Gibson, R.W. and J. Max Patrick. More: a preliminary bibliography. New Haven 1962.

UTOPIA. Louvain 1516 (*Latin original*); tr. Ralph Robynson, 1551, 1556; ed. J.H. Lupton, Oxford 1895 (*both versions*); ed. George Sampson and A.C. Guthkelch, 1910 (*both versions*).
EPIGRAMMATA. Basle 1518; ed. and tr. Leicester Bradner and Charles A. Lynch, Chicago 1953.
A DYALOGE OF THYNGES touchyng Luther and Tyndale. 1529; 1530. *Reply by Tindale,* An answere unto More's Dialoge, 1530, *and by More,* Confutacyon, *2 pts.* 1532–3.
APOLOGYE. 1533; ed. Arthur I. Taft, 1930 (EETS).
A DIALOGE OF COMFORT AGAINST TRIBULACION. 1553; 1910, 1951 (EL) (*with* Utopia).
HISTORY OF RICHARD THE THIRDE. 1544 (*in Hardyng's* Chronicle); 1548 (*in Hall's* Chronicle); 1557 (*in* Workes, *below*); 1565 (*Latin text in* Omnia opera, *below*); ed. J.R. Lumby, Cambridge 1883 (*English version*). *Both versions probably by More, the English probably the first.*
Workes in Englysh. Ed. William Rastell, 1557; ed. W.E. Campbell and A.W. Reed, 2 vols. 1927–31 (*with facs.*) (*7 vols. projected*).

Lucubrationes. Basle 1563; Omnia opera, Louvain 1565.

Poems. Ed. Sidney Lee, 1906 (*from* Workes).

Selections. Ed. P.S. and H.M.Allen, Oxford 1924.

English prayers. Ed. P.E.Hallett, 1938.

Correspondence. Ed. Elizabeth F.Rogers, Princeton 1947; Selected letters, ed. Rogers, New Haven 1961.

Roper, William. The mirrour of vertue: or the life of More. Paris 1625; ed. E.V.Hitchcock, 1935 (EETS); ed. Richard S.Sylvester and Davis P.Harding, New Haven 1962 (*with* George Cavendish, The life and death of Cardinal Wolsey); ed. Sylvester, 1959 (EETS) (*from MS.*).

Ba., Ro. The lyfe of More. Ed. Christopher Wordsworth, 1810 (*in* Ecclesiastical biography); ed. E.V.Hitchcock and P.E.Hallett, 1950 (EETS).

Campbell, W.E. More's Utopia and his social teaching. 1930.

Harpsfield, Nicholas. The life and death of Moore. Ed. E.V.Hitchcock, 1932 (EETS). *A biography written in 1557.*

Chambers, R.W. Thomas More. 1935.

Donner, H.W. Introduction to Utopia. 1945.

de Vocht, H. Acta Mori: history of the reports of his trial and death. Louvain 1947.

Hexter, J.H. Utopia: the biography of an idea. Princeton 1952.

THOMAS NASHE (1567 – 1601?)

THE UNFORTUNATE TRAVELLER. 1594; 1594; ed. H.F.B.Brett-Smith, Oxford 1920.

A PLEASANT COMEDIE called Summers last will and testament. 1600.

Nashe also collaborated with Marlowe in The tragedie of Dido, 1594.

Works. Ed. Ronald B.McKerrow, 5 vols. 1904–10; Oxford 1958 (rev. F.P.Wilson) (*with supplement*).

Hibbard, G.R. Nashe: a critical introduction. 1962.

GEORGE PEELE (1557? – 1596)

THE ARAYGNEMENT OF PARIS: a pastorall. 1584; ed. H.H.Child, 1910 (Malone Soc.).

EDWARDE THE FIRST. 1593; ed. W.W.Greg, 1907 (Malone Soc.).

THE BATTELL OF ALCAZAR. 1594; ed. W.W.Greg, 1907 (Malone Soc.).

THE OLD WIVES TALE: a comedie. 1595; ed. W.W.Greg, 1909 (Malone Soc.).

DAVID AND BETHSABE. 1599; ed. W.W.Greg, 1913 (Malone Soc.).

A number of plays, including Shakespeare's Henry VI *and* Titus Andronicus, *have been partly attributed to Peele.*

Works. Ed. A.H.Bullen, 2 vols. 1888; Life and works, ed. C.T. Prouty *et al.* New Haven 1952–.

PRAYER BOOK

THE BOOKE OF COMMON PRAYER. Ed. Thomas Cranmer, 1549, ed. J. Parker, 1883; 1552 (*a Puritan revision*), ed. Parker, 1883; 1559 (*Elizabethan version*); 1662 (*restored version*).

THE BOOKE OF COMMON PRAYER for the use of Church of Scotland. 1637; ed. J.Dowden, Edinburgh 1884 (*facs.*).

Procter, Francis. History of the Book of Common Prayer. 1855; 1901, 1902 (rev. Walter H.Frere).

Clarke, W.K.Lowther *et al.* Liturgy and worship: a companion to the Prayer Books. 1932.

Morison, Stanley. English prayer books. Cambridge 1943; 1949 (*enlarged*).

Donaldson, Gordon. The making of the Scottish Prayer Book of 1637. Edinburgh 1954.

GEORGE PUTTENHAM (*c.* 1530 – 1590)

THE ARTE OF ENGLISH POESIE. 1589; ed. G.Gregory Smith, Oxford 1904 (*in* Elizabethan critical essays); ed. Gladys D.Willcock and Alice Walker, Cambridge 1936. *Probably by Puttenham.*

FRANCIS QUARLES (1592 – 1644)

Horden, John. Quarles: a bibliography to 1800. Proc. Oxford Bibliog. Soc. new ser. ii (1953).

ARGALUS AND PARTHENIA. 1629.

DIVINE POEMS. 1630; 1634 (*enlarged*).

DIVINE FANCIES. 1632.

EMBLEMES. 1635; Hieroglyphikes of the life of man, 1638, 1639 (*with* Emblemes).

ENCHYRIDION. 1640; 1641 (*enlarged*).

Collected works. Ed. A.B.Grosart, 3 vols. 1880–1.

Praz, Mario. *In his* Studi sul concettismo, Milan 1934; tr. 2 vols. 1939–47 (*enlarged*).

Freeman, Rosemary. *In her* English emblem books, 1948.

SIR WALTER RALEGH (1552? – 1618)

Brushfield, T.N. A bibliography of Raleigh. Plymouth 1886; Exeter 1908 (*enlarged*).

THE REPORT OF THE FIGHT about the Açores. 1591; 1598 (*in Hakluyt's* Voyages).

THE DISCOVERIE OF GUIANA. 1596; 1598 (*in Hakluyt's* Voyages).

A HISTORIE OF THE WORLD. 1614; 1617; ed. William Oldys, 2 vols. 1736; Selections, ed. G.E.Hadow, Oxford 1917.

CYNTHIA. Ed. John Hannah, 1870 (*in* The courtly poets) (*from MS.*); ed. Walter Oakeshott, 1960 (*in his* The queen and the poet).
16 Ralegh poems appeared in The phoenix nest, 1593.

Remains. 10 vols. 1651; Works, 8 vols. Oxford 1829.

Poems. Ed. S.Egerton Brydges, 1813 (*from* Remains); ed. John Hannah, 1870; ed. Agnes M.C.Latham, 1929, 1951 (ML); ed. Gerald Bullett, 1947 (EL) (*in* Silver poets of the sixteenth century).

Oldys, William. Life of Raleigh. 1736 (*in* Historie, *above*).

Stebbing, William. Ralegh: a biography. 1891; 1899.

Bradbrook, M.C. The school of night: a study of the literary relationships of Ralegh. Cambridge 1936.

Strathmann, Ernest A. Ralegh: a study in Elizabethan skepticism. New York 1951.

Edwards, Philip. Sir Walter Ralegh. 1953.

Rowse, A.L. Ralegh and the Throckmortons. 1962.

THOMAS SACKVILLE, 1st EARL OF DORSET AND BARON BUCKHURST (1536 – 1608)

A MYRROURE FOR MAGISTRATES. Ed William Baldwin, 1559; 1563 (*enlarged*); 1571; The first parte, ed. John Higgins, 1587 (*with addns by Higgins*); The seconde part, by Thomas Blenerhasset, 1578; The mirour, ed. John Higgins, 1587 (*collected and enlarged*); ed. Richard Niccols, 1610 (*enlarged*); ed. Lily B.Campbell, 2 vols. Cambridge 1938–46. *The* Induction *and the* Complaint of Henry Duke of Buckingham *were contributed to 1559 by Sackville, ed. Marguerite Hearsey, New Haven 1936 (from MS.).*

THE TRAGEDIE OF GORBODUC. 1565; ed. J.W.Cunliffe, Oxford 1912 (*in* Early English classical tragedies). *First known English tragedy, with Thomas Norton.*

GEORGE SANDYS (1578 – 1644)

Bowers, Fredson and Richard B.Davis. Sandys: a bibliographical catalogue of printed editions to 1700. New York 1950.

OVIDS METAMORPHOSIS. 1621 (*bks i–v*) (*lost*); 1626 (*complete*): Oxford 1632 (*with* The first booke of Virgil's Aeneis).

A PARAPHRASE upon the Psalmes. 1636; 1638 (*re-entitled* A paraphrase upon the Divine Poems) (*enlarged*). *The text of* Henry Lawes, Chosen psalmes put into music, 1648.

A PARAPHRASE upon the Song of Solomon. 1641.

Poetical works. Ed. Richard Hooper, 2 vols. 1872.

Davis, Richard B. Sandys: poet-adventurer. 1955.

WILLIAM SHAKESPEARE (1564 – 1616)

Bartlett, John. A concordance to the dramatic works, with a supplementary concordance to the poems. 1894.

Onions, C. T. A Shakespeare glossary. Oxford 1911; 1953.

Bartlett, Henrietta C. and A. W. Pollard. A census of Shakespeare's plays in quarto, 1594–1709. New Haven 1916; 1939 (*enlarged*).

Ebisch, Walther and Levin L. Schücking. A Shakespeare bibliography. Oxford 1931; Supplement 1930–5, Oxford 1937.

Halliday, F. E. A Shakespeare companion, 1550–1950. 1952.

Annual bibliographies in Shakespeare survey, 1– (1948–) *and in* The Shakespeare quarterly, 1– (1950–).

Plays in order of composition according to Chambers; modern edns are listed in collections only, below.

[HENRY VI, pts i, ii and iii]. The first part of the contention betwixt the houses of Yorke and Lancaster. 1594 (pt ii) (*bad quarto*), 1623 (*in first folio*); The tragedie of Richard of Yorke, 1595 (pt iii) (*bad octavo*); 1623 (*in first folio*); pt i, 1623 (*in first folio*).

THE TRAGEDY of Richard the third. 1597; 1623 (*in first folio*).

THE COMEDY OF ERRORS. 1623 (*in first folio*).

THE TRAGEDIE of Titus Andronicus. 1594 (*good quarto*); 1623 (*with addn*) (*in first folio*). *With Peele?*

THE TAMING OF THE SHREW. 1623 (*in first folio*). The taming of a shrew, *probably a bad quarto of this play, was pbd in 1594.*

THE TWO GENTLEMEN OF VERONA. 1623 (*in first folio*).

LOVES LABORS LOST. 1596? (*lost*); 1598 (*good quarto*).

ROMEO AND JULIET. 1597 (*bad quarto*); 1599 (*good quarto*).

THE TRAGEDIE of Richard the second. 1597 (*good quarto*); 1608 (*with addn*).

A MIDSOMMER NIGHTS DREAME. 1600 (*good quarto*).

KING JOHN. 1623 (*in first folio*). *Perhaps based on the anon. play* The troublesome raigne of John, 2 pts. 1591.

THE MERCHANT OF VENICE. 1600 (*good quarto*).

THE HISTORIE of Henrie the fourth. 1598 (*good quarto*); The second part, 1600 (*good quarto*).

MUCH ADOE ABOUT NOTHING. 1600 (*good quarto*).

THE HISTORY of Henry the fift. 1600 (*bad quarto*); 1623 (*in first folio*).

JULIUS CAESAR. 1623 (*in first folio*).

AS YOU LIKE IT. 1623 (*in first folio*).

TWELFE NIGHT: or what you will. 1623 (*in first folio*).

HAMLET. 1603 (*bad quarto*); 1604–5 (*good quarto*); 1623 (*in first folio*).

A COMEDIE OF FALSTAFFE and the merrie wives of Windsor. 1602 (*bad quarto*); 1623 (*in first folio*).

THE HISTORIE of Troylus and Cresseida. 1609 (*good quarto*); 1623 (*in first folio*).

ALLS WELL, THAT ENDS WELL. 1623 (*in first folio*).

MEASURE FOR MEASURE. 1623 (*in first folio*).

OTHELLO, the Moore of Venice. 1622 (*good quarto, with omissions*); 1623 (*in first folio*).

KING LEAR. 1608 (*quarto, with omissions*); 1623 (*in first folio*).

MACBETH. 1623 (*in first folio*).

ANTHONY AND CLEOPATRA. 1623 (*in first folio*).

CORIOLANUS. 1623 (*in first folio*).

TIMON OF ATHENS. 1623 (*in first folio*).

CYMBELINE. 1623 (*in first folio*).

THE WINTERS TALE. 1623 (*in first folio*).

THE TEMPEST. 1623 (*in first folio*).

THE LIFE OF KING HENRY THE EIGHT. 1623 (*in first folio*). *Perhaps with John Fletcher.*

PERICLES. 1609 (*bad quarto*); 1664 (*in third folio*).

Facs. of many of the quartos have been pbd 1880–91, 1939– (Shakespeare Assoc.) and Oxford 1956–.

Attributed plays:

ARDEN OF FEVERSHAM. 1592; ed. Hugh Macdonald, 1947 (Malone Soc.). *Perhaps by Kyd.*

A YORKSHIRE TRAGEDY, written by Shakespeare. 1608; 1619. *Perhaps by Thomas Heywood.*

THE TWO NOBLE KINSMEN, by John Fletcher and Shakespeare. 1634.

THE BOOKE OF SIR THOMAS MOORE. Ed. Alexander Dyce, 1844; ed. W. W. Greg, 1911 (Malone Soc.).

Shakespeare apocrypha. Ed. C. F. Tucker Brooke, Oxford 1908.

Poems:

VENUS AND ADONIS. 1593; 1594.

LUCRECE. 1594.

THE PASSIONATE PILGRIME. 1599; 1612 (*with Heywood's* Love-epistles).

THE PHOENIX AND TURTLE. *In* Loves martyr, translated by Robert Chester, 1601; 1611 (*re-entitled* The annals of Great Brittaine).

SONNETS. 1609; 1640 (*in* Poems).

Comedies, histories and tragedies. Ed. John Heminge and Henry Condell, 1623; 1910 (*facs.*); ed. Helge Kökeritz and C.T.Prouty, New Haven 1955 (*facs.*). *First folio. The second, third and fourth folios were pbd in 1632, 1663–4 and 1685.*
Works. Ed. Nicholas Rowe, 7 vols. 1709–10.
Works. Ed. Alexander Pope, 6 vols. 1725; 10 vols. 1728 (*enlarged*); ed. Lewis Theobald, 7 vols. 1733; ed. William Warburton, 8 vols. 1747.
Plays. Ed. Samuel Johnson, 8 vols. 1765; 10 vols. 1773, 1778 (rev. George Steevens).
Plays and poems. Ed. Edmond Malone, 10 vols. 1790.
Variorum edition of the works. Ed. H.H.Furness *et al.*, Philadelphia 1871–.
Plays and poems in quarto. Ed. F.J.Furnivall *et al.*, 43 vols. 1880–91 (*facs.*).
Works. Ed. W.J.Craig, Oxford 1891 (OSA).
The Arden Shakespeare. Ed. W.J.Craig, R.H.Case *et al.*, 37 vols. 1899–1924; ed. Una Ellis-Fermor *et al.* 1951– (New Arden).
The Yale Shakespeare. Ed. Wilbur L.Cross, C.F.Tucker Brooke *et al.*, 40 vols. New Haven 1918–28.
Works. Ed. Arthur Quiller-Couch and J.Dover Wilson, Cambridge 1921– (New Cambridge).
Works. Ed. Herbert Farjeon, 7 vols. 1929–34 (Nonesuch Press).
Complete works. Ed. Peter Alexander, 1951.
Complete works. Ed. C.J.Sisson, 1954; New readings in Shakespeare, 2 vols. Cambridge 1956.
The London Shakespeare. Ed. John Munro, 6 vols. 1958.
For a collection of the sources and analogues of the plays see Narrative and dramatic sources of Shakespeare, ed. Geoffrey Bullough, 5 vols. 1957–. *See Muir, below.*

Johnson, Samuel. Preface. 1765 (*in his edn of the* Plays); Johnson on Shakespeare: essays and notes, ed. Walter Raleigh, Oxford 1908, 1925.
Morgann, Maurice. An essay on the dramatic character of Falstaff. 1777; ed. D.Nichol Smith, Glasgow 1903, Oxford 1963 (*in* Eighteenth-century essays on Shakespeare).
Hazlitt, William. Characters of Shakespeare's plays. 1817.
Coleridge, S.T. Notes and lectures upon Shakespeare. Ed. Sara Coleridge, 2 vols. 1849; Shakespearean criticism, ed. T.M.Raysor, 2 vols. Cambridge, Mass. 1930.
Dowden, Edward. Shakspere: his mind and art. 1874.
Boas, F.S. Shakspere and his predecessors. 1896.
Bradley, A.C. Shakespearean tragedy. 1904; 1905.
Raleigh, Walter. Shakespeare. 1907.

Adams, J.Q. A life of Shakespeare. Boston 1923.

Chambers, E.K. Shakespeare: a survey. 1925.

—— Shakespeare: a study of facts and problems. 2 vols. Oxford 1930; 1 vol. Oxford 1933 (abridged by Charles Williams).

Granville-Barker, Harley. Prefaces to Shakespeare. 5 sers. 1927–48; 2 vols. Princeton 1946–7.

—— and G.B.Harrison. Companion to Shakespeare studies. Cambridge 1934.

Stoll, Elmer E. Shakespeare studies. New York 1927; 1942.

—— Art and artifice in Shakespeare. New York 1933.

Wilson Knight, G. The wheel of fire: Shakespeare's sombre tragedies. Oxford 1930, 1949 (*with addns*); The imperial theme, Oxford 1931, 1951; The crown of life: Shakespeare's final plays, Oxford 1947.

Spurgeon, Caroline F.E. Shakespeare's imagery and what it tells us. Cambridge 1935.

Clemen, Wolfgang H. Shakespeares Bilder. Bonn 1936; tr. and rev. 1951 (The development of Shakespeare's imagery).

Greg, W.W. The editorial problem in Shakespeare. Oxford 1942; 1954.

—— The Shakespeare first folio. Oxford 1955.

Tillyard, E.M.W. Shakespeare's history plays. 1944.

Muir, Kenneth. Shakespeare's sources. 2 vols. 1957–.

Holloway, John. The story of the night: studies in Shakespeare's major tragedies. 1961.

Leishman, J.B. Themes and variations in Shakespeare's sonnets. 1961.

Rossiter, A.P. Angel with horns and other Shakespeare lectures. Ed. Graham Storey, 1961.

Shakespeare criticism: a selection, 1623–1840. Ed. D.Nichol Smith, Oxford 1916 (WC); Shakespeare criticism, 1919–35, ed. Anne Ridler, Oxford 1936 (WC).

Shakespeare and his critics. Ed. F.E.Halliday, 1949. *Includes an anthology of Shakespeare criticism. See* Augustus J.Ralli, A history of Shakespearian criticism, 2 vols. Oxford 1932.

JAMES SHIRLEY (1596–1666)

THE WEDDING. 1629. *First of 31 extant plays.*

THE WITTIE FAIRE ONE: a comedie. 1633.

THE TRAYTOR: a tragedie. 1635.

HIDE PARK: a comedie. 1637.

THE GAMESTER. 1637.

THE YOUNG ADMIRALL. 1637.

THE LADY OF PLEASURE. 1637.

POEMS. 1646.

SIX NEW PLAYES. 1653.

Dramatic works and poems. Ed. William Gifford and Alexander Dyce, 6 vols. 1833; [Six plays]. ed. Edmund Gosse, 1888 (Mermaid).

Nason, Arthur H. Shirley: a biographical and critical study. New York 1915.

SIR PHILIP SIDNEY (1554 – 1586)

THE COUNTESSE OF PEMBROKES ARCADIA. 1590 (*rev. version of bks i, ii and part of iii*); augmented and ended, 1593 (*adds bks iii–v*), ed. Ernest A.Baker, 1907 (*modernized*); *1577–80 MS. version*, ed. Albert Feuillerat, Cambridge 1926 (*in* Complete works, *below*).

ASTROPHEL AND STELLA. 1591; 1598 (*with* Arcadia *etc.*); ed. Sidney Lee, 1904 (*in* Elizabethan sonnets).

THE DEFENCE OF POESIE. 1595; 1595 (*entitled* The apologie for poetrie); ed. G.Gregory Smith, Oxford 1904 (*in* Elizabethan critical essays); ed. J.Churton Collins, Oxford 1907.

THE PSALMES translated into verse, begun by Sidney and finished by the Countess of Pembroke. 1823; ed. J.C.A.Rathmell, New York 1963.

Arcadia, with sundry new additions. 1598 (*with* Astrophel, *the* Defence *etc.*), 1655 (*enlarged*); Complete works, ed. Albert Feuillerat, 4 vols. Cambridge 1912–26, 1962; Poems, ed. William A.Ringler, Oxford 1962.

Greville, Fulke. The life of Sidney. 1652.
Wallace, Malcolm W. The life of Sidney. Cambridge 1915.
Zandvoort, R.W. Arcadia: a comparison between the two versions. Amsterdam 1929.
Wilson, Mona. Sir Philip Sidney. 1931; 1950.
Buxton, John. Sidney and the English Renaissance. 1954; 1964.
Boas, F.S. Sidney, representative Elizabethan: his life and writings. 1955.

JOHN SKELTON (1460? – 1529)

THE BOWGE OF COURTE. *c.* 1495–1500; 1945 (*facs.*).
BALETTYS AND DYTIES. *c.* 1525–30.
AGAINSTE A COMELY COYSTROWNE. *c.* 1525–30.
MAGNYFYCENCE: a goodly interlude. *c.* 1529–32; ed. R.L.Ramsay, 1908 (EETS).
COLLYN CLOUT. *c.* 1532–7.
PHYLLYP SPAROWE. *c.* 1542–6.
WHY COME YE NAT TO COURTE. *c.* 1542–6.
SPEKE PARROT. *c.* 1542–8.
HOW EDWARD [IV] SODAINLY DIED. *In* A myrroure for magistrates, ed. Thomas Baldwin, 1559. *See under Sackville, above.*

Workes. Ed. John Stow?, 1568; Poetical works, ed. Alexander Dyce, 2 vols. 1843; Complete poems, ed. Philip Henderson, 1931, 1959. *A selection ed. Robert Graves, 1927.*

BIBLIOTHECA HISTORICA of Diodorus Siculus. Ed. F.M.Salter and H.L.R.Edwards, 2 vols. 1956–7 (EETS). *A trn from a 1449 Latin version of the Greek.*

Auden, W.H. *In* The great Tudors, ed. Katharine Garvin, 1935.
Nelson, William. Skelton, laureate. New York 1939.
Gordon, I.A. Skelton, poet laureate. Melbourne 1943.
Edwards, H.L.R. John Skelton. 1949.

ROBERT SOUTHWELL (1561? – 1595)

SAINT PETERS COMPLAYNT, with other poems. 1595; 1602 (*enlarged*).
MAEONIAE: poems and hymns. 1595.
THE TRIUMPHS OVER DEATH. 1595; ed. J.W.Trotman, 1914 (*from MS.*).
AN HUMBLE SUPPLICATION to Her Majestie. 1600 ('1595'); ed. R.C. Bald, Cambridge 1953.
A FOURE-FOULD MEDITATION of the foure last things: a divine poeme by R.S. 1606. *Now attributed to his patron Philip, Earl of Arundel.*

Complete poems. Ed. A.B.Grosart, 1872.
Prose works. Ed. W.J.Walter, 1828.

Devlin, Christopher. Southwell: poet and martyr. 1956.

EDMUND SPENSER (1552? – 1599)

Osgood, C.G. A concordance to the poems. Washington 1915.
Whitman, Charles H. A subject-index to the poems of Spenser. New Haven 1918.
Carpenter, Frederic I. A reference guide to Spenser. Chicago 1923; Dorothy F.Atkinson, Supplement, Baltimore 1937.
Johnson, Francis R. A critical bibliography of Spenser before 1700. Baltimore 1933.

THE SHEPHEARDES CALENDER, conteyning twelve aeglogues. 1579.
THREE LETTERS between two Universitie men. 1580 (*letter i, dated April 1580, by Spenser, ii–iii by Gabriel Harvey*); Two other letters, 1580 (*letter i, 5 Oct. 1579, by Spenser, ii by Harvey*); ed. G. Gregory Smith, Oxford 1904 (*in* Elizabethan critical essays) (*extracts*).
THE FAERIE QUEENE. 1590 (*bks i–iii*); 2 vols. 1596 (*i–vi*); 1 vol. 1609 (*adds fragment of vii*).
COMPLAINTS. 1591. *Includes* The ruines of time, The teares of the Muses, Virgils gnat, Mother Hubberds tale, The ruines of Rome *etc.*

DAPHNAÏDA: an elegie upon Douglas Howard. 1591; 1596 (*with* Fowre hymnes, *below*).

AMORETTI; and EPITHALAMION. 1595; 1927 (*facs.*).

COLIN CLOUTS COME HOME AGAINE. 1595. *With elegies on Sidney by other hands.*

FOWRE HYMNES. 1596.

PROTHALAMION. 1596.

A VIEW of the present state of Ireland. Ed. James Ware, Dublin 1633.

The faerie queen and other works. 7 pts (*for 1 folio vol.*) 1611–13; Poetical works, ed. J.C. Smith and E. de Selincourt, 3 vols. Oxford 1909–10, 1 vol. 1912 (OSA); Works: a variorum edition, ed. Edwin Greenlaw, C.G. Osgood, F.M. Padelford *et al.*, 9 vols. Baltimore 1932–49, Index, Baltimore 1957.

[Minor works]. Ed. W.L. Renwick, 4 vols. 1928–34.

Warton, Thomas (1728–90). Observations on The faerie queene. 1754; 2 vols. 1762 (*enlarged*).

Hurd, Richard. *In his* Letters on chivalry and romance, 1762; ed. Edith J. Morley, 1911.

Renwick, W.L. Edmund Spenser. 1925.

Jones, H.S.V. A Spenser handbook. New York 1930.

Spens, Janet. Spenser's Faerie queene: an interpretation. 1934.

Lewis, C.S. *In his* The allegory of love, Oxford 1936.

Judson, Alexander C. The life of Spenser. Baltimore 1945 (*in* Works: a variorum edition, *above*).

Hamilton, A.C. The structure of allegory in The faerie queene. Oxford 1961.

Hough, Graham. A preface to The faerie queene. 1962.

SIR JOHN SUCKLING (1609 – 1642)

AGLAURA. 1638.

THE DISCONTENTED COLONELL. 1640?; 1646 (*re-entitled* Brennoralt) (*in* Fragmenta, *below*).

Fragmenta aurea: a collection. 4 pts. 1646; 1658. 1646 *adds to the two tragedies, above*, Poems *and the comedy* The goblins. 1658 *adds* Last remains, *i.e. poems, letters and the unfinished tragedy* The sad one.

Works. 1676; 1696 (*adds the four plays*); ed. A. Hamilton Thompson, 1910.

[Poems]. Ed. R.G. Howarth, 1931, 1953 (EL) (*in* Minor poets of the seventeenth century).

HENRY HOWARD, EARL OF SURREY (1517? – 1547)

SONGES AND SONETTES by Surrey and other. Ed. Richard Tottel,
1557; 1557; ed. Hyder E.Rollins, 2 vols. Cambridge, Mass. 1928–9.
Includes 40 poems attributed to Surrey.

CERTAIN BOKES [ii and iv] of Virgiles Aenaeis turned into English meter.
1557; Fourth boke, ed. Herbert Hartman, Oxford 1933 (*with facs.*).
First blank verse in English.

Poems. Ed. F.M.Padelford, Seattle 1920, 1928; ed. Emrys Jones,
Oxford 1964.

JEREMY TAYLOR (1613 – 1667)

THE GREAT EXEMPLAR OF SANCTITY. 1649.

THE RULE AND EXERCISES of holy living. 1650, ed. A.R.Waller, 2 vols.
1900; Of holy dying, 1651, 1656 (*with* Holy living).

XXVIII SERMONS preached at Golden Grove. 1651; XXV sermons, 1653.

THE GOLDEN GROVE: or a manuall of daily prayers and letanies. 1655.

DUCTOR DUBITANTIUM: or the rule of conscience. 2 vols. 1660.

Opuscula. 1675.

Whole works. Ed. Reginald Heber, 15 vols. 1822; 10 vols. 1847–52
(rev. Charles P.Eden).

Poems and verse-translations. Ed. A.B.Grosart, 1870.

The golden grove: selected passages. Ed. Logan Pearsall Smith,
Oxford 1930.

Heber, Reginald. The life of Taylor. 1822; 1854 (*in* Whole works,
above).

Gosse, Edmund. Jeremy Taylor. 1904 (EML).

Stranks, C.J. The life and writings of Taylor. 1952.

WILLIAM TINDALE (1494? – 1536)

[NEW TESTAMENT: the Cologne fragment]. Cologne 1525 (*c. 40 leaves,
suppressed*), ed. A.W.Pollard, Oxford 1926; Worms 1525 (1526?)
(*complete*), ed. Francis Fry, Bristol 1862 (*facs.*); Antwerp 1534, ed.
N. Hardy Wallis, Cambridge 1938; Antwerp 1535 (*second revision*).

THE OBEDIENCE of a Christen man. Antwerp? 1528; ed. H.Walter, 1848
(*in* Doctrinal treatises).

AN ANSWERE unto Sir T.More's Dialoge. Antwerp? 1530; ed. H.Walter,
1850.

THE PRACTYSE OF PRELATES. Antwerp? 1530.

AN EXPOSICION UPON MATHEW. Antwerp? 1530?; Of the fyrste epistle of
Jhon, Antwerp 1531; Of the epistles of Jhon, 1538.

JONAS. Antwerp? 1531?; ed. Francis Fry, Bristol 1863 (*facs.*). *Tindale tr. the O.T. as far as Chronicles; the material was used in Matthew's Bible, 1537.*

[PENTATEUCH]. Marburg 1531; 1534 (Genesis *rev.*); ed. J.I. Mombert, New York 1884.

THE RIGHT INSTITUTION of the sacraments. 1533?

Whole workes of Tyndall, John Frith and Doct. Barnes. Ed. John Foxe, 2 vols. 1573; Works, 3 vols. 1848–50.

Demaus, Robert. Tyndale: a biography. 1872; 1886 (rev. R. Lovett). Mozley, J.F. William Tyndale. 1937.

CYRIL TOURNEUR (1575? – 1626)

THE ATHEIST'S TRAGEDIE. 1611.
  The revengers tragaedie (1607) *is now attributed to Middleton.*

Plays and poems. Ed. J. Churton Collins, 2 vols. 1878; Complete works, ed. Allardyce Nicoll, 1930.

Eliot, T.S. *In his* Elizabethan essays, 1934.
Peter, John. *In his* Complaint and satire, Oxford 1956.

THOMAS TRAHERNE (1637 – 1674)

ROMAN FORGERIES. 1673.
CHRISTIAN ETHICKS. 1675.
POETICAL WORKS. Ed. Bertram Dobell, 1903 (*from MS.*).
CENTURIES OF MEDITATIONS. Ed. Bertram Dobell, 1908 (*from MS.*).
POEMS OF FELICITY. Ed. H.I. Bell, Oxford 1910 (*from MS.*). *Includes 39 poems not in* Poetical works, *above.*

Centuries, poems and thanksgivings. Ed. H.M. Margoliouth, 2 vols. Oxford 1958.
Poetical works. Ed. Gladys I. Wade, 1932.

Wade, Gladys I. Thomas Traherne. Princeton 1944; 1946.

NICHOLAS UDALL (1505 – 1556)

RALPH ROISTER DOISTER. 1577?; ed. W.W. Greg, 1935 (Malone Soc.); ed. G. Scheurweghs, Louvain 1939 (Bang). *First known English comedy.*

RESPUBLICA. Ed. John Payne Collier, 1866 (*in* Illustrations of old English literature); ed. W.W. Greg, 1952 (EETS). *An interlude of 1553 attributed to Udall.*

Dramatic writings. Ed. John S. Farmer, 1906.

SIR THOMAS URQUHART (1611 – 1660)

EPIGRAMS, DIVINE AND MORAL. 1641.

THE DISCOVERY of a most exquisite jewel. 1652. *Includes* The admirable Crichtoun, ed. Hamish Miles, Paris 1927.

THE FIRST BOOK of the works of Mr Francis Rabelais, translated into English. 1653; The second book, 1653; The third book, 1693 (*in* Works, *below*).

Works of Rabelais. 5 bks. 1693–4 (rev. and concluded (bks iv–v) by Peter Motteux); ed. Charles Whibley, 3 vols. 1900.

Tracts. Edinburgh 1774; Works [*excluding* Rabelais], ed. Thomas Maitland, Edinburgh 1834.

A challenge from Urquhart. Ed. C.H.Wilkinson, Oxford 1948.

HENRY VAUGHAN the Silurist (1622 – 1695)

Marilla, E.L. A comprehensive bibliography of Vaughan. Tuscaloosa, Ala. 1948.

POEMS, with the tenth satyre of Juvenal englished. 1646.

SILEX SCINTILLANS: sacred poems and private ejaculations. 1650; 1655 (*with bk ii*).

OLOR ISCANUS: select poems and translations. 1651.

THE MOUNT OF OLIVES: or solitary devotions. 1652; ed. Louise I. Guiney, 1902.

THALIA REDIVIVA. 1678.

Poems. Ed. E.K.Chambers, 2 vols. 1896 (ML).

Complete works. Ed. A.B.Grosart, 4 vols. 1870–1; Works, ed. L.C. Martin, 2 vols. Oxford 1914, 1 vol. Oxford 1958; Poetry and selected prose, ed. Martin, Oxford 1963 (OSA).

Blunden, Edmund. On the poems of Vaughan, with his principal Latin poems translated into English verse. 1927.

Holmes, Elizabeth. Vaughan and the Hermetic philosophy. Oxford 1932.

Hutchinson, F.E. Vaughan: a life and interpretation. Oxford 1947.

Pettet, E.C. Of paradise and light: a study of Vaughan's Silex scintillans. Cambridge 1960.

EDMUND WALLER (1606 – 1687)

POEMS. 1645; 1645; 1664; 1668 (*enlarged*); The second part, ed. Francis Atterbury, 1690. *Sixteen of the poems, including* Go, lovely rose!, *were first pbd in the third edn of the anthology* Witts recreations, 1645.

A PANEGYRICK to my Lord Protector. 1655.
THE PASSION OF DIDO. 1658. *With Sidney Godolphin.*
DIVINE POEMS. 1685.

Works. Ed. Elijah Fenton, 1729.
Poems. Ed. G.Thorn Drury, 1893; 2 vols. 1905 (ML).

Johnson, Samuel. *In his* Lives, 1779–81.

IZAAK WALTON (1593 – 1683)

Butt, John. A bibliography of Walton's Lives [to 1700]. Proc. Oxford
Bibliog. Soc. ii (1930).

THE LIFE and death of Dr Donne. 1640 (*in Donne's* LXXX sermons);
1658 (*enlarged*).
THE LIFE of Sir Henry Wotton. 1651; 1654; 1672 (*all in edns of*
Reliquiae Wottonianae).
THE COMPLEAT ANGLER: a discourse of fish and fishing. 1653; 1655;
1661 (*both enlarged*); The universal angler, 1676 (*enlarged, with*
Cotton's pt ii); ed. R.B.Marston, 2 vols. 1888; 1 vol. Oxford 1935
(WC). *For an anon. source see* The arte of angling, 1577, ed. Gerald
E.Bentley *et al.*, Princeton 1956.
THE LIFE of Mr Rich. Hooker. 1665; 1666 (*in Hooker's* Works,
enlarged). *See under Hooker, above.*
THE LIFE of Mr George Herbert. 1670; 1674 (*in Herbert's* Temple).
THE LIFE of Dr [Robert] Sanderson. 1678; 1681 (*in Sanderson's* XXXV
sermons, *enlarged*).

The lives of Donne, Wotton, Hooker, Herbert. 1670; 1675; ed.
Thomas Zouch, York 1796 (*adds* Life of Sanderson); ed. George
Saintsbury, Oxford 1927 (WC).
Waltoniana. Ed. R.H.Shepherd, 1878. *A collection of occasional*
verses, letters etc.
The complete angler and the Lives. Ed. A.W.Pollard, 1901; The
compleat Walton, ed. Geoffrey Keynes, 1929 (Nonesuch Press).

Novarr, David. The making of Walton's Lives. Ithaca, N.Y. 1958.

JOHN WEBSTER (1580? – 1625)

THE WHITE DIVEL. 1612; ed. F.L.Lucas, 1958; ed. John R.Brown,
1960.
THE TRAGEDY of the Dutchesse of Malfy. 1623; ed. F.L.Lucas, 1958.
THE DEVILS LAW-CASE: a tragecomoedy. 1623.
APPIUS AND VIRGINIA: a tragedy. 1654. *Also attributed to Thomas*
Heywood.

A CURE FOR A CUCKOLD: a pleasant comedy. 1661. *With William Rowley.*
Webster has also been ascribed a share in several Dekker plays, in Marston's
The malcontent *and in Tourneur's* The revengers tragaedie.

[Three tragedies]. Ed. A.H.Thorndike, New York 1912 (*in* Webster
and Tourneur); Works, ed. F.L.Lucas, 4 vols. 1927.

Stoll, Elmer E. John Webster. Boston 1905.
Brooke, Rupert. Webster and the Elizabethan drama. New York 1916.
Leech, Clifford. Webster: a critical study. 1951.
Bogard, Travis. The tragic satire of Webster. Berkeley, Cal. 1955.
Dent, R.W. Webster's borrowing. Berkeley, Cal. 1960.
Boklund, Gunnar. The Duchess of Malfi: sources, themes, characters.
Cambridge, Mass. 1962.

THOMAS WILSON (1525? – 1581)

THE RULE OF REASON, conteining the arte of logique. 1551.
THE ARTE OF RHETORIQUE. 1553; 1560; ed. G.H.Mair, Oxford 1909.

GEORGE WITHER (1588 – 1667)

ABUSES STRIPT AND WHIPT: or satirical essaies. 1613.
[TWO ECLOGUES]. *In William Browne's* Shepheards pipe, 1614; *rptd in*
The shepheards hunting, *below.*
FIDELIA. 1615.
THE SHEPHEARDS HUNTING: certain eclogues. 1615.
FAIRE-VIRTUE: a miscellany of epigrams, etc. 1622.
A COLLECTION OF EMBLEMES. 4 bks. 1634–5.
HALLELUJAH. 1641.

Workes. 1620 (*pirated*); Juvenilia, 1622; Miscellaneous works, 6 vols.
1872–3 (Spenser Soc.).
Poetry. Ed. Frank Sidgwick, 2 vols. 1902.

SIR HENRY WOTTON (1568 – 1639)

THE LIFE AND DEATH OF BUCKINGHAM. 1642.
You meaner beauties of the night *was first pbd in Michael East's* Sixt
set of bookes, 1624.

Reliquiae Wottonianae: or a collection of lives, letters, poems. Ed.
Izaak Walton (*with his* Life, *below*), 1651; 1654; 1672.
Letters and dispatches, 1617–20. Ed. George Tomline, 1850.
Poems. Ed. Alexander Dyce, 1842; ed. John Hannah, 1870 (*in* The
courtly poets).

Walton, Izaak. The life of Wotton. 1651; 1654; 1672 (*all in* Reliquiae, *above*).
Smith, Logan Pearsall. The life and letters of Wotton. 2 vols. Oxford 1907.

SIR THOMAS WYATT (1503 – 1542)

Hangen, Eva C. A concordance to the complete poetical works. Chicago 1941.

CERTAYN PSALMES. 1549.
SONGES AND SONETTES by Surrey and other. Ed. Richard Tottel, 1557; 1557; ed. Hyder E. Rollins, 2 vols. Cambridge, Mass. 1928–9. *Includes 97 poems attributed to Wyatt.*
[Poems in Egerton MS. 2711]. Ed. Ewald Flügel, Anglia, xviii–xix (1895–6).

Poems. Ed. Agnes K. Foxwell, 2 vols. 1913; Collected poems, ed. Kenneth Muir, 1949 (ML). *For a selection see Tillyard, below.*

UNPUBLISHED POEMS from the Blage manuscript. Ed. Kenneth Muir, Liverpool 1961.

Foxwell, Agnes K. A study of Wyatt's poems. 1911.
Tillyard, E. M. W. The poetry of Wyatt: a selection and a study. 1929.
Chambers, E. K. *In his* Wyatt and some collected studies, 1933.
Muir, Kenneth. Life and letters of Wyatt. Liverpool 1963.

THE RESTORATION TO THE ROMANTICS
(1660–1800)

THE RESTORATION TO THE ROMANTICS
(1660–1800)

Bibliographies

Williams, Iolo A. Seven xviiith-century bibliographies. 1924. *Akenside, Armstrong, Churchill, Collins, Goldsmith, Shenstone, Sheridan.*

Summers, Montague. A bibliography of the Restoration drama. 1935.

Block, Andrew. The English novel, 1740–1850: a catalogue. 1939; 1961.

Tobin, James E. Eighteenth-century English literature and its cultural background: a bibliography. New York 1939.

Wing, Donald. Short-title catalogue of books, 1641–1700. 3 vols. New York 1945–51; Paul G. Morrison, Index of printers, publishers and booksellers, Charlottesville, Va. 1955.

Crane, Ronald S., Louis A. Landa *et al.* English literature, 1660–1800: a bibliography of modern studies, 1926–50. 4 vols. Princeton 1950–62. *Annual lists collected from* Philological quarterly, *where they are continued.*

Pargellis, Stanley and D. J. Medley. The eighteenth century, 1714–89. Oxford 1951 (Bibliography of British history). *Ch. x: Cultural history.*

Avery, Emmett L. *et al.* The London stage, 1660–1800: a calendar of plays. 5 pts. Carbondale, Ill. 1960–.

Literary History and Criticism

Johnson, Samuel. Prefaces biographical and critical to the works of the English poets. 10 vols. 1779–81. *'Lives of the poets'.*

Nichols, John. Literary anecdotes of the eighteenth century. 9 vols. 1812–15.

—— Illustrations of the literary history of the eighteenth century. 8 vols. 1817–58.

Hazlitt, William. Lectures on the English comic writers. 1819.

Scott, Walter. Lives of the novelists. 4 vols. 1821–4.

Thackeray, W. M. The English humourists of the eighteenth century. 1853.

Beljame, Alexandre. Le public et les hommes de lettres en Angleterre, 1660–1744. Paris 1881; tr., ed. Bonamy Dobrée, 1948.

Gosse, Edmund. A history of eighteenth-century English literature, 1660–1780. 1889.

Dobson, Austin. Eighteenth-century vignettes. 3 ser. 1892–6.

—— Miscellanies. 2 ser. 1898–1901.

Stephen, Leslie. English literature and society in the eighteenth century. 1904.

Elton, Oliver. A survey of English literature, 1780–1830. 2 vols. 1912; 1730–80, 2 vols. 1928.

Saintsbury, George. The peace of the Augustans. 1916; Oxford 1946 (WC).

Nicoll, Allardyce. A history of Restoration drama, 1660–1700. Cambridge 1923; A history of eighteenth-century drama, 1700–50, Cambridge 1925; 1750–1800, Cambridge 1927.

Dobrée, Bonamy. Restoration comedy. Oxford 1924; Restoration tragedy, Oxford 1929.

—— English literature in the early eighteenth century. Oxford 1959 (Oxford history of English lit., vol. VII).

Willey, Basil. The seventeenth-century background. 1934; The eighteenth-century background, 1940.

Lovejoy, Arthur O. The great chain of being. Cambridge, Mass. 1936.

—— Essays in the history of ideas. Baltimore 1948.

From Anne to Victoria. Ed. Bonamy Dobrée, 1937.

Essays on the eighteenth century presented to David Nichol Smith. Oxford 1945.

Sutherland, James. A preface to eighteenth-century poetry. Oxford 1948.

—— English satire. Cambridge 1958.

Pope and his contemporaries: essays presented to George Sherburn. New York 1949.

The age of Johnson: essays presented to C. B. Tinker. New Haven 1949.

Wedgwood, C. V. Seventeenth-century English literature. Oxford 1950; R. P. McCutcheon, Eighteenth-century English literature, Oxford 1950 (Home univ. lib.).

Davie, Donald. Purity of diction in English verse. 1952.

Watt, Ian. The rise of the novel: studies in Defoe, Richardson and Fielding. 1957.

Eighteenth-century English literature: modern essays in criticism. Ed. James L. Clifford, New York 1959.

Collections and Anthologies

Dodsley, Robert. A collection of poems by several hands. 3 vols. 1748; 6 vols. 1758 (enlarged).

Johnson, Samuel. The works of the English poets. 68 vols. 1779–81; 75 vols. 1790 (enlarged).

Anderson, Robert. The works of the British poets, with prefaces. 14 vols. 1792–1807.

Chalmers, Alexander. The works of the English poets from Chaucer to Cowper, including the series edited by Johnson. 21 vols. 1810.

Spingarn, J.E. Seventeenth-century critical essays. 3 vols. Oxford 1908–9.

Williams, Iolo A. The shorter poems of the eighteenth century. 1923.

Campbell, Kathleen W. Poems on several occasions written in the eighteenth century. Oxford 1926.

Nichol Smith, D. The Oxford book of eighteenth-century verse. Oxford 1926.

Ault, Norman. Seventeenth-century lyrics from the original texts. 1928; 1950.

Rollins, Hyder E. The Pepys ballads. 8 vols. Cambridge, Mass. 1929–32.

Crane, Ronald S. A collection of English poems, 1660–1800. New York 1932.

Grierson, Herbert and Geoffrey Bullough. The Oxford book of seventeenth-century verse. Oxford 1934.

Davie, Donald. The late Augustans: longer poems of the later eighteenth century. 1958.

Dobrée, Bonamy. Five heroic plays. Oxford 1960 (WC).

Elledge, Scott. Eighteenth-century critical essays. 2 vols. Ithaca, N.Y. 1961.

Lord, George deF. *et al.* Poems on affairs of state: Augustan satirical verse, 1660–1714. 6 vols. New Haven 1963–.

JOSEPH ADDISON (1672 – 1719)

Wheeler, William. The spectator: a digest-index. 1892; Concordance, 1897.

REMARKS on several parts of Italy. 1705; 1718.

THE TATLER. April 1709–Jan. 1711; 4 vols. 1710–1; ed. George A. Aitken, 4 vols. 1898–9. *With Richard Steele.*

THE SPECTATOR. March 1711–Dec. 1712, cont. June–Dec. 1714; 8 vols. 1712–5 (*8vo and 12mo*); ed. Henry Morley, 1868; ed. G. Gregory Smith, 8 vols. 1897–8 and 4 vols. 1907, 1958 (EL); ed. Donald F. Bond, 5 vols. Oxford 1964. *With Steele.*

Notes upon the twelve books of Paradise lost. 1719; ed. Albert S. Cook, Boston 1892. *18 Milton papers, rev. from* Spectator (Jan.–May 1712).

THE GUARDIAN. March–Oct. 1713; 2 vols. 1714. *With Steele.*

CATO: a tragedy. 1713.

THE FREE-HOLDER. Dec. 1715–June 1716; 1716.

Works. Ed. Thomas Tickell, 4 vols. 1721; Miscellaneous works, ed. A.C. Guthkelch, 2 vols. 1914.

Essays. Ed. James George Frazer, 2 vols. 1915.

Letters. Ed. Walter Graham, Oxford 1941.

Johnson, Samuel. *In his* Lives, 1779–81.

Macaulay, Thomas. *In his* Critical and historical essays, 1843.

Dobrée, Bonamy. *In his* Essays in biography, 1680–1726, Oxford 1925.

Graham, Walter. The beginnings of English literary periodicals, 1665–1715. New York 1926.

—— English literary periodicals. New York 1930.

Lewis, C.S. *In* Essays on the eighteenth century presented to David Nichol Smith, Oxford 1945.

Smithers, Peter. The life of Addison. Oxford 1954.

MARK AKENSIDE (1721 – 1770)

THE PLEASURES OF IMAGINATION: a poem in three books. 1744; 1772 (*in* Poems, *with fragment of bk iv*).

ODES ON SEVERAL SUBJECTS. 1745; 1760.

Poems. 1772; ed. Alexander Dyce, 1835, 1894 (Aldine).

Johnson, Samuel. *In his* Lives, 1779–81.

Houpt, Charles T. Akenside: a biographical and critical study. Philadelphia 1944.

JOHN ARBUTHNOT (1667 – 1735)

THE HISTORY OF JOHN BULL. Edinburgh 1712; ed. Herman Teerink, Amsterdam 1925.

THE ART OF POLITICAL LYING. 1712.

MEMOIRS OF MARTINUS SCRIBLERUS. 1741 (*in* Works of Pope); ed. C. Kerby-Miller, New Haven 1950 (*facs.*).

Miscellanies. Ed. Alexander Pope and Jonathan Swift, 4 vols. 1727–32; 1 vol. Dublin 1739; 1746 (*enlarged*). *Vols. ii–iii contain* History, Art of political lying *etc.*

Life and works by George A. Aitken, Oxford 1892. *Incomplete.*

Beattie, Lester M. Arbuthnot: mathematician and satirist. Cambridge, Mass. 1935.

JOHN AUBREY (1626 – 1697)

MISCELLANIES. 1696; 1721 (*enlarged*).

THE NATURAL HISTORY and antiquities of Surrey. Ed. Richard Rawlinson, 5 vols. 1718–19.

LIVES. 1813; Brief lives, ed. Andrew Clark, 2 vols. Oxford 1898 (*from MS.*). *Abridged edns by Anthony Powell and Oliver L.Dick (1949).*

THE NATURAL HISTORY of Wiltshire. Ed. John Britton, 1847; Wiltshire: the topographical collections, ed. John E.Jackson, Devizes 1862.

Powell, Anthony. Aubrey and his friends. 1948; 1963.

WILLIAM BECKFORD (1760 – 1844)

Chapman, Guy and John Hodgkin. A bibliography of Beckford. 1930.

AN ARABIAN TALE. Tr. Samuel Henley, 1786 (*pirated trn from Fr.*); Lausanne 1787 (*re-entitled* Vathek) (*authorized trn*); Paris 1787 (*Fr. original*), ed. Guy Chapman, 2 vols. 1929. *The 1786 version is included in* Minor novels of the eighteenth century, 1930, 1953 (EL).

ITALY, with sketches of Spain and Portugal. 2 vols. 1834.

THE EPISODES OF VATHEK. Ed. 'Lewis Melville', 1912 (*Fr. text with trn*); ed. Guy Chapman (*with* Vathek, *above*).

Travel-diaries. Ed. Guy Chapman, 2 vols. Cambridge 1928.

Journal in Portugal and Spain, 1787–8. Ed. Boyd Alexander, 1954.

Life at Fonthill, 1807–22: from the correspondence. Ed. and tr. Boyd Alexander, 1957.

Chapman, Guy. Beckford. 1937; 1952.

Brockman, H.A.N. The Caliph of Fonthill. 1956.

Alexander, Boyd. England's wealthiest son: a study of Beckford. 1962.

APHRA BEHN (1640 – 1689)

THREE HISTORIES: Oroonoko, The fair jilt, Agnes de Castro. 1688.

Histories and novels. 1696; 1697 (*enlarged*).

Plays. 2 vols. 1702. *Pbd separately 1671–96.*

Works. Ed. Montague Summers, 6 vols. 1915.

Sackville-West, Victoria. Aphra Behn: the incomparable Astraea. 1927.

JEREMY BENTHAM (1748 – 1832)

A FRAGMENT ON GOVERNMENT. 1776; ed. W.Harrison, Oxford 1948.

AN INTRODUCTION to the principles of morals and legislation. 1789; ed. W.Harrison (*with* Fragment, *above*); The limits of jurisprudence defined: being part two, ed. C.W.Everett, New York 1945 (*from MS.*).

BOOK OF FALLACIES. 1824; ed. H.A.Larrabee, Baltimore 1952.

THEORY OF LEGISLATION. 1876; ed. C.K.Ogden, 1931.

Works. Ed. John Bowring, 11 vols. 1838–43; Economic writings, ed. W.Stark, 3 vols. Oxford 1952–4.

Mill, John Stuart. Bentham (1838). Ed. F.R.Leavis, 1950 (*in* Mill on Bentham and Coleridge).

Stephen, Leslie. *In his* The English utilitarians, vol. i, 1900.

Baumgardt, D. Bentham and the ethics of today. Princeton 1952.

Mack, Mary P. Jeremy Bentham. 2 vols. 1962–.

GEORGE BERKELEY (1685 – 1753)

Jessop, T.E. and A.A.Luce. A bibliography of Berkeley. Oxford 1934.

A NEW THEORY OF VISION. Dublin 1709; London 1732 (*in* Alciphron, *below*); ed. A.D.Lindsay, 1910 (EL) (*with* Principles *and* Three dialogues, *below*).

THE PRINCIPLES of human knowledge. Dublin 1710; London 1734; ed. T.E.Jessop, 1937.

THREE DIALOGUES between Hylas and Philonous. 1713.

ALCIPHRON: or the minute philosopher. 2 vols. 1732; 1752. *For Bernard Mandeville's reply see under Mandeville, below.*

THE THEORY OF VISION. 1733.

THE QUERIST. 3 pts. Dublin 1735–7; 1750; ed. Joseph M.Hone, Dublin 1935.

PHILOSOPHICAL REFLECTIONS and enquiries concerning the virtues of tar-water. 1744; Dublin 1744 (*entitled* Siris); Further thoughts on tar water, 1752 (*in* Miscellany).

COMMONPLACE BOOK. 1871 (*in* Works, *below*); ed. A.A.Luce, 1944 (*re-entitled* Philosophical commentaries).

Works. Ed. A.C.Fraser, 4 vols. Oxford 1871, 1901; ed. A.A.Luce and T.E.Jessop, 9 vols. 1948–57.

Selections, ed. A.C.Fraser, Oxford 1874, 1910; Philosophical writings, ed. T.E.Jessop, 1952.

Fraser, A.C. Life and letters of Berkeley. Oxford 1871 (*vol. iv of* Works, *above*); Berkeley, 1881.

Wild, John. Berkeley: a study of his life and philosophy. Cambridge, Mass. 1936.

Luce, A.A. The life of Berkeley. 1949.

Warnock, G.J. Berkeley. 1953 (Penguin).

SIR RICHARD BLACKMORE (1653 – 1729)

PRINCE ARTHUR: an heroick poem. 1695; 1695.

KING ARTHUR: an heroick poem. 1697.

A SATYR AGAINST WIT. 1700.

ADVICE TO POETS: a poem. 1706; 1706.

THE NATURE OF MAN: a poem. 1711.

CREATION: a philosophical poem. 1712.

ESSAYS UPON SEVERAL SUBJECTS. 1716.

ALFRED: an epick poem. 1723.

Dennis, John. Remarks on a book entitul'd Prince Arthur. 1696.
Johnson, Samuel. *In his* Lives, 1779–81.
Boys, R. C. Blackmore and the wits. Ann Arbor 1949.
Rosenberg, Alfred. Sir Richard Blackmore. Lincoln, Nebraska 1953.

WILLIAM BLAKE (1757 – 1827)

Keynes, Geoffrey. A bibliography of Blake. New York 1921; (*with* Edwin Wolf), Blake's illuminated books: a census, New York 1953.
Some dates in Blake's hand-printed books may indicate only the year in which he engraved the title-page.

POETICAL SKETCHES. 1783; 1926 (*facs.*).
SONGS OF INNOCENCE. 1789; 1954 (*facs.*).
THE BOOK OF THEL. 1789; 1928 (*facs.*).
THE FRENCH REVOLUTION. 1791.
THE MARRIAGE OF HEAVEN AND HELL. 1793; 1960 (*facs.*).
VISIONS of the daughters of Albion. 1793; 1959 (*facs.*).
AMERICA: a prophecy. 1793; 1963 (*facs.*).
SONGS OF INNOCENCE and experience. 1794; 1955 (*facs.*).
EUROPE: a prophecy. 1794.
THE FIRST BOOK OF URIZEN. 1794; 1958 (*facs.*).
THE BOOK OF AHANIA. 1795.
THE SONG OF LOS. 1795.
THE BOOK OF LOS. 1795.
THE FOUR ZOAS. 1797. *An expansion of* Vala, ed. H. M. Margoliouth, Oxford 1956 (*from MS.*); ed. G. E. Bentley, Oxford 1963 (*with facs.*).
MILTON: a poem. 1804–c. 1808.
JERUSALEM. 1804–c. 1820; 1951, 1952 (*facs.*).

Works. Ed. E. J. Ellis and W. B. Yeats, 3 vols. 1893; Writings, ed. Geoffrey Keynes, 3 vols. 1925, 1 vol. 1927, 1939 (Poetry and prose), 1957 (Complete writings with all the variant readings) (Nonesuch Press).
Poetical works. Ed. John Sampson, 2 vols. Oxford 1905; 1 vol. 1913 (OSA) (*incomplete*); Selected poems, ed. F. W. Bateson, 1957.
Note-book called The Rossetti manuscript. Ed. Geoffrey Keynes, 1935 (*with facs.*) (Nonesuch Press); Letters, ed. Keynes, 1956.

Gilchrist, Alexander. Life of Blake: 'pictor ignotus'. 2 vols. 1863; ed. Ruthven Todd, 1942, 1945 (EL).
Eliot, T. S. *In his* The sacred wood, 1920.
Damon, S. Foster. Blake: his philosophy and symbols. Boston 1924.
Wilson, Mona. The life of Blake. 1927 (Nonesuch); 1948.
Saurat, Denis. Blake and modern thought. 1929.

Frye, Northrop. Fearful symmetry: a study of Blake. Princeton 1947.
Keynes, Geoffrey. Blake studies. 1949.
Margoliouth, H.M. Blake. Oxford 1951 (Home univ. lib.).
Erdman, David V. Blake: prophet against empire. Princeton 1954.
Raine, Kathleen *et al*. The divine vision. Ed. V.de Sola Pinto, 1957.
Gleckner, Robert F. The piper and the bard. Detroit 1959.

HENRY ST JOHN, 1st VISCOUNT BOLINGBROKE
(1678 – 1751)

A DISSERTATION UPON PARTIES. 1735.
A COLLECTION of political tracts. Dublin 1748.
LETTERS on the spirit of patriotism; on the idea of a Patriot King; and on the state of the parties. 1749; ed. Arthur Hassall, Oxford 1917.
LETTERS on the study and use of history. 2 vols. 1752; vi–viii, ed. G.M.Trevelyan, Cambridge 1933.

Works. Ed. David Mallet, 5 vols. 1754.

Sichel, Walter. Bolingbroke and his times. 2 vols. 1901–2.
James, D.G. The life of reason: Hobbes, Locke, Bolingbroke. 1949.

JAMES BOSWELL (1740 – 1795)

Pottle, Frederick A. The literary career of Boswell. Oxford 1929.
Abbott, Claude C. A catalogue of papers relating to Boswell, Johnson and Sir William Forbes. Oxford 1936.

AN ACCOUNT OF CORSICA. Glasgow 1768; 1769; ed. S.C.Roberts, Cambridge 1923.
THE JOURNAL OF A TOUR to the Hebrides with Johnson. 1785; ed. R.W. Chapman, Oxford 1924 (*with Johnson's* Journey); ed. Frederick A.Pottle and C.H.Bennett, New York 1936 (*from MS.*); ed. L.F. Powell, Oxford 1950 (*in vol. v of the* Life of Johnson, *below*) and 1957 (EL).
THE LIFE OF SAMUEL JOHNSON. 2 vols. 1791; 4 vols. 1799; ed. G.Birkbeck Hill, 6 vols. Oxford 1887, 1934–50 (rev. L.F.Powell), 1964 (v–vi); ed. R.W.Chapman, Oxford 1953 (OSA).

Letters. Ed. C.B.Tinker, 2 vols. Oxford 1924.
Private papers. Ed. Geoffrey Scott and Frederick A.Pottle, 18 vols. New York 1928–34 (*private edn*); ed. Pottle *et al.*, *c.* 15 vols. New York 1950– ('*trade*' *edn; a research edn,* c. *30 vols., is also projected*); Index, Oxford 1937.

Macaulay, Thomas. Samuel Johnson (1831). *In his* Critical and historical essays, 1843.

Carlyle, Thomas. Boswell's Life of Johnson (1832). *In his* Critical and miscellaneous essays, Boston 1838.

Tinker, C.B. Young Boswell. Boston 1922.

GEORGE VILLIERS, 2ND DUKE OF BUCKINGHAM
(1628 – 1687)

THE REHEARSAL. 1672; 1675 (*with addns*), ed. Edward Arber, 1869. *Probably with Samuel Butler, Thomas Sprat and Martin Clifford. A satire upon Dryden.*

Works. Ed. Thomas Brown, 1704; 2 vols. 1715 (*enlarged*).

JOHN BUNYAN (1628 – 1688)

Harrison, Frank Mott. A bibliography of the works of Bunyan. 1932.

THE HOLY CITY. 1665.

GRACE ABOUNDING to the chief of sinners. 1666; ? (*3rd edn enlarged*); ed. John Brown, Cambridge 1907 (*with* Pilgrim's progress); ed. Roger Sharrock, Oxford 1962.

THE PILGRIM'S PROGRESS. 2 pts. 1678–84; ed. J.B.Wharey, Oxford 1928, 1960 (rev. Roger Sharrock); ed. G.B.Harrison, 1928 (*with* Mr Badman) (Nonesuch Press); illustr. William Blake, ed. G.B. Harrison, New York 1941.

THE LIFE AND DEATH OF MR BADMAN. 1680; ed. John Brown, Cambridge 1905 (*with* Holy war); Oxford 1929 (WC).

THE HOLY WAR. 1682.

THE HEAVENLY FOOTMAN. 1698; ed. Mabel Peacock, Oxford 1892 (*with* Holy war).

Works. 1692 (*incomplete*); ed. Henry Stebbing, 4 vols. 1859–60.

Brown, John. Bunyan; his life, times and work. 1885; 1928 (rev. F.M. Harrison).

Harrison, G.B. Bunyan: a study in personality. 1928.

Talon, Henri. Bunyan: l'homme et l'oeuvre. Paris 1948; tr. 1951.

Sharrock, Roger. John Bunyan. 1954.

EDMUND BURKE (1729 – 1797)

Copeland, Thomas W. and Milton S.Smith. A checklist of the correspondence of Burke. New York 1955 (Index Society).

A VINDICATION of natural society. 1756; 1757 (*with preface*). *A satire on Bolingbroke.*

A PHILOSOPHICAL ENQUIRY into the sublime and beautiful. 1757; 1759 (*with an introd. on taste*); ed. James T.Boulton, 1958.

THE ANNUAL REGISTER. 1759–. *Edited by Burke till 1789 and in large part written by him.*

THOUGHTS ON THE CAUSE of the present discontents. 1770.

SPEECH ON AMERICAN TAXATION. Bristol 1774; Speeches at Bristol, 1774; Speech on conciliation with the colonies, 1775.

Speeches and letters on American affairs. Ed. Hugh Law, 1908 (EL).

REFLECTIONS ON THE REVOLUTION in France. 1790; 1790 (*7th edn*); ed. Sidney Lee, 1905; ed. W.A. and C.B.Phillips, Cambridge 1912.

A LETTER to a member of the National Assembly. 1791.

AN APPEAL from the new to the old Whigs. 1791.

A LETTER to Sir Hercules Langrishe on the Roman Catholics of Ireland. 1792.

A LETTER to a noble lord. 1796.

TWO LETTERS on the proposals for peace with the regicide Directory of France. 1796. *Letter III pbd in 1796; IV (the first written, in 1795) pbd in 1812 in vol. v of Works, below.*

Works. Ed. French Laurence and William King, 8 vols. 1792–1827; ed. W.Willis and F.W.Raffety, 6 vols. 1906–7 (WC); Select works, ed. E.J.Payne, 3 vols. Oxford 1874–8.

Correspondence, 1744–97. Ed. Charles, Earl Fitzwilliam, 4 vols. 1844; Letters: a selection mainly political, ed. Harold Laski, Oxford 1922 (WC); Correspondence, ed. Thomas W.Copeland *et al.*, 10 vols. Cambridge 1958–.

Note-book. Ed. H.V.F.Somerset, Cambridge 1957. *Early poems, essays etc.*

Morley, John. Burke: an historical study. 1867.

—— Edmund Burke. 1879 (EML).

McCunn, John. The political philosophy of Burke. 1913.

Murray, Robert. Edmund Burke. 1931.

Magnus, Philip. Burke: a life. 1939.

Young, G.M. *In his* Today and yesterday, 1948.

Copeland, Thomas W. Our eminent friend Burke: six essays. New Haven 1949.

Boulton, James T. *In his* The language of politics in the age of Wilkes and Burke, 1963.

GILBERT BURNET (1643 – 1715)

A HISTORY of the reformation of the Church of England. 3 pts. 1679–1715; ed. Nicholas Pocock, 7 vols. Oxford 1865; Abridgement, 3 vols. 1718–9.

THE LIFE and death of Rochester. 1680.

BURNET–BURNS

HISTORY OF HIS OWN TIME. 4 vols. 1724–53; bks i–ii, ed. Osmund Airy,
Oxford 1897–1900; Supplement, ed. H.C.Foxcroft, Oxford 1902.
THOUGHTS ON EDUCATION. 1761; ed. John Clarke, Aberdeen 1914.

Ranke, Leopold von. *In his* Englische Geschichte, Berlin 1856–68, vol.
vi, appendix ii; tr. Oxford 1875.
Clarke, T.E.S. and H.C.Foxcroft. A life of Burnet. Cambridge 1907.

FRANCES BURNEY, later d'ARBLAY (1752 – 1840)

EVELINA. 3 vols. 1778; 1909 (EL); ed. F.D.Mackinnon, Oxford 1930.
CECILIA. 5 vols. 1782.
CAMILLA. 5 vols. 1796.
MEMOIRS OF DR BURNEY. 3 vols. 1832.
DIARY AND LETTERS, 1778–1840. 7 vols. 1842–6; ed. Charlotte Barrett
and Austin Dobson, 6 vols. 1904–5; Diary, 1940 (EL); Early diary,
1768–78, ed. Annie R.Ellis, 2 vols. 1889.

Macaulay, Thomas. *In his* Critical and historical essays, 1843.
Dobson, Austin. Fanny Burney. 1903 (EML).
Cecil, David. *In his* Poets and story-tellers, 1949.
Scholes, Percy. The great Dr Burney. 2 vols. Oxford 1948.
Hemlow, Joyce. The history of Fanny Burney. Oxford 1958.

ROBERT BURNS (1759 – 1796)

Reid, J.H. A concordance to the poems and songs. Glasgow 1889.
Angus, W.Craibe. The printed works of Burns. Glasgow 1899.

POEMS chiefly in the Scottish dialect. Kilmarnock 1786, Oxford 1911
(*facs.*); Edinburgh 1787; London 1787; 2 vols. Edinburgh 1793;
1794 (*both enlarged*).
THE SCOTS MUSICAL MUSEUM. 6 vols. Edinburgh 1787–1803. *This collec-
tion and the next contain some 300 Burns songs.*
A SELECT COLLECTION of original Scottish airs. 5 vols. 1793–1818.
TAM O'SHANTER. 1795.
THE COTTERS SATURDAY NIGHT. *In* Roach's Beauties of the poets, no. 21,
1795.
THE JOLLY BEGGARS: a cantata. Glasgow 1799.

Poetry. Ed. W.E.Henley and Thomas F.Henderson, 4 vols. Edin,
burgh 1896–7; Poetical works, ed. J.Logie Robertson, Oxford 1904
(OSA); Selected, ed. Laurence Brander, Oxford 1950 (WC).
Letters. Ed. J.De Lancey Ferguson, 2 vols. Oxford 1931; Selected-
ed. Ferguson, Oxford 1953 (WC).
Commonplace book, 1783–5. Ed. J.C.Ewing and Davidson Cook,
Glasgow 1938 (*facs.*).

Lockhart, John Gibson. Life of Burns. Edinburgh 1828.
Raleigh, Walter. *In his* Some authors, Oxford 1923.
Snyder, Franklin B. Life of Burns. New York 1932.
—— Burns: his personality, his reputation and his art. Toronto 1936.
Ferguson, J. De Lancey. Pride and passion: Burns. New York 1939.
Daiches, David. Robert Burns. 1952.
Crawford, Thomas. Burns: a study of the poems and songs. Edinburgh 1960.

JOSEPH BUTLER (1692 – 1752)

FIFTEEN SERMONS preached at the Chapel of the Rolls Court. 1726; 1729 (*with preface*), ed. W. R. Matthews, 1949; 1749 (*with six public sermons*).

THE ANALOGY OF RELIGION, natural and revealed, to the constitution and course of nature. 1736; 1736; ed. W. E. Gladstone, Oxford 1907 (WC).

Works. Ed. W. E. Gladstone, 2 vols. Oxford 1896; ed. J. H. Bernard, 2 vols. 1900.

SAMUEL BUTLER (1612 – 1680)

HUDIBRAS. 3 pts. 1663–78; ed. Zachary Grey, 2 vols. 1774.
Posthumous works in prose and verse. 3 vols. 1715–7. *Includes spurious material.*
Collected works. Ed. A. R. Waller and René Lamar, 3 vols. Cambridge 1905–28.

Johnson, Samuel. *In his* Lives, 1779–81.
Richards, Edward A. Hudibras in the burlesque tradition. New York 1937.

HENRY CAREY (1687? – 1743)

POEMS ON SEVERAL OCCASIONS. 1713; 1720; 1729 (*both enlarged*); Poems, ed. F. T. Wood, 1930.

THOMAS CHATTERTON (1752 – 1770)

POEMS supposed to have been written by Thomas Rowley. Ed. Thomas Tyrwhitt, 1777; 1778; ed. M. E. Hare, Oxford 1911.

Poetical works. Ed. Walter W. Skeat, 2 vols. 1871 (Aldine); Poems, ed. Sidney Lee, 2 vols. 1905.

Horace Walpole's correspondence with Chatterton. Ed. W. S. Lewis, *in* Walpole's correspondence, vol. xvi, New Haven 1951.

Meyerstein, E. H. W. A life of Chatterton. 1930.

PHILIP DORMER STANHOPE, 4TH EARL OF CHESTERFIELD (1694 – 1773)

Gulick, Sidney L. A Chesterfield bibliography to 1800. Pbns Bibliog. Soc. of America, xxix (1935).

THE ART OF PLEASING. Edinburgh Mag. (Feb.–June 1774); 1783.

LETTERS TO HIS SON, Philip Stanhope. Ed. Eugenia Stanhope, 2 vols. 1774, Supplement 1787; ed. Charles Strachey and Annette Calthrop, 2 vols. 1901.

LETTERS TO HIS FRIENDS. 3 vols. 1777–8.

CHARACTERS OF EMINENT PERSONAGES of his own time. 1777; 1778 (*enlarged*).

Letters. Ed. Viscount Mahon, 5 vols. 1845–53; ed. Bonamy Dobrée, 6 vols. 1932; Unpublished letters, ed. Sidney L. Gulick, Berkeley, Cal. 1937.

Wit and wisdom. Ed. William Ernst-Browning, 1875. *Other selections ed. R. K. Root, 1929 (EL), and Phyllis M. Jones, Oxford 1929 (WC).*

CHARLES CHURCHILL (1731 – 1764)

THE ROSCIAD. 1761; 1763. *First of 17 verse satires.*

THE APOLOGY, addressed to the critical reviewers. 1761.

THE GHOST. 4 bks. 1762–3.

THE NORTH BRITON. June 1762–April 1763; 3 vols. 1763. *With John Wilkes.*

THE DUELLIST: a poem. 1764.

GOTHAM: a poem. 3 bks. 1764.

THE CANDIDATE: a poem. 1764.

THE FAREWELL: a poem. 1764.

THE TIMES: a poem. 1764.

INDEPENDENCE: a poem. 1764.

Poetical works. Ed. William Tooke, 3 vols. 1804; 2 vols. 1868 (Aldine); ed. James Laver, 2 vols. 1933; ed. Douglas Grant, Oxford 1956.

Correspondence of Wilkes and Churchill. Ed. Edward H. Weatherly, New York 1954.

Brown, Wallace C. Churchill: poet, rake and rebel. Lawrence, Kansas 1953.

EDWARD HYDE, 1st EARL OF CLARENDON
(1609 – 1674)

THE HISTORY of the rebellion and civil wars in England. 3 vols. Oxford 1702–4; ed. W. Dunn Macray, 6 vols. Oxford 1888.

THE HISTORY of the rebellion and civil wars in Ireland. 1719; Dublin 1720.

LIFE. Oxford 1719; 2 vols. 1857. *Portions of the 1668–70 MS. not included in* History, *above.*

Selections. Ed. G. Huehns, Oxford 1955 (WC). *A brief selection in* Characters, ed. D. Nichol Smith, Oxford 1920.

State papers from 1621. 3 vols. Oxford 1767–86.

Ranke, Leopold von. *In his* Englische Geschichte, Berlin 1856–68, appendix ii; tr. Oxford 1875.

Craik, Henry. The life of Clarendon. 2 vols. 1911.

Wormald, B. H. G. Clarendon: politics, history and religion, 1640–60. Cambridge 1951.

WILLIAM COLLINS (1721 – 1759)

Booth, Bradford A. and Claude E. Jones. A concordance of the poetical works. Berkeley, Cal. 1939.

PERSIAN ECLOGUES. 1742; 1757 (*re-entitled* Oriental eclogues), Oxford 1925 (*facs.*).

ODES on several descriptive and allegoric subjects. 1747; 1926 (*facs.*).

AN ODE on the popular superstitions of the Highlands of Scotland. 1788.

Poetical works. Ed. Christopher Stone and A. L. Poole, Oxford 1917; 1937 (rev. Frederick Page) (OSA). *With Gray's poems.*

Poems. Ed. Edmund Blunden, 1929.

DRAFTS AND FRAGMENTS OF VERSE. Ed. J. S. Cunningham, Oxford 1956.

Johnson, Samuel. *In his* Lives, 1779–81.

Garrod, H. W. Collins. Oxford 1928.

WILLIAM CONGREVE (1670 – 1729)

INCOGNITA: a novel. 1692.

THE OLD BATCHELOUR: a comedy. 1693.

THE DOUBLE-DEALER: a comedy. 1694; 1706.

LOVE FOR LOVE: a comedy. 1695.

THE MOURNING BRIDE: a tragedy. 1697.

THE WAY OF THE WORLD: a comedy. 1700; 1706.

THE JUDGEMENT OF PARIS: a masque. 1701.

Works. 3 vols. 1710; ed. Montague Summers, 4 vols. 1923 (Nonesuch Press); ed. F.W.Bateson, 1930; ed. Bonamy Dobrée, 2 vols. Oxford 1925–8 (WC).

Johnson, Samuel. *In his* Lives, 1779–81.
Gosse, Edmund. Life of Congreve. 1888; 1924.
Taylor, D.Crane. William Congreve. Oxford 1931.
Hodges, John C. Congreve the man: a biography from new sources. New York 1941.

CHARLES COTTON (1630 – 1687)

THE COMPLEAT ANGLER [pt ii]. 1676 (*in* The universal angler); ed. R.B. Marston, 2 vols. 1888 (*with pt i*). *Pt i by Izaak Walton, pbd 1653*
ESSAYS OF MONTAIGNE newly rendred into English. 3 vols. 1685–6; ed. W. Carew Hazlitt, 4 vols. 1902.
POEMS ON SEVERAL OCCASIONS. 1689; Poems, ed. John Beresford, 1923 (*shorter poems*); ed. John Buxton, 1958 (ML).

Genuine works. 1715.

WILLIAM COWPER (1731 – 1800)

Neve, John. A concordance to the poetical works. 1887.
Russell, Norma. A bibliography of Cowper to 1837. Oxford 1963.

OLNEY HYMNS. 1779. *With John Newton.*
POEMS. 1782. *Contains* Table talk *etc.*
POEMS, vol. II. 1785. *Contains* The task, John Gilpin, *etc.* Gilpin *first pbd in* Public advertiser (Nov. 1782)

Poems. 2 vols. 1786; 1800.

THE ILIAD AND ODYSSEY of Homer, translated into English blank verse. 1791.
POEMS translated from the French of Madame Guion. 1801.
MEMOIR. 1816; 1835 (*re-entitled* Autobiography).

Life and letters, by William Hayley, 4 vols. 1803–6; Life and works, by Robert Southey, 15 vols. 1835–7.
Poetical works. Ed. Humphrey Milford, Oxford 1905; 1934 (*enlarged*) (OSA).
Correspondence. Ed. Thomas Wright, 4 vols. 1904; Unpublished and uncollected letters, ed. Wright, 1925; Selected letters, 1926 (EL).

Sainte-Beuve, C.-A. *In his* Causeries du lundi, vol. xi, Paris 1856.
Bagehot, Walter. *In his* Estimates of some Englishmen and Scotchmen, 1858.

Stephen, Leslie. Cowper and Rousseau. *In his* Hours in a library, ser. 3, 1879.

Cecil, David. The stricken deer. 1929.

Thomas, Gilbert. Cowper and the eighteenth century. 1935; 1948.

Ryskamp, Charles. Cowper of the Inner Temple, Esq.: a study of his life and works to 1768. Cambridge 1959.

Hartley, Lodwick. Cowper: the continuing revaluation. Chapel Hill, N.C. 1961.

GEORGE CRABBE (1754 – 1832)

THE CANDIDATE: a poetical epistle to The monthly review. 1780.

THE LIBRARY: a poem. 1781.

THE VILLAGE. 1783.

THE NEWSPAPER. 1785.

Poems. 1807. *Includes the above, with first edn of* The parish register *etc.*

THE BOROUGH: a poem in twenty-four letters. 1810.

TALES IN VERSE. 1812.

TALES OF THE HALL. 2 vols. 1819.

NEW POEMS. Ed. Arthur Pollard, Liverpool 1960.

Works. 4 vols. 1816; 5 vols. 1823; ed. George Crabbe [junior], 8 vols. 1834. *1823 includes final revisions of pbd tales, 1834 first edn of the Posthumous tales.*

Poems. Ed. A. W. Ward, 3 vols. Cambridge 1905–7; Poetical works, ed. A. J. and R. M. Carlyle, Oxford 1914 (OSA); Crabbe, ed. F. L. Lucas, Cambridge 1933 (*selection*).

Crabbe, George. The life of Crabbe by his son. 1834 (*in* Works, *above*); ed. E. M. Forster, Oxford 1932 (WC); ed. Edmund Blunden, 1947.

Stephen, Leslie. *In his* Hours in a library, ser. 2, 1876.

Saintsbury, George. *In his* Essays in English literature, 1780–1860, 1895.

Huchon, René. Un poète réaliste anglais. Paris 1906; tr. 1907.

Haddakin, Lilian. The poetry of Crabbe. 1955.

DANIEL DEFOE (1660 – 1731)

Moore, John R. A checklist of the writings of Defoe. Bloomington, Ind. 1960.

THE TRUE-BORN ENGLISHMAN: a satyr. 1701.

THE SHORTEST-WAY with the dissenters. 1702.

A collection of the writings. 1703 (*pirated*); 2 vols. 1703–5 (*enlarged*).

REVIEW. 1704–13; ed. A. W. Secord, 22 vols. New York 1938 (*facs.*), Index, New York 1948; Anthology, ed. W. L. Payne, New York 1951.

THE HISTORY of the union of Great Britain. Edinburgh 1709; London 1786.

THE LIFE and adventures of Robinson Crusoe, written by himself. 1719, ed. Austin Dobson, 1883 (*facs.*); Farther adventures, 1719; Serious reflections during the life of Robinson Crusoe, 1720.

MEMOIRS OF A CAVALIER. 1720.

THE LIFE of Captain Singleton. 1720; 1906 (EL).

THE FORTUNES and misfortunes of Moll Flanders. 1721, ed. Herbert Davis, Oxford 1961 (WC); 1722.

A JOURNAL of the plague year. 1722; 1908, 1953 (EL).

THE HISTORY of Col. Jack. 1722.

THE FORTUNATE MISTRESS: or a history of the Lady Roxana. 1724.

A TOUR THRO' GREAT BRITAIN. 3 vols. 1724–7; ed. G.D.H.Cole, 2 vols. 1927, 1928 (EL).

Novels and selected writings. 14 vols. Oxford 1927–8.

Letters. Ed. George H.Healey, Oxford 1955.

Lee, William. Defoe: his life and recently discovered writings. 3 vols. 1869.

Stephen, Leslie. De Foe's novels. *In his* Hours in a library, 1874.

Dottin, Paul. De Foe et ses romans. 3 vols. Paris 1924; tr. New York 1929.

Sutherland, James. Defoe. 1937; 1950.

Moore, John R. Defoe: citizen of the modern world. Chicago 1958.

JOHN DENNIS (1657 – 1734)

THE IMPARTIAL CRITICK: or some observations upon A short view of tragedy by Mr Rymer. 1693; ed. J.E.Spingarn, Oxford 1908–9 (*in* Critical essays of the seventeenth century). *Five critical dialogues.*

THE ADVANCEMENT and reformation of modern poetry. 1701.

THE GROUNDS of criticism in poetry. 1704.

THE GENIUS and writings of Shakespear. 1712.

ORIGINAL LETTERS, familiar, moral and critical. 2 vols. 1721.

Critical works. Ed. E.N.Hooker, 2 vols. Baltimore 1939–43.

Paul, H.G. Dennis: his life and criticism. New York 1911.

CHARLES SACKVILLE, 6TH EARL OF DORSET
(1638 – 1706)

WORKS OF THE LATE EARLS of Rochester and Roscommon. 1707; 2 vols. 1714. *1707 includes poems attributed to Dorset, 1714 adds his name to title-page. Some poems were pbd in miscellanies in his lifetime.*

Dorset also collaborated with Godolphin, Sedley and Waller in Pompey the
Great: a tragedy (1664), *a trn of Corneille's* Mort de Pompée (1644).

Johnson, Samuel. *In his* Lives, 1779–81.
Harris, Brice. Charles Sackville, Earl of Dorset. Urbana, Ill. 1940.

JOHN DRYDEN (1631 – 1700)

Macdonald, Hugh. Dryden: a bibliography of early editions and of
Drydeniana. Oxford 1939.
Montgomery, Guy. Concordance to the poetical works. Berkeley,
Cal. 1957.

ANNUS MIRABILIS: the year of wonders, 1666. 1667.
OF DRAMATICK POESIE: an essay. 1668; 1684; ed. D. Nichol Smith, 1900;
ed. D. D. Arundell, Cambridge 1929 (*in* Dryden and Howard, 1664–8).
THE CONQUEST OF GRANADA. 2 pts. 1672; Marriage à-la-mode, 1673, ed.
James Sutherland, 1934; Aureng-Zebe, 1676; The state of inno-
cence: an opera, 1677 (*from* Paradise lost); All for love, 1678; The
Spanish fryar, 1681. *Some 30 plays pbd 1663–94.*
ABSALOM AND ACHITOPHEL. 2 pts. 1681–2. *Pt ii largely by Nahum Tate.*
THE MEDALL: a satyre against sedition. 1682.
MACFLECKNOE: or a satyr upon T.S. 1682; 1684 (*in* Miscellany poems).
Against Thomas Shadwell.
RELIGIO LAICI. 1682.
TO MRS ANNE KILLIGREW: an ode. *In* Poems of Mrs Killigrew, 1686.
THE HIND AND THE PANTHER. 1687.
A SONG FOR ST CECILIA'S DAY. 1687.
THE SATIRES OF JUVENALIS translated into English verse; together with
the satires of Persius. 1693. *Satires i, iii, vi, x and xvi of Juvenal, and
all of Persius, by Dryden.*
ALEXANDER'S FEAST: an ode in honour of St Cecilia's Day. 1697.
THE WORKS OF VIRGIL translated into English verse. 1697; 1698; ed.
James Kinsley, Oxford 1961.
FABLES ANCIENT AND MODERN. 1700.

Works. Ed. Walter Scott, 18 vols. 1808, 1882–93 (rev. George
Saintsbury); ed. E. N. Hooker and H. T. Swedenberg, Berkeley,
Cal. 1956–; Poetry, prose and plays, ed. Douglas Grant, 1952 (RL).
Prose works. Ed. Edmond Malone, 4 vols. 1800; Essays, ed. W. P.
Ker, 2 vols. Oxford 1900; Of dramatic poesy and other critical
essays, ed. George Watson, 2 vols. 1962, 1964 (EL).
Poetical works. Ed. George R. Noyes, Cambridge, Mass. 1909, 1950
(*enlarged*); Poems, ed. James Kinsley, 4 vols. Oxford 1958; Poems

and fables, ed. Kinsley, Oxford 1962 (OSA); Prologues and epilogues, ed. W.B. Gardner, New York 1951.
Letters. Ed. Charles E. Ward, Durham, N.C. 1942.

Johnson, Samuel. *In his* Lives, 1779–81.
Saintsbury, George. Dryden. 1881 (EML).
Van Doren, Mark. The poetry of Dryden. New York 1920; 1946
(*re-entitled* Dryden: a study of his poetry).
Eliot, T.S. Homage to Dryden. 1924. *Rptd in his* Selected essays,
1932. *Reply by* C.S. Lewis *in his* Rehabilitations, Oxford 1939.
Bredvold, Louis I. The intellectual milieu of Dryden. Ann Arbor 1934.
Osborn, J.M. Dryden: some biographical facts and problems. New
York 1940.
Nichol Smith, D. Dryden. Cambridge 1950.
Proudfoot, L. Dryden's Aeneid and its seventeenth-century pre-
decessors. Manchester 1960.
Ward, Charles E. The life of Dryden. Chapel Hill, N.C. 1961.

JOHN DYER (1699 – 1758)

GRONGAR HILL. *In* Miscellaneous poems, ed. Richard Savage, 1726; *in*
Poems, 1761, 1765, *below.*
THE RUINS OF ROME: a poem. 1740.
THE FLEECE: a poem in four books. 1757.

Poems. 1761; 1765; ed. Edward Thomas, 1903; ed. Hugh I'Anson
Fausset (*in* Minor Poets of the eighteenth century, 1930 (EL)).

Johnson, Samuel. *In his* Lives, 1779–81.

SIR GEORGE ETHEREGE (1635 – 1691)

THE COMICAL REVENGE: or Love in a tub. 1664.
SHE WOU'D IF SHE COU'D: a comedy. 1668.
THE MAN OF MODE: or Sr Fopling Flutter. 1676.

Works. 1704; ed. A. Wilson Verity, 1888; Dramatic works, ed. H.F.B.
Brett-Smith, 2 vols. Oxford 1927; Poems, ed. James Thorpe,
Princeton 1962.
Letterbook. Ed. Sybil Rosenfeld, Oxford 1928 (*from MS.*).

Dobrée, Bonamy. *In his* Essays in biography, 1680–1726, Oxford 1925.
Underwood, Dale. Etherege and the seventeenth-century comedy of
manners. New Haven 1957.

JOHN EVELYN (1620 – 1706)

Keynes, Geoffrey. Evelyn: a study in bibliophily and a bibliography of his writings. Cambridge 1937.

A CHARACTER OF ENGLAND. 1659.

FUMIFUGIUM. 1662.

SCULPTURA. 1662; with second part, ed. C.F.Bell, Oxford 1906.

SYLVA: or a discourse of forest trees. 1664; 1706 (*enlarged*).

ACCOUNT OF ARCHITECTS and architecture. 1664 (*with a trn from the Fr. of Roland Freart*, A parallel of the antient architecture with the modern).

MISCELLANEOUS WRITINGS. Ed. William Upcott, 1825.

THE LIFE OF MRS GODOLPHIN. Ed. Samuel Wilberforce, 1847; ed. Harriet Sampson, Oxford 1939.

MEMOIRS, 1641–1706. Ed. William Bray, 2 vols. 1818; Diary, ed. E.S.de Beer, 6 vols. Oxford 1955 (*complete*), 1 vol. Oxford 1959 (OSA).

Ponsonby, Arthur. John Evelyn. 1933.

Hiscock, W.G. Evelyn and Mrs Godolphin. 1951; Evelyn and his family circle, 1955.

GEORGE FARQUHAR (1678 – 1707)

LOVE AND A BOTTLE. 1699. *First of eight comedies, pbd 1699–1707.*

THE RECRUITING OFFICER. 1706.

THE BEAUX STRATAGEM. 1707.

Works, 1711?; Complete works, ed. Charles A.Stonehill, 2 vols. 1930 (Nonesuch Press); [Four comedies], ed. William Archer, 1906 (Mermaid).

HENRY FIELDING (1707 – 1754)

TOM THUMB: a tragedy. 1730; 1731 (*re-entitled* The tragedy of tragedies); ed. James T.Hillhouse, New Haven 1918 (*both texts*). *A parody of the heroic play. 25 plays pbd 1728–78.*

AN APOLOGY for the life of Mrs Shamela Andrews. 1741; ed. Sheridan W.Baker, Berkeley, Cal. 1953. *A parody of Samuel Richardson's* Pamela.

JOSEPH ANDREWS. 2 vols. 1742; Oxford 1929 (WC).

THE LIFE of Mr Jonathan Wild the Great. 1743 (*in* Miscellanies, vol. iii, *below*); 1754; Oxford 1932 (WC).

THE HISTORY OF TOM JONES, a foundling. 6 vols. 1749; 4 vols. 1749.

AMELIA. 4 vols. 1752.

The four novels have been rptd, ed. George Saintsbury, 1910–30 (EL).

THE JOURNAL of a voyage to Lisbon. 1755; 1755; ed. Austin Dobson, 1892; Oxford 1907 (WC).

Miscellanies. 3 vols. 1743.
Works. Ed. Arthur Murphy, 4 vols. 1762, 10 vols. 1806 (rev. Alexander Chalmers); ed. George Saintsbury, 12 vols. 1893; Complete works, ed. W.E.Henley *et al.*, 16 vols. 1903 (*incomplete*).

Stephen, Leslie. *In his* Hours in a library, ser. 3, 1879.
Dobson, Austin. Fielding. 1883; 1925 (EML).
Cross, Wilbur L. The history of Fielding. 3 vols. New Haven 1918.
Digeon, Aurélien. Les romans de Fielding. Paris 1923; tr. 1925.
Crane, Ronald S. The concept of plot and the plot of Tom Jones. *In* Critics and criticism, ed. Crane, Chicago 1952.
Dudden, F.Homes. Fielding: his life, works and times. 2 vols. Oxford 1952.
Murry, J.Middleton. In defence of Fielding. *In his* Unprofessional essays, 1956.

GEORGE FOX (1624 – 1691)

A JOURNAL OF THE LIFE OF FOX. Ed. Thomas Ellwood, 1694; ed. John N. Nickalls, Cambridge 1952.

JOHN GAY (1685 – 1732)

THE PRESENT STATE OF WIT. 1711; ed. Donald F.Bond, Ann Arbor 1947 (Augustan Reprint Soc.).
THE SHEPHERD'S WEEK in six pastorals. 1714; ed. H.F.B.Brett-Smith, Oxford 1924.
TRIVIA: or the art of walking the streets of London. 1716; ed. W.H. Williams, 1922.
POEMS ON SEVERAL OCCASIONS. 2 vols. 1720; 1731.
FABLES. 2 vols. 1727–38.
THE BEGGAR'S OPERA. 1728; 1729, ed. F.W.Bateson, 1934; Polly: an opera, 1729, ed. Oswald Doughty, 1922.

Works, with Johnson's preface. 6 vols. 1795.
Poetical works. Ed. G.C.Faber, Oxford 1926 (OSA).

Johnson, Samuel. *In his* Lives, 1779–81.
Schultz, William E. Gay's Beggar's opera. New Haven 1923.
Irving, William H. Gay, favorite of the wits. Durham, N.C. 1940.
Sutherland, James. *In* Pope and his contemporaries: essays presented to George Sherburn, New York 1949.

EDWARD GIBBON (1737 – 1794)

Norton, J.E. Bibliography of the works of Gibbon. Oxford 1940.

THE HISTORY of the decline and fall of the Roman Empire. 6 vols. 1776–88; ed. J.B.Bury, 7 vols. 1896–1900, 1926–9; 1903–4 (WC).

MISCELLANEOUS WORKS, with memoirs of his life composed by himself. Ed. John, Earl of Sheffield, 2 vols. 1796; 5 vols. 1814 *(enlarged).* *Includes Sheffield's reconstructed version of the* Autobiography, *and parts of* Journal, *below, some tr. from Gibbon's French.*

AUTOBIOGRAPHIES. Ed. John Murray, 1896 *(six MS. drafts);* ed. G. Birkbeck Hill, 1900; ed. J.B.Bury, Oxford 1907 (WC).

JOURNAL to January 1763. Ed. D.M.Low, 1929; Le séjour de Gibbon à Paris, 1763, ed. Georges A.Bonnard, Lausanne 1952 *(in* Miscellanea Gibboniana); Le journal à Lausanne, 1763–4, ed. Bonnard, Lausanne 1945; Journey from Geneva to Rome: his journal from April to October 1764, ed. Bonnard, Edinburgh 1961.

Letters. Ed. J.E.Norton, 3 vols. 1956.

Sainte-Beuve, C.-A. *In his* Causeries du lundi, vol. viii, Paris 1855.

Bagehot, Walter. *In his* Estimates of some Englishmen and Scotchmen, 1858.

Young, G.M. Gibbon. 1932; 1948.

Low, D.M. Edward Gibbon. 1937.

Keynes, Geoffrey. The library of Gibbon: a catalogue of his books. 1940.

WILLIAM GODWIN (1756 – 1836)

THE PRINCIPLES of political justice. 2 vols. 1793; 1796; ed. F.E.L. Priestley, 3 vols. Toronto 1946 *(facs.).*

THE ADVENTURES of Caleb Williams. 3 vols. 1794. *A novel.*

ST LEON. 3 vols. 1799. *A novel.*

FLEETWOOD. 3 vols. 1805. *A novel.*

OLIVER GOLDSMITH (1730? – 1774)

Balderston, Katharine C. A census of the manuscripts of Goldsmith. New York 1926.

Paden, W.D. and Clyde K.Hyder. A concordance of the poems. Lawrence, Kansas 1940.

THE PRESENT STATE of polite learning in Europe. 1759; 1774.

THE BEE. Oct.–Nov. 1759; 1 vol. 1759; Oxford 1914 (OSA).

THE CITIZEN OF THE WORLD. 2 vols. 1762.

THE LIFE of Richard Nash of Bath. 1762; Oxford 1914 (OSA) *(with* The bee, *above).*

THE TRAVELLER: or a prospect of society. 1765; ed. W.B.Todd, 1954, Charlottesville 1956 *(first version of poem, from proofs).*

THE VICAR OF WAKEFIELD: a tale. 2 vols. 1766; 1 vol. 1901 (WC).

THE GOOD NATUR'D MAN: a comedy. 1768.

THE DESERTED VILLAGE. 1770; New York 1934 *(facs.).*

SHE STOOPS TO CONQUER: a comedy. 1773.

Miscellaneous works. 2 vols. Edinburgh 1791; Works, ed. J.W.M.
  Gibbs, 5 vols. 1884–6; Selected works, ed. Richard Garnett, 1950 (RL).
Poetical works. Ed. Austin Dobson, Oxford 1906 (OSA).
Collected letters. Ed. Katharine C. Balderston, Cambridge 1928.
Poems and plays. Ed. Austin Dobson, 1910 (EL).
New essays. Ed. Ronald S. Crane, Chicago 1927.

Boswell, James. *In his* The life of Samuel Johnson, 2 vols. 1791.
Forster, John. The life and adventures of Goldsmith. 1848.
Dobson, Austin. Life of Goldsmith. 1888.
Percy, Thomas. Memoir of Goldsmith. Ed. Katharine C. Balderston,
  Cambridge 1926 (*in her* The history and sources of Percy's Memoir).
Reynolds, Joshua. *In his* Portraits, ed. F.W.Hilles, New York 1952.
Wardle, Ralph M. Oliver Goldsmith. Lawrence, Kansas 1957. *A
  biography*.

THOMAS GRAY (1716 – 1771)

Cook, Albert S. A concordance of the English poems. Boston 1908.
Northup, Clark S. A bibliography of Gray. New Haven 1917.

ODE ON A DISTANT PROSPECT of Eton College. 1747; Oxford 1924 (*facs.*).
AN ELEGY WROTE in a country church yard. 1751; ed. George Sherburn,
  Los Angeles 1951 (Augustan Reprint Soc.) (*facs.*).
ODES. 1757. The progress of poetry *and* The bard.

Works. Ed. Edmund Gosse, 4 vols. 1884.
Poems. 1768; ed. William Mason, York 1775 (*enlarged*); English
  poems, ed. Duncan C. Tovey, Cambridge 1898; Poetical works, ed.
  A.L.Poole, Oxford 1917, 1937 (rev. Frederick Page) (OSA); Poems,
  ed. Leonard Whibley, Oxford 1939 (WC).
Correspondence. Ed. Paget Toynbee and Leonard Whibley, 3 vols.
  Oxford 1935; Selected, ed. John Beresford, Oxford 1925 (WC).

Johnson, Samuel. *In his* Lives, 1779–81.
Gosse, Edmund. Gray. 1882 (EML).
Arnold, Matthew. *In his* Essays in criticism, ser. 2, 1888.
Tovey, Duncan C. Gray and his friends: letters and relics. Cambridge
  1890.
Stephen, Leslie. Gray and his school. *In his* Hours in a library, 1892
  (*enlarged*).
Cecil, David. *In his* Two quiet lives, 1948.
Ketton-Cremer, R.W. Gray: a biography. Cambridge 1955.

MATTHEW GREEN (1696 – 1737)

THE GROTTO: a poem written by Peter Drake. 1733.
THE SPLEEN: an epistle. 1737; 1737; 1738 (*enlarged*); ed. W.H.
Williams, 1936.

The spleen and other poems. Ed. J.Aikin, 1796; ed. R.K.Wood, 1925.
Complete verse rptd in Minor poets of the eighteenth century, ed.
Hugh I'A.Fausset, 1930 (EL).

GEORGE SAVILE, 1ST MARQUESS OF HALIFAX
(1633 – 1695)

THE CHARACTER OF A TRIMMER. 1688. *Written late in 1684.*
ADVICE TO A DAUGHTER. 1688; 1688.

Miscellanies. 1700.
Complete works. Ed. Walter Raleigh, Oxford 1912.

Foxcroft, H.C. The life and letters of Halifax. 2 vols. 1898.

DAVID HUME (1711 – 1776)

Jessop, T.E. A bibliography of Hume and of Scottish philosophy
from Hutcheson to Balfour. 1938.

A TREATISE OF HUMAN NATURE. 3 vols. 1739–40; ed. L.A.Selby-Bigge,
Oxford 1888; ed. A.D.Lindsay, 2 vols. 1911 (EL).
ESSAYS MORAL AND POLITICAL. 2 vols. Edinburgh 1742; 1748 (*enlarged*).
PHILOSOPHICAL ESSAYS concerning human understanding. 1748.
THE HISTORY of Great Britain, [1603–49]. Edinburgh 1754; vol. II
[1649–88], 1757; The history of England from Julius Caesar to 1688,
6 vols. 1762, 8 vols. 1778.
FOUR DISSERTATIONS. 1757. *Includes* The natural history of religion,
Of the passions, Of tragedy, Of the standard of taste.

Essays and treatises. 4 vols. 1753–6, 2 vols. 1777; Enquiries, ed. L.A.
Selby-Bigge, Oxford 1894, 1902 (*enlarged*). *Vol. II of 1777 largely
a revision of the* Treatise, *above.*

DIALOGUES CONCERNING NATURAL RELIGION. 1779; ed. Norman Kemp
Smith, Oxford 1935, 1947.

Philosophical works. Ed. T.H.Green and T.H.Grose, 4 vols. 1874–5.
Letters. Ed. J.Y.T.Greig, 2 vols. Oxford 1932; New letters, ed.
Raymond Klibansky and Ernest C.Mossner, Oxford 1954.

Price, H.H. Hume's theory of the external world. Oxford 1940.

Kemp Smith, Norman. The philosophy of Hume. 1941.
Mossner, Ernest C. The life of Hume. Edinburgh 1954.
Hume: a symposium. Ed. D.F.Pears, 1963.

SAMUEL JOHNSON (1709 – 1784)

Courtney, W.P. and D.Nichol Smith. A bibliography of Johnson. Oxford 1915; 1925.
The R.B.Adam library relating to Johnson and his era. 4 vols. New York 1929–30.

LONDON: a poem. 1738; The vanity of human wishes, 1749, 1755 (*in Dodsley's* Collection). *Satires iii and x of Juvenal, imitated.*
AN ACCOUNT OF THE LIFE of Mr Richard Savage. 1744; 1748. *Rptd in an edn of Savage's* Works, 1775, *and in* Lives, 1779–81, *below.*
THE PLAN OF A DICTIONARY of the English language. 1747.
IRENE: a tragedy. 1749.
THE RAMBLER. 1750–2 (*twice weekly*); 6 vols. 1752; ed. S.C.Roberts, 1953 (EL) (*selection*).
A DICTIONARY of the English language. 2 vols. 1755; 1755–6; 1773 (*both rev.*); A modern selection, ed. E.L.McAdam and George Milne, 1963.
PROPOSALS FOR PRINTING the dramatick works of Shakespeare. 1756.
THE PRINCE OF ABISSINIA: a tale. 2 vols. 1759; 1759; ed. R.W. Chapman, Oxford 1927. *Ch. I headed 'The history of Rasselas'.*
THE IDLER. Universal chronicle (1758–60) (*weekly*); 2 vols. 1761.
THE PLAYS OF SHAKESPEARE. 8 vols. 1765; 10 vols. 1773, 1778 (rev. George Steevens); Preface, 1765.
Johnson on Shakespeare. Ed. Walter Raleigh, Oxford 1908; 1925. *The* Proposals, *above, with* Preface *and selected notes.*
A JOURNEY to the Western Isles of Scotland. 1775; ed. R.W.Chapman, Oxford 1924 (*with Boswell's* Journal of a tour to the Hebrides).
PREFACES BIOGRAPHICAL AND CRITICAL to the works of the English poets. 10 vols. 1779–81; 4 vols. 1781 (*re-entitled* Lives of the English poets); 1783; ed. G.Birkbeck Hill, 3 vols. Oxford 1905.

Works. Ed. John Hawkins *et al.*, 15 vols. 1787–9; ed. Allen T.Hazen *et al.*, New Haven 1958–; Prose and poetry, ed. Mona Wilson, 1950, 1957 (RL); Selections, ed. R.W.Chapman, Oxford 1955, 1962 (WC).
Poems. Ed. D.Nichol Smith and E.L.McAdam, Oxford 1941.
Letters. Ed. R.W.Chapman, 3 vols. Oxford 1952; Selected, ed. Chapman, Oxford 1925 (WC).
Prefaces and dedications. Ed. Allen T.Hazen, New Haven 1937.

Piozzi, Hester Lynch (Mrs Thrale). Anecdotes of Johnson. 1786.

Hawkins, John. The life of Johnson. 1787; 1787 (*in* Works, *above*); ed. Bertram Davis, 1962.

Boswell, James. The life of Johnson. 2 vols. 1791.

Raleigh, Walter. Six essays on Johnson. Oxford 1910.

Wimsatt, W.K. The prose style of Johnson. New Haven 1941.

—— Philosophic words: a study of style and meaning in the Rambler and Dictionary. New Haven 1948.

Krutch, Joseph W. Johnson. New York 1944.

Leavis, F.R. *In his* The common pursuit, 1952.

Bate, Walter J. The achievement of Johnson. New York 1955.

Clifford, James L. Young Samuel Johnson [1709–49]. New York 1955.

Eliot, T.S. Johnson as critic and poet. *In his* On poetry and poets, 1957.

New light on Dr Johnson. Ed. F.W.Hilles, New Haven 1959.

'JUNIUS'

LETTERS. Woodfall's Public advertiser (Jan. 1769–Jan. 1772); 2 vols. 1772; ed. C.W.Everett, 1927.

WILLIAM LAW (1686 – 1761)

THE UNLAWFULNESS of stage-entertainment. 1726.

A SERIOUS CALL to a devout and holy life. 1729; 1732; ed. Norman Sykes, 1955 (EL).

Works. 9 vols. 1753–76; Selected mystical writings, ed. Stephen Hobhouse, 1938, 1948.

Stephen, Leslie. *In his* Hours in a library, ser. 2, 1876.

Talon, Henri. Law: a study in literary craftsmanship. 1948.

NATHANIEL LEE (1649? – 1692)

THE TRAGEDY OF NERO. 1675. *First of 11 tragedies, pbd 1675–89.*

SOPHONISBA: or Hannibal's overthrow. 1675.

THE RIVAL QUEENS: or the death of Alexander the Great. 1675.

MITHRIDATES, KING OF PONTUS. 1678.

CAESAR BORGIA. 1679.

THEODOSIUS: or the force of love. 1680.

LUCIUS JUNIUS BRUTUS: father of his country. 1681.

CONSTANTINE THE GREAT. 1684.

Works. 1694; ed. T.B.Stroup and A.L.Cooke,2 vols. New Brunswick, N.J. 1954–5.

Ham, Roswell G. Otway and Lee. New Haven 1931.

JOHN LOCKE (1632 – 1704)

TWO TREATISES OF GOVERNMENT. 1690; 1698; ed. Peter Laslett, Cambridge 1960, 1964; Second treatise, ed. J.W.Gough, Oxford 1946.

AN ESSAY concerning humane understanding. 1690; 1700 (*enlarged*); ed. A.C.Fraser, 2 vols. Oxford 1894. *Drafts A and B (written 1671) pbd 1936, 1931.*

A SECOND LETTER concerning toleration. 1690; A third letter for toleration, 1692. *First letter pbd in Latin, Gouda, Holland, 1689, tr. 1689.*

SOME THOUGHTS concerning education. 1693; 1695 (*enlarged*); Educational writings, ed. J.W.Adamson, Cambridge 1912, 1922.

POSTHUMOUS WORKS. Ed. Peter King?, 1706.

ESSAYS ON THE LAW OF NATURE: the Latin text with a translation. Ed. W.von Leyden, Oxford 1954. *Written 1660–1.*

Fox Bourne, H.R. The life of Locke. 2 vols. 1876.
Aaron, Richard I. John Locke. Oxford 1937; 1955.
James, D.G. The life of reason: Hobbes, Locke, Bolingbroke. 1949.
Cranston, Maurice. Locke: a biography. 1957.
Tuveson, Ernest L. The imagination as a means of grace: Locke and the aesthetics of romanticism. Berkeley, Cal. 1960.

JAMES MACPHERSON (1736 – 1796)

FRAGMENTS OF ANCIENT POETRY collected in the Highlands of Scotland and translated from the Gallic. Edinburgh 1760.

FINGAL: an ancient epic poem. 1762.

TEMORA. 1763. *Also an heroic poem,* The Highlander (1758) *and a prose trn of Homer's* Iliad (1773).

Works of Ossian. 2 vols. 1765; ed. O.L.Jiriczek, 3 vols. Heidelberg 1940 (*facs. of 1762 and 1763, above*).

Blair, Hugh. A critical dissertation on the poems of Ossian. 1763.
Saunders, Thomas Bailey. The life and letters of Macpherson. 1894.

BERNARD MANDEVILLE (1670 – 1733)

SOME FABLES after the method of La Fontaine. 1703; 1704 (*with addn*) (*re-entitled* Æsop dress'd: or a collection of fables).

THE GRUMBLING HIVE: or knaves turn'd honest. 1705; 1714 (*in* The fable of the bees, *below, pt i*).

THE VIRGIN UNMASK'D: or female dialogues. 1709; 1714 (*re-entitled* The mysteries of virginity).

THE FABLE OF THE BEES: or private vices, publick benefits. 2 pts. 1714–29; 1724, 1732 (pt i); 1734? (pts i–ii); ed. F.B.Kaye, 2 vols. Oxford 1924.

A LETTER TO DION, occasion'd by his book call'd Alciphron. 1732; ed. Jacob Viner, Los Angeles 1953 (Augustan Reprint Soc.) (*facs.*); ed. Bonamy Dobrée, Liverpool 1954. *Reply to Berkeley.*

LADY MARY WORTLEY MONTAGU,
née PIERREPONT
(1689 – 1762)

LETTERS written during her travels. Ed. John Cleland?, 3 vols. 1763; vol. iv, 1767 (*both pirated*).

Letters and works. Ed. Baron Wharncliffe, 3 vols. 1837; ed. W.Moy Thomas, 2 vols. 1861; Letters, ed. R.Brimley Johnson, 1906 (EL).

Halsband, Robert. The life of Lady Mary Wortley Montagu. Oxford 1956.

SIR ISAAC NEWTON (1642 – 1727)

Gray, George J. A bibliography of the works of Newton. Cambridge 1888; 1907 (*enlarged*).

PHILOSOPHIAE NATURALIS PRINCIPIA MATHEMATICA. 1687; 1726; tr. Andrew Motte, 2 vols. 1729, rev. Florian Cajori, Berkeley, Cal. 1934.

OPTICKS. 1704; 1730.

ARITHMETICA UNIVERSALIS. 1707; tr. 1720, 1728.

Opera. Ed. Samuel Horsley, 5 vols. 1779–85.

Correspondence. Ed. J.Edleston, 1850; ed. H.W.Turnbull, 7 vols. Cambridge 1959–.

Papers and letters on natural philosophy. Ed. I.Bernard Cohen and Robert E.Schofield, Cambridge 1958 (*facs.*).

Unpublished scientific papers: a selection from the Portsmouth collection. Ed. A.Rupert Hall and M.B.Hall, Cambridge 1962.

Brewster, David. Memoirs of Newton. 2 vols. 1855.

More, Louis T. Newton: a biography. New York 1934.

Nicolson, Marjorie Hope. Newton demands the Muse: Newton's Opticks and the eighteenth-century poets. Princeton 1946.

THOMAS OTWAY (1652 – 1685)

ALCIBIADES. 1675. *First of 10 plays pbd 1675–84.*

DON CARLOS, Prince of Spain. 1676.

THE ORPHAN. 1680.

VENICE PRESERV'D. 1682.

Works. 2 vols. 1712; ed. Montague Summers, 3 vols. 1926 (Nonesuch Press); ed. J.C.Ghosh, 2 vols. Oxford 1932.

Johnson, Samuel. *In his* Lives, 1779–81.
Ham, Roswell G. Otway and Lee. New Haven 1931.

THOMAS PAINE (1737 – 1809)

RIGHTS OF MAN: being an answer to Mr Burke's attack on the French revolution. 2 pts. 1791–2; 1 vol. 1915 (EL).

THE AGE OF REASON. 2 pts. Paris 1794–London 1795; ed. J.M. Robertson, 1905.

Writings. Ed. M.D.Conway, 4 vols. 1894–6; ed. Philip S.Foner, New York 1945.

Aldridge, Alfred O. Man of reason: the life of Paine. 1960.

THOMAS PARNELL (1679 – 1718)

POEMS ON SEVERAL OCCASIONS. Ed. Alexander Pope, 1722; 1770 (*with Goldsmith's* Life).

Works. 1755. Glasgow 1767; ed. George A.Aitken, 1894 (Aldine); ed. Hugh I'Anson Fausset, 1930 (EL) (*in* Minor poets of the eighteenth century).

Johnson, Samuel. *In his* Lives, 1779–81.

SAMUEL PEPYS (1633 – 1703)

Tanner, J.R. *et al.* Bibliotheca Pepysiana: a descriptive catalogue of the library of Pepys. 4 pts. 1914–40.

MEMOIRS RELATING TO THE ROYAL NAVY [1679–88]. 1690; ed. J.R. Tanner, Oxford 1906 (*facs.*).

MEMOIRS. Ed. Richard, Baron Braybrooke. 2 vols. 1825, 1848–9 (*re-entitled* Diary, *enlarged*); ed. Mynors Bright, 6 vols. 1875–9, 10 vols. 1893–9 (rev. Henry B.Wheatley).

Private correspondence, 1679–1703; Further correspondence, 1662–79. Ed. J.R.Tanner, 3 vols. 1926–9.
Letters and second diary. Ed. R.G.Howarth, 1932.
Letters of Pepys and his family circle. Ed. Helen Heath, Oxford 1955.

Tanner, J.R. Mr Pepys: an introduction to the diary. 1925.
Ponsonby, Arthur. Samuel Pepys. 1928 (EML).
Bryant, Arthur. Samuel Pepys. 3 vols. Cambridge 1933–8.

THOMAS PERCY (1729 – 1811)

RELIQUES OF ANCIENT ENGLISH POETRY. 3 vols. 1765; 1794; ed. Henry B.Wheatley, 3 vols. 1876–7; 2 vols. 1906 (EL).

Letters. Ed. D.Nichol Smith, Cleanth Brooks et al., c. 10 vols. Baton Rouge, La. 1944–.

AMBROSE PHILIPS (1675? – 1749)

PASTORALS. 1710; Pastorals, epistles, odes and other poems, 1748.

Poems. Ed. M.G.Segar, Oxford 1937.

THE FREETHINKER. March 1718–July 1721; 3 vols. 1722.

Three tragedies. 1725. First pbd 1712–23.

Johnson, Samuel. In his Lives, 1779–81.

ALEXANDER POPE (1688 – 1744)

Abbott, Edwin. A concordance to the works. 1875.

Griffith, R.H. Pope: a bibliography. Vol. I (2 pts). Austin, Texas 1922–7.

PASTORALS. In Tonson's Poetical miscellanies, pt vi, 1709.

AN ESSAY ON CRITICISM. 1711; 1744.

THE RAPE OF THE LOCK. 1712 (in Lintot's Miscellaneous poems); 1714 (enlarged).

WINDSOR-FOREST. 1713.

THE ILIAD. 6 vols. 1715–20; 1 vol. 1902 (WC).

POEMS ON SEVERAL OCCASIONS. 1717; ed. Norman Ault, 1935 (Nonesuch Press). Pope's own miscellany of poems by his circle, including 37 unacknowledged poems of his own.

THE WORKS OF SHAKESPEAR collated and corrected. 6 vols. 1725.

THE ODYSSEY. 5 vols. 1725–6; 1 vol. 1903 (WC).

THE DUNCIAD: an heroic poem. 1728 (bks i–iii), The Dunciad variorum, 1729 (with notes etc.); The new dunciad, 1742 (bk iv); The Dunciad, 1743 (bks i–iv).

AN ESSAY ON MAN. 4 pts. 1733–4; 1 vol. 1734.

AN EPISTLE TO DR ARBUTHNOT. 1735.

IMITATIONS OF HORACE. In Works, vol. ii, 1738.

Works. 1717; 3 vols. 1735–6; 1737–8; ed. William Warburton, 9 vols. 1751 (with final revisions), Supplement, 1757; ed. W.Elwin and W.J.Courthope, 10 vols. 1871–89; Selected poetry and prose, ed. W.K.Wimsatt, New York 1951.

Poems: Twickenham edition. Ed. John Butt et al., 11 vols. 1939–; ed. Butt, 1963 (with selected notes).

Prose works. Ed. Norman Ault, vol. I, 1711–20. Oxford 1935.
Correspondence. Ed. George Sherburn, 5 vols. Oxford 1956; Letters, ed. John Butt, Oxford 1960 (WC) (*selection*).

Warton, Joseph. An essay on the writings and genius of Mr Pope. 2 pts. 1756–82.
Johnson, Samuel. *In his* Lives, 1779–81.
Spence, Joseph. Observations, anecdotes and characters. Ed. S. W. Singer, 1820.
Sitwell, Edith. Alexander Pope. 1930.
Sherburn, George. The early career of Pope. Oxford 1934. *To 1727.*
Root, R. K. The poetical career of Pope. Princeton 1938.
Tillotson, Geoffrey. On the poetry of Pope. Oxford 1938; 1950.
—— Pope and human nature. Oxford 1958.
Williams, Aubrey L. Pope's Dunciad. Baton Rouge, La. 1955.
Brower, Reuben A. Pope: the poetry of allusion. Oxford 1959.

MATTHEW PRIOR (1664 – 1721)

POEMS ON SEVERAL OCCASIONS. 1707, 1709; A second collection, 1716, 1718, 1720 (*enlarged*). 1707 *and* 1716 *were unauthorized.*

Writings. Ed. A. R. Waller, 2 vols. Cambridge 1905–7; Literary works, ed. H. Bunker Wright and Monroe K. Spears, 2 vols. Oxford 1959.

Johnson, Samuel. *In his* Lives, 1779–81.
Legg, L. G. Wickham. Prior: his public career and correspondence. Cambridge 1921.
Eves, Charles K. Prior, poet and diplomatist. New York 1939.

ALLAN RAMSAY (1686 – 1758)

Martin, Burns. Bibliography of Ramsay. Glasgow 1931.

POEMS. Edinburgh 1720; 2 vols. 1721–9; ed. H. Harvey Wood, Edinburgh 1940.
THE GENTLE SHEPHERD: a Scots pastoral comedy. Edinburgh 1725.

Works. Ed. Burns Martin, John W. Oliver, Alexander Kinghorn and Alexander Law, 4 vols. Edinburgh 1950– (Scottish Text Soc.).

Martin, Burns. Allan Ramsay. Cambridge, Mass. 1931.

SIR JOSHUA REYNOLDS (1723 – 1792)

SEVEN DISCOURSES delivered at the Royal Academy. 1778; 1797; 1809 (*in* Works, *below*); ed. Roger Fry, 1905; ed. Austin Dobson, Oxford 1907 (WC); 1924 (Royal Acad. of Arts). *Fifteen discourses, pbd separately 1769–91.*

Works. Ed. Edmond Malone, 2 vols. 1797; 3 vols. 1798, 1809.

PORTRAITS. Ed. F.W.Hilles, New York 1952.

Letters. Ed. F.W.Hilles, Cambridge 1929.

Boswell, James. *In his* The life of Samuel Johnson, 2 vols. 1791.

Malone, Edmond. An account of the life and writings. *In his edn of
the* Works, *1797, above.*

Hilles, F.W. The literary career of Reynolds. Cambridge 1936.

Hudson, Derek. Reynolds: a personal study; with Journey from
London to Brentford. 1958.

SAMUEL RICHARDSON (1689 – 1761)

Sale, William M. Richardson: a bibliographical record. New Haven
1936.

PAMELA: or virtue rewarded. 2 vols. 1740; ed. George Saintsbury,
2 vols. 1914 (EL); Introduction [to 2nd edn, 1741], ed. Sheridan W.
Baker, Los Angeles 1954 (Augustan Reprint Soc.) (*facs.*).

CLARISSA. 7 vols. 1748; 4 vols. 1932 (EL).

THE HISTORY of Sir Charles Grandison. 7 vols. 1754; ed. George Saintsbury, 1895.

Novels. 18 vols. Oxford 1929–31.

Correspondence. Ed. Anna L.Barbauld, 6 vols. 1804.

Stephen, Leslie. Richardson's novels. *In his* Hours in a library, 1874.

Dobson, Austin. Samuel Richardson. 1902 (EML).

McKillop, Alan D. Richardson, printer and novelist. Chapel Hill,
N.C. 1936.

Sale, William M. Richardson, master printer. Ithaca, N.Y. 1950.

JOHN WILMOT, 2ND EARL OF ROCHESTER
(1647 – 1680)

POEMS ON SEVERAL OCCASIONS. 'Antwerp' (London) 1680?, ed. James
Thorpe, Princeton 1950 (*facs.*); 1691 (*enlarged*).

Collected works. Ed. John Hayward, 1926 (Nonesuch Press); Poems,
ed. V.de Sola Pinto, 1953, 1964 (ML).

Burnet, Gilbert. Some passages of the life and death of Rochester.
1680.

Johnson, Samuel. *In his* Lives, 1779–81.

Prinz, Johannes. Rochester: his life and writings. Leipzig 1927.

Pinto, V.de Sola. Rochester. 1935; 1962 (*re-entitled* Enthusiast in wit).

WENTWORTH DILLON, 4TH EARL OF ROSCOMMON
(1633? – 1685)

HORACE'S ART OF POETRY made English. 1680; ed. John Bell, Edinburgh 1779 (*in* The poets of Great Britain).

AN ESSAY ON TRANSLATED VERSE. 1684; 1685 (*enlarged*), ed. J.E. Spingarn, Oxford 1908–9 (*in* Critical essays of the seventeenth century). *A verse essay.*

OVID'S ART OF LOVE made English. 1692.

A PROSPECT OF DEATH: a Pindarique essay. 1704.

Works of the late Earls of Rochester and Roscommon. 1707; 2 vols. 1714 (*with Dorset's works*); Poems, 1717.

The Christian poet: or remains by Roscommon. 1735.

Johnson, Samuel. *In his* Lives, 1779–81.

THOMAS RYMER (1641 – 1713)

THE TRAGEDIES of the last age. 1678.

A SHORT VIEW OF TRAGEDY. 1693. *Reply by Dennis, p. 121, above.*

Critical works. Ed. Curt A. Zimansky, New Haven 1956.

SIR CHARLES SEDLEY (1639? – 1701)

THE MULBERRY GARDEN: a comedy. 1668.

ANTONY AND CLEOPATRA: a tragedy. 1677.

BELLAMIRA: or the mistress. 1687.

THE GRUMBLER: a comedy. 1719.

Miscellaneous works. Ed. William Ayloffe, 1702; Poetical works, with large additions, 1707; Works, with memoirs [by Daniel Defoe?], 2 vols. 1722; Poetical and dramatic works, ed. V. de Sola Pinto, 2 vols. 1928.

Pinto, V. de Sola. Sir Charles Sedley. 1927.

ANTHONY ASHLEY COOPER, 3RD EARL OF SHAFTESBURY (1671 – 1713)

CHARACTERISTICKS OF MEN, manners, opinions, times. 3 vols. 1711; 1714; ed. J.M. Robertson, 2 vols. 1900; Second characters, ed. Benjamin Rand, Cambridge 1914. *Separate tracts pbd 1699–1710.*

The life, unpublished letters and Philosophical regimen. Ed. Benjamin Rand, New York 1900. *Includes* Life sketch *by his son.*

Fowler, Thomas. Shaftesbury and Hutcheson. 1882.

Brett, R. L. The third earl of Shaftesbury: a study in eighteenth-century literary theory. 1951.

WILLIAM SHENSTONE (1714 – 1763)

POEMS UPON VARIOUS OCCASIONS. Oxford 1737.
THE SCHOOL-MISTRESS: in imitation of Spenser. 1742; Oxford 1924
(*facs.*); 1748 (*enlarged*).

Works. 3 vols. 1764–9.
Letters. Ed. Marjorie Williams, Oxford 1939; ed. Duncan Mallam,
Minneapolis 1939.
Miscellany, 1759–63. Ed. I.A.Gordon, Oxford 1952.

Johnson, Samuel. *In his* Lives, 1779–81.
Graves, Richard. Recollections of Shenstone. 1788.
Williams, Marjorie. William Shenstone. Birmingham 1935.

RICHARD BRINSLEY SHERIDAN (1751 – 1816)

THE RIVALS. 1775; 1776; ed. R.L.Purdy, Oxford 1935 (*from Larpent
MS.*).
THE GOVERNESS. Dublin 1777 (*pirated*); London 1794 (*entitled* The
duenna).
THE SCHOOL FOR SCANDAL. Dublin 1780(*pirated*); 1799; ed. R. Crompton
Rhodes, Oxford 1930.
THE CRITIC. 1781.
SPEECHES. 5 vols. 1816.

Works. 2 vols. 1821; Plays and poems, ed. R.Crompton Rhodes,
3 vols. Oxford 1928.
Dramatic works. Ed. Joseph Knight, Oxford 1906 (WC); 1924 (OSA).

Moore, Thomas. Memoirs of the life of Sheridan. 1825; 2 vols. 1827.
Sichel, Walter. Sheridan, from new and original material. 2 vols. 1909.
Rhodes, R.Crompton. Harlequin Sheridan: the man and the legends.
Oxford 1933.

ALGERNON SIDNEY (1622 – 1682)

DISCOURSES CONCERNING GOVERNMENT. 1698.
LETTERS to Hon. Henry Savile. 1742.
PAPERS. *In* Letters and memorials of state, ed. Arthur Collins, vol. II,
1746.

CHRISTOPHER SMART (1722 – 1771)

POEMS ON SEVERAL OCCASIONS. 1752.
THE HILLIAD: an epic poem. 1753.
A SONG TO DAVID. 1763, Oxford 1926 (*facs.*); with other poems, ed.
Edmund Blunden, 1924.

HORACE TRANSLATED INTO VERSE. 4 vols. 1767.

REJOICE IN THE LAMB. Ed. William F. Stead, 1939; ed. William H. Bond, Cambridge, Mass. 1954 (*re-entitled* Jubilate agno).

Poems. 2 vols. Reading 1791; Collected poems, ed. Norman Callan, 2 vols. 1949 (ML); Selected poems, ed. Robert Brittain, Princeton 1950. *No complete collection.*

Devlin, Christopher. Poor Kit Smart. 1961.

ADAM SMITH (1723 – 1790)

THE THEORY OF MORAL SENTIMENTS. 1759.

AN INQUIRY into the nature and causes of the wealth of nations. 2 vols. 1776; ed. Edwin Cannan, 1904; 2 vols. 1910 (EL).

ESSAYS on philosophical subjects. 1795.

LECTURES on rhetoric and belles lettres, 1762–3. Ed. John M. Lothian, Edinburgh 1963 (*from MS.*).

Stewart, Dugald. Biographical memoir of Adam Smith. Trans. Royal Soc. of Edinburgh (1793).

Bagehot, Walter. *In his* Economic studies, 1880; *and in his* Biographical studies, 1881.

Hirst, Francis W. Adam Smith. 1904 (EML).

Scott, W. R. Adam Smith as student and professor. Glasgow 1937.

TOBIAS SMOLLETT (1721 – 1771)

THE ADVENTURES of Roderick Random. 2 vols. 1748; 1750; 1 vol. Oxford 1930 (WC). *First of five novels.*

THE ADVENTURES of Peregrine Pickle. 4 vols. 1751; 1758; ed. James L. Clifford, Oxford 1964.

THE ADVENTURES of Ferdinand, Count Fathom. 2 vols. 1753.

A COMPLETE HISTORY OF ENGLAND to 1748. 4 vols. 1757–8, 11 vols. 1758–9; Continuation [1748–65], 5 vols. 1760–5. *Often rptd in part as a continuation of Hume's* History (1762).

THE ADVENTURES of Sir Launcelot Greaves. 2 vols. 1762.

TRAVELS through France and Italy. 2 vols. 1766; 1 vol. Oxford 1907 (WC).

THE EXPEDITION of Humphry Clinker. 3 vols. 1771; 1 vol. Oxford 1925 (WC).

Also trns of Gil Blas (1749), Don Quixote (1755), *Fénelon's* Télémaque (1776) etc., *and editor of the* Critical review, 1756–62.

Select works, revised by the author. 8 vols. Dublin 1776; Works, ed. George Saintsbury, 12 vols. 1895; ed. W. E. Henley and Thomas Seccombe, 12 vols. 1899–1901.

Novels. 11 vols. Oxford 1925–6.

Letters. Ed. Edward S. Noyes, Cambridge, Mass. 1926.

Anderson, Robert. The life of Smollett. Edinburgh 1806.

Martz, Louis L. The later career of Smollett. New Haven 1942.

Kahrl, George M. Smollett: traveler-novelist. Chicago 1945.

Knapp, Lewis M. Smollett: doctor of men and manners. Princeton 1949.

THOMAS SPRAT (1635 – 1713)

OBSERVATIONS on Monsieur de Sorbier's Voyage into England. 1665. *A defence of England in reply to* Samuel de Sorbière, Relation d'un voyage en Angleterre (Paris 1664).

THE HISTORY of the Royal-Society of London. 1667; 1702; ed. Jackson I. Cope and Harold W. Jones, St Louis 1958 (*facs.*).

Also a collection of Pindaric verse, The plague of Athens (1659), *sermons and a life of Cowley in his edn of Cowley's works (1668).*

SIR RICHARD STEELE (1672 – 1729)

THE CHRISTIAN HERO. 1701; 1701 (*with addns*); 1710; ed. Rae Blanchard, Oxford 1932.

THE TATLER. April 1709–Jan. 1711; 4 vols. 1710–11; ed. George A. Aitken, 4 vols. 1898–9. *With Joseph Addison.*

THE SPECTATOR. March 1711–Sept. 1714; 8 vols. 1712–15; ed. Henry Morley, 1868; ed. G. Gregory Smith, 8 vols. 1897–8 and 4 vols. 1907, 1958 (EL); ed. Donald F. Bond, 5 vols. Oxford 1964. *With Addison.*

THE ENGLISHMAN: being the sequel to the Guardian. Oct. 1713–Nov. 1715; ed. Rae Blanchard, Oxford 1955.

Periodical literature, 1714–16: The lover, The reader [etc.], ed. Rae Blanchard, Oxford 1959.

[Plays]. Ed. George A. Aitken, 1894 (Mermaid). *The four comedies, pbd separately 1702–23, and two fragments.*

Correspondence. Ed. Rae Blanchard, Baltimore 1941.

Tracts and pamphlets. Ed. Rae Blanchard, Baltimore 1944.

Occasional verse. Ed. Rae Blanchard, Oxford 1952.

Dobson, Austin. Richard Steele. 1886.

Aitken, George A. Richard Steele. 2 vols. 1889.

Graham, Walter. The beginnings of English literary periodicals, 1665–1715. New York 1926.

—— English literary periodicals. New York 1930.

LAURENCE STERNE (1713 – 1768)

THE LIFE AND OPINIONS of Tristram Shandy. 9 vols. York (*later* London) 1760–7; ed. James A. Work, New York 1940.

THE SERMONS OF MR YORICK. 7 vols. 1760–9.

A SENTIMENTAL JOURNEY through France and Italy. 2 vols. 1768; ed. Virginia Woolf, Oxford 1928 (WC).

Works. 5 vols. 1773; [Selection], ed. Douglas Grant, 1950 (RL).

Letters. Ed. Lewis P. Curtis, Oxford 1935.

Bagehot, Walter. Sterne and Thackeray. *In his* Literary studies, 1879.

Stephen, Leslie. *In his* Hours in a library, 1892 (*enlarged*).

Cross, Wilbur L. Life and times of Sterne. New York 1909; New Haven 1929.

Fluchère, Henri. Sterne: de l'homme et de l'œuvre. Paris 1961.

Tuveson, Ernest L. Locke and Sterne. *In* Reason and the imagination, ed. J. A. Mazzeo, New York 1962.

JONATHAN SWIFT (1667 – 1745)

Williams, Harold. Dean Swift's library. Cambridge 1932.

Teerink, Herman. A bibliography of Swift. The Hague 1937; Philadelphia 1962.

A TALE OF A TUB; to which is added An account of a battel between antient and modern books. 1704; 1710; ed. A. C. Guthkelch and D. Nichol Smith, Oxford 1920, 1958.

THE CONDUCT OF THE ALLIES. 1711.

A PROPOSAL for correcting, improving and ascertaining the English tongue. 1712.

A LETTER of advice to a young poet. Dublin 1721.

A LETTER to the whole people of Ireland, by M. B. Drapier. Dublin 1724; The Drapier's letters, ed. Herbert Davis, Oxford 1935.

TRAVELS into several remote nations of the world by Lemuel Gulliver. 2 vols. 1726; Dublin 1735 (*in* Works, *below*); Oxford 1919 (OSA); ed. Harold Williams, 1926; ed. Herbert Davis, Oxford 1941, 1959.

A SHORT VIEW of the state of Ireland. Dublin 1727?

A MODEST PROPOSAL for preventing the children of poor people from being a burthen. Dublin 1729.

THE LIFE and genuine character of Doctor Swift. 1733; Dublin 1739 (*rev. and extended as* Verses on the death of Dr Swift).

A COMPLETE COLLECTION of genteel and ingenious conversation, in three dialogues. 1738; ed. Eric Partridge, 1963 (Polite conversation).

THE HISTORY of the four last years of the Queen. 1758. *Mainly written in 1712.*

JOURNAL TO STELLA. Ed. Harold Williams, 2 vols. Oxford 1948.
First pbd in part, 1766 and 1768.

Works. 4 vols. Dublin 1735; ed. Walter Scott, 19 vols. Edinburgh
1814; Gulliver's travels and selected writings, ed. John Hayward,
1934 (Nonesuch Lib.).

Prose works. Ed. Temple Scott, 12 vols. 1897–1908; ed. Herbert
Davis, 15 vols. Oxford 1939–64.

Poems. Ed. Harold Williams, 3 vols. Oxford 1937; 1958.

Letters to Charles Ford. Ed. D. Nichol Smith, Oxford 1935; Correspondence, ed. Harold Williams, 6 vols. Oxford 1963–.

Johnson, Samuel. *In his* Lives, 1779–81.

Scott, Walter. Memoirs of Swift. *In his edn of the* Works, *above,*
Edinburgh 1814.

Craik, Henry. The life of Swift. 1882; 2 vols. 1894.

Quintana, Ricardo. The mind and art of Swift. New York 1936; 1953.

Davis, Herbert. The satire of Swift. New York 1947: Oxford 1964
(*collected in his* Jonathan Swift).

Leavis, F. R. The irony of Swift. *In his* The common pursuit, 1952.

Landa, Louis A. Swift and the Church of Ireland. Oxford 1954.

Murry, J. Middleton. Swift: a critical biography. 1954.

Ehrenpreis, Irwin. The personality of Swift. 1958.

—— Swift: the man, his works, and the age. 3 vols. 1962–.

Williams, Kathleen. Swift and the age of compromise. Lawrence,
Kansas 1959.

Crane, Ronald S. *In* Reason and the imagination, ed. J. A. Mazzeo,
New York 1962. *On Gulliver bk iv.*

SIR WILLIAM TEMPLE (1628 – 1699)

POEMS. 1670.

AN ESSAY upon the advancement of trade in Ireland. Dublin 1673.

OBSERVATIONS upon the United Provinces of the Netherlands. 1673;
ed. G. N. Clark, Cambridge 1933.

Miscellanea. 3 pts. 1680–1701. *Pt i includes* Essay on government *and*
Survey of the Empire.

AN INTRODUCTION to the history of England. 1695; 1699.

LETTERS written during his being Ambassador at the Hague. 1699;
Letters, ed. Jonathan Swift, 2 vols. 1700; Memoirs, ed. Swift, 1709.

Works. 2 vols. 1720.

Early essays and romances. Ed. G. C. Moore Smith, Oxford 1930
(*from MS.*).

Bentley, Richard. Dissertation upon Phalaris. *In Wotton's* Reflections
upon ancient and modern learning, 1699 (2nd edn).

Giffard, Martha Lady. The life and character of Temple. 1728; ed.
  G.C.Moore Smith, Oxford 1930 (*in* Early essays and romances,
  above). *Two studies of Temple written in 1690 by his sister.*
Courtenay, Thomas P. Memoirs of the life, works and correspondence
  of Temple. 2 vols. 1836.
Osborne, Dorothy. Letters to Temple. Ed. E.A.Parry, 1888, 1903
  (*enlarged*); ed. G.C.Moore Smith, Oxford 1928 (*from MS.*).
  Letters from his future wife, written 1652–4.

JAMES THOMSON (1700 – 1748)

WINTER: a poem. 1726, 1726 (*enlarged*); Summer, 1727; Spring, 1728.
The seasons. 1730; 1744; 1746 (*both enlarged*); ed. Otto Zippel,
  Berlin 1908. *1730 includes the first edn of* Autumn.
BRITANNIA: a poem. 1729; 1730.
THE TRAGEDY OF SOPHONISBA. 1730. *Four other tragedies and a masque
  pbd 1738–49.*
LIBERTY: a poem. 5 pts. 1735–6.
THE CASTLE OF INDOLENCE: an allegorical poem written in imitation of
  Spenser. 1748; ed. Alan D.McKillop, Lawrence, Kansas 1961.

Works. Ed. George, Baron Lyttelton, 4 vols. 1750; Complete poetical
  works, ed. J.Logie Robertson, Oxford 1908 (OSA).
Letters and documents. Ed. Alan D.McKillop, Lawrence, Kansas
  1958.

Johnson, Samuel. *In his* Lives, 1779–81.
McKillop, Alan D. The background of Thomson's Seasons.
  Minneapolis 1942.
Grant, Douglas. James Thomson. 1951.

HESTER LYNCH THRALE, née SALUSBURY, later
PIOZZI (1741 – 1821)

ANECDOTES of the late Samuel Johnson. 1786; ed. S.C.Roberts,
  Cambridge 1925.
THRALIANA: the diary of Mrs Thrale, 1776–1809. Ed. Katharine C.
  Balderston, 2 vols. Oxford 1942; 1951.

Letters of Samuel Johnson, with Mrs Thrale's genuine letters to him.
  Ed. R.W.Chapman, 3 vols. Oxford 1952.

Clifford, James L. Hester Lynch Piozzi. Oxford 1941; 1952.

JOHN TILLOTSON (1630 – 1694)

SERMONS. 1694; ed. Thomas Birch, 3 vols. 1752 (*complete*).
The golden book of Tillotson: selections. Ed. James Moffatt, 1926.

SIR JOHN VANBRUGH (1664 – 1726)

THE RELAPSE. 1697. *First of nine plays, pbd 1697–1728.*
THE PROVOK'D WIFE. 1697.

Plays. 2 vols. 1719; [Four plays], ed. A.E.H.Swaen, 1896 (Mermaid);
Complete works, ed. Bonamy Dobrée and Geoffrey Webb, 4 vols.
1927–8.

Dobrée, Bonamy. *In his* Essays in biography, 1680–1726, Oxford 1925.
Whistler, Laurence. Vanbrugh: architect and dramatist. 1938.

HORACE WALPOLE, 4TH EARL OF ORFORD
(1717 – 1797)

Hazen, Allen T. A bibliography of the Strawberry Hill press. New
Haven 1942; A bibliography of Walpole, New Haven 1948.

A CATALOGUE of the royal and noble authors of England. 2 vols.
Strawberry Hill 1758; 1787 (*enlarged*); ed. Thomas Park, 5 vols.
1806 (*continued*).
ANECDOTES OF PAINTING in England. 4 vols. Strawberry Hill 1762–71;
1782 (*enlarged*); Anecdotes, 1760–95 (vol. v), ed. F.W.Hilles and
P.B.Daghlian, New Haven 1937.
THE CASTLE OF OTRANTO. 1765; 1765 (*with preface*); ed. W.S.Lewis,
Oxford 1964.
MEMOIRS AND PORTRAITS [1751–71]. Ed. Matthew Hodgart, 1963.

Works. Ed. Mary Berry *et al.*, 9 vols. 1798–1825.
Private correspondence. 4 vols. 1820; Letters, ed. Mrs Paget Toyn-
bee, 16 vols. Oxford 1903–5, Supplement, ed. Paget Toynbee, 3 vols.
Oxford 1918–25; Correspondence, ed. W.S.Lewis *et al.*, *c.* 50 vols.
New Haven 1937–; [Selected] letters, ed. W.S.Lewis, 1951.

Stephen, Leslie. *In his* Hours in a library, ser. 2, 1876.
Dobson, Austin. Horace Walpole. New York 1890; Oxford 1927 (rev.
Paget Toynbee).
Ketton-Cremer, R.W. Horace Walpole: a biography. 1940.
Lewis, W.S. Horace Walpole. New York 1961.

THOMAS WARTON the younger (1728 – 1790)

OBSERVATIONS ON THE FAIRY QUEEN. 1754; 2 vols. 1762 (*enlarged*).
THE HISTORY OF ENGLISH POETRY from the eleventh to the eighteenth
century. 3 vols. 1774–81; ed. Richard Price (d. 1833), 4 vols. 1824;
An unpublished continuation, ed. Rodney M.Baine, Los Angeles
1953 (Augustan Reprint Soc.). *Completed to c. 1600.*

Poetical works. Ed. Richard Mant, 2 vols. Oxford 1802; The three Wartons: a choice of their verse, ed. Eric Partridge, 1927. *Poems by Thomas Warton the elder, Joseph and Thomas Warton the younger.*

Correspondence of Thomas Percy and Warton. Ed. M. G. Robinson and Leah Dennis, Baton Rouge, La. 1951.

Ritson, Joseph. Observations on the History in a familiar letter to the author. 1782.

Nichol Smith, D. Warton's History of English poetry. Proc. Brit. Acad. xv (1929).

ISAAC WATTS (1674 – 1748)

HORAE LYRICAE. 1706; 1709 (*enlarged*).
HYMNS AND SPIRITUAL SONGS. 1707; 1709 (*enlarged*).
DIVINE SONGS for the use of children. 1715.
THE PSALMS IMITATED. 1719.

Johnson, Samuel. *In his* Lives, 1779–81.
Davis, Arthur Paul. Isaac Watts. New York 1943.

JOHN WESLEY (1703 – 1791)

Green, Richard. The works of John and Charles Wesley: a bibliography. 1896.

A COLLECTION of psalms and hymns. Charlestown 1737. *23 collections of hymns pbd 1737–86, with his brother Charles Wesley.*

JOURNAL. 21 pts. 1739–91; ed. Nehemiah Curnock, 8 vols. 1909–16.

Works. 32 vols. Bristol 1771–4.
Letters. Ed. John Telford, 8 vols. 1931.

Southey, Robert. Life of Wesley. 2 vols. 1820.
Dobrée, Bonamy. John Wesley. 1933.
Green, V. H. H. The young Mr Wesley: a study of John Wesley and Oxford. 1961.
Lawton, George. Wesley's English. 1962.

GILBERT WHITE (1720 – 1793)

Martin, Edward A. A bibliography of Gilbert White. 1897; 1934.

THE NATURAL HISTORY and antiquities of Selborne. 1789; 1813 (*poems added*); Oxford 1937 (WC).

JOURNALS. Ed. Walter Johnson, 1931.

Writings. Ed. H. J. Massingham, 2 vols. 1938 (*incomplete*).

Holt-White, Rashleigh. The life and letters of Gilbert White. 2 vols. 1901.

ANNE FINCH, COUNTESS OF WINCHILSEA,
née KINGSMILL
(1666? – 1720)

THE SPLEEN: a Pindarique ode. *In* A new miscellany, 1701; 1709 (*separately*).

MISCELLANY POEMS on several occasions. 1713.

Poems. Ed. Myra Reynolds, Chicago 1903; ed. Hugh I'Anson Fausset *in* Minor poets of the eighteenth century, 1930 (EL).

MARY WOLLSTONECRAFT (MRS WILLIAM GODWIN) (1759 – 1797)

THOUGHTS on the education of daughters. 1787.

A VINDICATION of the rights of woman, vol. I. 1792; 1929 (EL).

Posthumous works. Ed. William Godwin, 4 vols. 1798.

Love letters to Gilbert Imlay. Ed. Roger Ingpen, 1908.

ANTHONY WOOD (1632 – 1695)

HISTORIA ET ANTIQUITATES universitatis oxoniensis. Tr. and ed. John Fell, 2 vols. Oxford 1674; The history in English, ed. John Gutch, 4 vols. Oxford 1786–96 (*from MS.*).

ATHENAE OXONIENSES. 2 vols. 1691–2. *A biographical dictionary of Oxford writers and bishops, partly based on help from John Aubrey.*

SURVEY OF THE ANTIQUITIES of the City of Oxford. Ed. Andrew Clark, 3 vols. Oxford 1889–99.

THE LIFE AND TIMES of Anthony Wood described by himself: collected from his diaries and other papers [1657–95]. Ed. Andrew Clark, 5 vols. Oxford 1891–1900; Abridged, ed. Llewelyn Powys, 1932. *The autobiography, in its second version, was first pbd by Thomas Hearne in his edn of* Thomas Caii Vindiciae antiquitates academiae oxoniensis (1730).

WILLIAM WYCHERLEY (1640? – 1716)

LOVE IN A WOOD: or St James's Park. 1672.

THE GENTLEMAN DANCING MASTER. 1673.

THE COUNTRY-WIFE. 1675.

THE PLAIN-DEALER. 1677.

Posthumous works. Ed. Lewis Theobald, 2 vols. 1728–9; Complete works, ed. Montague Summers, 4 vols. 1924 (Nonesuch Press).

Plays. Ed. W. C. Ward, 1888 (Mermaid).

ARTHUR YOUNG (1741 – 1820)

A TOUR through the southern counties. 1768; 1769 (*enlarged*); through the east, 4 vols. 1770–1; through the north, 4 vols. 1771.

TOUR IN IRELAND. 2 vols. 1780; ed. Constantia Maxwell, Cambridge 1925 (*selection*).

TRAVELS DURING 1787–90 with a view to ascertaining the prosperity of France. 2 vols. Bury St Edmunds 1792–4; ed. Constantia Maxwell, Cambridge 1929 (*selection*).

EDWARD YOUNG (1683 – 1765)

THE COMPLAINT: or night-thoughts. 9 pts. 1742–5; 1 vol. 1747; illustr. William Blake, 1797.

CONJECTURES ON ORIGINAL COMPOSITION. 1759; ed. Edith J.Morley, Manchester 1918. *With Samuel Richardson.*

Works. 4 vols. 1757.

Johnson, Samuel. *In his* Lives, 1779–81. *Largely by Herbert Croft.*
'Eliot, George'. Worldliness and other-worldliness: the poet Young (1857). *In her* Essays and Leaves from a notebook, Edinburgh 1884.
Shelley, Henry C. The life and letters of Edward Young. 1914.

THE NINETEENTH CENTURY
(1800–1900)

THE NINETEENTH CENTURY
(1800–1900)

Bibliographies

Carter, John and Graham Pollard. An enquiry into the nature of certain nineteenth-century pamphlets. 1934. *Exposes forgeries by Thomas J. Wise of the Brownings, Morris, D. G. Rossetti, Ruskin, Swinburne etc.*

Ehrsam, T. G., R. H. Deily and R. M. Smith. Bibliographies of twelve Victorian authors. New York 1936. *Arnold, E. B. Browning, Clough, FitzGerald, Hardy, Kipling, Morris, Christina Rossetti, D. G. Rossetti, Stevenson, Swinburne, Tennyson.*

Graham, Walter *et al.* The romantic movement. ELH, iv–xvii (1937–49); Philological quarterly, xxix– (1950–). *Annual lists of modern studies since 1936 in European literature, 1800–37.*

Templeman, William D. (ed.). Bibliographies of studies in Victorian literature, 1932–44. Urbana, Ill. 1945; 1945–54, ed. Austin Wright, Urbana, Ill. 1956. *Annual lists collected from* Modern philology.

Raysor, T. M. (ed.). The English romantic poets: a review of research. New York 1950; 1956. *Byron, Coleridge, Keats, Shelley, Wordsworth.*

Sadleir, Michael. XIX century fiction: a bibliographical record. 2 vols. 1951.

Faverty, Frederic E. (ed.). The Victorian poets: a guide to research. Cambridge, Mass. 1956. *Arnold, the Brownings, Clough, FitzGerald, Hopkins, Swinburne, Tennyson.*

Houtchens, C. W. and L. H. (edd.). The English romantic poets and essayists: a review of research and criticism. New York 1957.

Townsend, Francis G. *et al.* Victorian bibliography. Victorian studies, i– (1958–). *Annual lists of modern studies since 1957.*

Literary History and Criticism

Jeffrey, Francis. Contributions to the Edinburgh review [1802–48]. 4 vols. 1844; Literary criticism, ed. D. Nichol Smith, Oxford 1910 (*selection*).

Saintsbury, George. A history of nineteenth-century literature, 1780–1895. 1896.

Elton, Oliver. A survey of English literature, 1780–1830. 2 vols. 1912; 1830–80, 2 vols. 1920.

Chesterton, G. K. The Victorian age in literature. 1913 (Home univ. lib.).

Nicoll, Allardyce. A history of nineteenth-century drama, 1800–50. 2 vols. Cambridge 1930; 1850–1900, 2 vols. Cambridge 1946.

Evans, B. Ifor. English poetry in the later nineteenth century. 1933.

Praz, Mario. The romantic agony. Oxford 1933; 1951.

—— The hero in eclipse in Victorian fiction. Oxford 1956.

Cecil, David. Early Victorian novelists. 1934. *The Brontës, Dickens, George Eliot, Mrs Gaskell, Thackeray, Trollope.*

Routh, H. V. Towards the twentieth century: essays in the spiritual history of the nineteenth century. Cambridge 1937.

Dobrée, Bonamy and Edith C. Batho. The Victorians and after. 1938; 1950.

Wilson Knight, G. The starlit dome. 1941; 1959 (*with addns*).

Essays mainly on the nineteenth century, presented to Sir Humphrey Milford. Oxford 1948.

James, D. G. The romantic comedy. 1948.

Leavis, F. R. The great tradition: George Eliot, Henry James, Joseph Conrad. 1948.

Hough, Graham. The last romantics. 1949. *Morris, Pater, Rossetti, Ruskin, Yeats etc.*

Willey, Basil. Nineteenth-century studies. 1949. *Arnold, Carlyle, Coleridge, George Eliot, Newman etc.*

—— More nineteenth-century studies: a group of honest doubters. 1956. *Froude, F. W. Newman, 'Mark Rutherford', John Morley etc.*

Tillotson, Geoffrey. Criticism and the nineteenth century. 1951. *Arnold, Wilkie Collins, Henry James, Newman, Pater, Tennyson.*

Abrams, M. H. The mirror and the lamp: romantic theory and the critical tradition. New York 1953.

Holloway, John. The Victorian sage. 1953. *Arnold, Carlyle, Disraeli, George Eliot, Hardy, Newman.*

Tillotson, Kathleen. Novels of the eighteen-forties. Oxford 1954. *Dombey and Son, Mary Barton, Vanity fair, Jane Eyre.*

House, Humphry. All in due time: collected essays. 1955.

Rowell, George. The Victorian theatre: a survey. Oxford 1956. *With chronology of plays and bibliography.*

Altick, Richard D. The English common reader: a social history of the mass reading public, 1800–1900. Chicago 1957.

Kermode, Frank. Romantic image. 1957.

Langbaum, Robert. The poetry of experience: the dramatic monologue in modern literary tradition. 1957.

English romantic poets: modern essays in criticism. Ed. M. H. Abrams, New York 1960.

Blackstone, Bernard. The lost travellers. 1962. *On myth and symbol in the romantic poets.*

Renwick, W.L. English literature, 1789–1815. Oxford 1963 (Oxford history of English lit., vol. ix).

Jack, Ian. English literature, 1815–32. Oxford 1963 (Oxford history of English lit., vol. x).

Collections and Anthologies

Beardsley, Aubrey and Henry Harland. The yellow book. 13 vols. 1894–7.

Quiller-Couch, Arthur. The Oxford book of Victorian verse. Oxford 1912.

Jones, Edmund D. English critical essays (nineteenth century). Oxford 1916 (WC).

Dover Wilson, J. The poetry of the age of Wordsworth. Cambridge 1927.

Milford, Humphrey. The Oxford book of Regency verse, 1798–1837. Oxford 1928; 1935 (*re-entitled* Romantic verse).

Bernbaum, Ernest. Anthology of romanticism and guide. 5 vols. New York 1930.

Hayward, John. Nineteenth-century poetry. 1932.

—— The Oxford book of nineteenth-century English verse. Oxford 1964.

Wain, John. Contemporary reviews of romantic poetry. 1953.

JOHN EMERICH EDWARD DALBERG ACTON, 1st BARON ACTON (1834 – 1902)

A LECTURE on the study of history. 1895.

Lectures on modern history. Ed. J.N.Figgis and R.V.Laurence, 1906; Historical essays and studies, ed. Figgis and Laurence, 1907; The history of freedom and other essays, ed. Figgis and Laurence, 1907; Lectures on the French revolution, ed. Figgis and Laurence, 1910; Essays on church and state, ed. Douglas Woodruff, 1952.

Selection from the correspondence, vol. i. Ed. Figgis and Laurence, 1917.

Essays on freedom and power. Ed. Gertrude Himmelfarb, New York 1955. *A selection.*

First editor of the Cambridge Modern History (1902–12) *from 1899.*

Gasquet, F.A. Acton and his circle. 1906.

Mathew, David. Acton: the formative years. 1946.

Fasnacht, G.E. Acton's political philosophy. 1952.

Himmelfarb, Gertrude. Acton: a study in conscience and politics. Chicago 1952.

Butterfield, Herbert. *In his* Man on his past, Cambridge 1955.

MATTHEW ARNOLD (1822 – 1888)

Smart, Thomas B. The bibliography of Arnold. 1892.

THE STRAYED REVELLER and other poems. 1849.

EMPEDOCLES ON ETNA and other poems. 1852; Poems, 1853, 1854, 1857; Second series, 1855. Sohrab and Rustum *and* The scholar-gipsy *first pbd in* 1853, Balder dead *in* 1855.

MEROPE. 1858.

NEW POEMS. 1867; 1868. *Includes* Thyrsis.

ON TRANSLATING HOMER: three lectures. 1861; Last words, 1862.

ESSAYS IN CRITICISM. 2 ser. 1865–88; ser. 1, 1869, 1875 (*with addn*), 1907 (*with two addns*). *A third but unauthorized collection from periodicals entitled* Essays in criticism: third series *was pbd Boston 1910.*

ON THE STUDY of Celtic literature. 1867; 1910 (EL).

CULTURE AND ANARCHY: an essay in political and social criticism. 1869; 1875; ed. J.Dover Wilson, Cambridge 1932.

LITERATURE AND DOGMA: an essay towards a better appreciation of the Bible. 1873; God and the Bible: a review of objections, 1875.

CIVILIZATION IN THE UNITED STATES. Boston 1888. *Three of the five lectures are rptd in* Five uncollected essays, ed. Kenneth Allott, Liverpool 1953.

Works. 15 vols. 1903–4; Poetry and prose, ed. John Bryson, 1954 (RL).

Poems. Ed. Humphrey Milford and Arthur Quiller-Couch, Oxford 1909; Poetical works, Oxford 1942 (*enlarged*); ed. C.B.Tinker and H.F.Lowry, Oxford 1950 (OSA).

Essays, including Essays in criticism 1865, On translating Homer [etc.]. Oxford 1914 (OSA); [Prose works], ed. R.H. Super, Ann Arbor 1960–.

Letters, 1848–88. Ed. G.W.E.Russell, 2 vols. 1895; Letters to Clough, ed. H.F.Lowry, Oxford 1932.

Note books. Ed. H.F.Lowry *et al.*, Oxford 1952.

Raleigh, Walter. *In his* Some authors, Oxford 1923.

Trilling, Lionel. Matthew Arnold. New York 1939; 1955.

Tinker, C.B. and H.F.Lowry. The poetry of Arnold: a commentary. New York 1940.

Brown, E.K. Arnold: a study in conflict. Chicago 1948.

Tillotson, Geoffrey. *In his* Criticism and the nineteenth century, 1951.

JANE AUSTEN (1775 – 1817)

Keynes, Geoffrey. Jane Austen: a bibliography. 1929 (Nonesuch Press).

Chapman, R.W. Jane Austen: a critical bibliography. Oxford 1953; 1955.

SENSE AND SENSIBILITY. 3 vols. 1811; 1813.
PRIDE AND PREJUDICE. 3 vols. 1813.
MANSFIELD PARK. 3 vols. 1814; 1816.
EMMA. 3 vols. 1816.
NORTHANGER ABBEY and PERSUASION. 4 vols. 1818.
   The six principal novels are all rptd Oxford 1907–31 (WC).

VOLUME THE FIRST. Ed. R.W.Chapman, Oxford 1933. *First of three vols. of MS. juvenilia, collected by the author c. 1793.*
LOVE AND FREINDSHIP and other early works. Ed. G.K.Chesterton, 1922; ed. B.C.Southam, Oxford 1963. *'Volume the second', 1790–3.*
LADY SUSAN. Ed. R.W.Chapman, Oxford 1925. *Written c. 1805, first pbd in Memoir (1871), below.*
THE WATSONS: a fragment. Ed. R.W.Chapman, Oxford 1927. *Written 1805 or later, first pbd in Memoir (1871), below.*
SANDITON: fragment of a novel written 1817. Ed. R.W.Chapman, Oxford 1925. *Extracts pbd in Memoir (1871), below.*
VOLUME THE THIRD. Ed. R.W.Chapman, Oxford 1951.

Novels. Ed. R.W.Chapman, 6 vols. Oxford 1923–54.
Letters. Ed. R.W.Chapman, 2 vols. Oxford 1932, 1 vol. 1952; Selected letters, ed. Chapman, Oxford 1955 (WC).

Austen-Leigh, James E. A memoir by her nephew. 1870; 1871; ed. R.W.Chapman, Oxford 1926.
Austen-Leigh, William and Richard A. Jane Austen: her life and letters. 1913.
Bradley, A.C. *In his* Miscellany, 1929.
Lascelles, Mary. Jane Austen and her art. Oxford 1939.
Leavis, Q.D. A critical theory of Jane Austen's writings. Scrutiny, X (1942), XIII (1944).
Chapman, R.W. Jane Austen: facts and problems. Oxford 1948.
Wright, Andrew H. Jane Austen's novels: a study in structure. 1953.

WALTER BAGEHOT (1826 – 1877)

ESTIMATES of some Englishmen and Scotchmen. 1858.
THE ENGLISH CONSTITUTION. 1867; 1872 (*enlarged*); ed. Arthur Balfour, Oxford 1928 (WC); ed. Richard Crossman, 1963.
   Edited The economist, *1859–77.*

Literary studies. Ed. R.H.Hutton, 2 vols. 1879; vol. iii, 1895, 1906 (*enlarged*).
Economic studies. Ed. R.H.Hutton, 1880.
Biographical studies. Ed. R.H.Hutton, 1881.

Biographical and literary studies. Ed. George Sampson, 2 vols. 1911 (EL).
Works and life. Ed. E. I. Barrington, 10 vols. 1915; A study, together with a selection from his political writings, ed. Norman St John-Stevas, 1959.

Stephen, Leslie. *In his* Studies of a biographer, 1898–1902.
Irvine, William. Walter Bagehot. New York 1939.
Young, G. M. The greatest Victorian. *In his* Today and yesterday, 1948.
Buchan, Alistair. The spare Chancellor: the life of Bagehot. 1959.

WILLIAM BARNES (1801? – 1886)

POEMS OF RURAL LIFE in the Dorset dialect. 3 pts. 1844–62; 1 vol. 1879.
POEMS PARTLY OF RURAL LIFE (in national English). 1846.
POEMS OF RURAL LIFE in common English. 1868.

Select poems. Ed. Thomas Hardy, 1908; Selected poems, ed. Geoffrey Grigson, 1950 (ML); Poems, ed. Bernard Jones, 2 vols. 1962.

Baxter, Lucy. The life of Barnes by his daughter. 1887.

SIR JAMES MATTHEW BARRIE (1860 – 1937)

Garland, Herbert. A bibliography of the writings of Barrie. 1928.

A WINDOW IN THRUMS. 1889.
THE LITTLE MINISTER. 1891.
QUALITY STREET: a comedy. 1913.
THE ADMIRABLE CRICHTON. 1914.
THE GREENWOOD HAT. 1937.

Uniform edition of the plays. 10 vols. 1918–38. *Includes first pbn of* What every woman knows (1918), Alice Sit-by-the-fire (1919), Dear Brutus (1922), Peter Pan (1928) *etc.*
Plays. Ed. A. E. Wilson, 1928; 1942.
Letters. Ed. Viola Meynell, 1942.

Darton, F. J. Harvey. Barrie. 1928.
Hammerton, J. A. Barrie: the story of a genius. 1929.
Mackail, Denis. The story of JMB. 1941.

THOMAS LOVELL BEDDOES (1803 – 1849)

THE IMPROVISATORE, with other poems. Oxford 1821.
THE BRIDE'S TRAGEDY. 1822.
DEATH'S JEST-BOOK: or the fool's tragedy. 1850.

Letters. Ed. Edmund Gosse, 1894.
Works. Ed. H.W.Donner, Oxford 1935; Plays and poems, ed. Donner, 1950 (ML); An anthology, ed. F.L.Lucas, Cambridge 1932.

The Browning box: or the life and works of Beddoes in letters by his friends. Ed. H.W.Donner, Oxford 1935.
Donner, H.W. Beddoes: the making of a poet. Oxford 1935.

ROBERT BLOOMFIELD (1766 – 1823)

THE FARMER'S BOY: a rural poem. 1800.
RURAL TALES, ballads and songs. 1802.
THE BANKS OF WYE. 1811.

Remains. Ed. Joseph Weston, 2 vols. 1824.
Poems. 3 vols. 1827.
Selections from the correspondence. Ed. W.H.Hart, 1870.

GEORGE BORROW (1803 – 1881)

Wise, Thomas J. A bibliography of the writings of Borrow. 1914.

THE BIBLE IN SPAIN. 3 vols. 1843; 1 vol. 1906 (WC).
LAVENGRO. 3 vols. 1851; 1 vol. 1904 (WC).
THE ROMANY RYE: a sequel. 2 vols. 1857; 1 vol. 1906 (WC); ed. Walter Starkie, 1949.
WILD WALES. 3 vols. 1862; 1 vol. Oxford 1920 (WC).

Works. Ed. Clement Shorter, 16 vols. 1923–4. *Norwich edition.*
Selections. Ed. Humphrey Milford, Oxford 1924.

Knapp, William I. Life, writings and correspondence of Borrow. 2 vols. 1899.
Shorter, Clement. Borrow and his circle. 1913.
Armstrong, Martin. George Borrow. 1950.

ROBERT SEYMOUR BRIDGES (1844 – 1930)

McKay, George L. A bibliography of Bridges. New York 1933.

POEMS. 1873; Second series, 1879; Third series, 1880; Shorter poems, 4 bks. Oxford 1890; Book v, Oxford 1893; ed. M.M.Bridges, Oxford 1931 (*enlarged*).
THE GROWTH OF LOVE. 1876; Oxford 1889 (*enlarged*).
PROMETHEUS THE FIREGIVER: a masque. Oxford 1884.
EROS AND PSYCHE: a narrative poem. 1885; 1894.
DEMETER: a masque. Oxford 1905.

POEMS WRITTEN IN 1913. 1914; October and other poems, 1920.
THE TESTAMENT OF BEAUTY. 5 pts. 1927–9; Oxford 1929; 1930.

Poetical works. 6 vols. Oxford 1898–1905; Poetical works excluding the eight dramas, Oxford 1912, 1936 (*enlarged*) (OSA).
Collected essays, papers etc. 30 pts. Oxford 1927–36.
Three friends: memoirs of Dolben, Dixon, Henry Bradley. Oxford 1932.
Correspondence of Bridges and Henry Bradley, 1900–23. Oxford 1940.
Poetry and prose. Ed. John Sparrow, Oxford 1955.

Smith, Nowell C. Notes on the Testament of beauty. 1932; 1940.
Hopkins, Gerard Manley. Letters to Bridges. Ed. Claude C. Abbott, Oxford 1935; 1955.
Guerard, Albert J. Bridges: a study of traditionalism. Cambridge, Mass. 1942.
Thompson, Edward. Robert Bridges. Oxford 1944.

ANNE BRONTË (1820 – 1849)
('Acton Bell')

POEMS by Currer, Ellis and Acton Bell. 1846. *With Charlotte and Emily.*
AGNES GREY. *Vol. iii of* Wuthering Heights, 3 vols. 1847.
THE TENANT OF WILDFELL HALL. 3 vols. 1848.

Complete poems. Ed. Clement Shorter and C. W. Hatfield, 1923.

Gérin, Winifrid. Anne Brontë: a biography. 1959.
See also under Charlotte Brontë, below.

CHARLOTTE BRONTË, later NICHOLLS (1816 – 1855)
('Currer Bell')

Wise, Thomas J. A bibliography of the writings of the Brontë family. 1917. *See* Parrish, *p. 174 below.*

POEMS by Currer, Ellis and Acton Bell. 1846. *With Anne and Emily.*
JANE EYRE: an autobiography, edited by Currer Bell. 3 vols. 1847; 1848 (*with preface*); 1848 (*with* Note).
SHIRLEY. 3 vols. 1849.
VILLETTE. 3 vols. 1853.
THE PROFESSOR. 2 vols. 1857. *Written 1846, first of four novels.*
LEGENDS OF ANGRIA, compiled from the early writings. Ed. Fannie E. Ratchford and W. C. DeVane, New Haven 1933.

Complete poems. Ed. Clement Shorter and C. W. Hatfield, 1923.
The Shakespeare head Brontë. Ed. Thomas J. Wise and J. Alex. Symington, 8 vols. Oxford 1932–8. *Poems, letters and miscellaneous writings.*

Gaskell, Elizabeth. The life of Charlotte Brontë. 2 vols. 1857; ed.
Clement Shorter, Oxford 1919 (WC).

Stephen, Leslie. *In his* Hours in a library, ser. 3, 1879.

Brontë Society. Transactions and publications. Bradford (*later*
Haworth) 1895–.

Shorter, Clement. Charlotte Brontë and her circle. 1896.

—— The Brontës: life and letters. 2 vols. 1908.

Sinclair, May. The three Brontës. 1912.

Ratchford, Fannie E. The Brontës' web of childhood. New York 1941.
On the MS. juvenilia, written 1829–45 and ed. as Legends of Angria,
above.

Bentley, Phyllis. The Brontës. 1947.

Hanson, Lawrence and Elisabeth. The four Brontës. Oxford 1949.

Lane, Margaret. The Brontë story: a reconsideration of Mrs Gaskell's
Life. 1953.

EMILY JANE BRONTË (1818 – 1848)
('Ellis Bell')

POEMS by Currer, Ellis and Acton Bell. 1846. *Includes 21 poems by Emily,*
WUTHERING HEIGHTS. 3 vols. 1847 (*vols. i–ii*); ed. Charlotte Brontë.
1850; ed. H.W.Garrod, Oxford 1930 (WC).

GONDAL POEMS. Ed. Helen Brown and Joan Mott, Oxford 1938;
Gondal's queen, ed. Fannie E.Ratchford, Austin, Texas 1955.

Complete poems. Ed. C.W.Hatfield, New York 1941.
See also under Charlotte Brontë, above.

ELIZABETH BARRETT BROWNING (1806 – 1861)

Wise, Thomas J. A bibliography of Elizabeth Barrett Browning. 1918.

POEMS. 2 vols. 1844; 1850 (*enlarged*). 1850 *includes first pbn of* Sonnets
from the Portuguese.

AURORA LEIGH. 1857.

A selection from the poetry. Ed. Robert Browning, 2 ser. 1866–80;
Poetical works, Oxford 1904 (OSA).

NEW POEMS by Robert and Elizabeth Barrett Browning. Ed. F.G.
Kenyon, 1914.

Letters. Ed. F.G.Kenyon, 2 vols. 1897; Letters of Robert and Elizabeth Barrett Browning, 1845–6, 2 vols. 1899; Elizabeth Barrett to
Miss Mitford, ed. Betty Miller, 1954.

Hewlett, Dorothy. Elizabeth Barrett Browning: a life. 1952.

Taplin, Gardner B. The life of Elizabeth Barrett Browning. New Haven 1957.

Hayter, Alethea. Mrs Browning. 1962.

ROBERT BROWNING (1812 – 1889)

Broughton, L.N. and B.F. Stelter. A concordance to the poems. 2 vols. New York 1925–6.

Broughton, L.N., Clark S. Northup and Robert Pearsall. Browning: a bibliography, 1830–1950. Ithaca, N.Y. 1953.

PAULINE. 1833; 1888 (*in* Poetical works, *below*); ed. N. Hardy Wallis, 1931.

PARACELSUS. 1835; 1863 (*in* Poetical works, *below*).

SORDELLO. 1840; 1863 (*in* Poetical works, *below*).

BELLS AND POMEGRANATES. 8 nos. 1841–6; 1 vol. 1846. *Includes* Pippa passes, Dramatic lyrics *etc.*

Poems. 2 vols. 1849. *A collection of* Paracelsus *and* Bells and pomegranates.

MEN AND WOMEN. 2 vols. 1855; ed. G.E. Hadow, Oxford 1911.

DRAMATIS PERSONAE. 1864.

THE RING AND THE BOOK. 4 vols. 1868–9; 1872; ed. Edward Dowden, Oxford 1912, 1940 (OSA). *For a facs. with trn of the source, see* The Old Yellow Book, ed. C.W. Hodell, Washington 1908.

THE AGAMEMNON OF AESCHYLUS, transcribed. 1877.

DRAMATIC IDYLS. 2 ser. 1879–80.

ASOLANDO. 1890.

NEW POEMS by Robert and Elizabeth Barrett Browning. Ed. F.G. Kenyon, 1914.

Poetical works. 3 vols. 1863; 17 vols. 1888–94; Poetical works 1833–65 and the shorter poems thereafter, Oxford 1940 (OSA); Selected, ed. Humphrey Milford, Oxford 1949 (WC).

Letters collected by Thomas J. Wise. Ed. Thurman L. Hood, New Haven 1933; New letters, ed. W.C. DeVane and K.L. Knickerbocker, New Haven 1950.

Works: centenary edition. Ed. F.G. Kenyon, 10 vols. 1912; Poetry and prose, ed. Simon Nowell-Smith, 1950 (RL).

James, Henry. The novel in The ring and the book. *In his* Notes on novelists, 1914.

Orr, Mrs Sutherland. Life and letters of Browning. 1891; 1908 (rev. F.G. Kenyon).

Chesterton, G.K. Robert Browning. 1903 (EML).

Griffin, H.W. and H.C.Minchin. The life of Browning. 1910.

DeVane, William Clyde. A Browning handbook. New York 1935; 1955.

Raymond, William O. The infinite moment and other essays in Browning. Toronto 1950.

Miller, Betty. Browning: a portrait. 1952.

SAMUEL BUTLER (1835 – 1902)

Hoppé, A.J. A bibliography of the writings of Butler and of writings about him. 1925.

EREWHON: or over the range. 1872, 1901 (*enlarged*); Erewhon revisited twenty years later, 1901; *both* ed. Desmond MacCarthy, 1932 (EL).

THE FAIR HAVEN: a work in defence of the miraculous element in our Lord's Ministry. 1873. *A parody.*

THE ILIAD rendered into English prose. 1898; Odyssey, 1900.

THE WAY OF ALL FLESH. Ed. R.A.Streatfeild, 1903; ed. Bernard Shaw, Oxford 1936 (WC); ed. A.J.Hoppé, 1954 (EL) (*from MS.*).

Essays on life, art and science. Ed. R.A.Streatfeild, 1904.

Notebooks: selections. Ed. Henry Festing Jones, 1912; ed. Geoffrey Keynes and Brian Hill, 1951.

Works: Shrewsbury edition. Ed. Henry Festing Jones and A.T. Bartholomew, 20 vols. 1923–6; The essential Butler, ed. G.D.H.Cole, 1950.

Jones, Henry Festing. Butler: a memoir. 2 vols. 1919.

Muggeridge, Malcolm. The earnest atheist. 1936. *Reply by* P.N. Furbank, Samuel Butler, Cambridge 1948.

Henderson, Philip. Butler: the incarnate bachelor. 1953.

Willey, Basil. Darwin and Butler. 1960.

GEORGE GORDON BYRON, 6TH BARON BYRON
(1788 – 1824)

Wise, Thomas J. A bibliography of the writings of Byron. 2 vols. 1932–3.

FUGITIVE PIECES. Newark 1806; Poems on various occasions, Newark 1807; Hours of idleness, Newark 1807. *Early poems.*

ENGLISH BARDS and Scotch reviewers: a satire. 1809; 1809 (*with addns*); 1816; 1936 (*facs. with MS. notes by Byron*).

CHILDE HAROLD'S PILGRIMAGE: a romaunt. Cantos i–ii, 1812; iii, 1816; iv, 1818; 2 vols. 1819; ed. A.Hamilton Thompson, Cambridge 1913.

THE GIAOUR: a fragment of a Turkish tale. 1813; 1813.

THE BRIDE OF ABYDOS: a Turkish tale. 1813.

THE CORSAIR: a tale. 1814.

LARA: a tale. 1814.

HEBREW MELODIES ancient and modern. 2 pts. 1815.

THE SIEGE OF CORINTH; Parisina. 1816.

THE PRISONER OF CHILLON and other poems. 1816.

MANFRED: a dramatic poem. 1817.

BEPPO: a Venetian story. 1818; 1818.

MAZEPPA: a poem. 1819.

DON JUAN. Cantos i–ii, 1819; iii–iv, 1821; i–v, 1822; v–xi, 1823; vi–viii, 1823; ix–xi, 1823; xii–xiv, 1823; xv–xvi, 1824; i–xvi, 2 vols. 1826; ed. Louis I. Bredvold, New York 1935; A variorum edition, ed. Truman G. Steffan and Willis W. Pratt, 4 vols. Austin, Texas 1957.

MARINO FALIERO: an historical tragedy; The prophecy of Dante. 1821.

SARDANAPALUS; The two Foscari; Cain. 1821.

THE VISION OF JUDGEMENT. Liberal, no. 1 (1822); Paris 1822; London 1822 (*with Southey's* A vision of judgement, *which it travesties, as* The two visions).

THE AGE OF BRONZE. 1823.

WERNER: a tragedy. 1823.

THE DEFORMED TRANSFORMED: a drama. 1824.

Letters and journals, with notices of his life by Thomas Moore. 2 vols. 1830; Correspondence, ed. John Murray, 2 vols. 1922; Letters, selected, ed. R. G. Howarth, 1936 (EL); A self-portrait: letters and diaries, 1798–1824, ed. Peter Quennell, 2 vols. 1950.

Works. Ed. E. H. Coleridge and Rowland E. Prothero, 13 vols. 1898–1904; Selections, ed. Peter Quennell, 1949 (Nonesuch Lib.).

Poetical works. Oxford 1896; 1904, 1945 (OSA).

Moore, Thomas. Life of Byron. *In* Letters and journals, *above.*

Trelawny, E. J. Recollections of the last days of Shelley and Byron. 1858; ed. J. E. Morpurgo, 1952.

Arnold, Matthew. *In his* Essays in criticism, ser. 2, 1888.

Quennell, Peter. Byron: the years of fame. 1935; Byron in Italy, 1941.

Eliot, T. S. *In* From Anne to Victoria, ed. Bonamy Dobrée, 1937.

Origo, Iris. The last attachment: Byron and Teresa Guiccioli. 1949.

Wilson Knight, G. Byron: Christian virtues. 1953; Byron's marriage, 1957.

Marchand, Leslie A. Byron: a biography. 3 vols. New York 1957.

Robson, W. W. Byron as poet. Proc. Brit. Acad. xliii (1957).

Moore, Doris L. The late Lord Byron. 1961. *On his reputation.*

Rutherford, Andrew. Byron: a critical study. Edinburgh 1961.

Auden, W. H. Don Juan. *In his* The dyer's hand, 1963.

Joseph, M. K. Byron the poet. 1964.

CHARLES STUART CALVERLEY, earlier BLAYDS
(1831 – 1884)

VERSES AND TRANSLATIONS. 1862; 1871.
TRANSLATIONS into English and Latin. Cambridge 1866; 1886.
THEOCRITUS translated into English Verse. 1869; 1883.
FLY LEAVES. Cambridge 1872.

Literary remains. Ed. Walter J. Sendall, 1885.
Complete works. Ed. Walter J. Sendall, 1901.

THOMAS CAMPBELL (1777 – 1844)

THE PLEASURES OF HOPE. Edinburgh 1799.
POEMS. 1803.
GERTRUDE OF WYOMING. 1809.

Complete poetical works. Ed. J. Logie Robertson, Oxford 1907.

Beattie, William. Life and letters of Campbell. 3 vols. 1849.

THOMAS CARLYLE (1795 – 1881)

Dyer, Isaac W. A bibliography of Carlyle's writings and ana. Portland, Maine 1928.

WILHELM MEISTER'S APPRENTICESHIP: a novel from the German of Goethe. 3 vols. Edinburgh 1824; ed. Edward Dowden, 1890.
THE LIFE OF SCHILLER. 1825.
SARTOR RESARTUS: the life and opinions of Herr Teufelsdröckh. Ed. Ralph Waldo Emerson, Boston 1836; ed. C. F. Harrold, New York 1937. *First pbd in* Fraser's mag. (1833–4).
THE FRENCH REVOLUTION: a history. 3 vols. 1837; ed. J. H. Rose, 3 vols. 1902; ed. Hilaire Belloc, 2 vols. 1906 (EL).
CRITICAL AND MISCELLANEOUS ESSAYS. 4 vols. Boston 1838.
ON HEROES, hero-worship and the heroic in history. 1841; ed. Archibald MacMechan, Boston 1901; London 1904 (WC).
PAST AND PRESENT. 1843; ed. A. M. D. Hughes, Oxford 1918.
LATTER-DAY PAMPHLETS. 1850.
LIFE OF JOHN STERLING. 1851; Oxford 1907 (WC).
FREDERICK THE GREAT. 6 vols. 1857–65; ed. A. M. D. Hughes, Oxford 1916 (*abridged*).
REMINISCENCES. Ed. J. A. Froude, 2 vols. 1881; ed. C. E. Norton, 2 vols. 1887; 1 vol. 1932 (EL).
UNPUBLISHED HISTORY of German literature. Ed. Hill Shine, Lexington, Va. 1951.

Works: centenary edition. Ed. H.D.Traill, 30 vols. 1896–9; Selected works, ed. Julian Symons, 1955 (RL); Selections, ed. A.M.D. Hughes, Oxford 1957.

Correspondence of Carlyle and Emerson, 1834–72. Ed. C.E.Norton, 2 vols. 1883; Correspondence between Goethe and Carlyle, ed. Norton, 1887; New letters, ed. A.J.Carlyle, 2 vols. 1904; Letters to Mill, Sterling and Browning, ed. A.J.Carlyle, 1923; Letters to his wife, ed. Trudy Bliss, 1953. *There is no collected edn of the letters.*

Froude, James Anthony. Thomas Carlyle. 4 vols. 1882–4.

Wilson, David A. Carlyle. 6 vols. 1923–34.

Neff, Emery. Carlyle and Mill. New York 1924; 1926.

—— Carlyle. New York 1932.

Harrold, C.F. Carlyle and German thought, 1819–34. New Haven 1934.

Symons, Julian. Carlyle: the life and ideas of a prophet. 1952.

'LEWIS CARROLL', i.e. CHARLES LUTWIDGE DODGSON (1832 – 1898)

Williams, S.H. A bibliography of the writings of Lewis Carroll. 1924; Oxford 1962 (*rev. Roger Lancelyn Green as* A Lewis Carroll handbook).

ALICE'S ADVENTURES IN WONDERLAND. 1865, 1897; Through the looking-glass, 1872, 1897.

PHANTASMAGORIA and other poems. 1869.

THE HUNTING OF THE SNARK. 1876.

SYLVIE AND BRUNO. 1889; Concluded, 1893.

Complete works. Ed. Alexander Woollcott, 1939; 1949 (Nonesuch Lib.).

Diaries. Ed. Roger Lancelyn Green, 2 vols. Oxford 1954.

Collingwood, S. Dodgson. The life and letters of Lewis Carroll. 1898. *A memoir by his nephew.*

Empson, William. Alice in Wonderland. *In his* Some versions of pastoral, 1935.

Green, Roger Lancelyn. The story of Lewis Carroll. 1949.

Sewell, Elizabeth. *In her* The field of nonsense, 1952.

Hudson, Derek. Lewis Carroll. 1954.

HENRY FRANCIS CARY (1772 – 1844)

THE INFERNO OF DANTE, with a translation in blank verse. 2 vols. 1805–6.

THE VISION: or Hell, Purgatory and Paradise of Dante translated. 3 vols. 1814; 1 vol. 1844; Oxford 1910 (OSA).

PINDAR IN ENGLISH VERSE. 1833.

Cary, Henry. Memoir of Cary, with his literary journal and letters. 2 vols. 1847. *By his son.*

Toynbee, Paget. *In his* Dante in English literature from Chaucer to Cary, 2 vols. 1909.

King, R.W. The translator of Dante: Cary. 1925.

JOHN CLARE (1793 – 1864)

POEMS descriptive of rural life and scenery. 1820.

THE VILLAGE MINSTREL and other poems. 2 vols. 1821.

THE SHEPHERD'S CALENDAR. 1827; ed. Eric Robinson and Geoffrey Summerfield, Oxford 1964 (*complete*).

THE RURAL MUSE. 1835.

SKETCHES IN THE LIFE of Clare written by himself. Ed. Edmund Blunden, 1931.

Poems. Ed. Edmund Blunden and Alan Porter, 1920; ed. J.W. Tibble, 2 vols. 1935; Selected, ed. Geoffrey Grigson, 1950 (ML); Selected poems, ed. James Reeves, 1954; Later poems, ed. Eric Robinson and Geoffrey Summerfield, Manchester 1964.

Prose. Ed. J.W. and Anne Tibble, 1951; Letters, ed. J.W. and Anne Tibble, 1951.

Tibble, J.W. and Anne. Clare: a life. 1932.

—— Clare: his life and poetry. 1956.

Murry, J.Middleton. *In his* Clare and other studies, 1950.

ARTHUR HUGH CLOUGH (1819 – 1861)

THE BOTHIE OF TOPER-NA-FUOSICH. Oxford 1848; London 1862 (*in* Poems, *below*) (*re-entitled* The bothie of tober-na-vuolich).

AMBARVALIA. 1849. *With Thomas Burbidge.*

AMOURS DE VOYAGE. Atlantic monthly (Feb.–May 1858).

Poems. Ed. Francis Palgrave, 1861, 1863; Poems and prose remains, ed. Mrs Clough, 2 vols. 1869; Poems, ed. H.F.Lowry, A.L.P. Norrington and F.L.Mulhauser, Oxford 1951.

Correspondence. Ed. F.L.Mulhauser, 2 vols. Oxford 1957.

Bagehot, Walter. Mr Clough's poems. *In his* Literary studies, 1879.
Garrod, H.W. *In his* Poetry and the criticism of life, Oxford 1931.
Chorley, Katharine. Clough: the uncommitted mind. Oxford 1962.
Houghton, Walter E. The poetry of Clough. New Haven 1963.

WILLIAM COBBETT (1762 – 1835)

Pearl, M.L. Cobbett: a bibliographical account of his life and times. Oxford 1953.

THE LIFE and adventures of Peter Porcupine. Philadelphia 1795; ed. G.D.H.Cole, 1927 (Nonesuch Press).
PORCUPINE'S WORKS: a faithful picture of the United States. 12 vols. 1801.
POLITICAL REGISTER. 88 vols. 1802–35. *A weekly edited by Cobbett.*
The opinions of Cobbett. Ed. G.D.H. and Margaret Cole, 1944. *Extracts from the* Register, *above.*
A GRAMMAR of the English language. New York 1818; ed. H.L. Stephen, 1906.
COTTAGE ECONOMY. 7 pts. 1821–2; 1822; ed. G.K.Chesterton, 1916.
ADVICE TO YOUNG MEN. 14 pts. 1829–30; 1 vol. Andover 1830; ed. E.E.Fisk, 1930.
RURAL RIDES. Political register (1821–34).
Rural rides in the [southern] counties. 1830. *From* Register (1822–6).
Tour in Scotland, 1832. 1833.
Rural rides, together with tours in Scotland and letters from Ireland. Ed. G.D.H. and Margaret Cole, 3 vols. 1930.
Selections. Ed. A.M.D.Hughes, Oxford 1923.
The progress of a ploughboy. Ed. William Reitzel, 1933; 1947 (*re-entitled* Autobiography). *A selection of autobiographical passages.*

Hazlitt, William. *In his* The spirit of the age, 1825.
Carlyle, E.I. Cobbett: a study of his life as shown in his writings. 1904.
Cole, G.D.H. The life of Cobbett. 1924; 1947.
Chesterton, G.K. William Cobbett. 1925.

MARY COLERIDGE (1861 – 1907)

FANCY'S FOLLOWING. 1896; Fancy's guerdon, 1897.

Poems. Ed. Henry Newbolt, 1908; Collected poems, ed. Theresa Whistler, 1954.

Bridges, Robert. *In his* Collected essays, pt vi, Oxford 1931.

SAMUEL TAYLOR COLERIDGE (1772 – 1834)

Wise, Thomas J. A bibliography of Coleridge. 1913; Supplement, 1919.

Logan, Eugenia. A concordance to the poetry. St Mary-of-the-Woods, Ind. 1940.

POEMS on various subjects. 1796; 1797; 1803 (*both with addns*).

LYRICAL BALLADS. 1798; 2 vols. 1800 (*with* Preface); The rime of the ancient mariner, ed. Robert Penn Warren, New York 1946. 1798 *and* 1800 *mainly by Wordsworth*.

THE FRIEND: a weekly paper. 28 nos. Penrith 1809–10; 1 vol. 1812; 3 vols. 1818 (*both enlarged*); ed. H.N.Coleridge, 3 vols. 1837.

CHRISTABEL; Kubla Khan; The pains of sleep. 1816; Christabel, ed. E.H.Coleridge, 1907 (*with MS. facs.*).

THE STATESMAN'S MANUAL: a lay sermon. 1816. *Second* Lay Sermon *pbd 1817*.

BIOGRAPHIA LITERARIA. 2 vols. 1817; ed. J.Shawcross, 2 vols. Oxford 1907; ed. George Watson, 1956, 1960 (EL).

SIBYLLINE LEAVES: a collection of poems. 1817; Poetical works, 3 vols. 1828, 1829, 1834.

AIDS TO REFLECTION. 1825; ed. H.N.Coleridge, 1839; 2 vols. 1843.

Table talk. Ed. H.N.Coleridge, 2 vols. 1835.

Anima poetae, from the unpublished notebooks. Ed. E.H.Coleridge, 1895; Inquiring spirit, ed. Kathleen Coburn, 1951; Notebooks, ed. Kathleen Coburn, 11 vols. New York 1957– (*complete*).

Shakespearean criticism. Ed. T.M.Raysor, 2 vols. Cambridge, Mass. 1930, London 1960 (EL); Miscellaneous criticism, ed. Raysor, Cambridge, Mass. 1936; Philosophical lectures, ed. Kathleen Coburn, 1949.

Letters. Ed. E.H.Coleridge, 2 vols. 1895; Collected letters, ed. E.L. Griggs, 6 vols. Oxford 1956–.

Complete poetical works. Ed. E.H.Coleridge, 2 vols. Oxford 1912; Poems, ed. E.H.Coleridge, Oxford 1912 (OSA).

Political thought. Ed. R.J.White, 1935.

Select poetry and prose. Ed. Stephen Potter, 1933; 1950 (*enlarged*) (Nonesuch Lib.).

Gillman, James. The life of Coleridge, vol. i. 1838. *Unfinished.*

Mill, John Stuart. Coleridge (1840). Ed. F.R.Leavis, 1950 (*in* Mill on Bentham and Coleridge).

Campbell, James Dykes. Coleridge: a narrative of the events of his life. 1894.

Lowes, John Livingston. The road to Xanadu. Boston 1927; 1930.

Richards, I.A. Coleridge on imagination. 1934; Bloomington, Ind. 1960 (*with comments by Kathleen Coburn*).

Chambers, E.K. Coleridge: a biographical study. Oxford 1938; 1950.

Nethercot, Arthur H. The road to Tryermaine: a study of Christabel. Chicago 1939.

House, Humphry. Coleridge: the Clark lectures. 1953.

Beer, J.B. Coleridge the visionary. 1959.

WILLIAM WILKIE COLLINS (1824 – 1889)

Parrish, M.L. Wilkie Collins and Charles Reade: first editions at Dormy House, New Jersey. 1940.

ANTONINA: or the fall of Rome. 3 vols. 1850.

HOUSEHOLD WORDS. Ed. Charles Dickens, 1850–9. *Includes short stories by Collins, 1853–9, fourteen collected as* Little novels, 3 vols. 1887.

THE WOMAN IN WHITE. 3 vols. 1860; 1861; 1 vol. Oxford 1921 (WC).

NO NAME. 3 vols. 1862.

ARMADALE. 2 vols. 1866.

THE MOONSTONE: a romance. 3 vols. 1868; ed. T.S.Eliot, Oxford 1928 (WC).

Eliot, T.S. Wilkie Collins and Dickens. *In his* Selected essays, 1932.

Dickens, Charles. *In his* Letters, ed. Walter Dexter, 3 vols. 1938 (Nonesuch edn).

Robinson, Kenneth. Wilkie Collins: a biography. 1951.

Davis, Nuel P. The life of Wilkie Collins. Urbana, Ill. 1956.

SIR ARTHUR CONAN DOYLE (1859 – 1930)

Locke, Harold. A bibliographical catalogue of the writings of Conan Doyle, 1879–1928. Tunbridge Wells 1928.

A STUDY IN SCARLET. *In* Beeton's Christmas annual, 28th season (1887). *The first Sherlock Holmes story.*

MYSTERIES AND ADVENTURES. 1889. *Re-issued in 1893 as* The gully of Bluemansdyke and other stories.

THE SIGN OF THE FOUR. 1890. *The second Holmes story.*

THE CAPTAIN OF THE POLESTAR and other tales. 1890.

THE WHITE COMPANY. 3 vols. 1891.

THE ADVENTURES OF SHERLOCK HOLMES. 1892. *12 stories.*

THE MEMOIRS OF SHERLOCK HOLMES. 1894. *An attempt to end the Holmes series.*

THE STARK MUNRO LETTERS. 1895.
THE EXPLOITS OF BRIGADIER GERARD. 1896.
THE GREEN FLAG and other stories. 1900.
THE HOUND OF THE BASKERVILLES. 1902.
ADVENTURES OF GERARD. 1903.
THE RETURN OF SHERLOCK HOLMES. 1905.
SIR NIGEL. 1906.
THROUGH THE MAGIC DOOR. 1907.
HIS LAST BOW. 1917.
MEMORIES AND ADVENTURES. 1924. *An autobiography.*
THE CASE-BOOK OF SHERLOCK HOLMES. 1927. *A final collection of Holmes stories.*
Many further stories and novels, mainly in the Strand magazine, *as well as a history of the South African War,* The great Boer War (1900), *and works on psychic research.*

Knox, Ronald. *In his* Essays in satire, 1928.
Lamond, John. Conan Doyle: a memoir. 1931.
Conan Doyle, Adrian. The true Conan Doyle. 1945.
'Carr, John Dickson'. The life of Conan Doyle. 1949.
Roberts, S.C. Holmes and Watson: a miscellany. Oxford 1953.

GEORGE DARLEY (1795 – 1846)

THE ERRORS OF ECSTASIE. 1822.
SYLVIA, or the May Queen. 1827.
NEPENTHE. 1835.

Complete poetical works. Ed. Ramsay Colles, 1908 (ML).

Abbott, Claude C. The life and letters of Darley. Oxford 1928.

CHARLES ROBERT DARWIN (1809 – 1882)

ON THE ORIGIN OF SPECIES by means of natural selection. 1859; 1872 (*with addns*); A variorum text, ed. Morse Peckham, Philadelphia 1959.
THE DESCENT OF MAN. 2 vols. 1871.
THE FOUNDATIONS of the Origin of species: two essays written in 1842 and 1844. Ed. Francis Darwin, Cambridge 1909.
The life and letters of Darwin, by Francis Darwin, 3 vols. 1887; abridged, 1892; More letters, ed. Francis Darwin and A.C. Seward, 2 vols. 1903.
Autobiography. Ed. Francis Darwin, 1929; ed. Nora Barlow, 1958 (*with addns*).

Huxley, Leonard. Charles Darwin. 1921.
Stevenson, Lionel. Darwin among the poets. Chicago 1932.
West, Geoffrey. Darwin: the fragmentary man. 1937.

THOMAS DE QUINCEY (1785 – 1859)

Green, J.A. De Quincey: a bibliography based on the Moss Side library. Manchester 1908.

CONFESSIONS of an English opium eater. London mag. (Sept.–Oct. 1821); 1822, ed. Edward Sackville-West, 1950 (*with selections from* Autobiographical sketches, *below*); Edinburgh 1856 (*enlarged*) (*in vol. v of* Selections, *below*), ed. George Saintsbury, 1927.

RECOLLECTIONS of the Lake poets. Tait's mag. (1834–40); Edinburgh 1854 (*vol. ii of* Selections, *below*); ed. Edward Sackville-West, 1948 (*enlarged from* Tait's). *On Coleridge, Southey, Wordsworth etc.*

AUTOBIOGRAPHIC SKETCHES. 2 vols. 1853–4 (*in vols. i–ii of* Selections, *below*). *A reconstruction of articles pbd in* Tait's mag. *etc.*

Selections grave and gay. 14 vols. Edinburgh 1853–60.
Collected writings. Ed. David Masson, 14 vols. Edinburgh 1889–90.
Memorials: letters and other records. Ed. Alexander H. Japp, 2 vols. 1891; Posthumous works, ed. Japp, 2 vols. 1891.
Uncollected writings. Ed. James Hogg, 2 vols. 1892.
Literary criticism. Ed. Helen Darbishire, Oxford 1909.
Diary, 1803. Ed. Horace A. Eaton, 1928.
De Quincey at work: new letters. Ed. W. H. Bonner, Buffalo, N.Y. 1936.

Stephen, Leslie. *In his* Hours in a library, 1874.
Japp, Alexander H. ('H.A. Page'). De Quincey: his life and writings. 2 vols. 1877; 1 vol. 1890.
Saintsbury, George. *In his* Essays in English literature, 1780–1890, 1890.
Eaton, Horace A. De Quincey: a biography. New York 1936.
Sackville-West, Edward. A flame in sunlight: the life and work of De Quincey. 1936.

CHARLES DICKENS (1812 – 1870)

Philip, Alexander J. A Dickens dictionary. Gravesend 1909; 1928 (*enlarged*).
Eckel, John C. The first editions of the writings of Dickens. New York 1913; 1932 (*enlarged*).

All the full-length novels first appeared in weekly or monthly parts, separately or in periodicals, immediately before their appearance as volumes.

SKETCHES BY 'BOZ'. 2 ser. (3 vols.) 1836.

THE POSTHUMOUS PAPERS OF THE PICKWICK CLUB, edited by 'Boz'. 1837.

OLIVER TWIST: or the parish boy's progress. 3 vols. 1838; 1841.

THE LIFE AND ADVENTURES OF NICHOLAS NICKLEBY. 1839.

MASTER HUMPHREY'S CLOCK. 3 vols. 1841.

THE OLD CURIOSITY SHOP. 1841.

BARNABY RUDGE: a tale of the riots of 'eighty. 1841.

A CHRISTMAS CAROL in prose. 1843; ed. G.K.Chesterton and B.W. Matz, 1922 (*facs.*).

THE LIFE AND ADVENTURES OF MARTIN CHUZZLEWIT. 1844.

DOMBEY AND SON. 1848.

THE PERSONAL HISTORY OF DAVID COPPERFIELD. 1850.

BLEAK HOUSE. 1853.

HARD TIMES. 1854.

LITTLE DORRIT. 1857.

A TALE OF TWO CITIES. 1859.

GREAT EXPECTATIONS. 3 vols. 1861; ed. Bernard Shaw, New York 1937.

OUR MUTUAL FRIEND. 2 vols. 1865.

THE MYSTERY OF EDWIN DROOD. 1870. *Unfinished; only six monthly pts appeared.*

Speeches, letters and sayings. New York 1870; Speeches, ed. R.H. Shepherd, 1870, 1884; ed. K.J.Fielding, Oxford 1960.

Letters. Ed. Georgina Hogarth and Mamie Dickens, 3 vols. 1880–2; Pilgrim edition, ed. Madeline House and Graham Storey, *c.* 11 vols. 1964– (*complete*).

Works. 17 vols. 1847–68. *First cheap edn.*

Gadshill edition. Ed. Andrew Lang, 36 vols. 1897–1908.

Novels. Ed. G.K.Chesterton, 22 vols. 1907–11 (EL).

The Nonesuch Dickens. Ed. Arthur Waugh, Walter Dexter *et al.*, 23 vols. 1937–8 (Nonesuch Press).

The Oxford illustrated Dickens. 21 vols. Oxford 1947–58.

Forster, John. The life of Dickens. 3 vols. 1872–4; ed. George Gissing, 1903 (*abridged*); ed. J.W.T.Ley, 1928.

Gissing, George. Dickens: a critical study. 1898.

Chesterton, G.K. Charles Dickens. 1906.

Wilson, Edmund. Dickens: the two Scrooges. *In his* The wound and the bow, Boston 1941.

'Orwell, George'. *In his* Inside the whale, 1940; *rptd in his* Critical essays, 1946.

House, Humphry. The Dickens world. Oxford 1941; 1942. *Also five essays and broadcasts in his* All in due time, 1955.

Johnson, Edgar. Dickens: his tragedy and triumph. 2 vols. New York 1952.

Ford, George H. Dickens and his readers. Princeton 1955.

—— and Lauriat Lane (edd.). The Dickens critics. Ithaca, N.Y. 1961. *An anthology.*

Butt, John and Kathleen Tillotson. Dickens at work. 1957.

Collins, Philip. Dickens and crime. 1962; Dickens and education, 1963.

Gross, John and Gabriel Pearson (edd.). Dickens and the twentieth century. 1962.

BENJAMIN DISRAELI, 1st EARL OF
BEACONSFIELD (1804 – 1881)

VIVIAN GREY. 5 vols. 1826–27; 1 vol. 1853.

THE YOUNG DUKE. 3 vols. 1831.

CONTARINI FLEMING: a psychological autobiography. 4 vols. 1832.

CONINGSBY: or the new generation. 3 vols. 1844; 1 vol. Oxford 1931 (WC).

SYBIL: or the two nations. 3 vols. 1845; 1 vol. Oxford 1926 (WC).

TANCRED: or the new crusade. 3 vols. 1847.

LORD GEORGE BENTINCK: a political biography. 1852; 1872; ed. Charles Whibley, 1905.

LOTHAIR. 3 vols. 1870.

ENDYMION. 3 vols. 1880.

Novels. 10 vols. 1870–1 (*with preface*).

TALES AND SKETCHES. Ed. J.Logie Robertson, 1891.

Selected speeches. Ed. T.E.Kebbel, 2 vols. 1882.

Letters, 1830–52. 1887; ed. Augustine Birrell, 1928.

Whigs and Whiggism: political writings. Ed. William Hutcheon, 1913.

Stephen, Leslie. Mr Disraeli's novels. *In his* Hours in a library, ser. 2, 1876.

Monypenny, W.F. and G.E.Buckle. The life of Disraeli. 6 vols. 1910–20; 2 vols. 1929.

CHARLES MONTAGU DOUGHTY (1843 – 1926)

TRAVELS IN ARABIA DESERTA. 2 vols. Cambridge 1888; ed. T.E. Lawrence, 2 vols. 1921; Passages from Arabia deserta, ed. Edward Garnett, 1931.

UNDER ARMS. 1900.

THE DAWN IN BRITAIN. 6 vols. 1906.

ADAM CAST FORTH. 1908.
MANSOUL: or the riddle of the world. 1920; 1923.

Fairley, Barker. Doughty: a critical study. 1927.
Hogarth, D.G. The life of Doughty. Oxford 1928.
Treneer, Anne. Doughty: a study of his prose and verse. 1935.

ERNEST CHRISTOPHER DOWSON (1867 – 1900)

VERSES. 1896.
DECORATIONS IN VERSE AND PROSE. 1899.

Poems. Ed. Arthur Symons, 1905; Poetical works, ed. Desmond Flower, 1934.
Stories. Ed. Mark Longaker, 1949.

Plarr, Victor. Dowson, 1888–97: reminiscences, unpublished letters and marginalia. 1914.
Longaker, Mark. Ernest Dowson. Philadelphia 1944.

MARIA EDGEWORTH (1767 – 1849)

Slade, Bertha C. Maria Edgeworth: a bibliographical tribute. 1937.

THE PARENT'S ASSISTANT: or stories for children. 3 vols. 1795?; 6 vols. 1800 (*enlarged*).
PRACTICAL EDUCATION. 2 vols. 1798; 3 vols. 1801. *With her father R.L. Edgeworth.*
CASTLE RACKRENT: an Hibernian tale. 1800; ed. George Watson, Oxford 1964.
BELINDA. 3 vols. 1801.
MORAL TALES FOR YOUNG PEOPLE. 5 vols. 1801; Popular tales, 3 vols. 1804; Tales of fashionable life, 2 ser. (6 vols.) 1809–12. *Vols. v–vi (1812) include* The absentee.
PATRONAGE. 4 vols. 1814.
HARRINGTON; and ORMOND. 3 vols. 1817; 1817.
MEMOIRS of Richard Lovell Edgeworth, concluded by Maria Edgeworth. 2 vols. 1820; 1 vol. 1844.

Tales and miscellaneous pieces. 14 vols. 1825; Tales and novels, 18 vols. 1832–3 (*with final revisions*); Tales, ed. Austin Dobson, 1903.
A memoir of Maria Edgeworth, with a selection from her letters by the late Mrs [Frances] Edgeworth. 3 vols. 1869; Chosen letters, ed. F.V.Barry, 1931.

Hare, Augustus J.C. The life and letters of Maria Edgeworth. 2 vols. 1894.

Newby, P.H. Maria Edgeworth. 1950.

'GEORGE ELIOT', i.e. MARY ANN EVANS, later CROSS (1819 – 1880)

Mudge, Isadore G. and M.E. Sears. A George Eliot dictionary. 1924.

Parrish, M.L. Victorian lady novelists: George Eliot, Mrs Gaskell, the Brontë sisters—first editions at Dormy House, New Jersey. 1933.

SCENES OF CLERICAL LIFE. 2 vols. Edinburgh 1858; 1 vol. Oxford 1909 (WC).

ADAM BEDE. 3 vols. Edinburgh 1859; 1 vol. 1904 (WC).

THE MILL ON THE FLOSS. 3 vols. Edinburgh 1860; 1 vol. 1903 (WC).

SILAS MARNER: the weaver of Raveloe. Edinburgh 1861; Oxford 1906 (WC) (*with* The lifted veil *and* Brother Jacob).

ROMOLA. 3 vols. 1863; 1 vol. Oxford 1913 (WC).

FELIX HOLT THE RADICAL. 3 vols. Edinburgh 1866; 1 vol. 1909 (EL).

MIDDLEMARCH: a study of provincial life. 4 vols. Edinburgh 1871–2; 1 vol. Oxford 1947 (WC); ed. Gordon S. Haight, Boston 1956.

THE LEGEND OF JUBAL and other poems. Edinburgh 1874.

DANIEL DERONDA. 4 vols. Edinburgh 1876; ed. F.R. Leavis, New York 1961.

Works: Warwick edition. 12 vols. Edinburgh 1901–3.

Letters. Ed. Gordon S. Haight, 7 vols. New Haven 1954–6.

Essays. Ed. Thomas Pinney, 1963.

Cross, John W. George Eliot's life as related in her letters and journals. 3 vols. 1885. *A memoir by her widower.*

James, Henry. *In his* Partial portraits, 1888. *A review of Cross.*

Stephen, Leslie. *In his* Hours in a library, 1892 (*enlarged*).

—— George Eliot. 1902 (EML).

Haight, Gordon S. George Eliot and John Chapman. New Haven 1940.

Bennett, Joan. George Eliot: her mind and her art. Cambridge 1948.

Leavis, F.R. *In his* The great tradition, 1948.

Hanson, Lawrence and Elisabeth. Marian Evans and George Eliot. Oxford 1952.

Hardy, Barbara. The novels of George Eliot. 1959.

Harvey, W.J. The art of George Eliot. 1961.

EDWARD FITZGERALD (1809 – 1883)

Prideaux, W.F. Notes for a bibliography of FitzGerald. 1901.

SIX DRAMAS OF CALDERÓN freely translated. 1853; 1928 (*with* Rubáiyát) (EL); Two plays from Calderón, 1865.
Eight dramas of Calderón. 1906.
RUBÁIYÁT OF OMAR KHAYYÁM, rendered into English verse. 1859; 1868; 1872; 1879; ed. N.H.Dole, 2 vols. 1898; ed. F.H.Evans, 1914 (*variorum text*).

Works. 2 vols. 1877; Letters and literary remains, ed. W.Aldis Wright, 3 vols. 1889, 7 vols. 1902–3 (*enlarged*); Variorum edition of the writings, ed. George Bentham, 7 vols. New York 1903; Letters, ed. J.M.Cohen, 1960; Selected works, ed. Joanna Richardson, 1962 (RL).

Wright, Thomas. The life of FitzGerald. 2 vols. 1904.
Benson, A.C. Edward FitzGerald. 1905 (EML).
Terhune, Alfred M. The life of FitzGerald. New Haven 1947.

SIR JAMES GEORGE FRAZER (1854 – 1941)

Besterman, Theodore. A bibliography of Frazer. 1934.

TOTEMICA. Edinburgh 1887.
THE GOLDEN BOUGH: a study in comparative religion. 2 vols. 1890; 3 vols. 1900; 12 vols. 1911–15 (*both enlarged*); Aftermath: a supplement, 1936. *Abridged edn, 1922.*
LECTURES on the early history of the kingship. 1905.
ADONIS, ATTIS, OSIRIS: studies in the history of oriental religion. 1906. *Pt iv of 3rd edn of* The golden bough, *above.*
PSYCHE'S TASK: the influence of superstition on the growth of institutions. 1909. *Re-entitled* The Devil's advocate, 1927.
TOTEMISM AND EXOGAMY: a treatise on superstition and society. 4 vols. 1910; A supplement, 1937.
THE BELIEF IN IMMORTALITY. 3 vols. 1913–24.
FOLK-LORE IN THE OLD TESTAMENT. 3 vols. 1918. *Abridged edn, 1923.*
MAN, GOD AND IMMORTALITY. 1927.
THE GORGON'S HEAD and other literary pieces. 1927.
MYTHS OF THE ORIGIN OF FIRE. 1930.
THE GROWTH of Plato's ideal theory. 1930.
GARNERED SHEAVES: essays. 1931.
THE FEAR OF THE DEAD in primitive religion. 3 vols. 1933–6.

Anthologia anthropologica: a selection from the MS. notebooks. Ed. R.Angus Downie, 4 vols. 1938-9.

Downie, R.Angus. Frazer: the portrait of a scholar. 1940.

JAMES ANTHONY FROUDE (1818 – 1894)

HISTORY OF ENGLAND from the fall of Wolsey to the death of Elizabeth. 12 vols. 1856-70; 1858-64 (vols. i–iv, vii–viii); 10 vols. 1909-12 (EL).
SHORT STUDIES ON GREAT SUBJECTS. 4 ser. (5 vols.) 1867-83.
THOMAS CARLYLE. 4 vols. 1882-4.
ENGLISH SEAMEN in the sixteenth century. 1895.

Dunn, W.H. Froude: a biography. 2 vols. Oxford 1961-3.

JOHN GALT (1779 – 1839)

THE AYRSHIRE LEGATEES. Edinburgh 1821.
ANNALS OF THE PARISH. Edinburgh 1821; ed. G.S.Gordon, 1908.
THE PROVOST. Edinburgh 1822.
THE ENTAIL. 3 vols. Edinburgh 1823; 1 vol. Oxford 1913 (WC).

Works. Ed. D.S.Meldrum and William Roughead, 10 vols. Edinburgh 1936.

Aberdein, Jennie W. John Galt. Oxford 1936.

ELIZABETH CLEGHORN GASKELL,
née STEVENSON (1810 – 1865)

Parrish, M.L. Victorian lady novelists: George Eliot, Mrs Gaskell, the Brontë sisters—first editions at Dormy House, New Jersey. 1933.

MARY BARTON: a tale of Manchester life. 2 vols. 1848.
CRANFORD. 1853.
NORTH AND SOUTH. 2 vols. 1855.
THE LIFE OF CHARLOTTE BRONTË. 2 vols. 1857; 1857.
WIVES AND DAUGHTERS. 2 vols. 1866. *Unfinished.*

Novels and tales. Ed. Clement Shorter, 11 vols. Oxford 1906-19 (WC).
Letters of Mrs Gaskell and C.E.Norton, 1855-65. Ed. Jane Whitehill, Oxford 1932.

Sanders, Gerald de W. Elizabeth Gaskell. New Haven 1929.
Cecil, David. *In his* Early Victorian novelists, 1934.
Hopkins, Annette B. Elizabeth Gaskell: her life and work. 1952.

SIR WILLIAM SCHWENK GILBERT (1836 – 1911)

Searle, Townley. A bibliography of Gilbert. 1931.

THE 'BAB' BALLADS. 1869; More 'Bab' ballads, 1873; Complete, 1874.
TRIAL BY JURY. 1875.
H.M.S. PINAFORE. 1878.
PATIENCE. 1881.
THE MIKADO. 1885.
THE GONDOLIERS. 1889.

Original plays. 4 ser. 1876–1911.
The Savoy operas. 1926; ed. Derek Hudson, 2 vols. Oxford 1962–3 (WC).

Dark, Sidney and Rowland Grey. Gilbert: his life and letters. 1923.
Pearson, Hesketh. Gilbert: his life and strife. 1957.

GEORGE ROBERT GISSING (1857 – 1903)

Danielson, Henry. *In his* Bibliographies of modern authors, 1921.

WORKERS IN THE DAWN. 3 vols. 1880. *First of 22 novels.*
THE UNCLASSED. 3 vols. 1884.
DEMOS. 1886.
THE NETHER WORLD. 3 vols. 1889.
NEW GRUB STREET. 3 vols. 1891; Oxford 1958 (WC).
CHARLES DICKENS: a critical study. 1898.
BY THE IONIAN SEA. 1901; ed. Virginia Woolf, 1933.
THE PRIVATE PAPERS of Henry Ryecroft. 1903.
VERANILDA: a romance. 1904; Oxford 1929 (WC).

Letters to members of his family. Ed. Algernon and Ellen Gissing, 1927; Gissing and H. G. Wells: their friendship and correspondence, ed. R. A. Gettmann, 1961.
Selections. Ed. Virginia Woolf and A. C. Gissing, 1929.

Roberts, Morley. The private life of Henry Maitland. 1912; ed. 'Morchard Bishop', 1958. *A novel based on Gissing's life by a friend.*
Swinnerton, Frank. Gissing: a critical study. 1912.
Murry, J. Middleton. *In his* Katherine Mansfield and other literary studies, 1959.
Korg, Jacob. Gissing: a critical biography. 1963.

THOMAS HARDY (1840 – 1928)

Purdy, Richard L. Hardy: a bibliographical study. Oxford 1954.

UNDER THE GREENWOOD TREE. 2 vols. 1872.
FAR FROM THE MADDING CROWD. 2 vols. 1874.
THE RETURN OF THE NATIVE. 3 vols. 1878.
TWO ON A TOWER. 3 vols. 1882.
THE MAYOR OF CASTERBRIDGE: the life and death of a man of character. 2 vols. 1886.
THE WOODLANDERS. 3 vols. 1887.
WESSEX TALES. 2 vols. 1888.
TESS OF THE D'URBERVILLES. 3 vols. 1891; 1892.
JUDE THE OBSCURE. 1896; Defence, Edinburgh 1928.
WESSEX POEMS and other verses. 1898 (*51 poems, one-third written in 1860's*); Poems of the past and present, 1902 (*99*); Time's laughing-stocks, 1902 (*94*); Satires of circumstance, 1914 (*107*); Moments of vision, 1917 (*159*); Late lyrics and earlier, 1922 (*151*); Human shows, 1925 (*152*); Winter words, 1928 (*105*).
THE DYNASTS: a drama of the Napoleonic wars. 3 pts. 1903–8; 1 vol. 1914.

Collected poems. 1919, 1930; Selected poems, ed. G.M.Young, 1940; ed. John Crowe Ransom, New York 1961; Love poems, ed. Carl J. Weber, 1963.
The Wessex novels. 16 vols. 1895–1913; 24 vols. 1912–31 (*rev. text*).
Short stories. 1928.
Notebooks. Ed. Evelyn Hardy, 1955.

Beach, Joseph W. The technique of Hardy. Chicago 1922.
Hardy, Florence E. The early life of Hardy, 1840–91. 1928; The later years, 1892–1928, 1930. *Probably an autobiography dictated to his wife; collected 1962.*
Lawrence, D.H. Study of Hardy. *In his* Phoenix, New York 1936.
Rutland, William R. Hardy: a study of his writings. Oxford 1938.
Cecil, David. Hardy the novelist. 1943.
Day Lewis, C. The lyrical poetry of Hardy. Proc. Brit. Acad. xxxvii (1951).
Holloway, John. Hardy's major fiction. *In his* The charted mirror, 1960.

WILLIAM HAZLITT (1778 – 1830)

Keynes, Geoffrey. Bibliography of Hazlitt. 1931 (Nonesuch Press).

THE ROUND TABLE: a collection of essays. 2 vols. Edinburgh 1817. *With Leigh Hunt.*

CHARACTERS OF SHAKESPEAR'S PLAYS. 1817; ed. Arthur Quiller-Couch, Oxford 1917 (WC).

A VIEW OF THE ENGLISH STAGE. 1818; ed. W.S.Jackson, 1906.

LECTURES on the English poets. 1818; ed. A.R.Waller, 1910 (EL) (*with* The spirit of the age, *below*); Oxford 1924 (WC).

LECTURES on the English comic writers. 1819; ed. R.Brimley Johnson, Oxford 1907 (WC).

LECTURES chiefly on the dramatic literature of the age of Elizabeth. 1820.

TABLE TALK. 2 vols. 1821–2; 1 vol. 1901 (WC).

LIBER AMORIS. 1823; ed. Richard Le Gallienne, 1894 (*enlarged*).

THE SPIRIT OF THE AGE: or contemporary portraits. 1825; 1825 (*with addns*); 2 vols. Paris 1825; 1 vol. 1904 (WC); ed. A.R.Waller, 1910 (EL).

THE PLAIN SPEAKER. 2 vols. 1826; ed. P.P.Howe, 1928 (EL).

THE LIFE OF NAPOLEON. 4 vols. 1828–30.

CONVERSATIONS of James Northcote, esq., R.A. 1830.

Complete works. Ed. P.P.Howe, 21 vols. 1930–4; Selected essays, ed. Geoffrey Keynes, 1930 (Nonesuch Lib.).

Hazlitt, W.Carew. Memoirs of Hazlitt. 2 vols. 1867.

Stephen, Leslie. *In his* Hours in a library, ser. 2, 1876.

Saintsbury, George. *In his* Essays in English literature, 1780–1860, 1890.

Howe, P.P. The life of Hazlitt. 1922; 1928; 1947 (*with introd.*).

Schneider, Elisabeth. The aesthetics of Hazlitt. Philadelphia 1933; 1952.

Baker, Herschel. William Hazlitt. Cambridge, Mass. 1962.

JAMES HOGG (1770 – 1835)

THE MOUNTAIN BARD. Edinburgh 1807; 1821 (*enlarged*).

THE FOREST MINSTREL. Edinburgh 1810.

THE QUEEN'S WAKE. Edinburgh 1813. *Includes* Kilmeny.

THE PRIVATE MEMOIRS and confessions of a justified sinner. 1824; ed. André Gide, 1947.

Poetical works. 4 vols. Edinburgh 1822; 5 vols. Glasgow 1838–40.

Tales and sketches. 6 vols. 1837.

Saintsbury, George. *In his* Essays in English literature, 1780–1860, 1890.

Batho, Edith C. The Ettrick shepherd. Cambridge 1927.

THOMAS HOOD (1799 – 1845)

ODES AND ADDRESSES to great people. 1825.
WHIMS AND ODDITIES. 2 ser. 1826–7.
THE PLEA of the midsummer fairies and other poems. 1827.
THE DREAM of Eugene Aram the murderer. Gem (1829); 1831.
HOOD'S OWN: or laughter from year to year. 1839; Hood and Lamb: the
    literary reminiscences, ed. Walter Jerrold, 1930 (*collected from* 1839).
WHIMSICALITIES. 1844.

Poetical works. Ed. Walter Jerrold, Oxford 1906.
Letters. Ed. Leslie A. Marchand, New Brunswick, N.J. 1945.

Saintsbury, George. *In his* Essays in English literature, 1780–1860,
    ser. 2, 1895.
Jerrold, Walter. Hood: his life and times. 1907.
Reid, J. C. Thomas Hood. 1963.

GERARD MANLEY HOPKINS (1844 – 1889)

POEMS. Ed. Robert Bridges, Oxford 1918; rev. W. H. Gardner, 1948,
    1956 (*enlarged*).
LETTERS TO ROBERT BRIDGES. Ed. Claude C. Abbott, Oxford 1935,
    1955; [to] R. W. Dixon, ed. Abbott, Oxford 1935, 1955; Further
    letters, ed. Abbott, Oxford 1937, 1956.
NOTE-BOOKS AND PAPERS. Ed. Humphry House, Oxford 1937; 2 vols.
    Oxford 1959 (*enlarged*).

Poems and prose, selected. Ed. W. H. Gardner, 1953 (Penguin);
    A Hopkins reader, ed. John Pick, Oxford 1953.

SERMONS and devotional writings. Ed. Christopher Devlin, Oxford 1959.

Leavis, F. R. *In his* New bearings in English poetry, 1932; 1950.
—— Hopkins; The letters of Hopkins. *In his* The common pursuit,
    1952.
Gardner, W. H. Gerard Manley Hopkins. 2 vols. 1944–9; 1948
    (vol. i).
Kenyon critics. Gerard Manley Hopkins. New York 1945.
Immortal diamond: studies in Hopkins. Ed. Norman Weyand, New
    York 1949.
House, Humphry. *In his* All in due time, 1955. *A broadcast and two
    reviews.*
Wain, John. Hopkins: an idiom of desperation. Proc. Brit. Acad.
    xlv (1959); *rptd in his* Essays on literature and ideas, 1963.
Winters, Yvor. The poetry of Hopkins. *In his* On modern poets, New
    York 1959.

ALFRED EDWARD HOUSMAN (1859 – 1936)

Carter, John and John Sparrow. Housman: an annotated hand-list. 1952. *See also Gow, below.*

A SHROPSHIRE LAD. 1896.
LAST POEMS. 1922.
MORE POEMS. Ed. Laurence Housman, 1936.

Collected poems. 1939, 1953; ed. John Sparrow, 1956 (Penguin).

MANUSCRIPT POEMS. Ed. Tom B.Haber, Minneapolis 1955.
Also edns of Manilius (5 vols. 1903–30) and Juvenal (1905).

Selected prose. Ed. John Carter, Cambridge 1961.

Gow, A.S.F. Housman: a sketch with a list of his writings and indexes to his classical papers. Cambridge 1936.
Housman, Laurence. AEH: some poems, some letters and a personal memoir. 1937.
Richards, Grant. Housman, 1897–1936. Oxford 1941.
Watson, George L. Housman: a divided life. 1957.

LEIGH HUNT (1784 – 1859)

CRITICAL ESSAYS on the performers of the London theatres. 1807.
THE EXAMINER: a Sunday paper. 1808–25. *Full of Hunt's contributions during this period, and edited by him till 1821.*
THE FEAST OF THE POETS, and other pieces in verse. 1814; 1815 *(enlarged)*.
THE STORY OF RIMINI. 1816.
THE ROUND TABLE: a collection of essays by Hazlitt. 2 vols. Edinburgh 1817. *Mainly by Hazlitt, but including ten Hunt essays.*
THE LIBERAL: verse and prose from the south. 2 vols. (4 nos.) 1822–3. *Edited and mainly written by Hunt.*
BYRON and some of his contemporaries. 1828, 2 vols. 1828 *(enlarged)*; Autobiography, 3 vols. 1850, 1860, ed. Edmund Blunden, Oxford 1928 (WC). *The* Autobiography *is a reconstruction of 1828.*
TABLE TALK. 1851.

Poetical works, revised by himself. Ed. Thornton Hunt, 1860; ed. Humphrey Milford, Oxford 1923 *(with addns)*.
Correspondence. Ed. Thornton Hunt, 2 vols. 1862; My Hunt library: the holograph letters, ed. Luther A.Brewer, Iowa City 1938.
[Selected] essays. Ed. J.B.Priestley, 1929 (EL); Dramatic criticism, 1808–31, ed. L.H. and C.W.Houtchens, New York 1949; Literary criticism, ed. Houtchens, New York 1957; Political and occasional essays, ed. Houtchens, New York 1962.

Saintsbury, George. *In his* Essays in English literature, 1780–1860, 1890.

Blunden, Edmund. Hunt's Examiner examined. 1928.

—— Hunt: a biography. 1930.

Landré, Louis. Leigh Hunt. 2 vols. Paris 1935–6.

HENRY JAMES (1843 – 1916)

Edel, Leon and Dan H. Laurence. A bibliography of James. 1957; 1961.

A PASSIONATE PILGRIM and other tales. Boston 1875.

RODERICK HUDSON. Boston 1876; 3 vols. London 1879; ed. Leon Edel, 1961.

THE AMERICAN. Boston 1877. *First London edn, 1877.*

FRENCH POETS AND NOVELISTS. 1878.

THE EUROPEANS: a sketch. 2 vols. 1878.

DAISY MILLER: a study. 2 vols. New York 1879. *First London edn, 1879. Three tales.*

HAWTHORNE. 1879 (EML).

WASHINGTON SQUARE. New York 1881. *First London edn, 2 vols. 1881.*

THE PORTRAIT OF A LADY. 3 vols. 1881; ed. Graham Greene, Oxford 1947 (WC).

THE BOSTONIANS: a novel. 3 vols. 1886.

THE PRINCESS CASAMASSIMA: a novel. 3 vols. 1886; ed. Lionel Trilling, New York 1948.

PARTIAL PORTRAITS. 1888. *Includes* The art of fiction *and reviews of George Eliot, R. L. Stevenson, Trollope.*

THE TRAGIC MUSE. 2 vols. Boston 1890. *First London edn, 3 vols. 1890.*

THE LESSON OF THE MASTER. New York 1892. *First London edn, 1892. Six short stories.*

THE SPOILS OF POYNTON. 1897.

WHAT MAISIE KNEW. 1897.

THE TURN OF THE SCREW. 1898 (*in* The two magics); 1935 (EL).

THE AWKWARD AGE. 1899.

THE WINGS OF THE DOVE. 2 vols. New York 1902. *First London edn, 1902.*

THE AMBASSADORS. 1903; 1948, 1959 (EL); ed. S. P. Rosenbaum, New York 1964.

THE GOLDEN BOWL. 2 vols. New York 1904. *First London edn, 1905.*

VIEWS AND REVIEWS. Boston 1908. *Includes reviews of Arnold, Browning, Dickens, George Eliot, Kipling, Morris, Ruskin, Swinburne, Tennyson.*

A SMALL BOY AND OTHERS. New York 1913; Notes of a son and brother, New York 1914; The middle years, 1917. *Collected as* Autobiography, ed. Frederick W. Dupee, New York 1956.

NOTES ON NOVELISTS. 1914. *Includes* The new novel, *studies of Browning's* The ring and the book, *R.L. Stevenson.*
THE IVORY TOWER. 1917. *Unfinished.*
THE SENSE OF THE PAST. 1917. *Unfinished.*

Novels and tales. 24 vols. New York 1907–9 (*rev. text with critical prefaces*); ed. Percy Lubbock, 35 vols. 1921–3; Uniform tales, 14 vols. 1915–20; The American novels and stories, ed. F.O. Matthiessen, New York 1947; Complete tales, ed. Leon Edel, 12 vols. 1962–.

Complete plays. Ed. Leon Edel, Philadelphia 1949. *12 complete plays etc., mainly written 1889–95 and 1907–9.*

Letters. Ed. Percy Lubbock, 2 vols. 1920; Selected letters, ed. Leon Edel, 1956; James and H.G. Wells: a record, ed. Edel and Gordon N. Ray, Urbana, Ill. 1958.

Notebooks. Ed. F.O. Matthiessen and Kenneth B. Murdock, New York 1947.

The art of the novel: critical prefaces. Ed. R.P. Blackmur, New York 1934; The art of fiction and other critical essays, ed. Morris Roberts, New York 1948; The scenic art: notes on acting and the drama, 1872–1901, ed. Allan Wade, New Brunswick, N.J. 1948; The painter's eye: notes and essays on the pictorial arts, ed. John L. Sweeney, 1956; The house of fiction: essays on the novel, ed. Leon Edel, 1957.

Beach, Joseph W. The method of James. New Haven 1918; Philadelphia 1954 (*with introd.*).
Brooks, Van Wycks. The pilgrimage of James. New York 1925.
Matthiessen, F.O. James: the major phase. New York 1944.
The legend of the Master. Ed. Simon Nowell-Smith, 1947. *An anthology of reminiscences.*
Leavis, F.R. *In his* The great tradition, 1948.
Dupee, F.W. Henry James. New York 1951; 1956 (*enlarged*).
Edel, Leon. Henry James. 4 vols. Philadelphia 1953–. *A biography.*
Jefferson, D.W. Henry James. Edinburgh 1960 (Writers & critics).
Krook, Dorothea. The ordeal of consciousness in James. Cambridge 1962.

HENRY ARTHUR JONES (1851 – 1929)

MICHAEL AND HIS LOST ANGEL. 1896. *Some 60 plays pbd 1879–1917.*
THE LIARS: an original comedy. New York 1901.

Representative plays. Ed. Clayton Hamilton, 4 vols. Boston 1925.

Jones, Doris. The life and letters of Jones. 1930.

JOHN KEATS (1795 – 1821)

Baldwin, D.L. *et al.* A concordance to the poems. Washington 1917.
MacGillivray, J.R. Keats: a bibliography and reference guide. Toronto
1949.

POEMS. 1817; 1927 (*facs.*).
ENDYMION: a poetic romance. 1818; Oxford 1927 (*facs.*).
LAMIA, ISABELLA, The eve of St Agnes and other poems. 1820.

Life, letters and literary remains. Ed. Baron Houghton, 2 vols. 1848,
1 vol. Oxford 1931 (WC); Letters, ed. Maurice Buxton Forman,
2 vols. Oxford 1931, 1 vol. Oxford 1952; Selected, ed. Lionel Trilling, New York 1951; ed. Frederick Page, Oxford 1954 (WC).
The Keats circle: letters and papers, 1816–78. Ed. Hyder E. Rollins,
2 vols. Cambridge, Mass. 1948; More letters and poems, ed. Rollins,
Cambridge, Mass. 1955.
Poetical works. Ed. H. Buxton Forman, Oxford 1908 (OSA); ed.
H.W. Garrod, Oxford 1939, 1958; 1956 (OSA); Poems in
chronological order, ed. J. Middleton Murry, 2 vols. 1930, 1 vol. 1949.

Arnold, Matthew. *In his* Essays in criticism, ser. 2, 1888.
Bridges, Robert. Keats: a critical essay. 1895; *rptd in his* Collected
essays, papers etc., Oxford 1927–36.
Garrod, H.W. Keats. Oxford 1926; 1939.
Murry, J. Middleton. Studies in Keats. Oxford 1930; 1955 (*re-entitled*
Keats, *enlarged*).
Ridley, M.R. Keats's craftsmanship. Oxford 1933; London 1963.
Fogle, Richard H. The imagery of Keats and Shelley. Chapel Hill,
N.C. 1949.
Wasserman, Earl R. The finer tone: Keats's major poems. Baltimore
1953.
Gittings, Robert. Keats: the living year, Sept. 1818–Sept. 1819. 1954.
Bate, Walter J. John Keats. Cambridge, Mass. 1963.
Ward, Aileen. Keats: the making of a poet. 1963.

JOHN KEBLE (1792 – 1866)

THE CHRISTIAN YEAR. 2 vols. Oxford 1827.
LYRA INNOCENTIUM. Oxford 1846.

The Christian year [etc.]. Oxford 1914 (OSA).
Occasional papers. Ed. E.B. Pusey, Oxford 1877.

Battiscombe, Georgina. Keble: a study in limitations. 1963.

ALEXANDER WILLIAM KINGLAKE (1809 – 1891)

EOTHEN. 1844; Oxford 1910 (WC).

THE INVASION OF THE CRIMEA. 8 vols. Edinburgh 1863–87; 9 vols. 1877–88.

CHARLES KINGSLEY (1819 – 1875)

Parrish, M.L. and Barbara K.Maun. Charles Kingsley and Thomas Hughes: first editions at Dormy House, New Jersey. 1936.

ALTON LOCKE. 2 vols. 1850; 1856, 1862 (*with prefaces*).

WESTWARD HO! 3 vols. Cambridge 1855.

THE WATER-BABIES. 1863.

HEREWARD THE WAKE. 2 vols. 1866.

Poems: collected edition. 1872; 2 vols. 1884 (*enlarged*).

Letters and memories of his life by his wife [Frances E.Kingsley]. 2 vols. 1877.

Life and works. 19 vols. 1901–3.

Stephen, Leslie. *In his* Hours in a library, ser. 3, 1879.

Pope-Hennessy, Una. Canon Charles Kingsley. 1948.

Martin, Robert B. The dust of combat: a life of Kingsley. 1959.

HENRY KINGSLEY (1830 – 1876)

THE RECOLLECTIONS of Geoffrey Hamlyn. 3 vols. 1859; 1 vol. Oxford 1924 (WC).

RAVENSHOE. 3 vols. 1861; 1 vol. Oxford 1925 (WC).

AUSTIN ELLIOTT. 2 vols. 1863; 1 vol. Oxford 1932 (WC).

Novels. Ed. Clement Shorter, 8 vols. 1894–5.

RUDYARD KIPLING (1865 – 1936)

Stewart, James McG. Kipling: a bibliographical catalogue. Ed. A.W. Yeats, Toronto 1960.

DEPARTMENTAL DITTIES and other verses. Lahore 1886 (*26 poems*); 1890 (*50*).

PLAIN TALES FROM THE HILLS. Calcutta 1888; London 1890.

THE LIGHT THAT FAILED. 1890.

BARRACK-ROOM BALLADS. 1892.

THE JUNGLE BOOK. 1894; Second jungle book, 1895.

RECESSIONAL. Times (July 1897); Recessional and other poems, 1899.

STALKY AND CO. 1899; The complete Stalky, 1929 (*five stories added*).

KIM. 1901. *The last novel.*

JUST SO STORIES. 1902.

PUCK OF POOK'S HILL. 1906; Rewards and fairies, 1910.
LAND AND SEA TALES for scouts and guides. 1923.
DEBITS AND CREDITS. 1926. *Fourteen stories, with poems.*
LIMITS AND RENEWALS. 1932. *Fourteen stories, with poems.*
SOMETHING OF MYSELF for my friends. 1937. *Autobiography, unfinished.*

Collected verse. New York 1907; Definitive edition, 1940 (*incomplete*);
A choice of Kipling's verse, ed. T. S. Eliot, 1941.
Works: Bombay edition. 31 vols. 1913–38.

Wilson, Edmund. The Kipling that nobody read. *In his* The wound and
the bow, Boston 1941.
'Orwell, George'. *In his* Critical essays, 1946.
Graves, Robert. *In his* The common asphodel, 1949.
Carrington, Charles. Kipling: his life and work. 1955.
Tompkins, J. M. S. The art of Kipling. 1959.
Lewis, C. S. *In his* They asked for a paper, 1962.
Bodelsen, C. A. Aspects of Kipling's art. Manchester 1964.
Rutherford, Andrew (ed.). Kipling's mind and art. 1964. *Collects*
Wilson, Orwell, *above.*

CHARLES LAMB (1775 – 1834)

Thomson, J. C. Bibliography of the writings of Charles and Mary
Lamb. Hull 1908.

TALES FROM SHAKESPEAR. 2 vols. 1807; ed. F. J. Furnivall, 2 vols. 1901.
Largely by his sister, Mary Lamb.
SPECIMENS OF ENGLISH DRAMATIC POETS who lived about the time of
Shakespeare. 1808; ed. Israel Gollancz, 2 vols. 1893.
ELIA: essays in the London magazine. 1823; The last essays of Elia,
1833; [both series], 2 vols. 1835; 1 vol. Oxford 1946 (WC).

Letters. Ed. E. V. Lucas, 3 vols. 1935. *With Mary Lamb's letters.*
Works. Ed. E. V. Lucas, 7 vols. 1903–5, 6 vols. 1912; Lamb's
criticism: a selection, ed. E. M. W. Tillyard, Cambridge 1923.

Lucas, E. V. Life of Lamb. 1905; 1921.
Blunden, Edmund. Lamb and his contemporaries. Cambridge 1933.
—— (ed.). Lamb recorded by his contemporaries. 1934.

WALTER SAVAGE LANDOR (1775 – 1864)

Wise, Thomas J. and Stephen Wheeler. A bibliography of Landor.
1919.
Super, R. H. The publication of Landor's works. 1954.

GEBIR: a poem. 1798; 1831.

POEMS. 1802.

IMAGINARY CONVERSATIONS. 3 vols. 1824–8; Second series, 2 vols. 1829; Selection, ed. E. de Selincourt, Oxford 1915 (WC). *Final, expanded version in* Works, 1846, *below.*

HELLENICS. 1847; 1859 (*enlarged*).

Letters. Ed. Stephen Wheeler, 1897; 1899; Last days, letters and conversations, ed. H. C. Minchin, 1934.

Poems. Ed. Stephen Wheeler, 3 vols. Oxford 1937.

Works. 2 vols. 1846; Complete works, ed. T. Earle Welby and Stephen Wheeler, 16 vols. 1927–36.

Forster, John. Landor: a biography. 2 vols. 1869.

Stephen, Leslie. Landor's Imaginary conversations. *In his* Hours in a library, ser. 3, 1879.

Colvin, Sidney. Landor. 1881 (EML).

Saintsbury, George. *In his* Essays in English literature, ser. 2, 1895.

Super, R. H. Landor: a biography. New York 1954.

EDWARD LEAR (1812 – 1888)

Osgood Field, William B. Lear on my shelves. Munich 1933.

VIEWS IN ROME and its environs. 1841. *First of seven travel-journals of Italy, Greece and Corsica, pbd 1841–70. Selection, ed. Herbert van Thal, 1952.*

A BOOK OF NONSENSE. 1846; 1861; 1863 (*both enlarged*).

NONSENSE SONGS, stories, botany and alphabets. 1871; More nonsense pictures, etc. 1872; Laughable lyrics, 1877.

Complete nonsense. Ed. Holbrook Jackson, 1947.

TEAPOTS AND QUAILS. Ed. Angus Davidson and Philip Hofer, Cambridge, Mass. 1953.

INDIAN JOURNAL, from the diary 1873–5. Ed. Ray Murphy, 1953.

Letters. Ed. Lady Strachey, 1907; Later letters, ed. Lady Strachey, 1911.

Davidson, Angus. Edward Lear. 1938.

Sewell, Elizabeth. *In her* The field of nonsense, 1952.

THOMAS BABINGTON MACAULAY, 1ST BARON MACAULAY (1800 – 1859)

LAYS OF ANCIENT ROME. 1842; 1848 (*enlarged*); ed. G. M. Trevelyan, 1928.

CRITICAL AND HISTORICAL ESSAYS. 3 vols. 1843; ed. F. C. Montague, 3 vols. 1903.

THE HISTORY OF ENGLAND FROM THE ACCESSION OF JAMES II. 5 vols. 1849–61; Oxford 1931 (WC).

Works. 9 vols. 1905–7; Prose and poetry, ed. G. M. Young, 1952 (RL).

Trevelyan, George Otto. The life and letters of Macaulay by his nephew. 2 vols. 1876; Oxford 1932 (WC).

Bagehot, Walter. *In his* Literary studies, 1879. *A review of the* History.

Stephen, Leslie. *In his* Hours in a library, ser. 3, 1879.

Bryant, Arthur. Macaulay. 1932.

FREDERICK MARRYAT (1792 – 1848)

PETER SIMPLE. 3 vols. 1834; ed. Michael Sadleir, 2 vols. 1929.

JACOB FAITHFUL. 3 vols. 1834; ed. George Saintsbury, 2 vols. 1928.

MR MIDSHIPMAN EASY. 3 vols. 1836; 1 vol. 1906 (EL).

MASTERMAN READY. 3 vols. 1841–2; 1 vol. 1907 (EL).

THE CHILDREN OF THE NEW FOREST. 2 vols. 1847; 1 vol. 1907 (EL).

Novels. Ed. R. Brimley Johnson, 24 vols. 1896–8; 25 vols. 1929–30.

Marryat, Florence. Life and letters of Captain Marryat. 2 vols. 1872.

Conrad, Joseph. Tales of the sea (1898). *In his* Notes on life and letters, 1921.

Warner, Oliver. Captain Marryat: a rediscovery. 1953.

GEORGE MEREDITH (1828 – 1909)

Buxton Forman, Maurice. A bibliography of Meredith. 1922; Meredithiana: a supplement, 1924.

THE SHAVING OF SHAGPAT: an Arabian entertainment. 1856.

THE ORDEAL OF RICHARD FEVEREL. 3 vols. 1859; 1899; 1 vol. 1935 (EL).

EVAN HARRINGTON. 3 vols. 1861.

MODERN LOVE and Poems of the English roadside, with poems and ballads. 1862.

RHODA FLEMING: a story. 3 vols. 1865.

VITTORIA. 3 vols. 1867.

THE ADVENTURES OF HARRY RICHMOND. 3 vols. 1871.

BEAUCHAMP'S CAREER. 3 vols. 1876; ed. G. M. Young, Oxford 1950 (WC).

ON THE IDEA OF COMEDY. 1877.

THE EGOIST. 3 vols. 1879; ed. Lord Dunsany, Oxford 1947 (WC).

THE TRAGIC COMEDIANS. 2 vols. 1880; 1892.

DIANA OF THE CROSSWAYS. 3 vols. 1885.

Works. 34 vols. 1896–8. *Revised text of early novels.*
Memorial edition. 27 vols. 1909–11.
Letters. Ed. W.M.Meredith, 2 vols. 1912.
Poetical works. Ed. G.M.Trevelyan, 1912.

Trevelyan, G.M. The poetry and philosophy of Meredith. 1906.
Priestley, J.B. George Meredith. 1926 (EML).
Sassoon, Siegfried. Meredith. 1948.
Stevenson, Lionel. The ordeal of George Meredith: a biography. New
York 1953.

ALICE MEYNELL, née THOMPSON (1847 – 1922)

POEMS. 1893; Other poems, 1896; Later poems, 1902; Ten poems,
1915; Last poems, 1923.

Poems. 1913; 1923; Oxford 1940 (OSA); ed. Francis Meynell, 1947.
Essays. 1914.
Prose and poetry. Ed. V.Sackville-West *et al.*, 1947.

Meynell, Viola. Alice Meynell: a memoir. 1929.

JOHN STUART MILL (1806 – 1873)

Bibliography of the published writings of Mill. Ed. Ney MacMinn
et al. Evanston 1945. *First pbn of Mill's own MS. list.*

THE SPIRIT OF THE AGE. Examiner (Jan.–May 1831); ed. F.A.Hayek,
Chicago 1942.
A SYSTEM OF LOGIC. 2 vols. 1843; 1872.
PRINCIPLES OF POLITICAL ECONOMY. 2 vols. 1848; 1871; ed. W.J.
Ashley, 1909.
ON LIBERTY. 1859; Oxford 1912 (WC); ed. Mary Warnock, 1962 (*with*
Utilitarianism *and* Bentham, *below*).
DISSERTATIONS AND DISCUSSIONS. 2 vols. 1859; 3 vols. 1867; 4 vols.
1875; On Bentham and Coleridge, ed. F.R.Leavis, 1950 (*from* 1859).
THOUGHTS ON PARLIAMENTARY REFORM. 1859.
REPRESENTATIVE GOVERNMENT. 1861; Oxford 1912 (WC) (*with*
Liberty, *above*).
UTILITARIANISM. 1863; ed. A.D.Lindsay, 1910 (EL) (*with* Liberty *and*
Representative government, *above*).
AN EXAMINATION of Sir William Hamilton's philosophy. 1865.
ON THE SUBJECTION OF WOMEN. 1869; Oxford 1912 (WC) (*with* Liberty,
above).
AUTOBIOGRAPHY. Ed. Helen Taylor, 1873; ed. Harold Laski, Oxford
1924 (WC); ed. Roger Howson, New York 1924 (*from MS.*).

The ethics of Mill. Ed. Charles Douglas, 1897.

Letters. Ed. Hugh S.R.Elliott, 1910; Mill and Harriet Taylor: their correspondence, ed. F.A.Hayek, 1951.

Collected works. Ed. F.E.L.Priestley, Francis E.Mineka *et al.*, 20 vols. Toronto 1963–.

Stephen, Leslie. *In his* The English utilitarians, 1900.
Britton, Karl. John Stuart Mill. 1953 (Pelican).
Packe, Michael St John. The life of Mill. 1954.

GEORGE MOORE (1852 – 1933)

CONFESSIONS OF A YOUNG MAN. 1888; 1926.
ESTHER WATERS. 1894; 1920.
'HAIL AND FAREWELL': a trilogy. 3 vols. 1911–14.
THE BROOK KERITH. 1916; 1927.

Works: Ebury edition. 20 vols. 1937.
Letters, 1895–1933, to Lady Cunard. Ed. Rupert Hart-Davis, 1957.

Yeats, W.B. *In his* Dramatis personae, Dublin 1935.
Hone, Joseph M. The life of George Moore. 1936.
Cunard, Nancy. GM: memories of George Moore. 1956.
Hough, Graham. *In his* Image and experience, 1960.

THOMAS MOORE (1779 – 1852)

A SELECTION OF IRISH MELODIES. 10 pts. 1808–34; 1 vol. 1821; ed. S.Gwynn, 1908 (ML).
LALLA ROOKH: an oriental romance. 1817.
LETTERS AND JOURNALS OF BYRON, with notices of his life. 2 vols. 1830.

Memoirs, journal and correspondence. Ed. John Russell, 8 vols. 1853–6; Diary: a selection, ed. J.B.Priestley, Cambridge 1925.
Poetical works. Ed. A.D.Godley, Oxford 1910 (OSA).

Hazlitt, William. *In his* The spirit of the age, 1825.
Saintsbury, George. *In his* Essays in English literature, 1780–1860, 1890.
Jones, Howard Mumford. The harp that once—: the life of Moore. New York 1937.

WILLIAM MORRIS (1834 – 1896)

Buxton Forman, H. The books of Morris. 1897.

THE DEFENCE OF GUENEVERE and other poems. 1858.
THE LIFE AND DEATH OF JASON. 1867.
THE EARTHLY PARADISE. 3 vols. 1868–70.

SIGURD THE VOLSUNG. 1877.
A DREAM OF JOHN BALL. 1888.
THE HOUSE OF THE WOLFINGS. 1889.
NEWS FROM NOWHERE. 1891.

Collected works. Ed. May Morris, 24 vols. 1910–15; Stories, shorter
poems, lectures and essays, ed. G. D. H. Cole, 1934 (Nonesuch Press);
Selected writings and designs, ed. Asa Briggs, 1962 (Penguin).
Poems. Oxford 1914 (WC).
Letters. Ed. Phillip Henderson, 1950. *Selection.*

Mackail, J. W. The life of Morris. 2 vols. 1899; 1 vol. Oxford 1950 (WC).
Morris, May. William Morris. 2 vols. Oxford 1936.
Lewis, C. S. *In his* Rehabilitations, Oxford 1939.

JOHN HENRY NEWMAN (1801 – 1890)

PAROCHIAL SERMONS. 6 vols. 1834–42.
LECTURES on the present position of Catholics. 1851.
THE SCOPE AND NATURE of university education. Dublin 1852, London
1859; The idea of a university, 1873 (*enlarged by addn of* Lectures
and essays), ed. C. F. Harrold, New York 1947.
APOLOGIA PRO VITA SUA. 1864; 1865 (*re-entitled* History of my religious
opinions) (*abridged*); ed. Wilfrid Ward, 1913 (*both versions*); ed. C. F.
Harrold, New York 1947; ed. Basil Willey, Oxford 1964 (WC).
THE DREAM OF GERONTIUS. 1866; 1909 (*with MS. facs.*).
VERSES ON VARIOUS OCCASIONS. 1868; The dream of Gerontius and
other poems, Oxford 1914 (OSA).
A GRAMMAR OF ASSENT. 1870.
Also two novels, Loss and gain (1848) *and* Callista (1856).

Works. 40 vols. 1874–1921; [Selected writings], ed. C. F. Harrold,
c. 20 vols. New York 1947–.
Prose and poetry. Ed. Geoffrey Tillotson, 1957 (RL).
Letters and diaries. Ed. C. S. Dessain, Edinburgh 1961–.

Ward, Wilfrid. The life of Cardinal Newman. 2 vols. 1912.
Harrold, C. F. Newman: a study of his mind, thought and art. New
York 1945.
Trevor, Meriol. Newman: the pillar of the cloud. 1962. Newman:
light in winter, 1962;

WALTER HORATIO PATER (1839 – 1894)

THE RENAISSANCE. 1873; 1877 (Conclusion *omitted*); 1888 (*with rev.*
Conclusion); ed. Kenneth Clark, 1961.

MARIUS THE EPICUREAN. 2 vols. 1885; 1 vol. 1934 (EL).
IMAGINARY PORTRAITS. 1887.
APPRECIATIONS. 1889. *Essays on style, Wordsworth, Coleridge, Lamb, Sir Thomas Browne, Shakespeare, D.G.Rossetti etc.*

Works. 9 vols. 1900–1, 10 vols. 1910; Selected works, ed. Richard Aldington, 1948.

Benson, A.C. Walter Pater. 1906 (EML).
Eliot, T.S. Arnold and Pater. *In his* Selected essays, 1932.
Cecil, David. Walter Pater. Cambridge 1955 (Rede lecture); *rptd in his* The fine art of reading, 1957.

COVENTRY KERSEY DIGHTON PATMORE
(1823 – 1896)

THE ANGEL IN THE HOUSE. 2 pts. 1854–6 (*unfinished*); 2 vols. 1858; 2 vols. 1863, 1866 (*with other poems*).
THE UNKNOWN EROS and other odes. 2 pts. 1877–8; 1890.

Poems. Ed. Frederick Page, Oxford 1949 (OSA); Selected poems, ed. Derek Patmore, 1931.

Champneys, Basil. Memoir and correspondence of Patmore. 2 vols. 1900.
Page, Frederick. Patmore: a study in poetry. Oxford 1933.
Hopkins, Gerard Manley. *In his* Further letters, ed. Claude C.Abbott, Oxford 1937, 1956.

THOMAS LOVE PEACOCK (1785 – 1866)

HEADLONG HALL. 1816; 1837 (*below*).
MELINCOURT. 3 vols. 1817.
NIGHTMARE ABBEY. 1818; 1837 (*below*).
THE FOUR AGES OF POETRY. 1820 (*in* Ollier's literary miscellany); ed. H.F.B.Brett-Smith, Oxford 1921 (*with Shelley's* Defence).
MAID MARIAN. 1822; 1837 (*below*).
THE MISFORTUNES OF ELPHIN. 1829; Oxford 1924 (WC) (*with* Crotchet Castle).
CROTCHET CASTLE. 1831; 1837 (*below*).

Bentley's standard novels, vol. lvii. 1837. *Rev. text of four of the novels, above.*

MEMOIRS OF SHELLEY. Fraser's mag. (1858–60); 1875; ed. H.F.B.Brett-Smith, Oxford 1909.
GRYLL GRANGE. 1861.

Works: Halliford edition. Ed. H.F.B.Brett-Smith and Claude E. Jones, 10 vols. 1924–34. *Vol. i includes the standard life by Brett-Smith.*

Novels. Ed. David Garnett, 1948.

Saintsbury, George. *In his* Essays in English literature, 1780–1860, 1890.
Brett-Smith, H.F.B. *See under* Works, *above.*
Priestley, J.B. Thomas Love Peacock. 1927 (EML).
Mayoux, J.-J. Un épicurien anglais: Peacock. Paris 1933.

SIR ARTHUR WING PINERO (1855 – 1934)

THE SECOND MRS TANQUERAY. 1895. *39 plays pbd 1891–1930.*
THE GAY LORD QUEX. 1900.

Social plays. Ed. Clayton Hamilton, 4 vols. New York 1917–22.

Archer, William. *In his* The old drama and the new, 1923.

WINTHROP MACKWORTH PRAED (1802 – 1839)

LILLIAN. 1823.
Most of the poems appeared in newspapers and periodicals and were not collected until after his death.

Poems. Ed. Derwent Coleridge, 2 vols. 1864.
Political and occasional pieces. Ed. George Young, 1888.
Selected poems. Ed. Kenneth Allott, 1953 (ML).

Saintsbury, George. *In his* Essays in English literature, 1780–1860, 1890.
Hudson, Derek. A poet in Parliament. 1939.

SIR ARTHUR QUILLER-COUCH (1865 – 1944) ('Q')

DEAD MAN'S ROCK: a romance. 1887; The astonishing history of Troy town, 1888; Hetty Wesley, 1903; Sir John Constantine, 1906. *Many novels pbd 1887–1918.*
GREEN BAYS: verses and parodies. 1893, 1930 *(enlarged)*; Poems and ballads, 1896, 1929 *(re-entitled* Poems, *enlarged).*
ADVENTURES IN CRITICISM. 1896, 1924 *(with omissions)*; On the art of writing, Cambridge 1916; Studies in literature, 3 ser. Cambridge 1918–29; On the art of reading, Cambridge 1920; The poet as citizen and other papers, Cambridge 1934. *Collections of articles and Cambridge lectures, selected in* Cambridge lectures, 1943 (EL).
FROM A CORNISH WINDOW. Bristol 1906.

SHAKESPEARE'S WORKMANSHIP. 1918.

CHARLES DICKENS AND OTHER VICTORIANS. Cambridge 1925.

MEMORIES AND OPINIONS: an unfinished autobiography. Ed. S.C. Roberts, Cambridge 1944.

Q anthology: a selection from the prose and verse. Ed. F.Brittain, 1948.

For some of his edns, see Index.

Brittain, F. Arthur Quiller-Couch: a biographical study of Q. Cambridge 1947.

CHARLES READE (1814 – 1884)

IT IS NEVER TOO LATE TO MEND. 3 vols. 1856.

THE CLOISTER AND THE HEARTH. 4 vols. 1861; 1 vol. 1906 (EL); ed. C.B.Wheeler, Oxford 1915.

HARD CASH. 3 vols. 1863.

Elwin, Malcolm. Reade: a biography. 1931.

DAVID RICARDO (1772 – 1823)

PRINCIPLES of political economy and taxation. 1817; ed. E.C.K. Gonner, 1891.

Works and correspondence. Ed. Piero Sraffa, 11 vols. Cambridge 1951–7.

SAMUEL ROGERS (1763 – 1855)

THE PLEASURES OF MEMORY: a poem in two parts. 1792.

ITALY: a poem. 2 pts. 1822–8; 1 vol. 1830.

Poetical works. 1856; ed. Edward Bell, 1875 (Aldine).

TABLE-TALK. Ed. Alexander Dyce, 1856; ed. 'Morchard Bishop', 1952.

CHRISTINA GEORGINA ROSSETTI (1830 – 1894)

GOBLIN MARKET and other poems. 1862; 1875 (*with* The prince's progress).

THE PRINCE'S PROGRESS and other poems. 1866; 1875.

SING-SONG. 1872.

A PAGEANT and other poems. 1881.

Poems. 1890.

VERSES. 1893.

NEW POEMS. Ed. William Michael Rossetti, 1896.

Poetical works. Ed. W.M.Rossetti, 1904.

Family letters. Ed. W.M.Rossetti, 1908; Three Rossettis: unpublished letters, ed. Janet C.Troxell, Cambridge, Mass. 1937.

Sandars, Mary F. The life of Christina Rossetti. 1930.
Packer, Lona M. Christina Rossetti. Berkeley, Cal. 1963.

DANTE GABRIEL ROSSETTI (1828 – 1882)

Rossetti, W.M. A bibliography of Rossetti, 1905.

THE EARLY ITALIAN POETS, 1100–1300, in the original metres. 1861; 1874 (*re-entitled* Dante and his circle).
POEMS. 1870; 1881 (*excluding* House of life *sonnets*).
The blessed damozel. Ed. P.F.Baum, Chapel Hill, N.C. 1937. *1847 MS., periodical versions (1850, 1856) and texts of* 1870, 1881.
BALLADS AND SONNETS. 1881.
The house of life: a sonnet-sequence. Ed. P.F.Baum. Cambridge Mass. 1928.
Family letters with a memoir. Ed. W.M.Rossetti, 2 vols. 1895.
Works. Ed. W.M.Rossetti, 1911.
Poems and translations. Oxford 1913 (OSA).
List of manuscripts in Duke University Library with unpublished verse and prose. Ed. P.F.Baum, Durham, N.C. 1931.

Pater, Walter. *In his* Appreciations, 1889.
Benson, A.C. Rossetti. 1904 (EML).
Doughty, Oswald. A Victorian romantic. 1949.

JOHN RUSKIN (1819 – 1900)

Wise, Thomas J. and J.P.Smart. A bibliography of Ruskin. 19 pts 1889–93.

MODERN PAINTERS. 5 vols. 1843–60; 1873.
THE SEVEN LAMPS OF ARCHITECTURE. 1849; 1880.
THE STONES OF VENICE. 3 vols. 1851–2; 1874.
UNTO THIS LAST: four essays on political economy. 1862.
SESAME AND LILIES. 1865; 1882.
THE ETHICS OF THE DUST. 1866; 1877.
THE CROWN OF WILD OLIVE. 1866; 1873.
FORS CLAVIGERA. 96 letters (8 vols.). 1871–84.
PRAETERITA. 28 pts. 1885–9; 3 vols. Orpington 1886–9; ed. Kenneth Clark, 1949. *An autobiography, vol. i partly based on* Fors, nos 10–65, *above.*

Works: library edition. Ed. E.T.Cook and Alexander Wedderburn, 39 vols. 1903–12. *Includes a selection of the letters, vols. xxxvi–xxxvii.*

Ruskin as literary critic. Ed. A.H.R.Ball, Cambridge 1928; Selected writings, ed. Peter Quennell, 1952; The lamp of beauty: writings on art, ed. Joan Evans, 1959.

Diaries, selected. Ed. Joan Evans and J.Howard Whitehouse, 3 vols. Oxford 1956–9.

Cook, E.T. The life of Ruskin. 2 vols. 1911.
Wilenski, R.H. John Ruskin. 1933.
Leon, Derrick. Ruskin: the great Victorian. 1949.
Evans, Joan. John Ruskin. 1954.

'MARK RUTHERFORD', i.e. WILLIAM HALE WHITE
(1831 – 1913)

Nowell-Smith, Simon. Mark Rutherford: a bibliography of the first editions. 1930.

THE AUTOBIOGRAPHY of Mark Rutherford, dissenting minister. 1881; Mark Rutherford's deliverance, 1885, 1888 (*enlarged, with* The autobiography). *A novel in two pts.*
THE REVOLUTION in Tanner's Lane. 1887.
MIRIAM'S SCHOOLING and other papers. 1890.
CATHARINE FURZE. 2 vols. 1893.
CLARA HOPGOOD. 1896.

Pages from a journal. 1900, 1910 (*enlarged*), Oxford 1930 (WC); More pages, 1910; Last pages, ed. Dorothy V.White, 1915.
The early life of Mark Rutherford. 1913. *An autobiography.*
Letters to three friends. Ed. Dorothy V.White, Oxford 1924.

White, Dorothy V. The Groombridge diary. Oxford 1925. *Includes extracts from her husband's letters.*
Stone, Wilfrid. Religion and art of W.H.White. Palo Alto, Cal. 1954.
Maclean, Catherine M. Mark Rutherford: a biography. 1955.
Stock, Irvin. William Hale White. 1956.

SIR WALTER SCOTT (1771 – 1832)

Worthington, Greville. A bibliography of the Waverley novels. 1931.
Corson, J.C. A bibliography of Scott: books and articles relating to his life and works, 1797–1940. Edinburgh 1943.

MINSTRELSY OF THE SCOTTISH BORDER. 2 vols. Kelso 1802; 3 vols. Edinburgh 1830 (*enlarged*); ed. J.G.Lockhart, 1833 (*with addns*).
THE LAY OF THE LAST MINSTREL. 1805; 1805.
MARMION. Edinburgh 1808.

THE LIFE OF JOHN DRYDEN. Edinburgh 1808. *Vol. i of his edn of the* Works, 1808.

THE LADY OF THE LAKE. Edinburgh 1810; 1810.

ROKEBY: a poem. Edinburgh 1813; 1813.

MEMOIRS OF SWIFT. *In his edn of the* Works, Edinburgh 1814.

WAVERLEY: or 'tis sixty years since. 3 vols. Edinburgh 1814.

THE LORD OF THE ISLES: a poem. Edinburgh 1815; 1815.

TALES OF MY LANDLORD. 4 ser. (16 vols.). Edinburgh 1817–32. *Ser. 1 includes* Old Mortality, *ser. 2 (1818)* The heart of Midlothian, ed. David Daiches, New York 1948.

ROB ROY. 3 vols. Edinburgh 1818.

IVANHOE. 3 vols. Edinburgh 1820.

THE MONASTERY. 3 vols. Edinburgh 1820.

KENILWORTH. 4 vols. Edinburgh 1821.

LIVES OF THE NOVELISTS. *Prefaces to* Ballantyne's Novelists' library, 4 vols. 1821–4; ed. George Saintsbury, 1910 (EL).

THE FORTUNES OF NIGEL. 4 vols. Edinburgh 1822.

PEVERIL OF THE PEAK. 4 vols. Edinburgh 1822.

QUENTIN DURWARD. 3 vols. Edinburgh 1823.

REDGAUNTLET. 3 vols. Edinburgh 1824.

TALES OF THE CRUSADERS. 4 vols. Edinburgh 1825. *Includes* The talisman.

WOODSTOCK: or the Cavalier. 3 vols. Edinburgh 1826.

CHRONICLES OF THE CANONGATE. 2 ser. (5 vols.). Edinburgh 1827–8.

TALES OF A GRANDFATHER. 2 ser. (6 vols.). Edinburgh 1828–31.

Poetical works. Ed. J. Logie Robertson, Oxford 1904 (OSA).

Novels and tales. 41 vols. Edinburgh 1819–33 (*rev. text*); 24 vols. Oxford 1912.

Letters. Ed. Herbert Grierson *et al.*, 12 vols. 1932–7.

Journal. Ed. J. G. Tait, 3 vols. Edinburgh 1939–46.

Lockhart, John Gibson. Memoirs of the life of Scott. 7 vols. Edinburgh 1837–8; 10 vols. Edinburgh 1839; 2 vols. Edinburgh 1848 (*rev. and abridged as* Narrative of the life of Scott). *Begins with Scott's fragment of autobiography to 1792, written 1808. The Edinburgh edn, 10 vols. 1902–3, reprints 1839 with addns of 1848.*

Bagehot, Walter. The Waverley novels (1858). *In his* Literary studies, 1879.

Stephen, Leslie. Some words about Scott. *In his* Hours in a library, 1874.

Muir, Edwin. Scott and Scotland. 1936.

Lukács, Georg. *In his* The historical novel, 1962, *pbd in Russian in 1937 and in the original German in 1955.*

Grierson, Herbert. Scott: a new life. 1938.
Young, G.M. Scott and the historians. *In his* Last essays, 1950.
Davie, Donald. The heyday of Scott. 1961.

GEORGE BERNARD SHAW (1856 – 1950)

Broad, C.Lewis and Violet M. Dictionary to the plays and novels of
Shaw, with bibliography. 1929.

THE QUINTESSENCE OF IBSENISM. 1891; 1913 (*enlarged*).
WIDOWERS' HOUSES. 1893: a comedy.
PLAYS PLEASANT AND UNPLEASANT. 2 vols. 1898. *Includes* Mrs Warren's
profession, Arms and the man, Candida.
THREE PLAYS FOR PURITANS: The Devil's disciple, Caesar and Cleopatra
and Captain Brassbound's conversion. 1901.
MAN AND SUPERMAN. 1903.
JOHN BULL'S OTHER ISLAND and Major Barbara. 1907.
DRAMATIC OPINIONS. 2 vols. 1907; Our theatres in the Nineties, 3 vols.
1932 (*complete*); Plays and players, ed. A.C.Ward, Oxford 1952
(WC); Shaw on Shakespeare, ed. Edwin Wilson, 1962.
ANDROCLES AND THE LION; Overruled; Pygmalion. 1916.
HEARTBREAK HOUSE [etc]. 1919.
BACK TO METHUSELAH. 1921.
SAINT JOAN. 1924.
THE INTELLIGENT WOMAN'S GUIDE to Socialism and Capitalism. 1928;
Everybody's political what's what, 1944.
THE APPLE CART. 1930.
PEN PORTRAITS AND REVIEWS. 1931; 1932.
ESSAYS IN FABIAN SOCIALISM. 1932; 1932.

Works. 33 vols. 1930–8; Complete plays, 1931; Prefaces, 1934.
Ellen Terry and Shaw: a correspondence. Ed. Christopher St John,
New York 1931.

Chesterton, G.K. George Bernard Shaw. 1909; 1935.
Henderson, Archibald. Shaw: playboy and prophet. New York 1932;
1956.
Wilson, Edmund. Shaw at eighty. *In his* The triple thinkers, New
York 1938.
Pearson, Hesketh. Shaw: his life and personality. 1942; Postscript,
1951.
Bentley, Eric. Shaw: a reconsideration. New York 1947; 1957.
Irvine, William. The universe of GBS. New York 1949.
Nethercot, Arthur H. Men and supermen: the Shavian portrait
gallery. Cambridge, Mass. 1954.

Ervine, St John. Shaw: his life, works and friends. 1956.
Meisel, Martin. Shaw and the nineteenth-century theater. Princeton, N.J. 1963.

MARY WOLLSTONECRAFT SHELLEY, née GODWIN (1797 – 1851)

FRANKENSTEIN: or the modern Prometheus. 3 vols. 1818; 1831. *First of six novels, pbd 1818–37.*

Tales and stories, now first collected. Ed. Richard Garnett, 1891.
Letters. Ed. Henry H. Harper, Boston 1918; ed. Frederick L. Jones, 2 vols. Norman, Oklahoma 1944.
Journal. Ed. Frederick L. Jones, Norman 1947.

Grylls, R. Glynn. Mary Shelley: a biography. Oxford 1938.
Nitchie, Elizabeth. Mary Shelley. New Brunswick, N.J. 1953.

PERCY BYSSHE SHELLEY (1792 – 1822)

Ellis, F. S. A concordance to the poetical works. 1892.
Granniss, Ruth S. A descriptive catalogue of the first editions. New York 1923.
de Ricci, Seymour. A bibliography of Shelley's letters. 1927.

QUEEN MAB: a philosophical poem. 1813.
ALASTOR. 1816.
LAON AND CYTHNA. 1818; 1818 (*re-entitled* The revolt of Islam).
THE CENCI: a tragedy. 1819.
PROMETHEUS UNBOUND: a lyrical drama. 1820; ed. Lawrence J. Zillman, Seattle 1958.
EPIPSYCHIDION. 1821.
ADONAIS: an elegy on the death of Keats. Pisa 1821.
HELLAS: a lyrical drama. 1822.
POSTHUMOUS POEMS. Ed. Mary Shelley, 1824. *Includes* Julian and Maddalo, The witch of Atlas, *and the unfinished* The triumph of life.
A DEFENCE OF POETRY. *In his* Essays, letters from abroad, translations and fragments, ed. Mary Shelley, vol. i, 1840. *A reply to Peacock, p. 192 above.*

Poetical works. Ed. Mary Shelley, 4 vols. 1839; ed. Thomas Hutchinson, Oxford 1905 (OSA); Selected poems, ed. John Holloway, 1960; Selected poems and prose, ed. G. M. Matthews, Oxford 1964.
Letters. Ed. Roger Ingpen, 2 vols. 1909, 1914; Shelley and his circle, 1773–1822, ed. Kenneth N. Cameron, 8 vols. Cambridge, Mass. 1960; Letters, ed. Frederick L. Jones, 2 vols. Oxford 1964.

Note books. Ed. H.Buxton Forman, 3 vols. St Louis 1911.

Hogg, Thomas Jefferson. The life of Shelley. 2 vols. 1858; ed. Edward Dowden, 1906.

Dowden, Edward. Life of Shelley. 2 vols. 1886; 1 vol. 1896 (*rev. and abridged*).

Arnold, Matthew. *In his* Essays in criticism, ser. 2, 1888.

Lewis, C.S. Shelley, Dryden and Mr Eliot. *In his* Rehabilitations, Oxford 1939.

White, Newman Ivey. Shelley. 2 vols. New York 1940; London 1947.

Blunden, Edmund. Shelley: a life story. 1946.

Baker, Carlos. Shelley's major poetry. Princeton 1948.

Rogers, Neville. Shelley at work. Oxford 1956.

SYDNEY SMITH (1771 – 1845)

THE LETTERS OF PETER PLYMLEY. 10 pts. 1807–8; 1 vol. 1808.

Co-founder of Edinburgh review (1802–1929).

Collected works. 3 vols. 1839.

A biography and a selection, by Gerald Bullett, 1951; Selected writings, ed. W.H.Auden, New York 1956.

A memoir by his daughter Lady Holland, with a selection from his letters by Mrs Austin. 2 vols. 1855; Letters, ed. Nowell C.Smith, 2 vols. Oxford 1953; Selected, ed. Smith, Oxford 1956 (WC).

ROBERT SOUTHEY (1774 – 1843)

JOAN OF ARC: an epic poem. Bristol 1796; London 1837 (*in* Poetical works, *below*).

POEMS. 2 vols. Bristol 1797–9.

THALABA THE DESTROYER. 2 vols. 1801; 1837 (*in* Poetical works, *below*).

MADOC. 1805.

LETTERS FROM ENGLAND. 3 vols. 1807; ed. Jack Simmons, 1951.

THE CURSE OF KEHAMA. 1810.

THE LIFE OF NELSON. 2 vols. 1813; 1830; ed. Geoffrey Callender, 1922.

RODERICK, the last of the Goths. 1814.

WAT TYLER: a dramatic poem. 1817 (*pirated*); 1817 (*with preface*). *Written in 1794.*

A VISION OF JUDGEMENT. 1821; 1822 (*in* The two visions, *with Byron's travesty*).

Poetical works. 10 vols. 1837–8; Poems, ed. Maurice H.Fitzgerald, Oxford 1909 (OSA).

Letters: a selection. Ed. Maurice H.Fitzgerald, Oxford 1912 (WC).

Hazlitt, William. *In his* The spirit of the age, 1825.
Dowden, Edward. Southey. 1879 (EML).
Simmons, Jack. Southey. 1945.
Carnall, Geoffrey. Southey and his age. Oxford 1960.

SIR LESLIE STEPHEN (1832 – 1904)

ESSAYS ON FREE THINKING and plain speaking. 1873.
HOURS IN A LIBRARY. 3 sers. 1874–9; 3 vols. 1892; 4 vols. 1907 (*both enlarged*). *For much of contents see Index.*
HISTORY OF ENGLISH THOUGHT in the eighteenth century. 2 vols. 1876.
SCIENCE OF ETHICS. 1882.
STUDIES OF A BIOGRAPHER. 4 vols. 1898–1902.
THE ENGLISH UTILITARIANS. 3 vols. 1900.
ENGLISH LITERATURE AND SOCIETY in the eighteenth century. 1904.
MEN, BOOKS AND MOUNTAINS: essays. Ed. S.O.A.Ullmann, Minneapolis 1956.
Also biographies of Johnson (1878), Pope (1880), Swift (1882), George Eliot (1902), Hobbes (1904) (EML). Stephen edited the Dictionary of national biography *from 1882 to 1891 and contributed 378 articles to it.*

MacCarthy, Desmond. Leslie Stephen. Cambridge 1937.
Dover Wilson, J. Stephen and Arnold as critics of Wordsworth. Cambridge 1939.
Annan, Noel. Stephen: his thought and character in relation to his time. 1951.

ROBERT LOUIS STEVENSON (1850 – 1894)

Prideaux, W.F. A bibliography of the works of Stevenson. New York 1903; 1917 (rev. Flora V.Livingston).
McKay, George L. A Stevenson library: catalogue of a collection formed by Edwin J.Beinecke. 2 vols. New Haven 1951–2.

TRAVELS WITH A DONKEY in the Cévennes. 1879.
VIRGINIBUS PUERISQUE and other papers. 1881.
NEW ARABIAN NIGHTS. 2 vols. 1882.
FAMILIAR STUDIES of men and books. 1882.
TREASURE ISLAND. 1883.
STRANGE CASE OF Dr Jekyll and Mr Hyde. 1886.
KIDNAPPED. 1886; Catriona: a sequel, 1893.
THE BLACK ARROW. New York 1888.
THE MASTER OF BALLANTRAE. 1889.
THE WRONG BOX. 1889. *With Lloyd Osbourne.*
THE WRECKER. 1892. *With Osbourne.*

THE EBB-TIDE. Chicago 1894. *With Osbourne.*

WEIR OF HERMISTON: an unfinished romance. 1896.

ST IVES. New York 1897. *First London edn, 1898.*

Collected poems. Ed. Janet A. Smith, 1950. *Pbd separately 1885–99.*

Letters, selected. Ed. Sidney Colvin, 2 vols. 1899; 4 vols. 1911 (*enlarged*); Henry James and Stevenson, ed. Janet A. Smith, 1948; Letters to Charles Baxter, ed. J. De Lancey Ferguson and Marshall Waingrow, New Haven 1956.

Works: Vailima edition. 26 vols. 1922–3; Tusitala edition, 35 vols. 1923–7; Novels and stories, ed. V. S. Pritchett, 1945.

James, Henry. Robert Louis Stevenson, 1894. *In his* Notes on novelists, 1914.

Balfour, Graham. The life of Stevenson. 2 vols. 1901.

Swinnerton, Frank. Stevenson: a critical study. 1914.

Smith, Janet A. R. L. Stevenson. 1937.

Furnas, Joseph C. Voyage to windward: the life of Stevenson. New York 1951.

ALGERNON CHARLES SWINBURNE (1837 – 1909)

Wise, Thomas J. A bibliography of Swinburne. 2 vols. 1919–20.

ATALANTA IN CALYDON. 1865; ed. Georges Lafourcade, 1930 (*facs.*).

CHASTELARD. 1865; Bothwell, 1874; Mary Stuart, 1881. *A dramatic trilogy.*

POEMS AND BALLADS. 1866; Second series, 1878; Third series, 1889.

A STUDY OF SHAKESPEARE. 1880.

TRISTRAM OF LYONESSE and other poems. 1882.

A MIDSUMMER HOLIDAY and other poems. 1884.

ROSAMUND, queen of the Lombards. 1899.

LESBIA BRANDON. Ed. Randolph Hughes, 1952. *A novel.*

Poems. 6 vols. 1904; Collected poems, 2 vols. 1924; Selected poems, ed. Laurence Binyon, Oxford 1939 (WC).

Letters. Ed. Cecil Y. Lang, 6 vols. New Haven 1959–62.

Complete works: Bonchurch edition. Ed. Edmund Gosse and Thomas J. Wise, 20 vols. 1925–7.

Gosse, Edmund. The life of Swinburne. 1917; 1927 (*vol. xix of Bonchurch edn, above*).

Eliot, T. S. *In his* The sacred wood, 1920.

Lafourcade, Georges. Swinburne: a literary biography. 1932.

Hyder, Clyde K. Swinburne's literary career and fame. Durham, N.C. 1933.

Hare, Humphrey. Swinburne: a biographical approach. 1949.

ALFRED, 1st BARON TENNYSON (1809 – 1892)

Wise, Thomas J. A bibliography of the writings of Tennyson. 2 vols. 1908.

Baker, Arthur E. A concordance to the poetical and dramatic works. 1914.

POEMS BY TWO BROTHERS. 1827; ed. Hallam Tennyson, 1893. *With his brothers Charles and Frederick Tennyson.*

POEMS CHIEFLY LYRICAL. 1830. *24 poems rev. for* 1842, *below.*

POEMS. 1833. *Includes* The lotos-eaters, The lady of Shalott; *16 poems rev. for* 1842, *below.*

POEMS. 2 vols. 1842; ed. J. Churton Collins, 1900.

THE PRINCESS. 1847; 1850 (*enlarged, with six new songs*).

IN MEMORIAM. 1850; 1851 (*with addn*); ed. A. W. Robinson, Cambridge 1901.

MAUD AND OTHER POEMS. 1855.

IDYLLS OF THE KING. 1859; 1869; 1889 (*both enlarged*).

ENOCH ARDEN. 1864.

TIRESIAS AND OTHER POEMS. 1885.

LOCKSLEY HALL sixty years after. 1886.

DEMETER AND OTHER POEMS. 1889.

Poems, 1830–70. Oxford 1912; 1953 (*re-entitled* Poetical works, including the dramas) (OSA).

Works: Eversley edition. Ed. Hallam Tennyson, 9 vols. 1907–8.

Tennyson, Hallam. Tennyson: a memoir. 2 vols. 1897.

Bradley, A. C. A commentary on In memoriam. 1901; 1902.

Nicolson, Harold. Tennyson: aspects of his character and poetry. 1923.

Tennyson, Charles. Alfred Tennyson. 1949.

Eliot, T. S. In memoriam. *In his* Selected essays, 1951 (*enlarged*).

Killham, John. Tennyson and The princess. 1958.

—— (ed.). Critical essays on the poetry of Tennyson. 1960.

Buckley, Jerome H. Tennyson: the growth of a poet. Cambridge, Mass. 1960.

WILLIAM MAKEPEACE THACKERAY (1811 – 1863)

van Duzer, Henry S. A Thackeray library. New York 1919.

VANITY FAIR: a novel without a hero. 1848; 1853, ed. Kathleen and Geoffrey Tillotson, 1963.

THE HISTORY OF PENDENNIS. 2 vols. 1849–50; 1863.

THE LUCK OF BARRY LYNDON. 2 vols. New York 1852 (*pirated*); 1856 (*in* Miscellanies). *The first novel, written 1843–4.*

THE HISTORY OF HENRY ESMOND. 3 vols. 1852; 1858.
THE ENGLISH HUMOURISTS of the eighteenth century. 1853.
THE NEWCOMES. 2 vols. 1854–5; 1863.
THE ROSE AND THE RING. 1855; ed. Gordon N.Ray, New York 1947 (*MS. facs.*).
THE VIRGINIANS. 2 vols. 1858–9; 1863. *A sequel to* Esmond, *above.*
THE FOUR GEORGES. New York 1860. *First London edn, 1861.*
ROUNDABOUT PAPERS. 1863; ed. J.E.Wells, New York 1925 (*from MS.*). *Essays first pbd in Cornhill mag., of which Thackeray was first editor (1860–2).*

Works. Ed. George Saintsbury, 17 vols. Oxford 1908.
Letters and private papers. Ed. Gordon N.Ray, 4 vols. Cambridge, Mass. 1945–6.

Trollope, Anthony. Thackeray. 1879 (EML).
'Melville, Lewis'. Thackeray: a biography. 2 vols. 1910.
Greig, J.Y.T. Thackeray: a reconsideration. Oxford 1950.
Ray, Gordon N. The buried life. Oxford 1952.
—— Thackeray. 2 vols. New York 1955–8.
Tillotson, Geoffrey. Thackeray the novelist. Cambridge 1954.

FRANCIS THOMPSON (1859 – 1907)

POEMS. 1893. *Includes* The hound of heaven, *first pbd 1890.*
SISTER-SONGS. 1895.
NEW POEMS. 1897.
EYES OF YOUTH. 1909.
UNCOLLECTED VERSE. 1917.

Works. Ed. Wilfrid Meynell, 3 vols. 1913; Poems, Oxford 1937 (OSA).
Literary criticisms. Ed. T.L.Connolly, New York 1948.

Meynell, Everard. The life of Thompson. 1913; 1926.
Reid, J.C. Francis Thompson: man and poet. 1959.

JAMES THOMSON (1834 – 1882) ('B.V.')

THE CITY OF DREADFUL NIGHT and other poems. 1880; ed. Edmund Blunden, 1932.
VANE'S STORY and other poems. 1881.
A VOICE FROM THE NILE and other poems. Ed. Bertram Dobell, 1884.

Poems, essays and fragments. Ed. J.M.Robertson, 1892; Poetical works, ed. Bertram Dobell, 2 vols. 1895; Poems and some letters, ed. Anne Ridler, 1963.

ANTHONY TROLLOPE (1815 – 1882)

Sadleir, Michael. Trollope: a bibliography. 1928; 1934.
Gerould, W.G. and J.T. A guide to Trollope. Princeton 1948.

There are three early novels: The Macdermots of Ballycloran (1847),
The Kellys and the O'Kellys (1848) *and* La Vendée (1850).
THE WARDEN. 1855; Barchester Towers, 3 vols. 1857; Doctor Thorne,
3 vols. 1858; Framley Parsonage, 3 vols. 1861; The last chronicle of
Barset, 2 vols. 1867. *The five Barsetshire novels.*
THE THREE CLERKS. 3 vols. 1858.
THE BERTRAMS. 3 vols. 1859.
ORLEY FARM. 2 vols. 1862.
THE SMALL HOUSE AT ALLINGTON. 2 vols. 1864.
CAN YOU FORGIVE HER? 2 vols. 1864; Phineas Finn, 2 vols. 1869; The
Eustace diamonds, 3 vols. 1873; Phineas Redux, 2 vols. 1874; The
Prime Minister, 4 vols. 1876; The Duke's children, 3 vols. 1880.
The six Plantagenet Palliser novels.
THE CLAVERINGS. 2 vols. 1867.
HE KNEW HE WAS RIGHT. 2 vols. 1869.
THE VICAR OF BULLHAMPTON. 1870.
RALPH THE HEIR. 3 vols. 1871.
THE WAY WE LIVE NOW. 2 vols. 1875.
THE AMERICAN SENATOR. 3 vols. 1877.
IS HE POPENJOY? 3 vols. 1878.
JOHN CALDIGATE. 3 vols. 1879.
AN AUTOBIOGRAPHY. 2 vols. 1883; ed. Michael Sadleir, Oxford 1923
(WC); ed. Frederick Page, Oxford 1950 (Illustr. Trollope), 1953 (WC).
*Also travel books on the West Indies (1859), North America (1862), South
Africa (1878) and Australia and New Zealand (1873), and a study of
Thackeray (1879) (EML).*

Shakespeare head edition: Barchester novels. Ed. Michael Sadleir,
14 vols. Oxford 1929; Oxford illustrated Trollope, ed. Sadleir and
Frederick Page, Oxford 1948–. *Both unfinished. Also Oxford 1907–*
(WC).
Letters. Ed. Bradford A. Booth, New York 1951.

James, Henry. *In his* Partial portraits, 1888.
Stephen, Leslie. *In his* Studies of a biographer, 1898–1902.
Sadleir, Michael. Trollope: a commentary. 1927; 1945.
Walpole, Hugh. Anthony Trollope. 1928 (EML).
Cockshut, A.O.J. Trollope: a critical study. 1955.

HERBERT GEORGE WELLS (1866 – 1946)

Wells, Geoffrey H. The works of Wells, 1887–1925: a bibliography, dictionary and subject-index. 1926.

THE TIME MACHINE: an invention. New York 1895; London 1895.
THE ISLAND OF DOCTOR MOREAU. 1896.
THE WHEELS OF CHANCE: a holiday adventure. 1896.
THE INVISIBLE MAN: a grotesque romance. 1897.
THE WAR OF THE WORLDS. 1898.
LOVE AND MR LEWISHAM. 1900.
KIPPS. 1905.
THE WAR IN THE AIR. 1908.
TONO-BUNGAY. 1909.
ANN VERONICA: a modern love story. 1909.
THE HISTORY OF MR POLLY. 1910.
THE NEW MACHIAVELLI. 1911.
THE COUNTRY OF THE BLIND and other stories. 1911. *A selection of 33 stories, five newly collected.*
BOON: being a first selection from the literary remains of George Boon. 1915. *Pbd anon.; authorship acknowledged in 1920 edn. A parody of Henry James. For correspondence see p. 183, above.*
MR BRITLING SEES IT THROUGH. 1916.
THE OUTLINE OF HISTORY: being a plain history of life and mankind. 24 pts. 1919–20; 2 vols. 1920; 1 vol. 1920, 1932 (*7th revision*); 1951 (rev. Raymond Postgate).
A SHORT HISTORY OF THE WORLD. 1922; 1945.
THE WORLD OF WILLIAM CLISSOLD: a novel at a new angle. 3 vols. 1926.

The Atlantic edition of the works. 28 vols. 1924–7. *Rev. text with new prefaces.*

Short stories. 1927.

THE KING WHO WAS A KING. 1929.
THE WORK, WEALTH and happiness of mankind. 2 vols. New York 1931. *First London edns, 1932, 1934.*
THE SHAPE OF THINGS TO COME. 1933.
EXPERIMENT IN AUTOBIOGRAPHY. 2 vols. 1934.
MIND AT THE END OF ITS TETHER. 1945.

Arnold Bennett and Wells. Ed. Harris Wilson, 1960; Gissing and Wells, ed. R.A.Gettmann, 1961.

Bergonzi, Bernard. The early Wells. Manchester 1961.

OSCAR FINGALL O'FLAHERTIE WILLS WILDE
(1854 – 1900)

'Mason, Stuart'. Bibliography of Wilde. 1908; 1914.

THE HAPPY PRINCE and other tales. 1888.

THE PICTURE OF DORIAN GRAY. 1891.

LORD ARTHUR SAVILE'S CRIME and other stories. 1891.

LADY WINDERMERE'S FAN. 1893; A woman of no importance, 1894; An ideal husband, 1899; The importance of being earnest, 1899, ed. Vyvyan Holland, 2 vols. New York 1957 (*original and longer version, from MS.*). *Four plays.*

THE BALLAD OF READING GAOL. 1898.

DE PROFUNDIS. Ed. Robert Ross, 1905; Suppressed portion, ed. Ross, New York 1913; ed. Vyvyan Holland, 1949; ed. Hart-Davis, 1962 (*in* Letters, *below*) (*complete*).

Works. 14 vols. 1908; Selected works, ed. Richard Aldington, 1946; Selected writings, ed. Richard Ellmann, Oxford 1961 (WC).

Letters. Ed. Rupert Hart-Davis, 1962.

Harris, Frank. Wilde: his life and confessions. New York 1918; ed. Bernard Shaw, 1938.

Pearson, Hesketh. The life of Wilde. 1946.

Ervine, St John. Oscar Wilde. 1951.

WILLIAM WORDSWORTH (1770 – 1850)

Cooper, Lane. A concordance to the poems. 1911.

Logan, J.V. Wordsworthian criticism: a guide and bibliography. Columbus, Ohio 1947.

Healey, G.H. The Cornell Wordsworth collection. Ithaca, N.Y. 1957.

AN EVENING WALK. 1793.

DESCRIPTIVE SKETCHES taken during a tour in the Alps. 1793.

LYRICAL BALLADS. Bristol and London 1798, ed. Harold Littledale, Oxford 1911 (*facs.*), ed. R.L.Brett and A.R.Jones, 1963 (*with* 1800); 2 vols. 1800, 1802, 1805 (*with addns and Preface*). *With Coleridge.*

POEMS in two volumes. 2 vols. 1807; ed. Helen Darbishire, Oxford 1915, 1952.

THE EXCURSION: a portion of the Recluse. 1814.

Poems, with a new preface and a supplementary essay. 2 vols. 1815.

THE WHITE DOE OF RYLSTONE. 1815.

PETER BELL. 1819.

THE WAGGONER. 1819.

Poems, including the Borderers. 1842.

THE PRELUDE: or the growth of a poet's mind. 1850; ed. E. de Selincourt, Oxford 1926 (*with first edn of 1805 MS. version in parallel texts*), 1959 (rev. Helen Darbishire); 1933 (OSA) (*1805 version only*).

Poetical works. 6 vols. 1836–7; 1849–50 (*with final revisions*); ed. Thomas Hutchinson, Oxford 1904, 1936 (rev. E. de Selincourt) (OSA); ed. E. de Selincourt and Helen Darbishire, 5 vols. Oxford 1940–9; 1952–.

Prose works. Ed. William Knight, 2 vols. 1896; Prefaces and essays, ed. George Sampson, Cambridge 1920 (*with Coleridge's* Biographia).

Letters of William and Dorothy Wordsworth. Ed. E. de Selincourt, 6 vols. Oxford 1935–9.

Coleridge, Samuel Taylor. *In his* Biographia literaria, 2 vols. 1817.

Crabb Robinson, Henry. Diary, reminiscences and correspondence. 3 vols. 1869; On books and their writers, ed. Edith J. Morley, 3 vols. 1938 (*selection*). *On Blake, Coleridge, Hazlitt, Lamb, Wordsworth etc.*

Wordsworth, Dorothy. Journals [1798–1828]. Ed. William Knight, 2 vols. 1897; ed. E. de Selincourt, 2 vols. 1941; ed. Helen Darbishire, Oxford 1958 (WC).

Arnold, Matthew. *In his* Essays in criticism, ser. 2, 1888.

Legouis, Emile. La jeunesse de Wordsworth, 1770–98. Paris 1896; tr. 1897, 1921.

Bradley, A. C. *In his* Oxford lectures on poetry, 1909.

Harper, G. M. Wordsworth: his life, works and influence. 2 vols. New York 1916; 1 vol. New York 1929.

Bateson, F. W. Wordsworth: a re-interpretation. 1954; 1956.

Jones, John. The egotistical sublime. 1954.

Moorman, Mary. Wordsworth: a biography. 2 vols. Oxford 1957–.

WILLIAM BUTLER YEATS (1865 – 1939)

Wade, Allan. A bibliography of the writings of Yeats. 1951; 1958.

Parrish, Stephen M. A concordance to the poems. Ithaca, N.Y. 1963.

THE WANDERINGS OF OISIN and other poems. 1889.

THE COUNTESS KATHLEEN. 1892. *First of 26 plays, collected below, with poems.*

THE CELTIC TWILIGHT. 1893; 1902 (*enlarged*).

THE LAND OF HEART'S DESIRE. 1894; 1903. *The second pbd play.*

Poems. 1895; 1927 (*with* Preface, *etc.*).

THE SECRET ROSE. 1897.

THE WIND AMONG THE REEDS. 1899.

CATHLEEN NI HOOLIHAN: a play in one act and in prose. 1902.

THE GREEN HELMET and other poems. 1910; 1912 (*enlarged*).

RESPONSIBILITIES: poems and a play. Dundrum 1914; London 1916 (*enlarged*).

REVERIES OVER CHILDHOOD AND YOUTH. Dundrum 1915; The trembling of the veil, 1922; Autobiographies, 1926 (*collected*), New York 1938, London 1955 (*with* Dramatis personae *etc., below*).

THE WILD SWANS AT COOLE. Dundrum 1917; London 1919 (*enlarged*).

MICHAEL ROBARTES AND THE DANCER. Dundrum 1920.

A VISION. 1925; 1937 (*much rev. and enlarged*); 1962.

Mythologies. 1925. *Collects* The Celtic twilight *and* The secret rose, *above, with other Irish stories.*

THE TOWER. 1928. *Includes* Sailing to Byzantium *and* Among school children.

THE WINDING STAIR. New York 1929; London 1933 (*with* Words for music, *below*).

WORDS FOR MUSIC, PERHAPS. Dublin 1932. *Includes* Byzantium, *the* Crazy Jane *poems and* I am of Ireland.

DRAMATIS PERSONAE. Dublin 1935; New York 1936 (*enlarged*).

NEW POEMS. Dublin 1938.

LAST POEMS and two plays. Dublin 1939; London 1940 (*with* New poems, *above*). *Includes* The death of Cuchulain *and* Purgatory.

Collected works. 8 vols. 1908.

Collected poems. New York 1933, 1950 (*enlarged*); The variorum edition of the poems, ed. Peter Allt and Russell K. Alspach, New York 1957.

Plays for an Irish theatre. 1911, 1922 (*enlarged*); Collected plays, 1934, 1952 (*complete*).

Letters. Ed. Allan Wade, 1954.

Essays and introductions. 1961. *Collects* Ideas of good and evil (1903), The cutting of an agate (1912) *and other critical essays.*

Explorations. Ed. Mrs W.B. Yeats, 1962. *Collects* The Irish dramatic movement, *dramatic forewords etc.*

MacNeice, Louis. The poetry of Yeats. Oxford 1941.

Hone, Joseph M. W.B. Yeats. 1942; 1962.

Ellmann, Richard. Yeats: the man and the masks. New York 1948; The identity of Yeats, New York 1954.

Jeffares, A. Norman. Yeats, man and poet. 1949.

Stauffer, Donald A. The golden nightingale: essays on some principles of poetry in the poems of Yeats. New York 1949.

The permanence of Yeats. Ed. James Hall and Martin Steinmann, New York 1950.

Henn, T.R. The lonely tower. 1950.

Stallworthy, Jon. Between the lines: Yeats's poetry in the making. Oxford 1963.

Ure, Peter. Yeats the playwright. 1963.

—— Yeats. Edinburgh 1963 (Writers & critics).

THE EARLY TWENTIETH CENTURY
(1900–1950)

THE EARLY TWENTIETH CENTURY
(1900–1950)

Bibliographies

Danielson, Henry. Bibliographies of modern authors. 1921; ser. 2, by Charles A. and H.W. Stonehill, 1925.

Manly, J.M. and Edith Rickert. Contemporary British literature. New York 1922; 1935 (rev. Fred B. Millett). *Bibliographies etc. of authors born after 1850.*

'Gawsworth, John'. Ten contemporaries: notes towards their definitive bibliography. 1932; ser. 2, 1933.

Literary History and Criticism

Ward, A.C. Twentieth-century literature. 1928; 1940 (*enlarged*).

Williams, Charles. Poetry at present. Oxford 1930.

Wilson, Edmund. Axel's castle: a study in the imaginative literature of 1870–1930. New York 1931.

Leavis, F.R. New bearings in English poetry. 1932; 1950 (*with addns*).

Bullough, Geoffrey. The trend of modern poetry. Edinburgh 1934; 1949.

Day Lewis, C. A hope for poetry. Oxford 1934. *On Auden, Spender etc.*

—— The poetic image: Clark lectures. 1947.

Swinnerton, Frank. The Georgian literary scene, 1910–35. 1935; 1950.

Roberts, Michael. Introduction. *In* The Faber book of modern verse, 1936.

Dobrée, Bonamy and Edith C. Batho. The Victorians and after. 1938; 1950.

MacNeice, Louis. Modern poetry; a personal essay. Oxford 1938.

Brooks, Cleanth. Modern poetry and the tradition. Chapel Hill, N.C. 1939. *On Auden, Eliot, Yeats etc.*

Muir, Edwin. The present age from 1914. 1939.

Daiches, David. The novel and the modern world. Chicago 1939; 1960.

—— Poetry and the modern world: a study of poetry in England, 1900–39. Chicago 1940.

—— The present age after 1920. 1958. *With bibliography.*

'Orwell, George'. Inside the whale. *In his* Inside the whale and other essays, 1940.

Scarfe, Francis. Auden and after: the liberation of poetry, 1930–41. 1942.

Routh, H.V. English literature and ideas in the twentieth century. 1946.

Savage, D.S. The withered branch: six studies in the modern novel. 1950. *On Forster, Aldous Huxley, Joyce, Virginia Woolf etc.*

Writers and their work. 1950–. *British Council pamphlets by various hands, mainly on twentieth-century writers.*

Isaacs, J. The assessment of twentieth-century literature. 1951.

Scott-James, R.A. Fifty years of English literature, 1900–50. 1951.

Durrell, Lawrence. Key to modern poetry. 1952.

Fraser, G.S. The modern writer and his world. 1953.

Johnstone, J.K. The Bloomsbury group: a study of Forster, Strachey, Virginia Woolf and their circle. 1954.

McCormick, John. Catastrophe and imagination: an interpretation of the recent English and American novel. 1957.

Alvarez, A. The shaping spirit: studies in modern English and American poets. 1958; 1963.

Donoghue, Denis. The third voice: modern British and American verse drama. Princeton 1959.

Hough, Graham. Image and experience: studies in a literary revolution. 1960.

Stewart, J.I.M. Eight modern writers. Oxford 1963 (Oxford history of English lit., vol. xii).

Allen, Walter. Tradition and dream: the English and American novel from the Twenties. 1964.

Anthologies and Periodicals

Ford, Ford Madox *et al.* The English review. 1908–37.

Marsh, Edward. Georgian poetry. 5 vols. 1912–22.

Sitwell, Edith. Wheels: an anthology of verse. 6 'cycles'. Oxford 1916–21.

Squire, J.C. The London Mercury. 1919–30. *Incorporated in* Life and letters, *below.*

Eliot, T.S. The criterion. 1922–39. *Eliot was also assistant editor of* The egoist, *1917–19.*

MacCarthy, Desmond. Life and letters. 1928–50.

Leavis, F.R. *et al.* Scrutiny. Cambridge 1932–53; 20 vols. Cambridge 1963 *(with index)*; The importance of Scrutiny, ed. Eric Bentley, New York 1948 *(anthology).*

Grigson, Geoffrey. New verse. 1933–9.

—— New verse: an anthology of poems in the first thirty numbers [1933–8]. 1939.

—— Poetry of the present: an anthology of the thirties and after. 1949.

Jones, Phyllis M. English critical essays: twentieth century. Oxford 1933 (WC); ser. 2, ed. Derek Hudson, Oxford 1958 (WC).

Roberts, Michael. New signatures: poems by several hands. 1932.
—— The Faber book of modern verse. 1936; 1951 (*with supplement by Anne Ridler*).
Lehmann, John. New writing. 8 vols. 1936–9; Penguin new writing, 40 vols. 1940–50.
—— Poems from New writing, 1936–46. 1946; English stories from New writing. 1951; Pleasures of New writing. 1952. *Three anthologies*.
—— The London magazine. 1953–.
Yeats, W.B. The Oxford book of modern verse. Oxford 1936.
Roberts, D.Kilham. Hopkins to Eliot. 1938 (Penguin Centuries' poetry, vol. v).
Tambimuttu. Poetry London. 1939–45.
—— Poetry London–New York. 1956–.
Connolly, Cyril. Horizon. 1940–9.
—— Horizon stories. 1943; Ideas and places, 1953; The golden Horizon, 1953. *Three anthologies from the quarterly*.
I believe: personal philosophies. 1940. *Essays by Auden, Forster, Bertrand Russell, Strachey, Wells et al.*
Day Lewis, C. and L.A.G. Strong. A new anthology of modern verse, 1920–40. 1941.
Ridler, Anne. A little book of modern verse. 1941.
Allott, Kenneth. Contemporary verse. 1950, 1962 (Penguin).
Bateson, F.W. Essays in criticism. Oxford 1951–.
New poems. 1952– (PEN). *An annual edited by various hands*.
Heath-Stubbs, John and David Wright. The Faber book of twentieth-century verse. 1953.
Spender, Stephen *et al.* Encounter. 1953–.
Day Lewis, C. and John Lehmann. The Chatto book of modern poetry, 1915–51. 1956.

WYSTAN HUGH AUDEN (b. 1907)

OXFORD POETRY. Oxford 1926–7. *An undergraduate annual edited in 1926 with Charles Plumb and in 1927 with C.Day Lewis*.
POEMS. 1930; 1933 (*with six omissions, seven addns*).
THE ORATORS: an English study. 1932. *Prose and verse*.
THE DANCE OF DEATH. 1933.
THE DOG BENEATH THE SKIN: or where is Francis? 1935. *A verse play with Christopher Isherwood*.
LOOK, STRANGER! POEMS. 1936. *Also New York 1937 as* On this island.
THE ASCENT OF F6: a tragedy. 1936. *A verse play with Isherwood*.
SPAIN. 1937.
LETTERS FROM ICELAND. 1937. *Prose and verse, with Louis MacNeice*.

ON THE FRONTIER: a melodrama. 1938. *A verse play with Isherwood.*
Since he settled in USA in Jan. 1939, Auden's books have been pbd in
London in the same year as the New York edn or in the following year.
JOURNEY TO A WAR. New York 1939. *A travel book on China, with*
Isherwood.
ANOTHER TIME: poems. New York 1940.
THE DOUBLE MAN. New York 1941. *Also London 1941 as* New Year
letter.
FOR THE TIME BEING. New York 1944. *Two poems*—The sea and the
mirror: a commentary on Shakespeare's The tempest; For the time
being: a Christmas oratorio.
THE AGE OF ANXIETY: a baroque eclogue. New York 1947.
THE ENCHAFÈD FLOOD: or the romantic iconography of the sea. New
York 1950.
NONES. New York 1951.
THE SHIELD OF ACHILLES. 1955.
HOMAGE TO CLIO. 1960.
THE DYER'S HAND and other essays. 1963.

Collected poetry. New York 1945; Collected shorter poems, 1930–44,
1950. *Similar collections with variations in the titles of some poems.*
Selected poems. 1938.

Auden double number. New verse (Nov. 1937). *Essays by Geoffrey*
Grigson, Isherwood, Day Lewis, Spender et al.
Hoggart, Richard. Auden: an introductory essay. 1951.
Beach, Joseph W. The making of the Auden canon. Minneapolis 1957.
Spears, Monroe K. The poetry of Auden: the disenchanted island.
New York 1963.
For reminiscences of Auden see Isherwood's autobiographical novel Lions
and Shadows (1938) *and Spender's autobiography* World within
world (1951).

GEORGE BARKER (b. 1913)

THIRTY PRELIMINARY POEMS. 1933.
POEMS. 1935.
CALAMITERROR. 1937.
LAMENT AND TRIUMPH. 1940.
EROS IN DOGMA. 1944.
THE DEAD SEAGULL. 1950.
THE TRUE CONFESSION OF GEORGE BARKER. 1950.
NEWS OF THE WORLD. 1950.
A VISION OF BEASTS AND GODS. 1954.
Collected poems, 1930–55. 1957.
Also two prose works, Alanna autumnal (1933) *and* Janus (1936).

SAMUEL BECKETT (b. 1906)

MORE PRICKS THAN KICKS. 1934.

MURPHY. 1938. *Fr. trn by Beckett, Paris 1947.*

MOLLOY. Paris 1951, tr. New York 1955; Malone meurt, Paris 1951, tr. Beckett, New York 1956; L'innommable, Paris 1953; Three novels, 1959 (Malone dies, The unnamable, tr. Beckett). *A trilogy of novels written in French.*

EN ATTENDANT GODOT: pièce en deux actes. Paris 1952; tr. Beckett, New York 1954 (Waiting for Godot: tragicomedy).

WATT. Paris 1953. *Extract in English trn in* Irish writing, March 1953.

NOUVELLES ET TEXTES POUR RIEN. Paris 1955.

ALL THAT FALL. 1957. *A radio drama.*

FIN DE PARTIE; Acte sans paroles. Paris 1957; tr. Beckett, New York 1958 (endgame; Act without words).

KRAPP'S LAST TAPE and Embers. 1959; New York 1960 (*with* All that fall, Act without words).

HAPPY DAYS. New York 1961.

POEMS IN ENGLISH [since 1930]. 1961.

COMMENT C'EST. Paris 1961; tr. Beckett, 1964 (How it is).

PLAY and two short pieces for radio. 1964.

Also a monograph on Proust (1931).

Esslin, Martin. *In his* The theatre of the Absurd, 1962.

Kenner, Hugh. Beckett: a critical study, 1962.

SIR MAX BEERBOHM (1872–1956)

Gallatin, Albert E. Beerbohm: bibliographical notes. Cambridge, Mass. 1944. 1952 (*below*) *contains a fuller collation of separate works only.*

—— and L. M. Oliver. A bibliography of Beerbohm. Cambridge, Mass. 1952.

WORKS, with a bibliography by John Lane. 1896.

THE HAPPY HYPOCRITE: a fairy tale for tired men. 1897.

MORE. 1899.

YET AGAIN. 1909.

ZULEIKA DOBSON: or an Oxford love story. 1911.

A CHRISTMAS GARLAND. 1912; 1950 (*with addn*). *18 parodies of Maurice Baring (added 1950), Belloc, Bennett, Chesterton, Conrad, Galsworthy, Edmund Gosse, Hardy, Henry James, Kipling, Meredith, George Moore, Shaw, Wells et al.*

SEVEN MEN. 1919; and two others, 1950 (*with one addn*).

AND EVEN NOW. 1920.

AROUND THEATRES. 2 vols. 1924; 1 vol. 1953 (*with* Note). *153 theatre reviews, first pbd 1898–1910.*

A VARIETY OF THINGS. 1928; New York 1928 (*with fuller discussion of piracy*); London 1953 (*with* Note, Hypocrite *omitted*).

MAINLY ON THE AIR. 1946; 1957 (*with addns*). *Six broadcasts made Dec. 1935–Oct. 1945.*

Riewald, J. G. Beerbohm: a critical analysis with a brief life and a bibliography. The Hague 1953.

HILAIRE BELLOC (1870 – 1953)

Cahill, Patrick. The English first editions of Belloc. 1953.

VERSES AND SONNETS. 1896.

THE BAD CHILD'S BOOK OF BEASTS: verses. 1896; More beasts, 1897; The modern traveller, 1898; A moral alphabet, 1899; Cautionary tales for children, 1907; New cautionary tales, 1930.

THE PATH TO ROME. 1902.

AVRIL: being essays on the poetry of the French Renaissance. 1904.

THE OLD ROAD. 1904.

ON NOTHING AND KINDRED SUBJECTS. 1908; On everything, 1909; On anything, 1910; On something, 1910; This and that and the other, 1912; On, 1923.

THE EYE-WITNESS. 1908.

VERSES. 1910.

THE FRENCH REVOLUTION. 1911 (Home univ. lib.).

THE GREEN OVERCOAT. 1912. *A novel.*

THE SERVILE STATE. 1912.

THE HISTORY OF ENGLAND TO GEORGE V. 11 vols. 1915. *Mainly by John Lingard. Vol. xi by Belloc.*

SONNETS AND VERSE. 1923; 1938, 1954 (*enlarged*).

A HISTORY OF ENGLAND [B.C. 55–A.D. 1612]. 4 vols. 1925–31 (*7 vols. projected*); A shorter history of England, 1934.

THE CRUISE OF THE 'NONA'. 1925.

A COMPANION to Mr Wells's Outline of history. 1926; Mr Belloc still objects, 1926. *The second a rejoinder to Wells's* Mr Belloc objects to the Outline, 1926.

BUT SOFT—WE ARE OBSERVED. 1928; 1929 (*re-entitled* Shadowed!). *A novel.*

AN HEROIC POEM in praise of wine. 1932.

THE CRISIS OF OUR CIVILIZATION. 1937.

THE GREAT HERESIES. 1938.

THE SILENCE OF THE SEA and other essays. 1941.

Also biographies of Danton (1899), Robespierre (1901), Marie Antoinette (1909), James II (1928), Joan of Arc (1929), Wolsey (1930), Cranmer (1931), Napoleon (1932), William the Conqueror (1933), Charles I (1933), Cromwell (1934), Milton (1935), Louis XIV (entitled Monarchy) (1938).

Selected essays. Ed. J.B. Morton, 1948; An anthology of prose and verse, ed. W.N. Roughead, 1951.

Verse. Ed. W.N. Roughead, 1954.

Letters, selected. Ed. Robert Speaight, 1958.

Woodruff, Douglas (ed.). For Belloc: essays in honour of his 72nd birthday. 1942.

Hamilton, Robert. Belloc: an introduction to his spirit and work. 1945.

Speaight, Robert. The life of Belloc. 1957.

ARNOLD BENNETT (1867 – 1931)

A MAN FROM THE NORTH. 1898.

ANNA OF THE FIVE TOWNS: a novel. 1902; ed. Frank Swinnerton, 1954 (Penguin).

THE GRAND BABYLON HOTEL: a fantasia on modern themes. 1902; ed. Swinnerton, 1954 (Penguin).

TALES OF THE FIVE TOWNS. 1905; The grim smile of the Five Towns, 1907; The matador of the Five Towns, 1912. *Short stories.*

THE OLD WIVES' TALE. 1908; 1912 (*with* Preface); 1935 (EL); ed. Swinnerton, 1954 (Penguin).

BURIED ALIVE. 1908.

LITERARY TASTE. 1909; Books and persons, 1917.

CLAYHANGER. 1910, ed. Swinnerton, 1954 (Penguin); Hilda Lessways, 1911; These twain, 1915. *A trilogy.*

THE CARD. 1911; The regent, 1913 (*sequel*).

THE REGENT: a Five Towns story in London. 1913.

RICEYMAN STEPS. 1923; ed. Swinnerton, 1954 (Penguin).

IMPERIAL PALACE. 1930.

Also a number of plays, pbd 1900–29, including dramatizations of some of the novels, as well as essays and travel-books.

Journals. Ed. Newman Flower, 3 vols. 1932–3; [Selection], ed. Swinnerton, 1954 (Penguin).

170 letters to Dorothy Cheston. 1935; Letters to his nephew, ed. Richard Bennett, 1936; Bennett and H.G. Wells, ed. Harris Wilson, 1960.

James, Henry. The new novel. *In his* Notes on novelists, 1914. *On Bennett, Conrad, Compton Mackenzie, Wells etc.*

Darton, F.J.Harvey. Arnold Bennett. 1915; 1924.

Woolf, Virginia. Mr Bennett and Mrs Brown. 1924 (Hogarth essays).

Lafourcade, Georges. Bennett: a study. 1939.

Allen, Walter. Arnold Bennett. 1948.

Wain, John. The quality of Bennett. *In his* Preliminary essays, 1957.

EDMUND BLUNDEN (b. 1896)

POEMS, 1913 and 1914. 1914.

PASTORALS: a book of verses. 1916.

THE WAGGONER and other poems. 1920.

THE SHEPHERD and other poems. 1922; 1928.

ENGLISH POEMS. 1925; 1929.

MASKS OF TIME: poems chiefly meditative. 1925.

UNDERTONES OF WAR. 1928; 1930. *Reminiscences.*

NEAR AND FAR: new poems. 1929.

Poems, 1914–30. 1930.

VOTIVE TABLETS: studies of English authors and books. 1931.

CHOICE OR CHANCE: new poems. 1934.

Poems, 1930–40. 1940.

SHELLS BY A STREAM. 1944.

AFTER THE BOMBING and other short poems. 1949.

Poems of many years. Ed. Rupert Hart-Davis, 1957. *A selection from the collected verse, 1920–49, with 20 uncollected poems.*

Also studies of Leigh Hunt (1930), Lamb (1932), Keats's publisher John Taylor (1936), Hardy (1941), Shelley (1946).

ELIZABETH BOWEN (b. 1899)

ENCOUNTERS: stories. 1923; Ann Lee's and other stories, 1926; Joining Charles and other stories, 1929; The cat jumps and other stories, 1934; Look at all those roses: stories, 1941; The demon lover and other stories, 1945.

THE HOTEL. 1927.

THE LAST SEPTEMBER. 1929.

FRIENDS AND RELATIONS. 1931.

TO THE NORTH. 1932.

THE HOUSE IN PARIS. 1935.

THE DEATH OF THE HEART. 1938.

SEVEN WINTERS. Dublin 1942.

WHY DO I WRITE? an exchange of views between Elizabeth Bowen, Graham Greene and V.S.Pritchett. 1948.

THE HEAT OF THE DAY. 1949.

COLLECTED IMPRESSIONS. 1950. *Includes studies of Barrie, Fanny Burney, Ivy Compton-Burnett, Conrad, Forster, Aldous Huxley, Ben Jonson, D.H.Lawrence, Trollope, Virginia Woolf.*

A WORLD OF LOVE. 1955.

THE LITTLE GIRLS. 1964.

Works: uniform edition. 1949–.

RUPERT BROOKE (1887 – 1915)

Keynes, Geoffrey. A bibliography of Brooke. 1954; 1959.

POEMS. 1911.

WAR SONNETS. New numbers (Dec. 1914).

1914 AND OTHER POEMS. 1915. *Includes* The old vicarage, Grantchester, *which was first pbd in* Basileon H (Cambridge) (June 1912) *and in* Georgian poetry, 1912.

LITHUANIA: a drama in one act. Chicago 1915. *First London edn, 1935*

JOHN WEBSTER and the Elizabethan drama. New York 1916. *A fellowship dissertation. First London edn, 1916.*

LETTERS FROM AMERICA. Ed. Henry James, New York 1916. *First London edn, 1916.*

FRAGMENTS. Ed. R.M.G.Potter, Hartford, Conn. 1925.

Collected poems. New York 1915; with a memoir by Edward Marsh, 1918 (*enlarged*); 1942; Poetical works, ed. Geoffrey Keynes, 1946.

Prose. Ed. Christopher Hassall, 1956.

Marsh, Edward. A memoir. *In* Collected poems, 1918, *above.*

de la Mare, Walter. Brooke and the intellectual imagination: a lecture. 1919; 1940 (*in his* Pleasures and speculations).

Stringer, Arthur. Red wine of youth: a life of Brooke. New York 1948.

Hassall, Christopher. Brooke: a biography. 1964.

JOHN BUCHAN, 1st BARON TWEEDSMUIR
(1875 – 1940)

PRESTER JOHN. 1910.

THE THIRTY-NINE STEPS. 1915; Greenmantle, 1916; Mr Standfast, 1919. *A trilogy.*

SALUTE TO ADVENTURERS. 1915.

POEMS, SCOTS AND ENGLISH. 1917; 1936 (*enlarged*).

A BOOK OF ESCAPES and hurried journeys. 1922.

JOHN MACNAB. 1925.

THE FOUR ADVENTURES of Richard Hannay. 1930.

A PRINCE OF THE CAPTIVITY. 1933.

MEMORY HOLD-THE-DOOR. 1940. *An autobiography.*

Also biographies of Montrose (1928), Cromwell (1934), Scott (1936), Augustus (1937).

Buchan, Anna. Unforgettable, unforgotten. 1945. *A biography by his sister.*

Tweedsmuir, Susan *et al.* Buchan by his wife and friends. 1947.

ROY CAMPBELL (1901 – 1957)

THE FLAMING TERRAPIN. 1924.

THE WAYZGOOSE: a South African satire. 1928.

ADAMASTOR: poems. 1930.

POEMS. Paris 1930. *Includes passages from* The Georgiad, *below.*

THE GEORGIAD: a satirical fantasy in verse. 1931.

FLOWERING REEDS: poems. 1933.

MITHRAIC EMBLEMS: poems. 1936.

FLOWERING RIFLE: a poem. 1939.

SONS OF THE MISTRAL. 1941.

TALKING BRONCO. 1946.

Collected poems. 3 vols. 1949–60.

Also autobiographies, Broken record (1934) *and* Light on a dark horse (1951); Portugal (1957); *and verse trns of St John of the Cross (1951), García Lorca (1952), Baudelaire (1952).*

JOYCE CARY (1888 – 1957)

AISSA SAVED. 1932.

AN AMERICAN VISITOR. 1933.

THE AFRICAN WITCH. 1936.

CASTLE CORNER. 1938.

MISTER JOHNSON. 1939.

CHARLEY IS MY DARLING. 1940.

THE HOUSE OF CHILDREN. 1941.

HERSELF SURPRISED. 1941; To be a pilgrim, 1942; The horse's mouth, 1944. *A trilogy of novels.*

THE MOONLIGHT. 1946.

A FEARFUL JOY. 1949.

PRISONER OF GRACE. 1952; Except the Lord, 1953; Not honour more, 1955. *Second trilogy.*

ART AND REALITY: Clark lectures. Cambridge 1958.

THE CAPTIVE AND THE FREE. 1959.

SPRING SONG and other stories. 1960.

Novels: Carfax edition. 1951– (*with prefaces*).

Adam international review (Nov.–Dec. 1950). *Studies on the novels by various hands, with his own articles on novel-writing.*

Wright, Andrew. Cary: a preface to his novels. 1958.

Bloom, Robert. The indeterminate world: a study of the novels of Cary. Philadelphia 1962.

Mahood, M.M. Joyce's Africa. 1964.

GILBERT KEITH CHESTERTON (1874–1936)

Sullivan, John. Chesterton: a bibliography. 1958.

THE NAPOLEON OF NOTTING HILL. 1904.

THE CLUB OF QUEER TRADES. 1905.

HERETICS. 1905.

THE MAN WHO WAS THURSDAY: a nightmare. Bristol 1908.

ORTHODOXY. 1909.

THE BALLAD OF THE WHITE HORSE. 1911.

THE INNOCENCE OF FATHER BROWN. 1911; The wisdom of Father Brown, 1914; The incredulity of Father Brown, 1926; The secret of Father Brown, 1927; The scandal of Father Brown, 1935. *Collections of detective stories.*

MANALIVE. 1912.

THE VICTORIAN AGE IN LITERATURE. 1913 (Home univ. lib.).

THE FLYING INN. 1914.

A SHORT HISTORY OF ENGLAND. 1917.

THE EVERLASTING MAN. 1925.

DO WE AGREE? a debate between Chesterton and Shaw. 1928.

AUTOBIOGRAPHY. 1936.

Also collections of essays and biographical studies of Browning (1903), Dickens (1906), Shaw (1910), St Francis of Assisi (1923), Cobbett (1925), Chaucer (1932), Aquinas (1933).

Collected poems. 1927.

Stories, essays and poems. 1935 (EL).

[Chesterton, Cecil]. G.K.Chesterton: a criticism. 1908. *An anon. study by his brother.*

Evans, Maurice. G.K.Chesterton. Cambridge 1939.

Belloc, Hilaire. On the place of Chesterton in English letters. 1940.

Ward, Maisie. Gilbert Keith Chesterton. 1944.

SIR WINSTON SPENCER CHURCHILL (b. 1874)

Woods, Frederick. A bibliography of the works of Churchill. 1963.

THE RIVER WAR: an historical account of the reconquest of the Soudan. Ed. F.Rhodes, 2 vols. 1899; I vol. 1902.

SAVROLA: a tale of the revolution in Laurania. New York 1900; 1956 (*with* Foreword). *First London edn, 1900. The only novel.*

IAN HAMILTON'S MARCH. 1900.

LORD RANDOLPH CHURCHILL. 2 vols. 1906; I vol. 1952 (*with addns*). *A biography of his father.*

LIBERALISM AND THE SOCIAL PROBLEM. 1909. *One of many Liberal pamphlets and speech-collections, pbd 1903–16, on free trade, Irish Home Rule, the suffragette movement, social policy, the Navy.*

THE WORLD CRISIS. 5 vols. 1923–31; I vol. 1931 (*abbreviated and rev.*). *An account of the years 1911–18.*

MY EARLY LIFE: a roving commission. 1930.

THOUGHTS AND ADVENTURES. 1932.

MARLBOROUGH. 4 vols. 1933–8.

THE GREAT WAR. 26 pts. 1933–4.

GREAT CONTEMPORARIES. 1937; 1938 (*with four addns*).

INTO BATTLE: speeches. Ed. Randolph Churchill, 1941; The unrelenting struggle, ed. Charles Eade, 1942; The end of the beginning, ed. Eade, 1943; Onwards to victory, ed. Eade, 1944; The dawn of liberation, ed. Eade, 1945; Victory, ed. Eade, 1946.

War speeches, 1940–5. 1946; ed. Charles Eade, 3 vols. 1951.

THE SECOND WORLD WAR. 6 vols. Boston 1948–53. *First London edn, 6 vols. 1948–54; abridged, I vol. 1959 (*with* Epilogue on the years 1945–57).*

EUROPE UNITE: speeches, 1947–8. Ed. Randolph Churchill, 1950; In the balance, 1949–50, ed. Randolph Churchill, 1951; Stemming the tide, 1951–2, ed. Randolph Churchill, 1953.

A HISTORY of the English-speaking peoples. 4 vols. 1956–8.

Selections from his writings and speeches. Ed. Guy Boas, 1952.

Guedalla, Philip. Mr Churchill: a portrait. 1941.

Broad, C.Lewis. Winston Churchill. 1941; 1951 (*rev. and extended*).

Eade, Charles (ed.). Churchill by his contemporaries. 1953.

Rowse, A.L. *In his* The later Churchills, 1958.

ROBIN GEORGE COLLINGWOOD (1889 – 1943)

For bibliographies of Collingwood as philosopher and historian see McCallum, below.

RELIGION AND PHILOSOPHY. 1916.

ROMAN BRITAIN. Oxford 1923; 1932.

SPECULUM MENTIS. Oxford 1924.

OUTLINES OF A PHILOSOPHY OF ART. 1925.

THE ARCHAEOLOGY OF ROMAN BRITAIN. 1930.

AN ESSAY ON PHILOSOPHICAL METHOD. Oxford 1933.

ROMAN BRITAIN and the English settlements. Oxford 1936, 1937 (Oxford history of England, vol. i). *Bk v*, The English settlements, *by J.N.L.Myres.*

THE PRINCIPLES OF ART. Oxford 1938.

AN AUTOBIOGRAPHY. Oxford 1939.

AN ESSAY ON METAPHYSICS. Oxford 1940.

THE NEW LEVIATHAN. Oxford 1942.

THE IDEA OF HISTORY. Ed. T.M.Knox, Oxford 1945.

THE IDEA OF NATURE. Ed. T.M.Knox, Oxford 1946.

McCallum, R.B., T.M.Knox and I.A.Richmond. Collingwood. Proc. Brit. Acad. xxix (1943). *An obituary, with bibliographies.*

Tomlin, E.W.F. R.G.Collingwood. 1953 (Brit. Council pamphlet).

IVY COMPTON-BURNETT (b. 1892)

There is an early novel, Dolores (1911).

PASTORS AND MASTERS. 1925.

BROTHERS AND SISTERS. 1929.

MEN AND WIVES. 1931.

MORE WOMEN THAN MEN. 1933.

A HOUSE AND ITS HEAD. 1935.

DAUGHTERS AND SONS. 1937.

A FAMILY AND A FORTUNE. 1939.

PARENTS AND CHILDREN. 1941.

ELDERS AND BETTERS. 1944.

MANSERVANT AND MAIDSERVANT. 1947.

TWO WORLDS AND THEIR WAYS. 1949.

DARKNESS AND DAY. 1951.

THE PRESENT AND THE PAST. 1953.

MOTHER AND SON. 1955.

A FATHER AND HIS FATE. 1957.

A HERITAGE AND ITS HISTORY. 1959.

THE MIGHTY AND THEIR FALL. 1961.

A GOD AND HIS GIFTS. 1963.

For a discussion of the novels see A conversation between I.Compton-Burnett and M.Jourdain, *in* Orion: a miscellany, I (1945).

Hansford Johnson, Pamela. I.Compton-Burnett. 1953 (Brit. Council pamphlet).

Liddell, Robert. The novels of I.Compton-Burnett. 1955.

CYRIL CONNOLLY (b. 1903)

THE ROCK POOL. Paris 1936; London 1947 (*with* Postscript). *The only novel.*

ENEMIES OF PROMISE. 1938; 1949.

THE UNQUIET GRAVE: a word cycle by Palinurus. 1944; 1951.

THE CONDEMNED PLAYGROUND: essays, 1927–44. 1945. *Reviews of Chesterfield, Housman, Joyce, Pope, Sterne, Swift etc.*

THE MISSING DIPLOMATS. 1952. *A pamphlet study of Burgess and Maclean.*

IDEAS AND PLACES. 1953; Previous convictions, 1963. *Essays, reviews, etc.*

> For Horizon *and its anthologies see p. 215, above.*

JOSEPH CONRAD, formerly JÓZEF KONRAD KORZENIOWSKI (1857 – 1924)

Wise, Thomas J. A bibliography of Conrad, 1895–1920, 1920; 1921 (*enlarged*); A Conrad library, 1928.

Lohf, Kenneth A. and Eugene P. Sheehy. Conrad at mid-century: editions and studies, 1895–1955. Minneapolis 1957.

ALMAYER'S FOLLY. 1895.

AN OUTCAST OF THE ISLANDS. 1896.

THE NIGGER OF THE 'NARCISSUS': a tale of the sea. 1898; Preface, 1902. *The first edn of the novel, New York 1897, was entitled* The children of the sea.

TALES OF UNREST. Edinburgh 1898.

LORD JIM. Edinburgh 1900.

YOUTH and two other stories. Edinburgh 1902. *With* Heart of darkness *and* The end of the tether.

TYPHOON. 1902; and other stories, 1903.

ROMANCE: a novel. 1903. *With Ford Madox Ford.*

NOSTROMO: a tale of the seaboard. 1904.

THE MIRROR OF THE SEA: memories and impressions. 1906.

THE SECRET AGENT: a simple tale. 1907.

A SET OF SIX. 1908.

UNDER WESTERN EYES. 1911.

SOME REMINISCENCES. 1912; 1916 (*re-entitled* A personal record).

'TWIXT LAND AND SEA: tales. 1912.

CHANCE: a tale in two parts. 1913.

WITHIN THE TIDES: tales. 1915.

VICTORY: an island tale. New York 1915. *First London edn, 1915.*

THE ARROW OF GOLD: a story between two notes. 1919.

THE RESCUE. New York 1920. *First London edn, 1920.*

NOTES ON LIFE AND LETTERS. 1921; Notes on my books, 1921; Last essays, 1926.

SUSPENSE: a Napoleonic novel. New York 1925; ed. Richard Curle, 1925. *Unfinished.*

Letters to his wife. 1927; Letters, 1895–1924, ed. Edward Garnett, 1928; Conrad to a friend: 150 selected letters to Richard Curle, ed. Curle, 1928; Letters to Marguerite Poradowska, 1890–1920, tr. and ed. John A. Gee and Paul J. Sturm, New Haven 1940; Letters to William Blackwood and David S. Meldrum, ed. William Blackburn, Durham, N.C. 1958.

Works: uniform edition. 22 vols. 1923–8.

James, Henry. The new novel. *In his* Notes on novelists, 1914.

Jean-Aubry, G. Conrad: life and letters. 2 vols. 1927; 1957 (*shortened and rev. as* The sea dreamer).

Crankshaw, Edward. Conrad: some aspects of the art of the novel. 1936.

Bradbrook, M. C. Conrad: Poland's English genius. Cambridge 1941.

Leavis, F. R. *In his* The great tradition, 1948.

Guerard, Albert J. Conrad the novelist. Cambridge, Mass. 1958.

Baines, Jocelyn. Conrad: a critical biography. 1959.

WALTER DE LA MARE (1873 – 1956)

Clark, Leonard. de la Mare: a check-list. 1956 (Nat. Book League pamphlet).

SONGS OF CHILDHOOD, by Walter Ramal. 1902.

HENRY BROCKEN: his travels and adventures. 1904; The three Mullamulgars, 1910; The return, 1910, 1945; Memoirs of a midget, 1921; The riddle, 1923; The connoisseur, 1926; On the edge, 1926; The wind blows over, 1936; The magic jacket, 1943; The scarecrow, 1945; The Dutch cheese, 1946; A beginning, 1955. *Tales.*

POEMS. 1906.

THE LISTENERS and other poems. 1912.

A CHILD'S DAY: a book of rhymes. 1912.

PEACOCK PIE: a book of rhymes. 1913.

THE SUNKEN GARDEN and other poems. 1917.

MOTLEY and other poems. 1918.

Poems, 1901 to 1918. 2 vols. 1920.

THE VEIL and other poems. 1921.

COME HITHER: a collection of rhymes and poems. 1923; 1928.

STUFF AND NONSENSE AND SO ON. 1927.

DESERT ISLANDS and Robinson Crusoe. 1930.

Poems, 1919 to 1934. 1935.

MEMORY and other poems. 1938.

PLEASURES AND SPECULATIONS. 1940. *Includes studies of Rupert Brooke, Shakespeare's* Midsummer night's dream, *Tennyson.*

BELLS AND GRASS: a book of rhymes. 1941.

THE BURNING-GLASS and other poems. 1945.

INWARD COMPANION: poems. 1950.

WINGED CHARIOT. 1951.

O LOVELY ENGLAND, and other poems. 1953.

PRIVATE VIEW. 1953. *A collection of reviews.*

Stories, essays and poems. 1938 (EL).

Collected poems. 1942.

Collected rhymes and verses. 1944.

Collected stories for children. 1947.

Mégroz, R.L. de la Mare: a biographical and critical study. 1924.

Reid, Forrest. de la Mare: a critical study. 1929.

Priestley, J.B., David Cecil, Graham Greene *et al.* Tribute to de la Mare on his seventy-fifth birthday. 1948. *38 tributes in prose and verse.*

NORMAN DOUGLAS (1868 – 1952)

McDonald, Edward D. A bibliography of Douglas, with notes by Douglas. 1927.

Woolf, Cecil. A bibliography of Douglas. 1954.

UNPROFESSIONAL TALES, by Normyx. 1901. *With his wife, Elsa Fitz-Gibbon.*

SIREN LAND. 1911; 1923.

OLD CALABRIA. 1915; New York 1928 *(with introd.)*; New York 1938 (WC) *(with new introd.).*

SOUTH WIND. 1917; New York 1925 *(with introd.).*

THEY WENT. 1920.

ALONE. 1921; Together, 1923; Experiments, Florence 1923, New York 1925 *(full text). Collections of reviews, essays etc.*

IN THE BEGINNING. Florence 1927; London 1928 *(incomplete)*; ed. Constantine FitzGibbon, 1953 *(complete).*

CAPRI: materials for a description of the island. Florence 1930.

Tomlinson, Henry Major. Norman Douglas. 1931; 1952.

'MacGillivray, Richard' (R.M.Dawkins). Norman Douglas. Florence 1933; London 1952 *(enlarged).*

Aldington, Richard. Pinorman: personal recollections of Douglas, Pino Orioli and Charles Prentice. 1954.

Cunard, Nancy. Grand man: memoirs of Douglas. 1954.

THOMAS STEARNS ELIOT (b. 1888)

Gallup, Donald. Eliot: a bibliography. 1952.

PRUFROCK and other observations. 1917.

POEMS. 1919.

Ara vos prec. 1920. *Adds* Gerontion *etc.*

THE SACRED WOOD: essays on poetry and criticism. 1920; 1928 (*with preface*). *Collects* The perfect critic, Tradition and the individual talent, The possibility of a poetic drama *and studies of Blake, Dante,* Hamlet, *Ben Jonson, Massinger, Swinburne. Largely rptd in Selected* essays, *below.*

THE WASTE LAND. New York 1922. *First London edn, 1923.*

HOMAGE TO JOHN DRYDEN: three essays. 1924. *Includes* Dryden, The metaphysical poets, Marvell.

Poems, 1909–25. 1925. *Adds* The hollow men.

FOR LANCELOT ANDREWES: essays on style and order. 1928. *Eight essays, including studies of Andrewes, Crashaw, Middleton.*

DANTE. 1929.

ASH-WEDNESDAY. 1930.

THOUGHTS AFTER LAMBETH. 1931.

Selected essays. 1932; 1951 (*with addns*). *1932 collects the five prose works above and adds studies of Arnold and Pater, Wilkie Collins, Dickens, Ford, Tourneur, Charles Whibley etc. 1951 adds* Marston, In memoriam *etc.*

SWEENEY AGONISTES: fragments of an Aristophanic melodrama. 1932.

THE USE OF POETRY and the use of criticism. 1933.

AFTER STRANGE GODS: a primer of modern heresy. 1934.

THE ROCK: a pageant play. 1934.

MURDER IN THE CATHEDRAL. 1935 (*acting text*); 1935; 1937.

Collected poems, 1909–35. 1936. *Adds* Burnt Norton *etc.*

THE FAMILY REUNION: a play. 1939.

OLD POSSUM'S BOOK OF PRACTICAL CATS. 1939.

THE IDEA OF A CHRISTIAN SOCIETY. 1939.

EAST COKER. 1940.

BURNT NORTON. 1941. *First pbd in* Collected poems, *above.*

THE DRY SALVAGES. 1941.

LITTLE GIDDING. 1942.

Four quartets. New York 1943. *First London edn, 1944. Collects* Burnt Norton, East Coker, The Dry Salvages, Little Gidding, *above.*

NOTES towards the definition of culture. 1948.

THE COCKTAIL PARTY: a comedy. 1950.

POETRY AND DRAMA. Cambridge, Mass. 1951 (Spencer lecture).

THE THREE VOICES OF POETRY. Cambridge 1953.

THE CONFIDENTIAL CLERK: a play. 1954.

THE ELDER STATESMAN: a play. 1959.

KNOWLEDGE AND EXPERIENCE in the philosophy of F.H.Bradley. 1964. *A Harvard thesis of 1916.*

Edited The criterion, *1922–39.*

On poetry and poets. 1957. *Sixteen lectures and articles, mainly pbd 1936–56.*

Complete poems and plays. New York 1952; Collected plays, 1962; Collected poems, 1909–62, 1963.

Selected prose. Ed. John Hayward, 1953 (Penguin).

Wilson, Edmund. *In his* Axel's Castle, New York 1931.

Leavis, F.R. *In his* New Bearings in English poetry, 1932; 1950.

—— Eliot's later poetry. *In his* Education and the university, 1943.

Matthiessen, F.O. The achievement of Eliot. 1935; 1947 (*enlarged*).

Winters, Yvor. Eliot: or the illusion of reaction. *In his* The anatomy of nonsense, Norfolk, Conn. 1943 *and in* In defense of reason, Denver 1947.

Gardner, Helen L. The art of Eliot. 1949.

Williamson, George. A reader's guide to Eliot: a poem-by-poem analysis. New York 1953.

Kenner, Hugh. The invisible poet. 1959.

Frye, Northrop. T.S.Eliot. Edinburgh 1963 (Writers & critics).

WILLIAM EMPSON (b. 1906)

SEVEN TYPES OF AMBIGUITY. 1930; 1947; 1953 (*with* Note).

POEMS. 1935; The gathering storm, 1940.

Collected poems. New York 1949. *First London edn, 1955.*

SOME VERSIONS OF PASTORAL. 1935.

THE STRUCTURE OF COMPLEX WORDS. 1951.

MILTON'S GOD. 1961.

RONALD FIRBANK (1886 – 1926)

Benkovitz, Miriam J. A bibliography of Firbank. 1963.

VAINGLORY. 1915.

INCLINATIONS. 1916.

CAPRICE. 1917.

VALMOUTH: a romantic novel. 1919.

THE PRINCESS ZOUBAROFF: a comedy. 1920.

SANTAL. 1921.

THE FLOWER BENEATH THE FOOT. 1923.

PRANCING NIGGER. New York 1924. *First London edn, 1925, entitled* Sorrow in sunlight.

CONCERNING THE ECCENTRICITIES of Cardinal Pirelli. 1926.

Collected works. Ed. Arthur Waley, 5 vols. 1929; The complete Firbank, ed. Anthony Powell, 1961.

THE ARTIFICIAL PRINCESS. Ed. Coleridge Kennard, 1934. *An early work, written before* Vainglory.

Fletcher, Ifan Kyrle. Firbank: a memoir, with reminiscences by Lord Berners, V.B. Holland, Augustus John and Osbert Sitwell. 1930.

Forster, E.M. *In his* Abinger harvest, 1936.

Brooke, Jocelyn. Ronald Firbank. 1951.

JAMES ELROY FLECKER (1884 – 1915)

THIRTY-SIX POEMS. 1910; Forty-two poems, 1911, 1924 (*with* The Grecians).

THE GOLDEN JOURNEY TO SAMARKAND. 1913.

THE KING OF ALSANDER. 1914. *The only novel.*

THE OLD SHIPS. 1915.

HASSAN: a play. 1922.

DON JUAN: a play. 1925.

Collected poems. Ed. J.C. Squire, 1916; 1946.

Collected prose. 1920. *Excluding* Alsander, *above.*

Letters to Frank Savery. 1920.

Hodgson, Geraldine E. The life of Flecker. 1925. *With the text of many letters.*

FORD MADOX FORD, formerly HUEFFER (1873 – 1939)

ROMANCE: a novel. 1903. *With Joseph Conrad.*

THE FIFTH QUEEN. 1906; Privy Seal, 1907; The fifth queen crowned, 1908. *A trilogy of romances on Katherine Howard.*

MR FLEIGHT. 1913.

THE GOOD SOLDIER: a tale of passion. 1915.

SOME DO NOT—. 1924; No more parades, 1925; A man could stand up—, 1926; Last post, 1928. *The Tietjens Saga, collected as* Parade's end, New York 1950.

RETURN TO YESTERDAY: reminiscences, 1894–1914. 1931; It was the nightingale, 1934. *Autobiography.*

PORTRAITS FROM LIFE: memories and criticisms. Boston 1937. *First London edn, 1938 (re-entitled* Mightier than the sword). *On Conrad,*

Galsworthy, James, D.H.Lawrence et al. *Also studies of James (1913) and Conrad (1924).*

The Bodley Head Ford. Ed. Graham Greene, 4 vols, 1962–3. *Founded and edited* The English review, 1908–10.

Goldring, Douglas. The last Pre-Raphaelite. 1948.
Cassell, Richard A. Ford: a study of his novels. Baltimore 1961.

EDWARD MORGAN FORSTER (b. 1879)

WHERE ANGELS FEAR TO TREAD. 1905.
THE LONGEST JOURNEY. 1907; Oxford 1960 (WC) *(with introd.).*
A ROOM WITH A VIEW. 1908.
HOWARDS END. 1910.
THE CELESTIAL OMNIBUS and other stories. 1911; The story of the siren, 1920; The eternal moment and other stories, 1928; Collected short stories, 1947.
ALEXANDRIA: a history and a guide. Alexandria 1922, 1938, New York 1961 *(with introd.);* Pharos and Pharillon, 1923.
A PASSAGE TO INDIA. 1924; 1924, 1957 (EL) *(with notes).*
ASPECTS OF THE NOVEL. 1927. *On Jane Austen, the Brontës, Defoe, Dickens, Hardy, Henry James, Joyce, Meredith, Scott etc.*
GOLDSWORTHY LOWES DICKINSON. 1934. *A biography.*
ABINGER HARVEST. 1936; Two cheers for democracy, 1951. *Collections of essays and reviews.*
THE HILL OF DEVI: being letters from Dewas State Senior. 1953.
MARIANNE THORNTON, 1797–1887: a domestic biography. 1956.

Macaulay, Rose. The writings of Forster. 1938.
Trilling, Lionel. E.M.Forster. Norfolk, Conn. 1943.
Leavis, F.R. *In his* The common pursuit, 1952.
McConkey, James. The novels of Forster. Ithaca, N.Y. 1957.
Gransden, K.W. E.M.Forster. Edinburgh 1962 (Writers & critics).

CHRISTOPHER FRY (b. 1907)

THE BOY WITH A CART: Cuthman, saint of Sussex. Oxford 1939.
THE FIRSTBORN: a play. Cambridge 1946; Oxford 1952.
A PHOENIX TOO FREQUENT: a comedy. Oxford 1946.
THOR, WITH ANGELS: a play. Oxford 1949.
THE LADY'S NOT FOR BURNING: a comedy. Oxford 1949.
RING ROUND THE MOON: a charade with music. 1950; 1952 *(acting version). An English adaptation of* Jean Anouilh, L'invitation au château (Paris 1948).

VENUS OBSERVED: a play. Oxford 1950.

A SLEEP OF PRISONERS: a play. Oxford 1951.

THE DARK IS LIGHT ENOUGH: a winter comedy. Oxford 1954.

CURTMANTLE: a play. Oxford 1961.

ROGER FRY (1866 – 1934)

VISION AND DESIGN. 1920. '*A selection from my writings on Art extending over a period of twenty years.*'

TRANSFORMATIONS: essays on art. 1926. *A second collection.*

CÉZANNE: a study of his development. 1927.

FLEMISH ART. 1927; Characteristics of French art, 1932; Reflections on British painting, 1934. *Lectures on Royal Academy exhibitions, collected 1951.*

HENRI MATISSE. Paris 1930.

LAST LECTURES. Cambridge 1939. *Rev. text and notes of lectures delivered as Slade Professor at Cambridge, 1933–4.*

Also an edn of Reynolds's Discourses (1905) *and a verse trn of Mallarmé's poems* (1936).

Woolf, Virginia. Fry: a biography. 1940.

JOHN GALSWORTHY (1867 – 1933)

Marrot, H.V. A bibliography of Galsworthy. 1928.

THE MAN OF PROPERTY. 1906; In chancery, 1920; To let, 1921.

The Forsyte saga. 1922. *The above trilogy, with two connecting interludes,* Indian summer of a Forsyte *and* Awakening.

PLAYS: The silver box; Joy; Strife. 1909. *Six further play collections, 1912–30.*

FRATERNITY. 1909.

JUSTICE: a tragedy. 1910.

THE PATRICIAN. 1911.

THE DARK FLOWER. 1913.

FIVE TALES. 1915.

THE SKIN GAME: a tragi-comedy. 1920.

LOYALTIES: a drama. 1922.

THE WHITE MONKEY. 1924; The silver spoon, 1926; Swan song, 1928. *A second Forsyte trilogy, collected as* A modern comedy, 1928.

OLD ENGLISH: a play. 1924.

ESCAPE: an episodic play. 1926.

End of the chapter. 1934. *A final Forsyte collection, containing* Maid in waiting (1931), Flowering wilderness (1932), Over the river (1933).

Caravan: assembled tales. 1925.

Plays. New York 1928. *First London edn, 1929.*
Collected poems. 1934.
Autobiographical letters: a correspondence with Frank Harris. 1933;
Letters, 1900–32, ed. Edward Garnett, 1934.

Archer, William. *In his* The old drama and the new, 1923.
Marrot, H.V. The life and letters of Galsworthy. 1935.
Lawrence, D.H. *In his* Phoenix, New York 1936.
Barker, Dudley. The man of principle: a view of Galsworthy. 1963.

ROBERT GRAVES (b. 1895)

OVER THE BRAZIER. 1916; Country sentiment, 1920. *Poems.*
POETIC UNREASON and other studies. 1925.
Poems, 1914–26. 1927. *A rev. selection from 11 vols. pbd 1916–25.*
GOOD-BYE TO ALL THAT: an autobiography. 1929; 1957 (Penguin) *(rev. and extended).*
POEMS, 1929. 1929; Ten poems more, 1930.
Poems, 1926–30. 1931; 1930–3, 1933.
I, CLAUDIUS. 1934; Claudius the god, 1934; Count Belisarius, 1938. *Historical novels.*
Poems, 1938–45. 1946.
WIFE TO MR MILTON. 1943.
THE GOLDEN FLEECE. 1944.
KING JESUS. 1946.
THE WHITE GODDESS. 1948; 1952 *(enlarged).*
POEMS AND SATIRES. 1951.
POEMS, 1953. 1953.
THE COMMON ASPHODEL: collected essays on poetry, 1922–49. 1949.
Collected poems. 1938; Collected poems, 1914–47, 1948; Collected poems, 1959, 1959. *Successive selections, with rev. texts.*
THE GREEK MYTHS. 2 vols. 1955, 1962 (Penguin); 1 vol. 1958.
THE CROWNING PRIVILEGE: Clark lectures, 1954–5; also various essays and sixteen new poems. 1955.
STEPS: stories, talks, essays, poems, studies in history. 1958.
THE ANGER OF ACHILLES: Homer's Iliad translated. 1960; Pharsalia, 1961.
OXFORD ADDRESSES on poetry. 1962.
MORE POEMS. 1961.
NEW POEMS. 1962.
MAN DOES, WOMAN IS. 1964.

'HENRY GREEN', i.e. HENRY VINCENT YORKE
(b. 1905)

There is an undergraduate novel, Blindness *(1926).*

LIVING. 1929.
PARTY GOING. 1939.
PACK MY BAG: a self-portrait. 1940.
CAUGHT. 1943.
LOVING. 1945.
BACK. 1946.
CONCLUDING. 1948.
NOTHING. 1950.
DOTING. 1952.

Stokes, Edward. The novels of Henry Green. 1959.

GRAHAM GREENE (b. 1904)

There are three early novels, The man within *(1929),* The name of
action *(1930)* and Rumour at nightfall *(1931).*

STAMBOUL TRAIN. 1932; A gun for sale, 1936; The confidential agent,
1939; The ministry of fear, 1943; Our man in Havana, 1958.
'Entertainments.'

IT'S A BATTLEFIELD. 1934.

THE BASEMENT ROOM and other stories. 1934. *A film play based on* The
basement room *entitled* The fallen idol, *pbd 1950, below.*

ENGLAND MADE ME. 1935.

JOURNEY WITHOUT MAPS. 1936. *A travel book on Liberia.*

BRIGHTON ROCK. 1938.

THE LAWLESS ROADS. 1939; 1950 *(with* Note). *A travel book on religious
persecution in Mexico.*

THE POWER AND THE GLORY. 1940.

NINETEEN STORIES. 1947. *Includes the eight stories of* The basement
room, *above.*

THE HEART OF THE MATTER. 1948.

THE THIRD MAN, and The fallen idol. 1950. *Two stories.*

THE END OF THE AFFAIR. 1951.

THE LOST CHILDHOOD and other essays. 1951. *Studies in Buchan, de la
Mare, Dickens, Fielding, F.M.Ford, Henry James, Rolfe, Sterne etc.*

THE LIVING ROOM: a play. 1953.

THE QUIET AMERICAN. 1956.

THE POTTING SHED: a play. 1959; The complaisant lover: a comedy,
1959.

A BURNT-OUT CASE. 1961.
A SENSE OF REALITY. 1963. *Four stories.*
[Works]: uniform edition. 14 vols. 1947–55.

Allen, Walter. The novels of Greene. Penguin new writing, xviii (1943).
Allott, Kenneth and Miriam Farris. The art of Greene. 1951.

ISABELLA AUGUSTA, LADY GREGORY,
née PERSSE (1852 – 1932)

CUCHULAIN OF MUIRTHEMNE. 1902; Poets and dreamers, Dublin 1903;
   Gods and fighting men, 1904; A book of saints and wonders,
   Dundrum 1907. *English adaptations of Irish sagas, poems etc.*
SPREADING THE NEWS. Dublin 1904. *Seven short plays.*
SEVEN SHORT PLAYS. Dublin 1910.
IRISH FOLK-HISTORY PLAYS. 2 ser. New York 1912.
NEW COMEDIES. New York 1913.
OUR IRISH THEATRE: a chapter of autobiography. 1914.
THE GOLDEN APPLE. 1916.
THE DRAGON: a wonder play. 1920.
VISIONS AND BELIEFS in the West of Ireland. New York 1920.
ARISTOTLE'S BELLOWS. 1923.
THREE WONDER PLAYS. 1924.
THE STORY BROUGHT BY BRIGIT. 1924. *A Passion play.*

*Lady Gregory wrote 27 original plays, as well as adaptations of Molière
   and Goldoni, and collaborated in others with Douglas Hyde and W.B.
   Yeats.*

Journals. Ed. Lennox Robinson, 1946 (*selection*).
Selected plays. Ed. Elizabeth Coxhead, 1962.

Malone, Andrew E. *In his* The Irish drama, 1929.
Ellis-Fermor, Una. *In her* The Irish dramatic movement, 1939; 1954.
Coxhead, Elizabeth. Lady Gregory: a literary portrait. 1961.
   Also George Moore's autobiography, Hail and farewell (1911–14).

LESLIE POLES HARTLEY (b. 1895)

NIGHT FEARS and other stories. 1924.
SIMONETTA PERKINS. 1925. *The first novel.*
THE KILLING BOTTLE. 1932. *A second collection of stories.*
THE SHRIMP AND THE ANEMONE. 1944; The sixth heaven, 1946; Eustace
   and Hilda, 1947. *A trilogy, collected as* Eustace and Hilda, 1958.
THE BOAT. 1949.
THE TRAVELLING GRAVE and other stories. 1951.

MY FELLOW DEVILS. 1951.
THE GO-BETWEEN. 1953.
THE WHITE WAND and other stories. 1954.
A PERFECT WOMAN. 1955.
THE HIRELING. 1957.
THE BRICKFIELD. 1964.

Bien, Peter. L.P.Hartley. 1963.

THOMAS ERNEST HULME (1883 – 1917)

SPECULATIONS: essays on humanism and the philosophy of art. Ed. Herbert Read, 1924, 1936; Further speculations, ed. Sam Hynes, Minneapolis 1955.
Also a trn of Georges Sorel, Réflections sur la violence (Paris 1912). The complete poetical works of Hulme (*five short poems*) *are appended to* Ezra Pound, Ripostes (1912), *rptd in* Speculations, *above; see also Roberts, below.*

Roberts, Michael. T.E.Hulme. 1938.

ALDOUS HUXLEY (1894 – 1963)

Eschelbach, C.J. and J.C.Schober. Huxley: a bibliography, 1916–59. Berkeley, Cal. 1961.

LIMBO. 1920; Mortal coils, 1922; Little Mexican, 1924; Two or three graces, 1926; Brief candles, 1930. *Short stories.*
CROME YELLOW. 1921.
ANTIC HAY. 1923.
ON THE MARGIN. 1923; Do what you will, 1929. *First of many essay-collections.*
THOSE BARREN LEAVES. 1925.
JESTING PILATE: the diary of a journey. 1926.
POINT COUNTER POINT. 1928. *Dramatized as* This way to Paradise, 1930.
BRAVE NEW WORLD. 1932, New York 1950 (*with foreword*); Brave New World revisited, 1958.
TEXTS AND PRETEXTS: an anthology with commentaries. 1932.
EYELESS IN GAZA. 1936.
Huxley settled in USA in 1939.
GREY EMINENCE: a study in religion and politics. 1941.
TIME MUST HAVE A STOP. New York 1944. *First London edn, 1945.*
THE PERENNIAL PHILOSOPHY. New York 1945. *First London edn, 1946.*
THE GIOCONDA SMILE: a play. 1948. *Adapted from a short story of that title in* Mortal coils, *above. First New York edn, 1948* (Mortal coils).

APE AND ESSENCE. New York 1948. *First London edn, 1949.*
THE DEVILS OF LOUDUN. New York 1952. *First London edn, 1952.*
THE GENIUS AND THE GODDESS. 1955.

Stories, essays and poems. 1937 (EL).
The world of Huxley: an omnibus. Ed. Charles J.Rolo, New York 1947.

CHRISTOPHER ISHERWOOD (b. 1904)

For collaborations with W.H.Auden see under Auden, above.

ALL THE CONSPIRATORS. 1928; 1957 (*with* Foreword). *The first novel.*
THE MEMORIAL: portrait of a family. 1932.
MR NORRIS CHANGES TRAINS. 1935.
LIONS AND SHADOWS. 1935. *An autobiographical novel of England in the 1920's.*
SALLY BOWLES. 1937.
GOODBYE TO BERLIN. 1939. *Six narrative sketches of pre-Hitler Berlin, including* Sally Bowles, *above.*

Isherwood settled in USA in Jan. 1939.

PRATER VIOLET. New York 1945. *First London edn, 1946.*
THE CONDOR AND THE COWS: a South American travel diary. New York 1947. *First London edn, 1949.*
THE WORLD IN THE EVENING. New York 1954. *First London edn, 1954.*
DOWN THERE ON A VISIT. New York 1962. *First London edn, 1962.*
A SINGLE MAN. New York 1964. *First London edn, 1964.*

Also edns in trn of Bhagavad-gita (Hollywood 1944), Vedanta (Hollywood 1945) *etc.*

JAMES JOYCE (1882 – 1941)

Slocum, John J. and Herbert Cahoon. A bibliography of Joyce. New Haven 1953.

CHAMBER MUSIC. 1907; ed. W.Y.Tindall, New York 1954. *36 poems.*
DUBLINERS. 1914. *15 short stories.*
A PORTRAIT OF THE ARTIST as a young man. New York 1916. *First London edn, 1917 (ptd in USA). See* Stephen hero, *below.*
EXILES: a play. 1918; including hitherto unpublished notes, ed. Padraic Colum, New York 1951.
ULYSSES. Paris 1922. *First London edn, 1922 (ptd in France); first ptd in England, 1936.* Hamburg 1932, *text rev. Stuart Gilbert at Joyce's request, is probably the most accurate.*
POMES PENYEACH. Paris 1927. *13 poems.*
WORK IN PROGRESS. 5 pts. New York 1927–30. *Materials from* Finnegans wake (*below*), *ptd in limited edns for copyright purposes but not pbd.*

ANNA LIVIA PLURABELLE. New York 1928. *From* Finnegans wake, *below. First London edn, 1930.*

TALES TOLD OF SHEM AND SHAUN: three fragments from Work in progress. Paris 1929. *From* Finnegans wake, *below. First London edn (two stories only), 1932.*

FINNEGANS WAKE. 1939; Corrections of misprints, New York 1945 (*included in London edns since 1946*); A skeleton key by Joseph Campbell and H.M.Robinson, 1947; A first draft, ed. David Hayman, 1963; A concordance by Clive Hart, Minneapolis 1963.

STEPHEN HERO: part of the first draft of A portrait of the artist. Ed. Theodore Spencer, 1944; New York 1955 (*with addn*).

Collected poems. New York 1936.

Introducing Joyce: a selection of prose. Ed. T.S.Eliot, 1942.

The portable Joyce. Ed. Harry Levin, New York 1947. *London edn, 1948 (entitled* The essential Joyce).

Letters. Ed. Stuart Gilbert, 1957.

Critical writings. Ed. Ellsworth Mason and Richard Ellmann, 1959.

Gilbert, Stuart. Joyce's Ulysses: a study. 1930; 1952.

Wilson, Edmund. *In his* Axel's castle, New York 1931.

Gorman, Herbert S. James Joyce. New York 1939.

Levin, Harry. Joyce: a critical introduction. Norfolk, Conn. 1941; 1960 (*enlarged*).

Kenner, Hugh. Dublin's Joyce. 1956.

Joyce, Stanislaus. My brother's keeper. Ed. Richard Ellmann, New York 1958; Dublin diary [1903–5], ed. George H.Healey, New York 1962.

Ellmann, Richard. James Joyce. New York 1959.

Goldberg, Samuel L. The classical temper: a study of Joyce's Ulysses. 1961.

Adams, Robert M. Surface and symbol: the consistency of Joyce's Ulysses. New York 1962.

JOHN MAYNARD KEYNES, 1st BARON KEYNES
(1883 - 1946)

THE ECONOMIC CONSEQUENCES of the peace. 1919; A revision of the Treaty: a sequel, 1922.

A TREATISE ON PROBABILITY. 1921.

A TRACT ON MONETARY REFORM. 1923.

A SHORT VIEW OF RUSSIA. 1925.

THE ECONOMIC CONSEQUENCES of Mr Churchill. 1925; Can Lloyd George do it? 1928 (*with Hubert Henderson*). *Two of his pamphlets.*

THE END OF LAISSEZ-FAIRE. 1926.

BRITAIN'S INDUSTRIAL FUTURE: being the report of the Liberal Industrial Inquiry. 1928. *The 'Yellow Book': Keynes was a member of the Inquiry.*

A TREATISE ON MONEY. 2 vols. 1930.

ESSAYS IN PERSUASION. 1931; Essays in biography, 1933, 1951 (*with three addns*).

THE GENERAL THEORY OF EMPLOYMENT, interest and money. 1936.

TWO MEMOIRS: Dr Melchior and My early beliefs. 1949.

Edited The economic journal, 1911–44.

Harrod, R.F. The life of Keynes. 1951.

ARTHUR KOESTLER (b. 1905)

SPANISH TESTAMENT. 1937. *Pt ii*, Dialogue with death (*1955*), *is based on a diary kept in English in a Spanish prison in 1937. The* Testament *is tr. from a German version written after his release.*

THE GLADIATORS. 1939. *A novel, tr. from German.*

DARKNESS AT NOON. 1940. *A novel, tr. from German.*

Since settling in England in 1940 all his books have been written in English.

SCUM OF THE EARTH. 1941; 1955 (*with preface*). *His first book to be written in English. Autobiography.*

ARRIVAL AND DEPARTURE. 1943. *A novel.*

TWILIGHT BAR. 1945. *A play.*

THE YOGI AND THE COMMISSAR, and other essays. 1945.

THIEVES IN THE NIGHT. 1946. *A novel.*

PROMISE AND FULFILMENT: Palestine 1917–19. 1949.

INSIGHT AND OUTLOOK: an enquiry into the common foundations of science, art and social ethics. 1949.

THE AGE OF LONGING. 1951. *A novel.*

ARROW IN THE BLUE: an autobiography [to 1931]. 1952; The invisible writing: the second volume [1931–40], 1954. *Also an autobiographical essay in* The god that failed: six studies in Communism, ed. Richard Crossman, 1950. Scum of the earth, *above, continues the story into the Second World War.*

THE TRAIL OF THE DINOSAUR and other essays. 1955.

REFLECTIONS ON HANGING. 1956.

THE SLEEPWALKERS: a history of man's changing view of the universe. 1959.

THE ACT OF CREATION. 1964.

DAVID HERBERT LAWRENCE (1885 – 1930)

Roberts, Warren. A bibliography of Lawrence. 1963.

THE WHITE PEACOCK. New York 1911. *First London edn, 1911 (bowdlerized).*

THE TRESPASSER. 1912.

LOVE POEMS AND OTHERS. 1913; Amores, 1916; Look! we have come through!, 1917, 1958 *(with memoir by Frieda Lawrence)*; New poems, 1918; Bay, 1919; Tortoises, 1921; Birds, beasts and flowers, 1923. Collected poems. 2 vols. 1928.

SONS AND LOVERS. 1913.

THE WIDOWING OF MRS HOLROYD: a drama. 1914. *Three further plays pbd 1920–34, three collected as* Plays, 1933.

THE PRUSSIAN OFFICER. 1914. *Short stories.*

THE RAINBOW. 1915.

TWILIGHT IN ITALY. 1916. *Travel sketches.*

WOMEN IN LOVE. New York 1920. *First London edn, 1921.*

THE LOST GIRL. 1920.

PSYCHOANALYSIS AND THE UNCONSCIOUS, New York 1921; Fantasia of the unconscious, New York 1922. *First London edns, 1923.*

SEA AND SARDINIA. New York 1921. *First London edn, 1923. A travel-book on Sardinia and Sicily.*

AARON'S ROD. New York 1922. *First London edn, 1922.*

ENGLAND MY ENGLAND and other stories. 1922.

THE LADYBIRD. 1923. *Includes* The fox *and* The captain's doll.

STUDIES IN CLASSIC AMERICAN LITERATURE. New York 1923. *First London edn, 1924. An earlier version of 1918–21 collected as* The symbolic meaning, ed. Armin Arnold, 1962.

KANGAROO. 1923.

ST MAWR; together with THE PRINCESS. 1925.

REFLECTIONS ON THE DEATH OF A PORCUPINE and other essays. Philadelphia 1925. *First London edn, 1934.*

THE PLUMED SERPENT. 1926.

THE WOMAN WHO RODE AWAY and other stories. 1928.

LADY CHATTERLEY'S LOVER. Florence 1928 *(third version). First London edn, 1928 (expurgated), 1960* (Penguin) *(complete). A pirated version was pbd Paris 1929. The first, unfinished version of the novel* (The first Lady Chatterley) *was pbd Berne, Paris and New York 1944; the second, Verona 1954.*

PANSIES: poems. 1929. Fire, San Francisco 1940.

PORNOGRAPHY AND OBSCENITY. 1929; ed. Harry T. Moore, 1955 *(in* Sex, literature and censorship: essays).

THE VIRGIN AND THE GIPSY. 1930.

THE MAN WHO DIED. 1931.

LAST POEMS. Ed. Richard Aldington and Giuseppe Orioli, 1932; The ship of death, 1933.

THE LOVELY LADY and other stories. 1933.

A MODERN LOVER. 1934. *A collection of early stories.*

Novels: uniform pocket edition. 20 vols. 1927–34; Tales, 1934.

Works: uniform pocket edition. 33 vols. 1936–9; 22 vols. 1945–60 (Penguin).

Letters. Ed. Aldous Huxley, 1932; Selected by Richard Aldington, 1950 (Penguin); Letters to Bertrand Russell, ed. Harry T. Moore, New York 1948; Collected letters, ed. Moore, 2 vols. New York 1962 (*incomplete*).

Phoenix: posthumous papers. Ed. Edward D. McDonald, 1936; Selected essays, ed. Richard Aldington, 1950 (Penguin); Selected literary criticism, ed. Anthony Beal, 1955.

Complete poems. 3 vols. 1957.

Potter, Stephen. Lawrence: a first study. 1930.

Murry, J. Middleton. Lawrence: son of woman. 1931; 1954 (*with introd.*).

Carswell, Catherine. The savage pilgrimage: a narrative of Lawrence. 1932; 1932.

Lawrence, Frieda. 'Not I, but the wind...'. Santa Fe, New Mexico 1934. *By his widow.*

Moore, Harry T. The intelligent heart: the story of Lawrence. New York 1954.

Leavis, F. R. D. H. Lawrence, novelist. 1955.

Hough, Graham. The dark sun: a study of Lawrence. 1956.

Lawrence: a composite biography. Ed. Edward Nehls, 3 vols. Madison, Wis. 1957–9.

Moynahan, Julian. The deed of life: the novels and tales of Lawrence. Princeton 1963.

THOMAS EDWARD LAWRENCE, later SHAW
(1888 – 1935)

Duval, Elizabeth W. Lawrence: a bibliography. New York 1938.

SEVEN PILLARS OF WISDOM: a triumph. 1926. *Abridged as* Revolt in the desert, 1927.

THE ODYSSEY OF HOMER. 1932; ed. Maurice Bowra, Oxford 1955 (WC). *A prose trn.*

THE MINT: notes made in the RAF depot, 1922, and at Cadet College in 1925. New York 1936. *First London edn, 1955.*

Diary. 1937.

Letters. Ed. David Garnett, 1938; Selected by Garnett, 1952; Home letters to his brothers, ed. M.R.Lawrence, Oxford 1954.

Men in print: essays in literary criticism. Ed. A.W.Lawrence, 1939. *Reviews of Doughty, Flecker, Landor, D.H.Lawrence, Wells etc.*

The essential T.E.Lawrence. Ed. David Garnett, 1951; 1956 (Pelican).

Graves, Robert. Lawrence and the Arabs. 1927. *Reply*, Lawrence to his biographer Graves: letters, 1938.

Hart, B.H.Liddell. Lawrence in Arabia and after. 1934; 1935 (*enlarged*). *Reply*, Lawrence to his biographer Hart: letters, 1938, *collected with the above reply as* Lawrence to his biographers, 1963.

Lawrence by his friends. Ed. A.W.Lawrence, 1937; 1954 (*abridged*).

Aldington, Richard. Lawrence of Arabia: a biographical enquiry. 1955.

CECIL DAY LEWIS (b. 1904)

There are two early volumes of verse, Beechen vigil (1925) *and* Country comets (1928).

TRANSITIONAL POEM. 1929.

FROM FEATHERS TO IRON. 1931.

THE MAGNETIC MOUNTAIN. 1933.

A HOPE FOR POETRY. Oxford 1934; 1936 (*with postscript*).

A TIME TO DANCE and other poems. 1935.

Collected poems, 1929–33. 1935; 1929–36, 1948.

OVERTURES TO DEATH and other poems. 1938.

POEMS, 1943–7. 1948.

Collected poems [1929–53]. 1954; Selected poems, 1951 (Penguin).

THE GEORGICS OF VIRGIL. 1941; The Aeneid, 1952; The Eclogues, 1963. *Verse trns.*

THE POETIC IMAGE: the Clark lectures, 1946. 1947.

AN ITALIAN VISIT. 1953. *A poem.*

PEGASUS and other poems. 1957.

THE BURIED DAY. 1960.

THE GATE and other poems. 1962.

Also a number of detective novels since 1935 under the pseudonym 'Nicholas Blake'.

CLIVE STAPLES LEWIS (1898–1963)

DYMER. 1926; 1950. *A verse allegory.*

THE PILGRIM'S REGRESS. 1933; 1943. *A prose allegory.*

THE ALLEGORY OF LOVE: a study in medieval tradition. Oxford 1936.

OUT OF THE SILENT PLANET. 1938; Perelandra, 1943; That hideous strength, 1945. *A trilogy of science-fiction novels.*

REHABILITATIONS and other essays. Oxford 1939; They asked for a paper, 1962.

THE PERSONAL HERESY: a controversy by E. M. W. Tillyard and C. S. Lewis. Oxford 1939. *Six essays, the first three rptd from* Essays and studies, xix–xxi (1934–6).

THE PROBLEM OF PAIN. 1940.

THE SCREWTAPE LETTERS. 1942; 1961 *(with addns).*

BROADCAST TALKS. 1942; Christian behaviour, 1943; Beyond personality, 1944. *Rev. and collected as* Mere Christianity, 1952.

A PREFACE TO PARADISE LOST. Oxford 1942.

THE ABOLITION OF MAN. Oxford 1943; 1946.

THE GREAT DIVORCE. 1945.

MIRACLES. 1947.

ENGLISH LITERATURE in the sixteenth century, excluding drama. Oxford 1954 (Oxford history of English lit., vol. iii).

DE DESCRIPTIONE TEMPORUM: an inaugural lecture. Cambridge 1955.

SURPRISED BY JOY: the shape of my early life. 1955.

TILL WE HAVE FACES: a myth retold. 1956.

STUDIES IN WORDS. Cambridge 1960.

AN EXPERIMENT IN CRITICISM. Cambridge 1961.

THE DISCARDED IMAGE: an introduction to medieval and Renaissance literature. Cambridge 1964.

> *Also many critical essays and children's books.*

PERCY WYNDHAM LEWIS (1884 – 1957)

TARR. 1918; 1928. *A novel.*

TIME AND WESTERN MAN. 1927.

THE LION AND THE FOX: the role of hero in the plays of Shakespeare. 1927.

THE CHILDERMASS. 1928, 1956; The human age [pts ii and iii], 1955. *A tetralogy entitled* The human age: Childermass, Monstre-gai, Malign fiesta, The trial of man *(projected).*

PALEFACE: the philosophy of the melting-pot. 1929.

THE APES OF GOD: a novel. 1930.

MEN WITHOUT ART. 1934.

BLASTING AND BOMBARDIERING, 1937; Rude assignment: a narrative of my career up-to-date, 1950. *Autobiographies.*

THE REVENGE FOR LOVE. 1937. *A novel.*

ROTTING HILL. 1951. *Short stories.*

THE WRITER AND THE ABSOLUTE. 1952.

SELF CONDEMNED. 1954. *A novel.*

THE DEMON OF PROGRESS in the arts. 1954.

THE RED PRIEST. 1956. *A novel.*

Also edited Blast: review of the great English Vortex (1914–15) *with Ezra Pound*, Tyro: a review of the arts of painting, sculpture and design (1921–2) *and* The enemy: a review of art and literature (1927–9).

Letters. Ed. W. K. Rose, 1963.

Handley-Read, Charles. The art of Wyndham Lewis. 1951.

Kenner, Hugh. Wyndham Lewis. 1954.

Wagner, Geoffrey. Wyndham Lewis. 1957. *With bibliography.*

LOUIS MacNEICE (1907 – 1963)

BLIND FIREWORKS. 1929.

POEMS. 1935.

LETTERS FROM ICELAND. 1937. *Prose and verse, with W. H. Auden.*

THE EARTH COMPELS: poems. 1938.

MODERN POETRY: a personal essay. Oxford 1938; The poetry of W. B. Yeats, Oxford 1941. *Literary criticism.*

AUTUMN JOURNAL: a poem. 1939.

Selected poems. 1940.

PLANT AND PHANTOM. 1941.

SPRINGBOARD: poems, 1941–4. 1944.

THE DARK TOWER and other radio scripts. 1947.

HOLES IN THE SKY: poems, 1944–7. 1948.

Collected poems, 1925–49. 1949; Eighty-five poems, 1959 (*selection*).

TEN BURNT OFFERINGS. 1952.

AUTUMN SEQUEL: a rhetorical poem in xxvi cantos. 1954.

VISITATIONS. 1957.

THE BURNING PERCH. 1963.

Also trns of the Agamemnon *of Aeschylus* (1936) *and Goethe's* Faust (1951).

'KATHERINE MANSFIELD', i.e. KATHLEEN MANSFIELD BEAUCHAMP (1888 – 1923)

Mantz, Ruth Elvish. The critical bibliography of Katherine Mansfield. 1931.

IN A GERMAN PENSION. 1911. *13 short stories.*

PRELUDE, 1918; Je ne parle pas français, 1919. *Two short stories.*

BLISS and other stories. 1920. *14 short stories, including the two above.*

THE GARDEN PARTY and other stories. 1922.

THE DOVE'S NEST and other stories. 1923. *A posthumous collection of 21 stories, 15 unfinished.*

POEMS. 1923.
SOMETHING CHILDISH and other stories. 1924. *25 stories.*

Stories: a selection. Ed. J.Middleton Murry, New York 1930;
Collected stories, 1945; Selected stories, ed. D.M.Davin, Oxford
1953 (WC).
Journal. Ed. J.Middleton Murry, 1927; 1954 *(enlarged).*
Letters. Ed. J.Middleton Murry, 2 vols. 1928; Letters to Murry
1913–22, ed. Murry, 1951.
Novels and novelists. Ed. J.Middleton Murry, 1930. *A collection of
her reviews from* The Athenaeum, 1919–20.

Mantz, Ruth Elvish and J.Middleton Murry. The life of Katherine
Mansfield. 1933.
Murry, J.Middleton. *In his* Katherine Mansfield and other literary
portraits, 1949.
—— *In his* Katherine Mansfield and other literary studies, 1959.
Alpers, Antony. Katherine Mansfield. 1954.

JOHN MASEFIELD (b. 1878)

Simmons, Charles H. A bibliography of Masefield. New York 1930.

SALT-WATER BALLADS. 1902; Ballads, 1903; Ballads and poems, 1910.
THE MAINSAIL HAUL. 1905; 1913 *(enlarged)*; A tarpaulin muster, 1907.
Short stories.
THE TRAGEDY OF MAN and other plays. 1909; The tragedy of Pompey the
Great, 1910; The trial of Jesus, 1925; The coming of Christ, 1928.
THE EVERLASTING MERCY. 1911.
DAUBER: a poem. 1913.
SONNETS AND POEMS. 1916; Cholsey, Berkshire 1916 *(four sonnets
replaced).*
LOLLINGDON DOWNS and other poems. 1917.
REYNARD THE FOX: or the ghost heath run. 1919. *Poems.*
ENSLAVED and other poems. 1920.

Selected poems. 1922; 1950.
Collected poems. 1923; 1932, 1938 *(enlarged)*; Poems, 1946.

SARD HARKER. 1924; Odtaa, 1926; The bird of dawning, 1933. *Novels.*
THE WANDERER OF LIVERPOOL. 1930.

Collected works. 5 vols. 1935–7.

WILLIAM SOMERSET MAUGHAM (b. 1874)

Stott, Raymond T. The writings of Maugham: a bibliography. 1956.

Eight early novels pbd 1897–1908.

A MAN OF HONOUR: a play. 1903. *24 further plays pbd separately 1904–53.*

OF HUMAN BONDAGE. New York 1915. *First London edn, 1915.*

THE MOON AND SIXPENCE. 1919.

THE TREMBLING OF A LEAF: little stories of the South Sea Islands. New York 1921. *First London edn, 1921. Rptd as* Sadie Thompson *in 1928; includes* Rain.

THE PAINTED VEIL. New York 1925. *First London edn, 1925.*

ASHENDEN: or the British agent. 1928.

CAKES AND ALE. 1930; 1950 *(with introd.)*; 1954 *(with preface).*

SIX STORIES WRITTEN IN THE FIRST PERSON SINGULAR. New York 1931. *First London edn, 1931.*

THE NARROW CORNER: a novel. 1932.

East and west. New York 1934. *First London edn, 1934 (entitled* Altogether: being the collected stories).

THE SUMMING UP. 1938. *Autobiography.*

CHRISTMAS HOLIDAY. 1939.

THE RAZOR'S EDGE: a novel. New York 1944. *First London edn, 1944.*

GREAT NOVELISTS AND THEIR NOVELS. Philadelphia 1948; *First London edn, 1954 (entitled* Ten novels and their authors), New York 1955 *(rev. and enlarged, re-entitled* The art of fiction).

QUARTET: [four] stories. 1948; Trio, 1950; Encore, 1952. *With film adaptations.*

A WRITER'S NOTEBOOK. 1949.

Here and there: selected short stories. 1949.

Collected plays. 6 vols. 1931–4; 3 vols. 1952.

Complete short stories. 3 vols. 1951.

Selected novels. 3 vols. 1953.

Dottin, Paul. Maugham et ses romans. Paris 1928; Le théâtre de Maugham, Paris 1937.

Cordell, Richard A. W.Somerset Maugham. New York 1937.

Ward, Richard Heron. William Somerset Maugham. 1937.

Papejewski, Helmut. Die Welt-, Lebens- und Kunstanschauung Maughams. Cologne 1952.

The Maugham enigma. Ed. Klaus W.Jonas, New York 1954. *A collection of 29 essays and reviews pbd 1908–50.*

GEORGE EDWARD MOORE (1873 – 1958)

PRINCIPIA ETHICA. Cambridge 1903.

ETHICS. 1912 (Home univ. lib.).

PHILOSOPHICAL STUDIES. 1922.

SOME MAIN PROBLEMS OF PHILOSOPHY. 1953.
PHILOSOPHICAL PAPERS. 1959.

Commonplace book, 1919–53. Ed. Casimir Lewy, 1962 (*from MS.*).
The philosophy of Moore. Ed. Paul A. Schilpp, Evanston, Ill. 1942;
New York 1952. *With autobiography, bibliography and a reply by Moore to essays by various hands.*

CHARLES MORGAN (1894–1958)

MY NAME IS LEGION. 1925.
PORTRAIT IN A MIRROR. 1929.
THE FOUNTAIN. 1932.
SPARKENBROKE. 1936.
THE FLASHING STREAM: a play. 1938; 1948.
THE VOYAGE. 1940.
THE EMPTY ROOM. 1941.
REFLECTIONS IN A MIRROR. 1944; Second series, 1946; Liberties of the mind, 1951. *Essays.*
THE JUDGE'S STORY. 1947.
THE RIVER LINE. 1949. *A novel; a play-adaptation pbd 1952.*
A BREEZE OF MORNING. 1951.
THE BURNING GLASS: a play. 1953.

EDWIN MUIR (1887 – 1959)

FIRST POEMS. 1925.
TRANSITION: essays on contemporary literature. 1926. *Essays on Eliot, Graves, Aldous Huxley, Joyce, D. H. Lawrence, Edith Sitwell, Strachey, Virginia Woolf etc.*
CHORUS OF THE NEWLY DEAD. 1926.
THE MARIONETTE. 1927; The three brothers, 1931; Poor Tom, 1932. *Novels.*
THE STRUCTURE OF THE NOVEL. 1928.
VARIATIONS ON A TIME THEME. 1934.
JOURNEYS AND PLACES. 1937.
THE PRESENT AGE FROM 1914. 1939.
THE STORY AND THE FABLE: an autobiography [to 1922]. 1940; 1954 (*completed as* An autobiography).
THE NARROW PLACE. 1943.
THE VOYAGE and other poems. 1946.
ESSAYS ON LITERATURE AND SOCIETY. 1949. *Essays on Browning, Burns, Chapman, Hardy, Henryson, Scott, Sterne,* King Lear *etc.*
THE LABYRINTH. 1949.
ONE FOOT IN EDEN. 1956.

Collected poems, 1921–51. Ed. J. C. Hall, 1952; 1921–58, 1960, 1964 (*with addn*).

Also a biography of John Knox (1929) and trns with his wife Willa Anderson of Hauptmann (1924), Feuchtwanger (1926–32), Kafka (1930–8) etc.

GILBERT MURRAY (1866 – 1957)

A HISTORY of ancient Greek literature. 1897.

HIPPOLYTUS and The Bacchae of Euripides, and the Frogs of Aristophanes. 1902; Electra, 1905; The Trojan women, 1905; Medea, 1906; Iphigenia in Tauris, 1910; Rhesus, 1913; Alcestis, 1915. *Verse trns of eight plays of Euripides etc.*

THE RISE OF THE GREEK EPIC. Oxford 1907; 1924.

THE EARLY GREEK EPIC. Oxford 1908.

OEDIPUS, KING OF THEBES. 1911. *A verse trn of Sophocles.*

FOUR STAGES OF GREEK RELIGION. New York 1912; London 1925 (*enlarged as* Five stages).

EURIPIDES AND HIS AGE. 1913; Oxford 1946 (Home univ. lib.).

HAMLET AND ORESTES: a study in traditional types. 1914.

ARISTOPHANES AND THE WAR PARTY. 1919.

AGAMEMNON. 1920; The Choëphoroe, 1923; The Eumenides, 1925; The suppliant women, 1930; Prometheus bound, 1931. *Verse trns of five Aeschylus plays, the first three collected as* The Oresteia, 1928.

ARISTOPHANES: a study. Oxford 1933.

AESCHYLUS, THE CREATOR OF TRAGEDY. Oxford 1940.

GREEK STUDIES. Oxford 1946.

AN UNFINISHED AUTOBIOGRAPHY, with contributions by his friends. 1960.

Also two original plays, Andromache (1900) *and* Carlyon Sahib (1900), *edns of Greek classics and many books and pamphlets on Liberalism and the League of Nations.*

Eliot, T. S. Euripides and Professor Murray. *In his* The sacred wood, 1920.

Essays in honour of Gilbert Murray. 1936. *18 essays by H. A. L. Fisher, Harley Granville-Barker, Masefield, Arnold Toynbee et al.*

LEOPOLD HAMILTON MYERS (1881 – 1944)

THE ORISSERS. 1921.

THE 'CLIO'. 1925.

THE NEAR AND THE FAR. 1929; Prince Jali, 1931. *Pts 1 and 2 of* The root and the flower, *below.*

THE ROOT AND THE FLOWER. 1935. *Adds pt 3*, Rajah Amar.
THE POOL OF VISHNU. 1940.

The near and the far, containing The root and the flower and The pool
of Vishnu. 1943. *The four novels set in sixteenth-century India,
above, collected.*

STRANGE GLORY. 1936.

Bantock, G.H. Myers: a critical study. Leicester 1956.

SEAN O'CASEY (b. 1884)

TWO PLAYS: Juno and the paycock, The shadow of a gunman. 1925.
THE PLOUGH AND THE STARS. 1926.

Five Irish plays. 1935. *The three plays above, with two one-act comedies.*

THE SILVER TASSIE: a tragi-comedy. 1928.
WITHIN THE GATES: a play. 1933.
THE STAR TURNS RED. 1940.
PURPLE DUST: a wayward comedy. 1940.
PICTURES IN THE HALLWAY. 1942. *Autobiography.*
RED ROSES FOR ME: a play. 1942.
DRUMS UNDER THE WINDOWS. 1945.
OAK LEAVES AND LAVENDER: or a warld on wallpaper. 1948.
COCK-A-DOODLE DANDY. 1949.
ROSE AND CROWN. 1952.

Collected plays. 4 vols. 1949–51.

'GEORGE ORWELL', i.e. ERIC ARTHUR BLAIR
(1903 – 1950)

DOWN AND OUT IN PARIS AND LONDON. 1933. *Autobiographical.*
BURMESE DAYS: a novel. New York 1934. *First London edn, 1935.*
A CLERGYMAN'S DAUGHTER. 1935. *A novel.*
KEEP THE ASPIDISTRA FLYING. 1936. *A novel.*
THE ROAD TO WIGAN PIER. 1937.
HOMAGE TO CATALONIA. 1938; ed. Lionel Trilling, New York 1952.
COMING UP FOR AIR. 1939. *A novel.*
INSIDE THE WHALE and other essays. 1940; Critical essays, 1946;
  Shooting an elephant and other essays, 1950; England your
  England and other essays, 1953; Such, such were the joys, New
  York 1953; Selected essays, 1957 (Penguin); Collected essays, 1961
  (*incomplete*).
ANIMAL FARM: a fairy tale. 1945.
NINETEEN EIGHTY-FOUR. 1949. *A novel.*

UNPUBLISHED NOTEBOOKS. World review (June 1950). *With essays by Malcolm Muggeridge, Bertrand Russell, Spender et al.*

Hollis, Christopher. A study of Orwell. 1956.
Rees, Richard. George Orwell. 1961.
Wain, John. *In his* Essays on literature and ideas, 1963.

WILFRED OWEN (1893 – 1918)

POEMS. Ed. Siegfried Sassoon, 1920; A new edition including many pieces now first published, ed. Edmund Blunden, 1931, 1933; Collected poems, ed. C.Day Lewis, 1963 (*with Blunden's* Memoir).

Only four of the poems were pbd in his lifetime, in periodicals; seven were included by Edith Sitwell in Wheels: fourth cycle (1919).

Blunden, Edmund. Memoir. *In* Poems, 1931, *above.*
Welland, D.S.R. Owen: a critical study. 1960.
Owen, Harold. Journey from obscurity: memoirs of the Owen family. 3 vols. Oxford 1963–. *By his brother.*

JOHN BOYNTON PRIESTLEY (b. 1894)

FIGURES IN MODERN LITERATURE. 1924. *Bennett, de la Mare, Housman etc.*

THE ENGLISH COMIC CHARACTERS. 1925. *Studies in Jane Austen, Dickens, Fielding, Peacock, Shakespeare, Sterne.*

THE ENGLISH NOVEL. 1927. *Also biographical studies of Meredith (1926) and Peacock (1927) (EML).*

THE GOOD COMPANIONS. 1929.

ANGEL PAVEMENT. 1930.

DANGEROUS CORNER: a play. 1932.

ENGLISH JOURNEY, autumn 1933. 1934.

EDEN END: a play. 1934.

THEY WALK IN THE CITY. 1936.

TIME AND THE CONWAYS: a play. 1937; I have been here before, 1937. *Collected as* Two time plays, 1937.

JOHNSON OVER JORDAN: the play and all about it. 1939.

LET THE PEOPLE SING. 1939.

POSTSCRIPTS. 1940; Delight, 1949. *Collected essays.*

THREE MEN IN NEW SUITS. 1945.

THE LINDEN TREE: a play. 1948.

HOME IS TOMORROW: a play. 1949.

FESTIVAL AT FARBRIDGE. 1951.

JOURNEY DOWN A RAINBOW. 1955. *A study of contrasting societies in Texas and Mexico, with his wife Jacquetta Hawkes.*

Plays. 3 vols. 1948–50.

KATHLEEN RAINE (b. 1908)

STONE AND FLOWER: poems. 1943.
LIVING IN TIME: poems. 1946.
THE PYTHONESS AND OTHER POEMS. 1949.
THE YEAR ONE: poems. 1953.

Collected poems. 1956. *Includes the whole of* The Year One, *with selections from the previous collections.*

FORREST REID (1875 – 1947)

Burlingham, Russell. A bibliography of Reid. *In his study, below.*

There are two early novels, The kingdom of twilight (1904) *and* The garden god (1905).

THE BRACKNELS: a family chronicle. 1911; 1947 (*re-entitled* Denis Bracknel, *largely rewritten*).

FOLLOWING DARKNESS. 1912; 1937 (*re-entitled* Peter Waring, *largely rewritten*).

THE GENTLE LOVER: a comedy of middle age. 1913.
AT THE DOOR OF THE GATE. 1915.
THE SPRING SONG. 1916.
PIRATES OF THE SPRING. Dublin 1919.
PENDER AMONG THE RESIDENTS. 1922.
APOSTATE. 1926; Private road, 1940. *Autobiographies.*
DEMOPHON: a traveller's tale. 1927.
UNCLE STEPHEN. 1931; The retreat, 1936; Young Tom, 1944. *A trilogy on boyhood.*
BRIAN WESTBY. 1934.
RETROSPECTIVE ADVENTURES. 1941; Notes and impressions, Newcastle, co. Down 1942; The milk of paradise: some thoughts on poetry, 1946.

Also critical studies of Yeats (1915) and de la Mare (1929).

Forster, E.M. *In his* Abinger harvest, 1936 *and* Two cheers for democracy, 1951.

Burlingham, Russell. Reid: a portrait and a study. 1953.

IVOR ARMSTRONG RICHARDS (b. 1893)

THE FOUNDATIONS OF AESTHETICS. 1922. *With C.K.Ogden and James Wood.*

THE MEANING OF MEANING: a study of the influence of language upon thought and of the science of symbolism. 1923; 1936. *With Ogden.*

PRINCIPLES OF LITERARY CRITICISM. 1924; 1926 (*with two appendices*).

SCIENCE AND POETRY. 1926; 1935 (*enlarged*).
PRACTICAL CRITICISM: a study of literary judgment. 1929.
COLERIDGE ON IMAGINATION. 1934; 1950.
THE PHILOSOPHY OF RHETORIC. New York 1936.
BASIC ENGLISH AND ITS USES. 1943.
SPECULATIVE INSTRUMENTS. 1955.
GOODBYE EARTH and other poems. 1959; The screens, 1961.

FREDERICK ROLFE, 'BARON CORVO' (1860 – 1913)

Woolf, Cecil. A bibliography of Baron Corvo. 1957.

STORIES TOTO TOLD ME. 1898; In his own image, 1901. *Two overlapping collections of saint stories, some rptd from the* Yellow book.
CHRONICLES OF THE HOUSE OF BORGIA. 1901.
HADRIAN THE SEVENTH: a romance. 1904; The desire and pursuit of the whole: a romance of modern Venice, ed. A.J.A.Symons, 1934 (*pt iii*). *Pt ii of this trilogy of autobiographical novels*, Nicholas Crabbe: or The one and the many, ed. Cecil Woolf, 1960.
DON TARQUINIO: a kataleptic phantasmatic romance. 1905.
DON RENATO: an ideal content. 1909 (*ptd but never pbd*); ed. Cecil Woolf, 1963. *The first novel.*
HUBERT'S ARTHUR: being certain curious documents of Mr N.C. Ed. A.J.A.Symons, 1935.

Also a prose trn of Omar Khayyám (1903) *from the Fr. of Nicolas.*

Letters to Grant Richards. St Ives 1952; Centenary edition of the letters, ed. Cecil Woolf, 3 vols. 1959–.

Symons, A.J.A. The quest for Corvo. 1934; 1952 (*with addns by Julian Symons*).

BERTRAND RUSSELL, 3RD EARL RUSSELL (b. 1872)

A CRITICAL EXPOSITION of the philosophy of Leibniz. Cambridge 1900.
THE PRINCIPLES OF MATHEMATICS, vol. 1. Cambridge 1903.
PRINCIPIA MATHEMATICA. 3 vols. Cambridge 1910–13. *With Alfred North Whitehead.*
PHILOSOPHICAL ESSAYS. 1910.
THE PROBLEMS OF PHILOSOPHY. 1912 (Home univ. lib.).
THE PRACTICE AND THEORY OF BOLSHEVISM. 1920.
THE ANALYSIS OF MIND. 1921.
ON EDUCATION. 1926; Education and the social order, 1932.

SCEPTICAL ESSAYS. 1928; In praise of idleness and other essays, 1935; Unpopular essays, 1950.

THE CONQUEST OF HAPPINESS. 1930.

FREEDOM AND ORGANIZATION, 1814–1914. 1934.

POWER: a new social analysis. 1938.

AN INQUIRY INTO MEANING AND TRUTH. 1940.

A HISTORY OF WESTERN PHILOSOPHY. New York 1945. *First London edn, 1946.*

HUMAN KNOWLEDGE: its scope and limits. 1948.

AUTHORITY AND THE INDIVIDUAL: Reith lectures. 1949.

NEW HOPES FOR A CHANGING WORLD. 1951.

SATAN IN THE SUBURBS and other stories, 1953; Nightmares of eminent persons and other stories, 1954.

PORTRAITS FROM MEMORY and other essays. 1956. *Includes portraits of Conrad, D.H.Lawrence, Shaw, Wells.*

LOGIC AND KNOWLEDGE: essays, 1901–50. Ed. R.C.Marsh, 1956.

MY PHILOSOPHICAL DEVELOPMENT. 1959.

The philosophy of Russell. Ed. Paul A.Schilpp, Evanston, Ill. 1944. *With autobiography, bibliography and a reply by Russell to essays by various hands.*

HON. VICTORIA SACKVILLE-WEST (1892 – 1962)

THE LAND. 1926. *Several collections of poems pbd 1914–31;* Collected poems, vol. i *pbd 1933,* Selected poems, 1941.

THE EDWARDIANS. 1930.

ALL PASSION SPENT. 1931.

FAMILY HISTORY. 1932.

THE DARK ISLAND. 1934.

THE EAGLE AND THE DOVE: St Teresa of Avila and St Thérèse of Lisieux. 1943.

THE EASTER PARTY. 1953.

Also short stories, two travel-books on Persia (1926–8) and studies of Aphra Behn (1927), Marvell (1929), Joan of Arc (1936).

'SAKI', i.e. HECTOR HUGH MUNRO (1870 – 1916)

THE WESTMINSTER ALICE. 1902.

REGINALD. 1904; Reginald in Russia and other sketches, 1910.

THE CHRONICLES OF CLOVIS. 1912.

THE UNBEARABLE BASSINGTON. 1912.

WHEN WILLIAM CAME: a story of London under the Hohenzollerns. 1914.

BEASTS AND SUPER-BEASTS. 1914.

THE TOYS OF PEACE and other papers. 1919. *A posthumous collection with a memoir by Rothay Reynolds.*

THE SQUARE EGG and other sketches, with three plays. 1924. *With a biography by his sister, Ethel M. Munro, rptd in* Short stories, *below.*

Short stories. 1930; 1948 *(with addn).*

Novels and plays. 1933.

SIEGFRIED SASSOON (b. 1886)

Keynes, Geoffrey. A bibliography of Sassoon. 1962.

WAR POEMS. 1919. *64 poems, mostly collected from three previous volumes, 1917–19.*

Selected poems. 1925; Poems newly selected, 1916–35, 1940.

SATIRICAL POEMS. 1926; 1933 *(with five addns).*

MEMOIRS OF A FOX-HUNTING MAN. 1928.

MEMOIRS OF AN INFANTRY OFFICER. 1930.

SHERSTON'S PROGRESS. 1936.

The complete memoirs of George Sherston. 1937. *A collection of the three books of reminiscences, above.*

SIEGFRIED'S JOURNEY, 1916–20. 1945.

Collected poems. 1947; 1961 *(with* Sequences, *below).*

SEQUENCES. 1956. *62 poems, first pbd 1950–4.*
Also a study of Meredith (1948).

DAME EDITH SITWELL (b. 1887)

Fifoot, Richard. A bibliography of Edith, Osbert and Sacheverell Sitwell. 1963.

There are three early verse-collections: The mother (1915), Twentieth century harlequinade (1916) *(with Osbert Sitwell) and* Clown's houses (1918).

THE WOODEN PEGASUS. Oxford 1920.

FAÇADE. 1922.

BUCOLIC COMEDIES. 1923.

THE SLEEPING BEAUTY. 1924.

TROY PARK. 1925.

POOR YOUNG PEOPLE. 1925. *With her brothers Osbert and Sacheverell.*

RUSTIC ELEGIES. 1927.

FIVE POEMS. 1928.

GOLD COAST CUSTOMS. 1929.

Collected poems. 1930.

FIVE VARIATIONS ON A THEME. 1933.

Selected poems. 1936.

I LIVE UNDER A BLACK SUN. 1937.

TRIO: dissertations on natural genius. 1937. *With Osbert and Sacheverell Sitwell.*

POEMS NEW AND OLD. 1940.

STREET SONGS. 1942.

GREEN SONG and other poems. 1944.

THE SONG OF THE COLD. 1945.

THE OUTCASTS. 1962.

The canticle of the rose: selected poems, 1920–47. 1949.

Façade and other poems, 1920–35. 1950.

Collected poems. 1957.

Also studies of Pope (1930), The English eccentrics (1933), Aspects of modern poetry (1934), Victoria (1936), A poet's notebook (1943), Fanfare for Elizabeth (1946) *and* A notebook on Shakespeare (1948).

SIR OSBERT SITWELL (b. 1892)

For collaborations with his sister, and bibliography, see under Edith Sitwell, above.

THE WINSTONBURG LINE: 3 satires. 1919.

ARGONAUT AND JUGGERNAUT. 1919.

TRIPLE FUGUE. 1924; Dumb-animal and other stories, 1930; Open the door! 1941; Death of a god and other stories, 1949.

DISCURSIONS ON TRAVEL, art and life. 1925; Winters of content, 1932, 1950 (*with addns on the Mediterranean from* Discursions); Four continents: being more discursions, 1954.

BEFORE THE BOMBARDMENT. 1926; The man who lost himself, 1929; Miracle on Sinai, 1933. *Novels.*

ENGLAND RECLAIMED: a book of eclogues. 1927; Wrack at Tidesend: being the second volume, 1952; On the Continent, 1958.

Collected satires and poems. 1931.

PENNY FOOLISH: tirades and panegyrics. 1935.

MRS KIMBER. 1937. *A poem.*

THOSE WERE THE DAYS. 1938.

A PLACE OF ONE'S OWN. 1941. *A ghost story.*

Selected poems old and new. 1943.

SING HIGH! SING LOW! a book of essays. 1944.

LEFT HAND, RIGHT HAND! Boston 5 vols. 1944–50. *Vols. ii–v of the autobiography entitled* The scarlet tree, Great Morning!, Laughter in the next room, Noble essences. *First London edns, 1945–50.*

DEMOS THE EMPEROR: a secular oratorio. 1949.

Collected stories. 1953.

STEPHEN SPENDER (b. 1909)

TWENTY POEMS. Oxford 1930.

POEMS. 1933.

VIENNA. 1934.

THE DESTRUCTIVE ELEMENT, 1935; The creative element, 1953; The struggle of the modern, 1963. *Studies in modern literature.*

THE BURNING CACTUS. 1936. *Short stories.*

THE TRIAL OF A JUDGE. 1938. *A play.*

THE STILL CENTRE. 1939.

Selected poems. 1940.

RUINS AND VISIONS: poems. 1942.

POEMS OF DEDICATION. 1947.

THE EDGE OF BEING. 1949.

WORLD WITHIN WORLD: autobiography. 1951. *Also an autobiographical essay in* The god that failed: six studies in Communism, ed. Richard Crossman, 1950.

LEARNING LAUGHTER. 1952. *A travel-diary on Israel.*

Collected poems. 1955.

Co-editor of Oxford poetry (1929–30) *and of* Encounter (1953–). *Also trns of Büchner (1939), Lorca (1939), Rilke (1939) etc.*

LYTTON STRACHEY (1880 – 1932)

LANDMARKS IN FRENCH LITERATURE. 1912 (Home univ. lib.).

EMINENT VICTORIANS. 1918.

QUEEN VICTORIA. 1921.

BOOKS AND CHARACTERS, French and English. 1922. *Studies of Beddoes, Blake, Sir Thomas Browne, Johnson, Racine, Shakespeare's final period etc.*

ELIZABETH AND ESSEX. 1928.

PORTRAITS IN MINIATURE and other essays. 1931. *On Aubrey, Boswell, Carlyle, Froude, Gibbon, Sir John Harington, Hume, Macaulay.*

CHARACTERS AND COMMENTARIES. Ed. James Strachey, 1933. *A posthumous collection including studies of Chesterfield, Cowper, Disraeli, Gray, Mary Wortley Montagu, Pope, Shakespeare, Horace Walpole.*

Collected works. 6 vols. 1948–.

Virginia Woolf and Strachey: letters. Ed Leonard Woolf and James Strachey, 1956.

House, Humphry. The present art of biography. *In his* All in due time, 1955.

Sanders, Charles P. Strachey: his mind and art. New Haven 1957.

JOHN MILLINGTON SYNGE (1871 – 1909)

THE SHADOW OF THE GLEN and Riders to the sea. 1905.
THE WELL OF THE SAINTS. Dublin 1905; ed. W.B.Yeats, 1905.
THE PLAYBOY OF THE WESTERN WORLD. Dublin 1907.
DEIRDRE OF THE SORROWS. Dundrum 1910.

Poems and translations. Ed. W. B. Yeats, Dundrum 1909.
Works. 4 vols. Dublin 1910; Plays, poems and prose, 1941 (EL);
    Collected works, ed. Robin Skelton *et al.*, 5 vols. Oxford 1962–;
    Plays and poems, ed. T. R. Henn, 1963.
Autobiography. Ed. Alan Price, Dublin 1963.

Yeats, W. B. Synge and the Ireland of his time. Dundrum 1911.
—— The death of Synge. Dublin 1928.
Bourgeois, Maurice. Synge and the Irish theatre. 1913.
Gregory, Isabella. Our Irish theatre. 1914.
Greene, David H. and Edward M. Stephens. J. M. Synge. New York
    1959.

DYLAN THOMAS (1914 – 1953)

Rolph, J.Alexander. Dylan Thomas: a bibliography. 1956.

18 POEMS. 1934.
TWENTY-FIVE POEMS. 1936.
THE MAP OF LOVE: verse and prose. 1939.

The world I breathe. Norfolk, Conn. 1939. *A selection of poems and
    stories.*

PORTRAIT OF THE ARTIST AS A YOUNG DOG. 1940. *Ten autobiographical
    stories.*

NEW POEMS. Norfolk, Conn. 1943.

Selected writings. Ed. John L.Sweeney, Norfolk, Conn. 1946.

DEATHS AND ENTRANCES: poems. 1946.

Collected poems, 1934–52. 1952.

THE DOCTOR AND THE DEVILS. 1953. *A film-play from a story by Donald
    Taylor.*

UNDER MILK WOOD: a play for voices. 1954.

QUITE EARLY ONE MORNING: broadcasts. 1954; Norfolk, Conn. 1954
    (*with omissions and addns*).

ADVENTURES IN THE SKIN TRADE and other stories. Norfolk, Conn. 1955.
    Eight stories newly collected, with others from The map of love, *above.
    First London edn of the unfinished novel* The skin trade (*only*), 1955.

A prospect of the sea and other stories and prose writings. 1955.
A selection of 15 prose pieces.
Letters to Vernon Watkins. 1957.

Treece, Henry. Dylan Thomas: 'dog among the fairies'. 1949; 1956.
Olson, Elder. The poetry of Dylan Thomas. Chicago 1954.
Brinnin, John Malcolm. Dylan Thomas in America: an intimate
journal. Boston 1955.
Thomas, Caitlin. Leftover life to kill. 1957. *An autobiography by his
widow.*
Jones, T.H. Dylan Thomas. Edinburgh 1963 (Writers & critics).

EDWARD THOMAS (1878 – 1917)

Eckbert, Robert P. Edward Thomas: a biography and a bibliography.
1937.

POEMS BY EDWARD EASTAWAY. 1917.
POEMS. 1917.
LAST POEMS. 1918.

Collected poems. Ed. Walter de la Mare, 1920; 1928 *(with four addns)*.
Selected poems. Ed. Edward Garnett, Newtown 1927.
*The poems were all written 1915–17. Also many prose works, pbd 1897–
1928, including studies of Swinburne (1912), Borrow (1912), Pater
(1913), Keats (1916).*

Moore, John. The life and letters of Edward Thomas. 1939.
Coombes, H. Edward Thomas. 1956.

ARNOLD JOSEPH TOYNBEE (b. 1889)

NATIONALITY AND THE WAR. 1915. *Many further books on the War and
the League of Nations, and Chatham House pbns.*
A JOURNEY TO CHINA. 1931.
A STUDY OF HISTORY. 12 vols. Oxford 1934–61. *Vols. i–x abridged by
D.C. Somervell, 2 vols. Oxford 1946–57.*
CIVILIZATION ON TRIAL. 1948.
THE WORLD AND THE WEST: Reith lectures. Oxford 1953.
EAST TO WEST. Oxford 1958. *A travel book.*

GEORGE MACAULAY TREVELYAN (1876 – 1962)

ENGLAND IN THE AGE OF WYCLIFFE. 1899; 1909.
ENGLAND UNDER THE STUARTS. 1904; 1947.

GARIBALDI'S DEFENCE of the Roman Republic. 1907; Garibaldi and the Thousand, 1909; Garibaldi and the making of Italy, 1911. *Three studies collected as* Garibaldi, 1933.

CLIO A MUSE, and other essays. 1913; 1919 (Recreations of an historian); 1930 (*re-entitled* Clio) (*both enlarged*).

LORD GREY OF THE REFORM BILL. 1920.

BRITISH HISTORY in the nineteenth century (1782–1901). 1922; 1937.

HISTORY OF ENGLAND. 1926; 1945 (*enlarged*).

ENGLAND UNDER QUEEN ANNE. 3 vols. 1930–4.

GREY OF FALLODON: being the life of Sir Edward Grey. 1937.

THE ENGLISH REVOLUTION, 1688–9. 1938.

ENGLISH SOCIAL HISTORY, Chaucer to Queen Victoria. 1942. *Illustr. edn, 4 vols. 1949–52.*

AN AUTOBIOGRAPHY and other essays. 1949.

A LAYMAN'S LOVE OF LETTERS: Clark lectures. 1954.

ARTHUR WALEY (b. 1889)

A HUNDRED AND SEVENTY CHINESE POEMS, translated. 1918.

MORE TRANSLATIONS FROM THE CHINESE. 1919.

THE NŌ PLAYS OF JAPAN. 1921.

THE TEMPLE and other poems. 1923.

THE TALE OF GENJI, by Lady Murasaki. 6 vols. 1925–33.

THE PILLOW-BOOK OF SEI SHŌNAGON. 1928.

THE LADY WHO LOVED INSECTS, translated from the Japanese. 1929.

THE BOOK OF SONGS. 1937.

THE ANALECTS OF CONFUCIUS, translated. 1938.

MONKEY. 1942. *A trn of a sixteenth-century Chinese novel.*

THE REAL TRIPITAKA and other pieces. 1951.

Chinese poems, selected. 1946.

SIR HUGH WALPOLE (1884 – 1941)

MR PERRIN AND MR TRAILL. 1911; 1935 (EL) (*with preface*).

FORTITUDE. 1913.

THE DARK FOREST. 1916; The secret city, 1919. *Two novels on Russia.*

JEREMY. 1919; Jeremy and Hamlet, 1923; Jeremy at Crale, 1927. *A trilogy.*

THE CATHEDRAL. 1922; 1937 (*dramatized*).

ROGUE HERRIES. 1930; Judith Paris, 1931; The fortress, 1932; Vanessa, 1933. *Collected as* The Herries chronicle, 1939; *continued as* The bright pavilions, 1940.

ROMAN FOUNTAIN. 1940.

Hart-Davis, Rupert. Walpole: a biography. 1952.

EVELYN WAUGH (b. 1903)

DECLINE AND FALL. 1928; 1962 (*original version*). *The first novel.*

LABELS: a Mediterranean journal. 1930; Remote people, 1931; Ninety-two days, 1934; Waugh in Abyssinia, 1936. *Extracts from the four travel-books pbd as* When the going was good, 1946.

VILE BODIES. 1930.

BLACK MISCHIEF. 1932; 1962 (*with preface*).

A HANDFUL OF DUST. 1934; 1964.

MR LOVEDAY'S LITTLE OUTING and other stories. 1936.

SCOOP. 1938.

WORK SUSPENDED: two chapters of an unfinished novel. 1942; 1949 (*with* Mr Loveday, *above, etc.*).

PUT OUT MORE FLAGS. 1942.

BRIDESHEAD REVISITED. 1945; 1960.

SCOTT-KING'S MODERN EUROPE. 1947.

THE LOVED ONE. 1949.

HELENA. 1950.

MEN AT ARMS. 1952; Officers and gentlemen, 1955; Unconditional surrender, 1961.

LOVE AMONG THE RUINS. 1953.

THE ORDEAL OF GILBERT PINFOLD. 1957.

Also studies of D.G.Rossetti (1928), Edmund Campion (1935), and Ronald Knox (1959).

Stopp, Frederick J. Evelyn Waugh: portrait of an artist. 1958.

CHARLES WILLIAMS (1886 – 1945)

POETRY AT PRESENT. Oxford 1930. *Essays on 15 poets.*

WAR IN HEAVEN. 1930; Many dimensions, 1931; The place of the lion, 1931; The greater trumps, 1932; Descent into hell, 1937; All Hallows' Eve, 1945. *Six novels.*

THREE PLAYS. Oxford 1931; Collected plays, ed. John Heath-Stubbs, Oxford 1963.

THE ENGLISH POETIC MIND. Oxford 1932.

REASON AND BEAUTY IN THE POETIC MIND. Oxford 1933.

TALIESSIN THROUGH LOGRES, Oxford 1938; The region of the summer stars, 1944. *Arthurian poems.*

THE DESCENT OF THE DOVE: a short history of the Holy Spirit in the Church. 1939.

THE FIGURE OF BEATRICE: a study in Dante. 1943.

SEED OF ADAM and other plays. Ed. Anne Ridler, Oxford 1948.

ARTHURIAN TORSO: containing the posthumous fragment of The figure of Arthur, and a commentary on the Arthurian poems by C. S. Lewis. Oxford 1948.

THE IMAGE OF THE CITY and other essays. Ed. Anne Ridler, Oxford 1958.

VIRGINIA WOOLF, née STEPHEN (1882 – 1941)

Kirkpatrick, B. J. A bibliography of Virginia Woolf. 1957.

THE VOYAGE OUT. 1915; New York 1920. *First of the nine novels.*

NIGHT AND DAY. 1919.

JACOB'S ROOM. 1922.

THE COMMON READER. 2 ser. 1925–32. *Studies in Addison, Jane Austen, the Brontës, Conrad, Defoe, George Eliot, Evelyn, Paston letters etc.; E. B. Browning, Chesterfield, Defoe, De Quincey, Donne, Gissing, Hardy, Hazlitt, Meredith, Dorothy Osborne, Christina Rossetti, Sidney, Sterne, Swift etc.*

MRS DALLOWAY. 1925.

TO THE LIGHTHOUSE. 1927.

ORLANDO: a biography. 1928. *A novel as fantasy.*

A ROOM OF ONE'S OWN. 1929. *Two lectures on women and fiction.*

THE WAVES. 1931.

FLUSH: a biography. 1933.

THE YEARS. 1937.

THREE GUINEAS. 1938. *A tract against war and dictatorship.*

ROGER FRY: a biography. 1940.

BETWEEN THE ACTS. 1941. *A posthumous and unrevised novel.*

THE DEATH OF THE MOTH and other essays. Ed. Leonard Woolf, 1942. *Essays on Forster, Gibbon, Henry James, George Moore etc.*

A HAUNTED HOUSE and other short stories. 1943.

THE MOMENT and other essays. Ed. Leonard Woolf, 1947. *Essays on Lewis Carroll, Congreve, Dickens, Roger Fry, D. H. Lawrence, Scott, Spenser, Sterne, Mrs Thrale etc.*

THE CAPTAIN'S DEATH BED and other essays. Ed. Leonard Woolf, New York 1950. *First London edn, 1950. Essays on Arnold Bennett, Conrad, Crabbe, Goldsmith, Hardy, Ruskin, Leslie Stephen, Gilbert White etc.*

GRANITE AND RAINBOW: essays. Ed. Leonard Woolf, 1958.

Uniform edition. 14 vols. 1929–52.

A writer's diary: extracts. Ed. Leonard Woolf, 1953.

Virginia Woolf and Lytton Strachey: letters. Ed. Leonard Woolf and James Strachey, 1956.

Daiches, David. Virginia Woolf. Norfolk, Conn. 1942.

Forster, E.M. Virginia Woolf: Rede lecture. Cambridge 1942.

Bennett, Joan. Virginia Woolf: her art as a novelist. Cambridge 1945.

Blackstone, Bernard. Virginia Woolf: a commentary. 1949.

Brewster, Dorothy. Virginia Woolf. 1963.

Woolf, Leonard. Beginning again. 1964. *A portrait by her widower.*

INDEX

of primary names, together with the titles of many works of unknown, uncertain and mixed authorship. Bold type indicates a main entry.

Acton, Baron, 153
Addison, Joseph, 84, **107**, 140, 262
Aelfric, **17–18**
Aeschylus, 160, 245, 249
Akenside, Mark, 105, **108**
Alexander romances, **31**
Alfred, King, **18–19**, 110
Allott, Robert, 53
Ancrene riwle, **32**
Andrewes, Lancelot, 55, 229
Anglo-Saxon Chronicle, **21–2**
Annual Register, 114
Anouilh, Jean, 232
Arbuthnot, John, **108**, 134
Arden of Feversham, 78, 90
Ariosto, Ludovico, 71, 73
Aristophanes, 249
Armstrong, John, 105
Arnold, Matthew, 127, 151, 152, **154**, 162, 182, 184, 200, 208, 229
Arthurian literature, **32–3**, 110–11, 203, 261–2
Ascham, Roger, **55**
Assembly of ladies, **39**
Aubrey, John, 66, 76, 77, 84, 108, 146, 257
Auden, W. H., 7, 94, 162, 200, 213, **215–16**, 245
Austen, Jane, **154–5**, 232, 251, 262
Ayenbite of inwyt, **33**

Bacon, Francis, 52, **56**
Bagehot, Walter, 119, 126, 139, 141, **155–6**, 166, 188, 197
Bale, John, **56–7**, 78
ballads, **7**
Barbour, John, 31, **33**
Barclay, Alexander, 57
Barker, George, 216
Barnes, William, **156**
Barnfield, Richard, 53, 57
Barrie, Sir James, **156**, 221
Bartholomew Anglicus, 47
Baudelaire, Charles, 222
Beaumont, Francis, **57–8**
Beckett, Samuel, **217**
Beckford, William, **109**
Beddoes, Thomas Lovell, **156–7**, 257
Bede, Venerable, 18, **19**, 20, 21
Beerbohm, Sir Max, **217–18**
Behn, Aphra, **109**, 254
Belloc, Hilaire, 163, 217, **218–19**, 223
Bennett, Arnold, 206, 217, **219–20**, 251, 262

Bentham, Jeremy, **109**
Bentley, Richard, 83, 142
Beowulf, 17, **20**
Berkeley, George, **110**, 132
Berners, Baron (John Bourchier), **58**
Bestiary (ME), **34**
Bible, **17–18**, 20–1, 23 (OE); 46 (ME); 58–9, 89, 93, 96–7
Blackmore, Sir Richard, **110–11**
Blake, William, **111–12**, 113, 147, 208, 229, 257
Blickling homilies, **20**
Bloody brother, 58
Bloomfield, Robert, **157**
Blunden, Edmund, 98, 118, 120, 138, 165, 181, 182, 186, 200, 204, 220, 251
Bolingbroke, Viscount (Henry St John), **112**, 113
Book of common prayer, **87**
Borrow, George, **157**, 259
Boswell, James, **112–13**, 127, 129, 130, 136, 257
Bowen, Elizabeth, **220–1**
Bradley, F. H., 230
Breton, Nicholas, **60**
Bridges, Robert, 8, **157–8**, 167, 180, 184
Brontë, Anne, 152, **158**, 174
Brontë, Charlotte, 152, **158–9**, 174, 176, 232, 262
Brontë, Emily, 152, **159**, 174, 232, 262
Brooke, Rupert, 100, **221**, 228
Browne, Sir Thomas, **60–1**, 192, 257
Browne, William of Tavistock, 41, 52, **61**, 100
Browning, Elizabeth Barrett, 151, **159–60**, 262
Browning, Robert, 151, 159, **160**, 164, 182, 183, 223, 248
Brunanbur (OE), **24**
Buchan, John, **221–2**, 235
Büchner, Georg, 257
Buckingham, 2nd Duke of (George Villiers), **113**
Bunyan, John, **113**
Burbidge, Thomas, 165
Burke, Edmund, **113–14**, 133
Burnet, Gilbert, **114–15**, 136
Burney, Charles, 115
Burney, Fanny, **115**, 221
Burns, Robert, **115–16**, 248
Burton, Robert, **61–2**
Butler, Joseph, **116**
Butler, Samuel (d. 1680), 113, **116**
Butler, Samuel (d. 1902), **161**

Byrthnoth, 24
Byrthferth, 20
Byron, Baron (George Gordon), 151, 161–2, 181, 200

Caedmon, 17, 20–1
Calverley, Charles Stuart, 163
Camden, William, 62
Campbell, Roy, 222
Campbell, Thomas, 163
Campion, Thomas, 62, 64
Carew, Thomas, 54, 62
Carey, Henry, 116
Carlyle, Thomas, 113, 152, 163–4, 176, 257
'Carroll, Lewis', 164, 262
Cary, Henry Francis, 165
Cary, Joyce, 222–3
Cavendish, George, 86
Caxton, William, 34–5, 39, 43, 47, 58
Cervantes Saavedra, Miguel de, 139
Chapman, George, 57, 62–3, 80, 81, 248
Charlemagne romances, 35
Charms (OE), 21
Charters (OE), 21
Chatterton, Thomas, 116
Chaucer, Geoffrey, 30, 34, 35–7, 39, 40, 41, 47, 106, 165, 223, 260
Cheke, Sir John, 59
Chepman and Myllar prints, 38, 40
Chesterfield, Earl of, 117, 226, 257, 262
Chesterton, G. K., 151, 155, 160, 166, 171, 198, 217, 223
Chronicle, Anglo-Saxon, 21–2
Churchill, Charles, 105, 117
Churchill, Sir Winston, 223–4, 239
Clare, John, 165
Clarendon, Earl of, 69, 118
Cleanness (14th cent.), 46
Clifford, Martin, 113
Clough, Arthur Hugh, 151, 154, 165–6
Cobbett, William, 166, 223
Coleridge, Mary, 166
Coleridge, S. T., 61, 71, 74, 91, 151, 152, 167–8, 170, 192, 207, 208, 253
Collier, Jeremy, 52
Collingwood, R. G., 224–5
Collins, Wilkie, 152, 168, 229
Collins, William, 105, 118
Common prayer, Book of, 87
Compton-Burnett, Ivy, 221, 225
Conan Doyle, Sir Arthur, 168–9
Congreve, William, 118–19, 262
Connolly, Cyril, 226
Conrad, Joseph, 152, 188, 217, 220, 221, 226–7, 231, 232, 254
'Corvo, Baron' (F. Rolfe), 235, 253
Cotton, Charles, 119
Coverdale, Miles, 59–60
Cowley, Abraham, 63–4, 140
Cowper, William, 84, 106, 119–20, 257
Crabb Robinson, Henry, 208
Crabbe, George, 120, 262
Cranmer, Thomas, 59, 87, 219

Crashaw, Richard, 53, 64, 229
Croft, Herbert, 147
Cromwell, Thomas, 59
Cynewulf, 22–3

Daniel, Samuel, 62, 64–5
Dante Alighieri, 165, 195, 229, 261
Darley, George, 169
Darwin, Charles, 167–70
Davenant, Sir William, 65, 75
Davies, Sir John, 55, 65, 80
Day Lewis, C., 178, 213, 215, 216, 243
Defoe, Daniel, 106, 120–1, 137, 232, 262
Dekker, Thomas, 52, 65–6, 70, 81, 82, 100
de la Mare, Walter, 221, 227–8, 235, 251, 252, 259
Deloney, Thomas, 66
Denham, Sir John, 66
Dennis, John, 111, 121
Deor's lament, 23
De Quincey, Thomas, 170, 262
Dickens, Charles, 152, 168, 170–1, 177, 182, 194, 223, 229, 232, 235, 251, 262
Dictionary of national biography, 4, 201
Disraeli, Benjamin, 152, 172, 257
Dodgson, C. L. ('Lewis Carroll'), 164, 262
Dodsley, Robert, 53, 106, 129
Donne, John, 52, 53, 66–7, 99, 262
Dorset, 1st Earl of (Thomas Sackville), 88
Dorset, 6th Earl of (Charles Sackville), 121–2, 137
Doughty, Charles Montagu, 172–3, 243
Douglas, Gavin, 37
Douglas, Norman, 228
Dowson, Ernest, 173
Doyle, Sir Arthur Conan, 168–9
Drayton, Michael, 68
Drummond of Hawthornden, William, 68–9, 77
Dryden, John, 36, 55, 77, 113, 122–3, 197, 200, 229
Dunbar, William, 38–9
Dyer, John, 123

Earle, John, 69
East, Michael, 100
Eastward hoe, 63, 81
Edgeworth, Maria, 173–4
Edgeworth, Richard Lovell, 173
'Eliot, George', 147, 152, 174, 182, 262
Eliot, T. S., 6, 52, 55, 64, 67, 70, 75, 77, 80, 81, 82, 83, 84, 97, 111, 123, 130, 162, 168, 192, 200, 201, 202, 203, 213, 214, 229–30, 239, 249
Elyot, Sir Thomas, 69
Empson, William, 85, 164, 230
Etherege, Sir George, 123
Euripides, 249
Evelyn, John, 124, 262
Everyman, 37–8
Exeter book, 17, 22

Fairfax, Edward, 69
Farquhar, George, 124
Fénelon, François de, 139
Feuchtwanger, Lion, 249
Field, Nathaniel, 82
Fielding, Henry, 106, 124–5, 235, 251
Finnsburg, 20
Firbank, Ronald, 230–1
FitzGerald, Edward, 151, 175
Flecker, James Elroy, 231, 243
Fletcher, Giles, 69
Fletcher, John, 52, 57–8, 82, 90
Fletcher, Phineas, 70
Florio, John, 70
Floure and leafe, 39
Ford, Ford Madox, 214, 226, 231–2, 235
Ford, John, 70, 229
Forster, E. M., 120, 214, 215, 221, 231, 232, 262, 263
Fortescue, Sir John, 39
Fox, George, 125
Foxe, John, 23, 48, 71, 97
Fraunce, Abraham, 53
Frazer, James George, 107, 175–6
Froude, J. A., 73, 152, 163, 164, 176, 257
Fry, Christopher, 232–3
Fry, Roger, 135, 233, 262
Fuller, Thomas, 71

Galsworthy, John, 217, 232, 233–4
Galt, John, 176
Gascoigne, George, 71–2
Gaskell, Elizabeth, 152, 159, 174, 176
Gawayne and the grene knight, Sir, 46
Gay, John, 125
Geoffrey of Monmouth, 32
Gibbon, Edward, 125–6, 257, 262
Gilbert, W. S., 177
Gildas, 32
Gissing, George, 171, 177, 206, 262
Glanvill, Joseph, 85
Gnomic verses (OE), 23
Godolphin, Sidney, 99, 122
Godwin, Mary (Mrs Shelley), 199
Godwin, William, 126, 146
Goethe, Johann Wolfgang, 163, 164, 245
Golden legend, 34, 58
Goldsmith, Oliver, 105, 126–7, 133, 262
Gorges, Arthur, 55
Gospels (OE), 23
Gosson, Stephen, 79
Gower, John, 34, 39–40
Graves, Robert, 94, 186, 234, 243, 248
Gray, Thomas, 118, 127, 257
'Green, Henry', 235
Green, Matthew, 128
Greene, Graham, 182, 220, 228, 232, 235
Greene, Robert, 72, 79
Gregory, Lady, 236, 258
Greville, Fulke (Baron Brooke), 72, 93

Habington, William, 72
Hakluyt, Richard, 72–3, 88

Hali meiðhad, 32, 42
Halifax, Marquess of (George Savile), 128
Hall, Edward, 85
Hall, Joseph, 73, 80
Hardy, Thomas, 151, 152, 156, 178, 217, 220, 232, 248, 262
Hardyng, John, 85
Harington, Sir John, 73, 257
Harley lyrics, 31
Harrington, James, 73
Hartley, L. P., 236–7
Harvey, Christopher, 74
Harvey, Gabriel, 94
Hauptmann, Gerhard, 249
Havelok, Lay of, 40
Hawes, Stephen, 40
Hawkes, Jacquetta, 251
Hawkins, John, 130
Hazlitt, William, 5, 51, 91, 105, 166, 178–9, 181, 190, 201, 208, 262
Henderson, Hubert, 239
Henryson, Robert, 40, 248
Herbert, Edward of Cherbury, Baron, 54, 73
Herbert, George, 52, 53, 74, 99
Herrick, Robert, 74
Hesiod, 63
Heywood, John, 74–5
Heywood, Thomas, 52, 75, 90, 99
Higden, Ranulf, 47
Hilton, Walter, 41
Hobbes, Thomas, 52, 65, 75–6, 112, 201
Hoccleve, Thomas, 41
Hogg, James, 179
Homer, 63, 119, 131, 134, 154, 161, 234, 242
Hood, Thomas, 180
Hooker, Richard, 76, 99
Hopkins, Gerard Manley, 151, 158, 180, 192, 215
Horace, 134, 137, 139
Housman, A. E., 181, 226, 251
Howard, Sir Robert, 122
Hughes, Thomas, 185
Hulme, T. E., 237
Hume, David, 128–9, 139, 257
Hunt, Leigh, 178, 181–2, 220
Hurd, Richard, 95
Hutcheson, Francis, 137
Huxley, Aldous, 214, 221, 237–8, 242, 248
Hyde, Douglas, 236

Ibsen, Henrik, 198
Isherwood, Christopher, 215, 216, 238

James I, King of England, 59
James I, King of Scotland, 41
James, Henry, 52, 152, 160, 174, 182–3, 202, 205, 206, 217, 220, 221, 227, 232, 235, 262
Jeffrey, Francis, 151
John of Trevisa, 34, 47

Johnson, Samuel, 5, 7, 10, 61, 64, 66, 84, 91, 99, 105, 106, 108, 111, 112–13, 116, 118, 119, 122, 123, 125, 127, 129–30, 133, 134, 135, 136, 137, 138, 142, 143, 145, 147, 201, 257
Jones, Henry Arthur, 183
Jonson, Ben, 52, 57, 63, 65, 69, 76–7, 81, 221, 229
Joyce, James, 214, 226, 232, 238–9, 248
Judith (OE), 24
Julian of Norwich, 41
'Junius', 130
Juvenal, 122, 129, 181

Kafka, Franz, 249
Katherine group (ME), 42
Keats, John, 151, 184, 199, 259
Keble, John, 76, 184
Kempe, Margaret, 42
Keynes, John Maynard, 239–40
King Hart (ME), 37
Kinglake, Alexander William, 185
Kingsley, Charles, 185
Kingsley, Henry, 185
Kipling, Rudyard, 151, 182, 217
Koestler, Arthur, 240
Kyd, Thomas, 78, 90

Lesage, A. R., 139
La Fontaine, Jean de, 131
Laʒamon, 32
Lamb, Charles, 53, 180, 186, 192, 208, 220
Lamb, Mary, 186
Lampit, Juliana, 41
Landor, Walter Savage, 186–7, 243
Langland, William, 30, 42–3
Lawes, Henry, 89
Law, William, 130
Lawrence, D. H., 178, 221, 232, 234, 241–2, 243, 248, 254, 262
Lawrence, T. E., 172, 242–3
Laws (OE), 21
Lay of Havelok, 40
Lear, Edward, 187
Lee, Nathaniel, 130
Leland, John, 78
Lewis, C. Day, 178, 213, 215, 216, 243
Lewis, C. S., 7, 8, 29, 36, 40, 53, 59, 63, 68, 84, 95, 108, 123, 186, 191, 200, 243–4, 262
Lewis, P. Wyndham, 244–5
Lindisfarne gospels, 23
Lindsay, Sir David, 78
Ling, Nicholas, 53
Lingard, John, 218
Locke, John, 112, 131, 141
Lockhart, John Gibson, 116, 196, 197
Lodge, Thomas, 79
Lorca, Garcia, 222, 257
Lovelace, Richard, 54, 79
Lydgate, John, 43
Lyly, John, 79

Macaulay, Thomas, 56, 108, 112, 115, 187–8, 257
Mackenzie, Compton, 220
MacNeice, Louis, 209, 213, 215, 245
Macpherson, James, 131
Maldon (OE), 24
Malone, Edmond, 91, 122, 136
Mallarmé, Stéphane, 233
Malory, Sir Thomas, 34, 43–4
Mandeville, Bernard, 131–3
'Mandeville, Sir John', 44
Mannyng of Brunne, Robert, 44
Marlowe, Christopher, 53, 62, 72, 80, 86
Marryat, Frederick, 188
Marston, John, 63, 65, 80–1, 100, 229
Martin, Gregory, 59
Marvell, Andrew, 81, 229, 254
Masefield, John, 72, 246, 249
Massinger, Philip, 52, 57, 81–2, 229
Matthew, Thomas, 59, 97
Maugham, Somerset, 246–7
medieval drama, 37–8
Meredith, George, 188–9, 217, 232, 251, 255, 262
Meynell, Alice, 189
Michael of Northgate, 33
Middleton, Thomas, 52, 66, 82–3, 97, 229
Mill, John Stuart, 109, 164, 167, 189–90
Milton, John, 52, 53, 83–5, 107, 111, 122, 219, 230, 234, 244
Minot, Laurence, 44
Montagu, Lady Mary Wortley, 132, 257
Montaigne, Michel de, 70
Moore, George, 190, 217, 236, 262
Moore, G. E., 247–8
Moore, Thomas, 138, 162, 190
More, Henry, 52, 85
More, Sir Thomas, 85–6, 90, 96
Morgan, Charles, 248
Morley, John, 152
Morris, William, 151, 152, 182, 190–1
Morte Arthur, Le, 33
Morte Arthure, 33
Muir, Edwin, 197, 213, 248–9
Mum and the sothsegger, 42
Murray, Gilbert, 249
Myers, L. H., 249–50

Nashe, Thomas, 80, 86
Nennius, 32
Newman, F. W., 152
Newman, John Henry, 55, 152, 191
Newton, Sir Isaac, 132
Newton, John, 119
Nicholas of Guildford, 45

O'Casey, Sean, 250
Occam, William of, 47
Occleve, Thomas, 41
Ogden, C. K., 252
Orfeo, Sir, 45
Orrmulum, 45
'Orwell, George', 171, 186, 213, 250–1

Osborne, Dorothy, 143, 262
Osbourne, Lloyd, 201, 202
'Ossian', 131
Otway, Thomas, 132–3
Ovid, 34, 65, 80, 89, 137
Owen, Wilfred, 251
Owl and nightingale, 45
Oxford English dictionary, 10

Paine, Thomas, 133
Parker, Matthew, 59
Parlement of the three ages, 42
Parker, Samuel, 81
Parnell, Thomas, 133
Pastons, 45, 262
Pater, Walter, 152, 191–2, 195, 229, 259
Patience (14th cent.), 46
Patmore, Coventry, 192
Peacock, Thomas Love, 192–3, 199, 251
Pearl (14th cent.), 45–6
Pecock, Reginald, 46
Peele, George, 86–7, 89
Pembroke, Mary Countess of, 60, 93
Pepys, Samuel, 133
Percy, Thomas, 127, 134, 145
Persius, 122
Philips, Ambrose, 134
Pinero, Sir Arthur Wing, 193
Plutarch, 69
Pope, Alexander, 91, 106, 108, 133, 134–5, 201, 226, 256, 257
Pound, Ezra, 24, 237, 245
Praed, W. M., 193
Prayer book, 87
Priestley, J. B., 181, 189, 190, 193, 228, 251
Prior, Matthew, 135
Proverbs of Alfred (12th cent.), 46
Purity (14th cent.), 46
Puttenham, George, 87

Quarles, Francis, 87
Quiller-Couch, Sir Arthur, 7, 91, 153, 154, 179, 193–4

Rabelais, François, 98
Raine, Kathleen, 252
Ralegh, Sir Walter, 53, 55, 88
Ramsay, Allan, 39, 135
Reade, Charles, 168, 194
Reid, Forrest, 252
Reynolds, Sir Joshua, 127, 135–6, 233
Ricardo, David, 194
Richards, I. A., 252–3
Richardson, Samuel, 106, 124, 136, 147
Riddles (OE), 24
Rilke, Rainer Maria, 257
Robinson, Henry Crabb, 208
Rochester, Earl of (John Wilmot), 114, 136, 137
Rogers, John, 59
Rogers, Samuel, 194
Rolfe, Frederick ('Baron Corvo'), 235, 253

Rolle, Richard, 46–7
Rollo, 58
Roscommon, Earl of (Wentworth Dillon), 121, 137
Rossetti, Christina, 151, 194–5, 262
Rossetti, Dante Gabriel, 151, 152, 192, 195, 261
Rowe, Nicholas, 91
Rowley, William, 70, 82, 100
'Rowley, Thomas', 116
Ruin (OE), 24
Ruskin, John, 151, 152, 182, 195–6, 262
Russell, Bertrand, 215, 242, 251, 253–4
'Rutherford, Mark', 152, 196
Rymer, Thomas, 121, 137

Sackville, Thomas, 1st Earl of Dorset, 88
Sackville-West, Victoria, 254
St John of the Cross, 222
'Saki' (H. H. Munro), 254–5
Sandys, George, 88–9
Sassoon, Siegfried, 189, 251, 255
Savage, Richard, 123, 129
Schiller, Friedrich, 163
Scott, Sir Walter, 105, 122, 142, 196–7, 222, 232, 248, 262
Seafarer (OE), 24
Sedley, Sir Charles, 122, 137
Selden, John, 39
Shadwell, Thomas, 122
Shaftesbury, 3rd Earl of, 137
Shakespeare, William, 52, 53, 54, 58, 63, 72, 79, 82, 87, 89–91, 121, 129, 134, 179, 186, 192, 194, 198, 202, 244, 248, 249, 251, 256, 257, 228, 229
Shaw, George Bernard, 171, 198–9, 207, 217, 223, 254
Shelley, Mary Wollstonecraft, 199
Shelley, Percy Bysshe, 151, 199–200, 220
Shenstone, William, 105, 138
Sheridan, Richard Brinsley, 105, 138
Shirley, James, 92–3
Short-title catalogue, 51, 105
Sidney, Sir Philip, 53, 55, 64, 72, 93, 95, 262
Sidney, Algernon, 138
Sitwell, Edith, 135, 214, 248, 251, 255–6
Sitwell, Osbert, 231, 255, 256
Sitwell, Sacheverell, 255, 256
Skelton, John, 93–4
Smart, Christopher, 138–9
Smith, Adam, 139
Smith, Sydney, 200
Smollett, Tobias, 139–40
Sophocles, 249
Sorbière, Samuel de, 140
Sorel, Georges, 237
Southey, Robert, 7, 119, 145, 162, 170, 200–1
Southwell, Robert, 53, 94
Spence, Joseph, 135
Spender, Stephen, 213, 215, 216, 251, 257

Spenser, Edmund, 52, 70, 94–5, 138, 143, 144, 262
Sprat, Thomas, 63, 64, 113, 140
Stationers' register, 51
Steele, Sir Richard, 107, 140
Stephen, Leslie, 4, 61, 82, 106, 109, 120, 121, 125, 127, 130, 136, 141, 144, 156, 159, 170, 172, 174, 179, 185, 187, 188, 190, 197, 201, 205, 262
Sterling, John, 163, 164
Strachey, Lytton, 214, 215, 248, 257, 262
Sterne, Laurence, 141, 226, 235, 248, 251, 262
Stevenson, Robert Louis, 151, 182, 183, 201–2
Suckling, Sir John, 54, 95
Surrey, Earl of (Henry Howard), 53, 55, 96, 101
Swift, Jonathan, 108, 141–2, 197, 201, 226, 262
Swinburne, Algernon Charles, 63, 151, 182, 202, 229, 259
Synge, John Millington, 258

Tasso, Torquato, 69
Tate, Nahum, 122
Taverner, Richard, 59
Taylor, Jeremy, 96
Temple, Sir William, 142–3
Tennyson, Alfred Baron, 24, 151, 182, 203, 228, 229
Tennyson, Charles, 203
Tennyson, Frederick, 203
Thackeray, William Makepeace, 105, 152, 203–4
Theocritus, 163
Thomas, Dylan, 258–9
Thomas, Edward, 123, 259
Thompson, Francis, 204
Thomson, James (d. 1748), 143
Thomson, James (d. 1882), 204
Thrale, Mrs (Hester Lynch Piozzi), 129, 143, 262
Tindale, William, 23, 59, 85, 96–7
Tottel, Richard, 53, 96, 101
Tourneur, Cyril, 82, 97, 100, 229
Toynbee, Arnold, 249, 259
Traherne, Thomas, 97
Trelawny, E. J., 162
Trevelyan, G. M., 48, 112, 187, 189, 259–60
Trevisa, John of, 34, 47
Trollope, Anthony, 152, 182, 204, 205, 221
Two noble kinsmen, 58, 82, 90
Tyndale, William, 23, 59, 85, 96–7

Udall, Nicholas, 97
Urquhart, Sir Thomas, 98
Usk, Thomas, 47

Vanbrugh, Sir John, 144
Vaughan, Henry, 98
Vercelli book, 17, 22
Vergil, Polydore, 32, 78
Virgil, 34, 37, 89, 96, 99, 122–3, 243

Wace, 32
Waldere (OE), 25
Waley, Arthur, 231, 260
Waller, Edmund, 98–9
Walpole, Horace, 73, 116, 144, 257
Walpole, Hugh, 205, 260
Walton, Izaak, 67, 74, 76, 99, 100, 101
Wanderer (OE), 25
Warton, Joseph, 135, 145
Warton, Thomas the elder, 145
Warton, Thomas the younger, 5, 29, 31, 95, 144–5
Watkins, Vernon, 259
Watts, Isaac, 145
Waugh, Evelyn, 261
Webster, John, 81, 99–100, 221
Wells, H. G., 177, 183, 206, 215, 217, 218, 219, 220, 243, 254
Wesley, Charles, 145
Wesley, John, 145
White, Gilbert, 145, 262
Whitehead, A. N., 253
Whittingham, William, 59
Wiclif, John, 23, 47–8, 59, 259
Widsið (OE), 25
Wilde, Oscar, 207
William of Occam, 47
Williams, Charles, 33, 84, 92, 213, 261–2
Wilson, Thomas, 100
Winchilsea, Countess of, 146
Witch of Edmonton, 70
Wither, George, 61, 100
Wollstonecraft, Mary, 146
Wood, Anthony, 61, 84, 146
Wood, James, 252
Woolf, Virginia, 141, 177, 214, 220, 221, 233, 248, 257, 262–3
Wordsworth, Dorothy, 208
Wordsworth, William, 151, 153, 167, 170, 192, 201, 207–8
Wortley Montagu, Lady Mary, 132, 257
Wotton, Sir Henry, 99, 100–1
Wulfstan, 25
Wyatt, Sir Thomas, 55, 101
Wycherley, William, 146
Wycliffe, John, 23, 47–8, 59, 259
Wynnere and Wastoure, 42

Yeats, W. B., 52, 111, 152, 190, 208–10, 213, 215, 236, 245, 252, 258
Yellow book (1894–7), 153, 253
Yellow book (Liberal), 240
Yorkshire tragedy, 90
Young, Arthur, 147
Young, Edward, 147